KU-544-378

The Archaeology of Ulster
from Colonization to Plantation

by

J.P. Mallory and T.E. McNeill

Illustrations under the supervision of B.N. Hartwell

The Institute of Irish Studies
The Queen's University of Belfast

Published 1991
Institute of Irish Studies
The Queen's University of Belfast

Reprint 1995

© J.P. Mallory and T.E. McNeill

All rights reserved. No part of this system may be reproduced, stored.
in a retrieval system, or transmitted in any form or by any means,
electronic, mechanical, photocopying, recording, or otherwise, without
the permission of the Institute of Irish Studies.

Hardback ISBN 0 85389 352 7
Paperback ISBN 0 85389 353 5

Printed by W.G. Baird Ltd, Antrim.

CONTENTS

Chapter 1

The Colonization of Ulster (7000 - 4000 BC)

Aerial demons	1
Ulster before man	3
Background to colonization	5
The evidence	7
The Early Mesolithic: 7000- 5500 BC	11
Who were the first colonists?	20
The Later Mesolithic: 5500 - 3500 BC	22

Chapter 2

The First Farmers (4000 - 2500 BC)

Introduction	29
Neolithic settlement	31
Neolithic economy and environment	38
Neolithic technology	43
Axes	44
Flint tools	49
Ceramics	51
Ornament and dress	54
Neolithic tombs and ritual	55
Court tombs	56
Portal tombs	63
Passage tombs	65
Wedge tombs	69
Stone circles	71
Henges	74
Society in Neolithic Ulster	77
Megaliths and society	79

Chapter 3

Metal and Wealth (2500 - 1200 BC)

Three ages	85
New people?	87
Beaker settlement	88
Beaker burials	89
Beaker technology	90
Food Vessels and Urns	91
Early Bronze Age settlement	95

Early Bronze Age burial   96
Early Bronze Age technology   99
Stone monuments   103
Middle Bronze Age   105
Industrial changes   109
Social changes   111

Chapter 4

Arms and Aristocracy (1200 - 300 BC)

Introduction   115
The Navan Complex   116
Settlement   124
Environment   127
Technology   129
The outfitting of a warrior   131
Dress and ornament   133
Tools, vessels and musical instruments   135
Burial   138
Later Bronze Age ritual   139
Final Bronze Age collapse   140

Chapter 5

From Uluti to Ulster (300 BC - 400 AD)

Ptolemy and Ulster   143
Emain Macha   146
Iron Age settlements   150
Linear earthworks of Ulster   150
Economy and industry   153
The Iron Age warrior   155
Iron Age clothes and ornaments   158
Religion and art   160
Burial   163
The dawn of Ulster   164
The Ulster cycle and the Iron Age   167
The origins of Gaelic Ulster   171
The Cruthin   176
The Romans and Ulster   178

Chapter 6

Kings, Christians and Vikings (c. 400 - 1177 AD)

Christianity, archaeology and the historical record   181
The arrival of Christianity   183
Types of sites   184

Farming and the appearance of the landscape 188
Buildings 191
Outside the houses 193
The purpose of enclosures 196
Towards a framework of dates 200
Patterns of the distribution of sites 202
The early Christian church in Ulster 204
Metalworking 208
Manuscripts 211
Stone carving 213
Pottery 217
Towards and overview of the 7th to 9th century Ulster 219
The context of Ulster settlement 224
Ulster and the Vikings: invasions or colonization? 226
The impact of the Vikings 228
Craftsmanship after the Vikings 234
The new kings 238
The reform of the church and Irish romanesque building 243
New monasteries and cathedrals 245

Chapter 7

English Earls and Irish Lords (1177 - 1550 AD)

The establishing of the English earldom of Ulster 249
The earl's castles 252
The castles of the barons 259
Farming and settlement in the earldom 262
Towns 264
Mediaeval industry 266
English and Irish 269
The remains of the church 274
Abbeys and Friaries 276
The secular church 279
The fourteenth century divide 282
The Late Middle Ages 285
The towns of the 15th and 16th centuries 286
Trade in the 15th century 288
The lords' sites in the countryside 288
Tower houses 289
The archaeology of the late mediaeval church 292

Chapter 8

Planters and Capitalists (1550 - 1800 AD)

Introduction 299
Sites of the Plantation 304

Fortifications   307
Settlement and houses   309
Towns   316
17th and 18th century industry   317
Detecting immigration   319

Chapter 9
Retrospect and Prospect

The Identity of Ulster   325
Retrospect   326
Prospect   334

Guide to further reading   338
Illustration credits   353
Index   357

PREFACE

Archaeology is the science of explaining the past through the study of physical remains. These remains may come to our attention by accident - a holiday visit, something dug up in our garden (or rediscovered in a roof space), or a newspaper account of a controversy concerning a site threatened with destruction - or by design - a visit to the local museum. However we may come into contact with the world of the archaeologist, the proliferation of local museums and interpretative centres, the increasing membership in local historical societies, and the Northern Ireland government's emphasis on the 'cultural heritage' in the schools, a rapidly growing interest in the past of our province is obvious. Yet the last two attempts to treat the entire archaeology of Ulster, Henry Lawlor's *Ulster: Its Archaeology and Antiquities* (1928) and Oliver Davies' "A Summary of the Archaeology of Ulster" which was published in *The Ulster Journal of Archaeology* 11 (1948), 1-41 and 12 (1949) 43-76, are now very much out of date and hardly easy of access to the general reader. The justification for producing a more up-to-date survey then should hardly require much discussion but perhaps a few points could do with some emphasis.

The archaeology treated within this volume is essentially confined to the modern nine counties of Ulster. As anyone familiar with Irish history will realize, Ulster has always been a very fluid geographical entity, waxing and waning according to political circumstances. From an archaeological standpoint neither of us are entirely happy with the concept of Ulster as a major well-defined cultural entity and the reader will periodically witness our attempts to wrestle with the concept of an Ulster cultural province. On the other hand, general surveys of Irish archaeology by their very nature tend to generalize for the entire island and pass over the very real evidence for regionalism within Ireland. If archaeologists in Cork set out to produce a survey of Munster, for example, it would be a very different account than our own. For this reason we find a regional archaeology as the appropriate framework to discuss not only to what extent the cultural history of Ulster may differ from the other provinces but also to emphasize how far regions within Ulster itself differ from one another.

Finally, we have attempted to discuss our material as much as we could although we are fully aware how far short our interpretations may fall in accounting for all the 'facts'. We have not tried to compete with other accounts whose primary purpose is to list and describe the various sites and monuments of Ulster but rather we hope to provide the general reader, especially the beleaguered teacher suddenly thrust into teaching 'cultural heritage', with some sort of guide as to what the archaeology of Ulster is all about; what sites 'mean' and what are the problems that interest the current generation of archaeologists. Armed with such goals, such a survey will inevitably tend to be a personal account and it is not merely a bold archaeologist but a deceitful one who imagines that he or she can consistently represent received opinion much less the answers to every problem (or worse, imagine that there are no problems).

The publication of this volume has been greatly assisted by generous subventions from the following organizations: the Belfast Natural History and Philosophical Society who helped pioneer archaeological research in Ulster; the Esme Mitchell Trust which has generously supported local studies in Ulster; the Cultural Traditions Programme of the Community Relations Council which aims to encourage acceptance and understanding of cultural diversity; the School of Geosciences in Queen's University; and the Northern Bank for its contribution to the Ulster Archaeological Society which initiated this project. The authors would especially like to thank Maura Pringle of the School of Geosciences for the preparation of maps, Emma Brennan, Derry Warner and Stephen Conlin for many of the illustrations and reconstructions, and Barrie Hartwell for his photography, drawings, and supervision of the illustrations of this book. We have also been assisted by a number of our colleagues who read either whole chapters - Peter Woodman, Derek Simpson, Greer Ramsey, Richard Warner, Michael Avery, Chris Lynn - or sections - Mike Baillie, Brian Williams, Seamus Caulfield, Jonathan Pilcher. The president of the Ulster Archaeological Society, Bobby Dickinson, did full service in reading chapters 1 to 8. Any infelicities of fact or interpretation are naturally the fault of the authors.

1 The Colonization of Ulster 7000 – 4000 B.C.

Aerial demons

Who were the first Ulstermen, where did they come from and when did they settle in Ulster? It is ironic that all these questions seemed to have been a lot easier to answer in the 17th century than they are today. This was the century that not only saw the collapse of Gaelic Ulster but also a major attempt to preserve the earlier traditional history of this island. For example, during the 1630s Michael O'Cleary and his three assistants were labouring in Donegal to produce an outline history of Ireland from the earliest times up to their own. Their account, *The Annals of the Kingdom of Ireland,* more commonly known as the *Annals of the Four Masters,* was based on their studies of the various mediaeval Irish annals. According to these 'Four Masters', the annals and other sources of native tradition revealed that the Irish first arrived on this island about 1700 BC when they seized it from its previous inhabitants, the Tuatha Dé Danann, who were driven underground. From these texts we would also learn that Ireland had been colonized on a number of earlier occasions by various peoples and that the

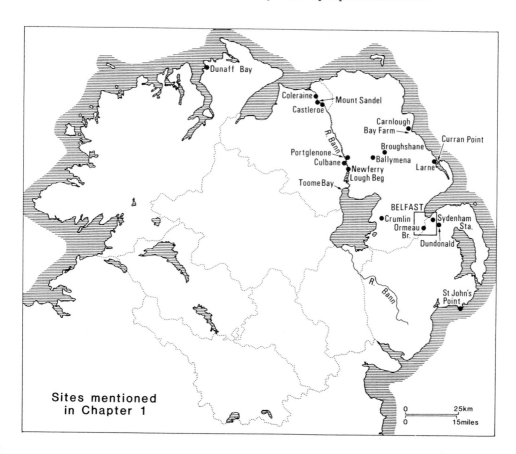

Sites mentioned in Chapter 1

first person to set foot in Ireland, Cessair, a granddaughter of Noah, did so 2242 years after the creation of the world (and forty days before 'The Flood'), that is, about 3000 BC according to the calculations of the 'Four Masters'. Writing in the same century, Geoffrey Keating tells us that the territory of Ulster was first set out as a province by the Fir Bolg whom the Four Masters reckoned to have ruled Ireland about 1900 BC and the first ruler of Ulster was Rudraige (Rury).

Had all of this been told to an Ulster planter from the Scottish Lowlands or England, he may well have accepted such answers since it would not have been far off his own estimate of when such events might have happened. However, like Geoffrey Keating he may have been more than a little perplexed how the mediaeval annalists 'obtained tidings of the people whom they assert to have come into Ireland before the deluge' unless they were informed by 'aerial demons' or someone wrote all this out on flagstones before the flood.

Now, towards the end of the 20th century we realize that we cannot depend on the information gained from the 'old books' for what happened in prehistoric Ulster although, to some extent, at least some of our story is to be found in stones. The written record will not really serve us until Christianity spreads throughout Ireland and creates a partially literate society. For the prehistoric period our evidence must be purely archaeo-logical - the reconstruction of the past through the analysis of objects, settlements, burials, and past environments. These do not provide us with the precise dates that one would have taken for granted in the 17th century nor can we call the actors of Ulster's ancient past by their names. But if we seem to be less precise, we are at least far more accurate. We can confidently assert that the traditional reckoning of man's arrival in Ireland is at least 4000 years off the mark and that the initial colonization of Ulster dated to about 7000 BC. We have no written sources to prove this (such a date is about 3000 years earlier than the invention of writing anywhere in the world), and we depend on a different type of 'aerial demon' than Keating had in mind. The radio-active carbon that permeates our atmos-phere enters all organic matter. On the death of any living thing, be it plant or animal, radio-active carbon begins to disintegrate at a known rate and the measurement of the amount of residual radiocarbon (Carbon 14) in something such as charcoal from a prehistoric hearth provides us with a date for when the tree died that produced the charcoal. This is the type of evidence that indicates that man has been in Ulster for about 9,000 years.

While such a date would have appeared preposterously early to anyone in the 17th century, it is actually a remarkably late event in prehistory. People had been living in southern Britain from about 250,000 years ago and early mammoth hunters and their families had already crossed from Siberia into the New World and spread the entire length of the Americas before man set foot in Ireland (Ill. 1-1). Indeed, the evidence for man in Patagonia is nearly two thousand years earlier than that for Ireland. In terms of human settlement Ulster is a very young land and the reasons why

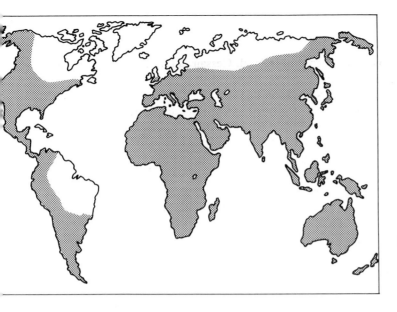

1-1. *Areas of the world settled before the colonization of Ireland.*

it took people so long to settle here can only be understood if we go back to a period long before our earliest evidence for the human colonization of this island.

Ulster before man

For much of the past two million years the northern half of Europe has experienced long periods of intense cold that frequently resulted in massive glaciers covering large stretches of land. This period is commonly called the Ice Age. The more technical name is the Pleistocene from the Greek words *pleistos* 'most' and *keinos* 'recent', that is, it was the most recent of the geological eras. During the colder periods, Ireland like most of northern Europe (and much of North America) was largely covered by extensive sheets of ice. Even during periods of somewhat less intense cold, the Irish landscape was still much like northern Siberia today.

Naturally, when Ulster was covered with glaciers, possibly up to 350 metres thick, this would have been more than enough to discourage people from settling here (Ill. 1-2). But there were also relatively warmer periods when there would have been open steppe lands with grass enough to feed such animals as mammoths, reindeer and wild horse, the same game that was being hunted by people elsewhere in Europe. Indeed, the remains of mammoths have been recently uncovered near Crumlin, Co. Antrim, that date over 40,000 years ago. Moreover, it was probably much easier for people to travel to Ireland during the Pleistocene than one might first imagine. During the colder periods, the waters of the world which would have otherwise been in the seas, were locked up in the great glaciers. With much less water in the oceans, the level of the sea dropped between both Britain and the Continent and between Ireland and Britain. Here the sea beds between them are not particularly deep and so a drop in sea level of 90 metres would have exposed the land between them. During some

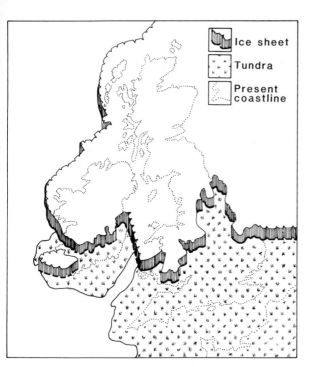

1-2. Ulster during major glaciation.

Ice sheet

Tundra

Present coastline

0   5cm

1-3. Palaeolithic flake from near Drogheda.

periods of the Pleistocene, it may have been possible to walk much of the distance between say France or Holland across to Britain and then further on into Ireland where one would only encounter the occasional river. Man had been crossing from the Continent to Britain for many thousands of years.

The archaeological period that prevailed during the Pleistocene is commonly called the Old Stone Age or Palaeolithic (Greek *palaeo* 'old' and *lithos* 'stone'). This is the period of the world's great big game hunters whose economies were based on pursuing the herds of mammoths, wild horses, wild cattle and reindeer that grazed on the open grasslands and steppe which were characteristic of the Ice Age. We have considerable evidence for the existence of these hunters in southern Britain but really no solid evidence for them in either Scotland or Ireland. This is certainly not for lack of searching since a number of Ulster antiquaries of the late nineteenth and early twentieth centuries believed (or certainly wished) that they had actually found traces of Palaeolithic man in Ulster. Mammoth teeth and sometimes bones have been found both along the Antrim coast from Larne to Glenariff and in County Cavan but there is not the slightest evidence that they had been hunted by man. Stone tools from many sites along the Antrim coast were once claimed to derive from glacial times but it soon became clear that they only dated about 7000 years ago or less. Other crude chopping tools, interpreted as traces of Palaeolithic man, have long been dismissed as 'eoliths', natural pieces of flint that have only a vague resemblance to early Palaeolithic tools. Most archaeologists have been forced to conclude, therefore, that the conditions in Ireland were never attractive enough to tempt hunters to cross over until long after the end of the last glacial period. A few, however, suspect that early hunters may have come here before the last great cold period of the Pleistocene and we simply haven't been able to find any trace of them yet. The only evidence so far is a simple flint flake found in gravels near Drogheda which appears similar to the type of flakes produced by men in southern Britain several hundred thousand years ago (Ill. 1-3). It would most likely have been dropped by someone camping in what is now the Irish Sea basin and after many thousands of years it had been redeposited by the glaciers on the Irish coast.

Finally, if evidence for Palaeolithic man is ever discovered in Ireland, it is most unlikely that it will be in Ulster. Here the ice sheets would not only have prevented settlement but in their advance over the land and their subsequent melting in their retreat they would have scoured away any traces of previous settlements. It is much more likely that evidence for Palaeolithic people (if they were indeed ever here) will eventually be discovered in the south such as in the Blackwater Valley in Munster which lay beyond the ice sheets of the last glaciation. As for Ulster, our starting point must still remain about nine thousand years ago for the beginning of human settlement.

Background to colonization

By about 12,000 BC the climate had become increasingly warmer and the ice sheets were well on their way to melting. These new conditions permitted the spread of trees from southern Europe northwards into Britain and then into Ireland. The expansion of these trees and other plants was made easier by the fact that the sea level was still so low that landbridges existed between the Continent and Britain and probably between Britain and Ireland. The first trees to appear on the newly formed landscape were juniper and willow, trees which are not only tolerant of cold conditions but which could also survive on the very poor soils of a landscape recently scoured by ice. At the end of the Ice Age, the soils of Ulster were little more than gravels and clays until trees and other plants could establish themselves and begin the process of soil formation by adding the organic matter that renders the earth fertile. Following the willow there appeared the juniper and then there was again a cold snap that reduced the spread of trees until warming conditions returned and saw the addition of first birch and then hazel to these early Ulster forests. The colonization of Ireland by trees and other plants permitted the further colonization by animals that could not have survived earlier in the barren wastes of Ice Age Ulster.

If we consider the reasons why plants and animals were able to expand into Ireland, we can readily see how this process of colonization was a race against time. The same warm climatic conditions that had permitted the spread of new plants and animals were also melting the glaciers of Scandinavia and North America. The melt water was continually running back into the seas and the level of the world's seas was continually rising. By the 7th millennium BC, the sea level had risen so high that Ireland was

Native Irish Fauna		X Fish with limited economic value
MAMMALS		
Irish Hare	Badger	Wolf
Irish Stoat	Otter	Brown Bear
Pigmy Shrew	Pine Marten	Wild Cat
Red Squirrel	Red Deer	Lynx
Fox	Wild Pig	
FISH		
Trout	Bream	xStone Loach
Salmon	Rudd	Eels
Charr	xGudgeon	Perch
Pollan	xStickleback	Marine Lampreys
Tench	xMinnow	River Lampreys

1-4. The native Irish fauna.

well separated from Britain. The Irish Sea then proved to be an ever-widening barrier for continued colonization. This helps explain why Ireland is far poorer in the number of its native plants and animals than Britain. For example, even today of the 32 species of mammals native to Britain, only 14 of them are known in Ireland (Ill. 1-4). Perhaps the only benefit Ireland derived from this rising sea level was that it kept the snakes out of Ireland. But it also made it a poorer country for hunters and fishers.

The climatic changes that produced such dramatic alterations in the landscape of northern Europe also stimulated changes in culture. With the end of the Pleistocene we also see the end of the Palaeolithic. Without the vast expanses of grasslands, the great herds that once existed and supplied Palaeolithic hunters with their food supply ceased to exist. The mammoths and many other animals became extinct while the reindeer migrated further to the north. Now with a landscape becoming increasingly forested, we find new animals expanding northwards. These included the large red deer, elk, and the aurochs, the great wild cattle of Europe. Also, there was the much smaller roe deer and wild pig. Of these animals only the wild pig and red deer made it as far as Ireland. In addition, fishing and shellfish collecting as well as the gathering of wild plants and nuts played increasingly important parts in people's diets. New weapons and tools were designed to help capture and kill these animals. One of the most striking changes is the shift to much smaller tools than were known in the Palaeolithic. These new stone tools are known as microliths (Greek *mikros* 'small' and *lithos* 'stone') and the period that these hunter-fishers dominated Europe is known as the Mesolithic (Greek *mesos* 'middle' and *lithos* 'stone').

In Britain, the Mesolithic inhabitants appear to have lived in small bands consisting of several families. Because the food available to them fluctuated from one season to the next, the people of the Mesolithic usually

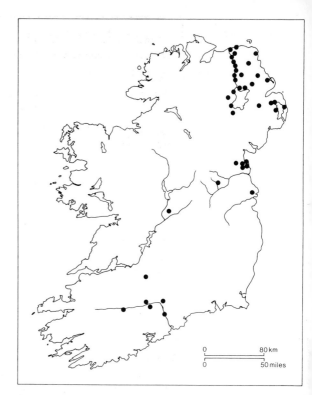

1-5. Early Mesolithic sites in Ireland.

moved about following the seasonal migrations of animals like the red deer or attempting to catch fish such as salmon in their annual runs upriver. Mesolithic camp sites are known from many localities in England and Wales and somewhat later they begin to appear in Scotland and Ireland.

The evidence

What type of evidence do we have for the first settlers in Ulster? If one considers their way of life then we soon see that the evidence will not be particularly abundant. We imagine that like hunters and gatherers today, Mesolithic people in Ulster would have had tools and containers of wood, plants and animal skin, all of which would have long disintegrated in the ground. Furthermore, soils in Ulster are often so acidic that they dissolve bone that has laid buried for a long time unless it has been charred by fire, or been preserved in a wet environment such as a bog. The only really indestructable material that they used and carried with them would be their stone tools. It is just such tools, normally made of flint, that provide us with most of our evidence for the earliest colonists and have to serve as Keating's hypothetical flagstone messages from before the Deluge. These chipped flakes of flint are normally discovered by both archaeologists and amateur collectors by walking over newly ploughed fields or examining the walls of drainage ditches or river banks. When a number of them have been found in the same vicinity this constitutes an archaeological site. It is convenient for our purposes to begin our survey of the earlier Mesolithic period in Ireland by first examining a map of the Early Mesolithic sites of Ireland (Ill. 1-5).

1-6. Flint nodules in chalk near
Ballycastle, Co. Antrim.

At a glance we can see several very interesting things about their distribution. First of all, the great majority of them are located in Ulster, especially in counties Antrim and Down, with only a few sites along the Leinster coast or well within the interior of Ireland. From this we might wish to draw several conclusions. For example, if most of the early Mesolithic sites are located in Ulster, this should mean that most of the first colonists lived in Ulster rather than in the rest of Ireland. In addition, if the sites are especially concentrated in Antrim and Down, i.e., the eastern counties, and we recall that the shortest crossing from Britain to Ireland is into these very same counties, then this should indicate that the earliest settlers probably crossed over from Scotland to Antrim like a modern passenger on the Stranraer-Larne ferry. All of these conclusions, however, seem to be wrong.

In order to understand better the distribution map we must recall that most of the sites marked on the map indicate the presence of flint tools. Given this, we must now ask ourselves where did the flint come from?

1-7. Flint-bearing chalk deposits
covered and protected by basalt.

8

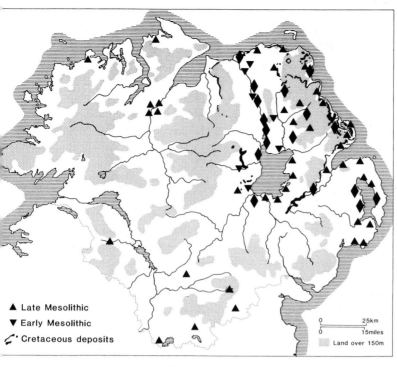

▲ Late Mesolithic
▼ Early Mesolithic
⌒˙ Cretaceous deposits

0   25km
0   15miles
Land over 150m

1-8. Mesolithic sites and flint (Cretaceous) outcrops in Ulster.

About 100 million years ago Ireland lay under the sea and at the bottom of this sea there accumulated deep layers of chalk in which there were also formed nodules of flint. These layers can be easily seen by anyone from the beaches near Glenarm or Ballycastle (Ill. 1-6). The chalk layers that measured about 100 metres thick completely covered all Ireland at one time but they are now limited to northeast Ulster. Here molten rock pushed through the chalk about 65 to 50 million years ago and sealed it with a protective layer of basalt which we can also see along the north coast overlying the chalk (Ill. 1-7). While the northeast Ulster chalk and flint was preserved, the chalk that covered much of this island was eroded away over millions of years. For this reason flint is limited primarily to northeast Ulster except for smaller amounts that were scattered over the countryside by the movement of glaciers. If we compare the map of the Mesolithic sites with that showing the distribution of flint deposits we can see that most of the early sites are in the areas where flint was abundant and very few are far beyond this range (Ill. 1-8). Many people would naturally conclude then that the earliest colonists in Ireland only lived in those areas close to the supplies of flint since this was their main source of tools and Henry Lawlor even suggested that the first colonists came to Ulster in order to procure flint. But food supply is always far more important than the raw materials of tools and there is no reason why people could not have occupied all Ireland during the Mesolithic. We are now learning that different stones were used to make tools in other parts of Ireland. For example, in Munster and Connacht where there was very little good flint available, chert and rhyolite were used to make the same types of tools that we find in the flint-rich areas of Ulster. Now chert and other stones are

9

1-9. Rev. J. Grainger.   *1-10. William Gray.*

usually much more difficult to recognize on the ground than flint and, therefore, we may have simply not yet found many of the chert sites that were spread over Ireland. What the map shows is that Mesolithic sites are not confined to Ulster; they are just easier to find here.

There is another reason why most of these early prehistoric sites are known in Ulster - modern Ulstermen! The majority of sites have not been discovered by professional archaeologists (there are too few of them) but rather by amateur collectors, frequently members of the Belfast Natural History and Philosophical Society or the Ballymena Field Club, who especially towards the end of the last century walked the fields of Ulster in pursuit of the flint implements of Ulster's past. These 'Northern Collectors' as they are often termed included Rev. J. Grainger of Broughshane (Ill. 1-9) whose own collections became the basis of what is now the Ulster Museum, the Belfast engineer William Gray and the Ballymena land agent William Knowles who discovered a number of important sites. It should be mentioned that one of the negative aspects of all this collecting was that it did turn flint-working into a cottage industry in some areas. Even as early as 1891, William Wakeman could write that 'as the spirit of collecting increased, prices for these relics of a long past, but mysterious period advanced in due proportion; so much so as to induce certain native "Flint Jacks" to produce counterfeits, which were, and are, eagerly purchased by unsuspecting strangers, of which body, wonderful to say, American tourists are, it would appear, the most gullible.'

10

Nevertheless, the tradition of fieldwalking and collecting, when carried out in a systematic way, has provided an invaluable aid to professional archaeologists, and still survives today - it was a fieldwalker who uncovered the two most recently discovered Early Mesolithic sites in Ulster near Dundonald, Co. Down - and so we should not be too surprised if Ulster is far better represented than any other province in Ireland.

The Early Mesolithic: 7000-5500 BC

The most famous Early Mesolithic site in Ulster is Mount Sandel near Coleraine, Co. Londonderry. It was occupied about 7000 BC and provides us with our best evidence for how the first colonists in Ireland lived.

The site was first reported in the 1880s by one of the more meticulous of the early collectors, William Gray (Ill. 1-10). But its real importance was not recognized until it was threatened with destruction by an expanding housing development in the 1970s. In order to determine that nothing important would be destroyed, the site was excavated by Peter Woodman, then of the Ulster Museum, who quite unexpectedly discovered at Mount Sandel the earliest man-made structures in Ireland. In a small hollow a Mesolithic community had erected a series of huts one after another. The evidence for the structure of the huts is indicated by the pattern of post- and stake-holes (Ill. 1-11). Archaeologists can often recognize where a post has been driven into the earth because when a post rots away in the ground, the hole in which it sat generally fills up with earth or top-soil, or, if the hut burns down, with charcoal. All of these fillings tend to be of a darker colour than the surrounding natural soil and so a dark patch of stained earth may mark where a post previously stood. At Mount Sandel the evidence of the post-holes indicated that a series of huts, each measuring about six metres across, had been erected with another series of hearths in the centre. As the

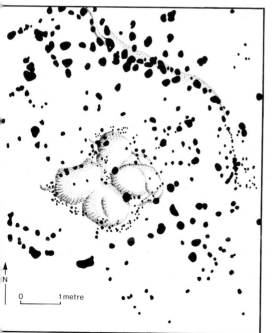

1-11. Stake-holes and hearths from Mount Sandel.

1-12. Reconstruction of Mount Sandel hut.

11

postholes were only found on the periphery of the huts, we suspect that a hut was built by ramming poles or saplings into the ground and then bending them over at an angle so that they could be tied in place at the centre. We have no evidence for what was used to cover the walls: it may have been brush or skins and there may have been an outer covering of earth to help insulate the hut against the cold (Ill. 1-12).

The plan of the structure is made more complicated by the fact that several huts, possibly four, were erected in the same place one after another. Although this makes it more difficult for the archaeologist to interpret their shape, it does indicate that the inhabitants of Mount Sandel returned to this site and rebuilt their huts in the same place over a number of seasons. From this we conclude that Mesolithic communities did not wander aimlessly over Ulster from one season to another but probably kept to a basic annual pattern year after year that took them back to the same settlement.

How many people lived in the hut? To answer this question our only recourse is to look at the evidence of hunter-gatherers who have been studied by anthropologists which suggests that about 6 to 9 people may have occupied the Mount Sandel huts. There were also some possible traces of other huts at Mount Sandel but it is impossible to determine whether they were occupied at precisely the same time as the huts described above.

In addition to the huts, Peter Woodman also discovered many pits in the ground that had probably been used to store food supplies and, after they had been emptied, they filled with rubbish from the site. These pits give us some evidence for what the people of Mount Sandel ate (Ill. 1-13). The burnt bones of mammals, especially wild pig, were found as well as fish bones such as eel, salmon and trout, all of which could be caught in the river Bann. Bird bones were also found which indicate the hunting or trapping of birds. Some of the pits contained the charred remains of hazel nut shells which had probably been stored in them. Even the carbonized seeds of water lilies and possibly wild apples were recovered.

All of this evidence for plants and animals tells us more than simply what the people ate but they also provide us clues about when Mount Sandel was occupied. People who live by hunting, fishing and gathering very rarely live in the same location all year round since they are seldom able to obtain sufficient food in the same place throughout the four seasons. Generally they must move from one season to the next to obtain their food. In order to determine during what season people lived at Mount Sandel the archaeologist must play detective and examine any clues that might suggest that the site was occupied during a particular part of the year.

Hazel nuts ripen only in the autumn so we know from their charred remains on the site that people probably occupied Mount Sandel during the autumn. Since they were stored in the ground it is also possible that the camp was occupied into the winter with the hazel nuts serving to insure that the people did not starve during the lean season. The pig bones generally

Species found at Mount Sandel		
MAMMALS		
Sus Scrofa (wild boar)	322	[6]
Lepus cf. *timidus* (hare)	6	[3]
Canis sp. (wolf/dog)	1	
Felis silvestris (wild cat)	-	
BIRDS		
Gavia stellata (red-thr. diver)	3	
Anas platyrhynchos (mallard)	15	
Anas cf. *crecca* (teal)	2	
Anas penelope (wigeon)	2	
Accipiter gentilis (goshawk)	6	
Aquila/Haliaeetus (eagle)	2	
Falco peregrinus (peregrine)	-	
Tytonidae/Strigidae (owls)	-	
Tetrao urogallus (capercaillie)	1	
Lagopus/Lyrurus (grouse)	7	
Fulica atra (coot)	1	
Scolopacidae (snipe/woodcock)	8	
Columba palumbus (wood pigeon)	24	
Garrulus glandarius (jay)	-	
Turdus sp. (thrush)	8	
FISH		
Salmo salar (salmon)	894	
Salmo trutta (trout)	568	
Salmo sp. (salmonid)	43	
Anguilla anguilla (eel)	122	
Diecentrarchus labrax (seabass)	144	
Pleuronectidae (flatfish)	13	
[ ] = identification uncertain		

1-13. Food remains recovered from Mount Sandel.

came from young animals somewhat less than two years old. We know this because in the young pig, or any other mammal including ourselves, certain bones of the body only join together, or fuse, or teeth develop as the animal matures. Zoologists know at approximately what age the various bones of a pig will fuse and the pattern of fusion from Mount Sandel indicates that most of the pigs were juveniles when they were killed. Since we know that sows bear their young in April to May, we can then estimate

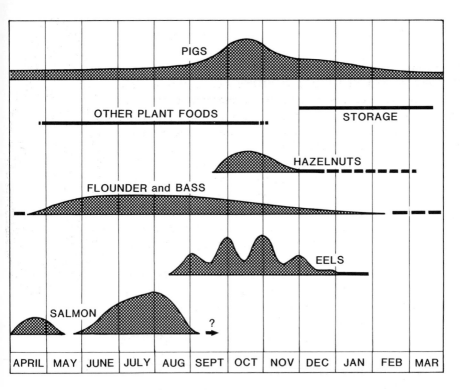

1-14. The seasonal availabilty of different food resources at Mount Sandel.

their age when they were butchered. The evidence from Mount Sandel suggests that the pigs were generally killed during the late winter.

The remains of salmon, however, suggest that the community was fishing in the spring and summer while the bones of eels are best associated with autumn occupation when the eels run downstream. From all of this we can see that the basic resources at Mount Sandel changed from one season to the next and Peter Woodman suspects that the site may have been occupied for several seasons in succession since the site is superbly located to take advantage of a variety of different resources (Ill. 1-14).

Whether the same community occupied the site all year round or whether it was used seasonally over a period of years is very difficult to determine. The seasons of plentiful food, for example, may have seen several families at Mount Sandel while the winter season may have required some to move off to other sites as resources dwindled. Indeed, Peter Woodman excavated another Early Mesolithic site at Castleroe, only 2 kilometres away from Mount Sandel. It is possible that the group at Mount Sandel was only a part of a larger community settled over a broad area of the Bann estuary that shrunk or expanded as the seasons permitted.

We can say very little about the social organization of these Mesolithic communities since we lack much of the most basic evidence for social structure. For example, we do not have a single burial dating to the first 3000 years of human settlement of this island. But the evidence of social anthropology indicates that Mesolithic Ulster would have obviously been

14

a far cry from the more complex societies that we will later encounter in the historic period where some parts of Ulster would find themselves under the power of an earl, barons and petty lords or native Gaelic kings. In contrast, hunter-gathering societies are typically egalitarian and the main social unit beyond the family would be the band, a number of families related to one another. One's position within this type of society was determined by your age, sex and what you yourself accomplished. This means that you might have enjoyed the esteem of your fellows because you had either acquired a reputation for wisdom with your years or you had demonstrated particular prowess at finding and hunting wild pigs or picking the best fishing spots. What you would not have enjoyed was much power and any aspiring leader would have to inspire his followers by example rather than appealing to either moral authority or physical coercion.

So far, no other site in Ulster has produced such excellent evidence for huts or diet during the Early Mesolithic. Normally, we only find the remains of stone tools. These were recovered in abundance at Mount Sandel. The largest of these tools were flint axes that were flaked into shape and used for chopping wood and possibly fashioning wooden tools. The axes occur in two forms - core axes and flake axes. The core axes have rounded symmetrical edges that were generally sharpened by striking a transverse blow across the edge (Ill. 1-15). This meant that whenever the edge became dull from use, one needed only to knock off another flake on the edge to resharpen it. Microscopic analysis of the damage done to the edge of the core axes indicates that they were used for chopping. The other flint axe type, the flake axe, has a broad straight edge and was prepared from a large flake (Ill. 1-16). Its adze-like (asymmetrical) blade coupled with the evidence for microscopic use marks on the edge, indicates that it was used for planing or as a chisel. In addition, there were several polished stone axes that would eventually come to dominate axe production in later periods. A number of picks and adzes were also discovered. But the most typical tools for the Early Mesolithic were microliths.

The microliths were small splinters or blades of flint that were fashioned into a number of different shapes. The most frequent were scalene triangles, rods and needle points. In order to form such small and slender blades of flint, the person manufacturing them, the flint-knapper, had to use a technique known as indirect percussion. This involved knocking off flakes of flint by striking a bone or antler tool with a hammer against a pre-shaped nodule of flint, a core (Ill. 1-17). Generally, such small slivers of blades of flint were not whole tools themselves but were only parts of larger tools. Small bladelets, for example, averaging about 4 centimetres in length, could be inserted into the end of a pointed shaft of wood to form arrow points or the barbs on an arrow or harpoon or they might be set into a wooden handle to form a saw-like instrument (Ill. 1-18). The small size of these tools makes them very difficult to find and they are normally recovered on excavations by passing all of the soil through sieves. The excavators at Mount Sandel discovered over 1000 deliberately shaped

1-16. Flake axe (l. 6 cm).

1-17. Indirect percussion technique with antler hammer.

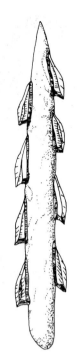

1-18. Harpoon barbed with microliths.

microliths and over 6000 small blades that could have been turned into microliths.

Although archaeologists can determine the shape of the various microliths, one might well ask why they were made in different shapes? Why were some scalene triangles and others made to look like rods or needle points? Peter Woodman investigated this by examining how the various tools correlated with each other and with the different animal remains. He discovered that the scalene triangles (Ill. 1-19), for example, were not found with rods. The former were found in pits that also included pig bones and this suggested that the triangles were employed in some form of weapon used to hunt pig. Once embedded in the pig or, perhaps used to skewer joints of pig, the scalene triangles came to rest in the same pits as the pig bones. The use of the rods (Ill. 1-20) was more problematic and Peter Woodman suggests that they may have been used primarily in fishing or possibly in processing plant remains.

There were also larger flint flakes that could be used as a tool by themselves. One of these was the scraper which would be used to clean hides since the edge could scrape and work the skin of animals without damaging the surface of the hide (Ill. 1-21). Scrapers are often found on prehistoric sites and the interesting thing about the Mount Sandel scrapers is their small number. Only seven of them were recovered and this suggests that scraping hides was probably a very minor activity on the site. The same type of tool would be fairly abundant on a British Mesolithic site where we might expect to find red deer. At Mount Sandel there is no evidence for red deer remains and this may explain why there are so few scrapers on the site. Flint gravers or what archaeologists term 'burins' were found (Ill. 1-22) which were used to work bone or antler into shape so that it could be used as tools. Like the scrapers, they number so few that we can again suspect that red deer was not the standard prey of the Mount Sandel hunters.

How typical of the Early Mesolithic is Mount Sandel? If we look back again to the map showing the distribution of Early Mesolithic sites, we can see that most of them are, like Mount Sandel, situated in lowland areas and near rivers, lakes or the sea coast. There are about ten sites along the Lower Bann. All of these locations suggest that the economy of these earliest colonists was primarily based on fishing, shellfish collecting, trapping wild birds, and hunting the main lowland mammal, the wild pig. It is also interesting to note where we do *not* seem to find Early Mesolithic sites. There is really no evidence for sites in the upland regions of Ulster such as the Antrim plateau, the Mournes, or the mountainous regions west of the Bann. Since surveys show that prehistoric man did occupy these highland areas in later times, we believe that our inability to discover sites in these regions dating to the Early Mesolithic is probably because Mesolithic people had little to do with the upland regions of Ulster. Now it is these very areas where we might expect to find herds of red deer, the largest mammal that man could have hunted in Ireland and one of the main sources of food of Mesolithic man in Britain. In Ireland, red deer remains seem to be much

1-19. Scalene triangle (l. 2 cm).

1-20. Rod (2 cm).

rarer and the number of red deer in Ireland may not have been sufficient to make it an important part of the hunting economy of the earliest colonists of Ireland. Indeed, as as we shall see below, red deer may not have arrived in Ireland until after man had colonized it.

Meagre though our evidence may be, it does give us a hint as to what life may have been like in Ulster during the Early Mesolithic (Ill. 1-23). During the spring time a group of families or perhaps only a single family would camp near the sea coast where there were supplies of fish and shellfish, and sea birds could be trapped while they were nesting. Also, the coasts of Antrim and Down would have provided a ready source of flint for making tools. During the summer and early autumn, families would have moved inland along the rivers and established their camps in the best fishing places such as where a river narrows or discharges from a lake. This would be the best season for catching fish like salmon moving upstream and for gathering wild plants. Hazel nuts might be of special importance since these could be readily stored. By the beginning of winter the camp site would have to be made secure against the harsher weather and so Mount Sandel is probably a good example of the type of huts that people built during these months. The late autumn was a good time to catch eels as they moved back down river but probably hunting wild pig became one of the main sources of food as the winter progressed. In addition, if enough wild nuts were gathered it was always possible to use them to get through this harshest part of the year. By spring time some families might then again move back towards the coast. This, at least, is the pattern that fits well enough with the evidence for Mount Sandel but we should always be wary of generalizing from a single archaeological site. For example, it would be a mistake to imagine that pigs were hunted only in the winter time as the Mount Sandel evidence suggests. An Early Mesolithic site at Lough Boora in County Offaly also yielded primarily the remains of pigs but here the evidence of their age and the presence of sows suggested that they had been hunted in the summer when mother and brood would have been least mobile.

In general, we should emphasize that life during the Early Mesolithic did involve seasonal movements of individual families or small bands of several families together. We should also not imagine this as a life of unendurable hardship. Even today where hunter-fisher-gathering societies often live in the most uninviting areas, they obtain their subsistence with less effort and greater free-time than their supposedly more civilized neighbours, including the professional archaeologists and anthropologists who are paid to study them. Moreover, we should also imagine that these Mesolithic societies were not solely concerned with obtaining their next meal but rather they possessed their own rituals, beliefs, ceremonies and art, all of which still lies beyond our limited ability to retrieve.

1-22. Burin (l. 5 cm).

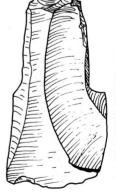

17

1-23. The four seasons of the Mesolithic:

spring

summer

autumn

...d winter.

Who were the first colonists?

Where did the first colonists in Ulster come from? It used to be immediately assumed that Scotland was the most likely place since the sea crossing is narrowest between western Scotland and Ulster. The location of so many sites in Antrim and Down also seemed to indicate that the earliest inhabitants of Ireland came from Scotland. But there are problems with this theory. We see them most clearly when we ask ourselves what evidence we might use to trace the path of the earliest colonists.

The only evidence we now have that might link the earliest Ulstermen with anywhere else in the world is their stone tools, especially the microliths such as those discovered at Mount Sandel. These tools appear in both Ulster and in the Irish midlands at the site of Lough Boora about 6500 BC. We may suppose that the potential colonists of Ireland lived somewhere along the western coast of Britain or Scotland. But when we examine the Scottish or British tool-kits for the same type of microlithic narrow-blade industries that we find in Ireland, so far they appear to date somewhat later than those known in Ireland. Moreover, there is no evidence that people occupied Scotland any earlier than Ireland which one must expect if Ulster was settled by communities coming from there. The only place in Europe where we find somewhat similar stone tools at a date earlier than those found in Ireland is France and it has even been proposed that hunter-gathering communities might have walked from France around the southern coast of Britain and then crossed what was gradually becoming an ever widening sea into Ireland. This is obviously not the easiest solution to the problem of the earliest Ulstermen and another possibility is probably a little more likely.

As we have already seen, there are also similarities between the stone industries of Ulster and those of Britain, particularly northern Britain. While the British evidence is still somewhat later than that for Ireland, it is quite possible that new discoveries will push back the antiquity of narrow-blade industries in Britain. The area that we are most concerned with is probably the area from Cumbria south to northwest Wales. At the time of the colonization of Ireland, this area was radically different from how it appears today (Ill. 1-24). The sea level would have still been quite low and it is thought that land was exposed all the way out to the west of the Isle of Man. From there one could have easily seen across to the Mournes and would realize that there was another land which might be occupied beyond the narrow sea that separated Britain from Ireland at that time. In addition, the people occupying this region would have been coastal dwellers experienced in the making and use of boats, a prerequisite to the earliest settlement of Ireland. It is possible then that the remains of the direct ancestors of those people who first colonized Ireland now lie at the bottom of the Irish Sea or are still preserved somewhere on the Isle of Man.

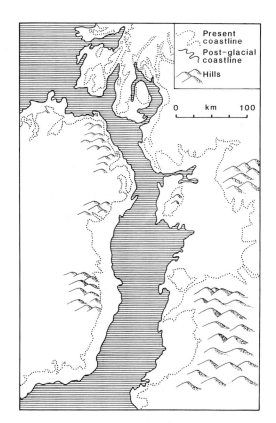

1-24. The Irish Sea at the time of colonization.

These first settlers would have had to cross by boat, either skin boats somewhat similar to those still used by eskimos or dugout canoes. It is unlikely that these earliest colonists in their small boats would have crossed to Ireland in any great number. Not only is this a matter of logistics but Peter Woodman regards the similarity between the earliest Mesolithic tool-kits in Ireland as evidence that Ireland was colonized by a small group of related people rather than by waves of peoples coming from different parts of Britain (who would, presumably, have introduced a greater variety of tool-types into Ireland). On the other hand, a single band numbering about 25 people, something like the colonization by Cessair as related by the Four Masters, would have been insufficient to have maintained a viable population that would have survived to colonize the entire island (Cessair's band drowned in the Deluge!). Possibly we should think in terms of a number of bands, comprising a total of several hundred people, entering Ireland over a period of years. It is likely that they landed on the south Down or Leinster coast and eventually spread out from there across the rest of the island wherever coastal and river resources permitted settlement. We know that they reached the Blackwater region of Munster and as far into the interior of Ireland as County Offaly. Clearly, they also came north into Ulster where we still find most of the evidence for these first colonists in Ireland.

The Later Mesolithic: 5500-3500 BC

We divide the Mesolithic into two main periods because of the very marked change in tool-kits that begins to appear about 5500 BC. In the Early Mesolithic the small microlithic tools were common but by the Later Mesolithic such tools were completely abandoned and communities began to fashion much larger implements made from long flint flakes. These did not require the more complicated technique of indirect percussion but rather the much simpler means of direct percussion. A nodule of flint could be picked up from the beach and after a chunk of it was knocked off to form a striking platform, the flint knapper could then remove a series of flakes in a matter of seconds by striking the platform with a hard stone such as quartzite (Ill. 1-25). In addition to large flint flakes, the earlier type of axes that were flaked from flint began to disappear and they were ultimately replaced by stone axes made from schist and baked mudstone whose surface had been ground or polished. It is difficult to explain the reason for these changes since many of them seem to indicate a shift from a sophisticated set of flint implements in the earlier period to much simpler and cruder tools in the Later Mesolithic. Some have suggested that the Early Mesolithic people had died out or were replaced by a second wave of colonists who brought with them simpler tools. This, however, would seem to be very unlikely since the Later Mesolithic tools are almost unique to Ireland (they can also be found on the Isle of Man) and are unlike the tools being made at that time anywhere in Britain or the Continent. There is no place outside of Ireland that can explain where these new tools came from and so we are forced to assume that the Later Mesolithic peoples of Ireland descended from their earlier predecessors.

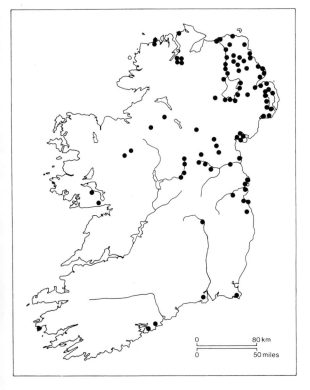

0 ____ 80 km

0 ____ 50 miles

1-26. Later Mesolithic sites in Ireland.

7. A Later Mesolithic coastal
settlement is first inundated
by the rising sea and is then
left on a raised beach
as the land rises faster
than the sea.

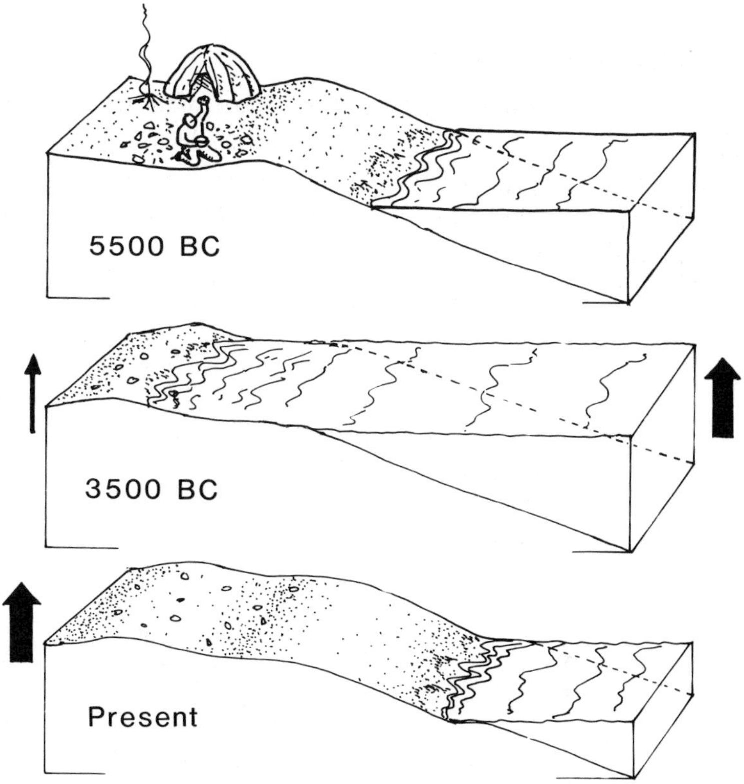

5500 BC

3500 BC

Present

Many of the Later Mesolithic sites are to be found along the Irish coast, especially the Antrim coast, along the raised beaches (Ill. 1-26). Communities apparently came to work nodules of flint along the flint-rich coast from about 5500 BC onwards. But the constant rise of the sea after the Ice Age, especially around 3500 BC, meant that the sea rose higher with respect to the shore than it is today and the Later Mesolithic coastal sites were heavily battered by waves (Ill. 1-27). Then the land itself began to rise (it literally sprang back from having been weighed down by the earlier glaciers) faster than the rise in sea level and by the time things became relatively stable again, the ancient beaches of the Later Mesolithic in Ulster were left about 8 metres above present sea level. The heavily battered remains of these industrial work camps were observed as long ago as 1865 by the 'Northern Collectors' such as William Gray of Belfast. The various east Antrim sites, especially those around Larne, were periodically investigated by the Belfast Naturalists' Field Club and fierce debate broke out as to whether they represented evidence of Palaeolithic man in Ulster. William Knowles, the Ballymena estate agent who proved to be one of Ulster's greatest collectors, continually argued that the flint implements found in the raised beaches were probably the oldest known in the British Isles while others such as Gray himself believed that they dated to the 'New Stone Age', the Neolithic (the whole idea of a Mesolithic was not even invented until 1895). Ultimately, it was conclusively shown that the flint flakes were deposited after the end of the Ice Age and could not possibly

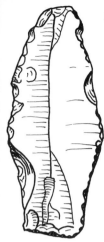

1-28. Typical 'Larnian' flake (l. 8 cm).

be Palaeolithic. Since so much of the material had been found near Larne, archaeologists came to refer to the Later Mesolithic as the Larnian culture, and professional archaeologists such as Hallam Movius of Harvard University came to Larne to carry out extensive scientific excavations of this disputed material. In 1935 at the Curran Point in Larne he recovered 15,000 flints from the raised beach. Today, we know that there was no special Larnian culture, just heavily battered and rolled flakes scattered along the coasts that were originally produced by striking flakes off large single-platformed cores using a hard hammerstone (Ill. 1-28). Only in a few special circumstances such as at Bay Farm I near Carnlough, Co. Antrim, do we find the remains of Later Mesolithic flint-working stations with their flint in fresh condition.

It should be clear from all this that these coastal sites do not provide the best evidence for Later Mesolithic communities in Ulster since they generally appear to have served as specialist industrial sites that may have been occupied for only a matter of days from one year to the next. We must turn to the inland sites if we wish to learn more about these people than the battered remains of their flint-working stations. Most inland sites are situated along rivers and the most important of these is Newferry, Co. Antrim. Here Peter Woodman excavated a series of sites situated where Lough Beg disgorges into the river Bann and provided exceptionally good conditions for Mesolithic fishermen. Later Mesolithic communities occupied this site on and off for nearly 2000 years from about 5500 to 3500 BC. The tools accumulated in the diatomaceous earth that is typical for this area and in the different layers of the site we can trace the development of tools of these Later Mesolithic people.

In contrast to the Early Mesolithic tool kit of microliths, the Later Mesolithic hunters and fishers utilized as their classic tool a flint instrument generally known as the Bann flake because many thousands have been found along the river Bann. This is a simple leaf-shaped flake that resembles a spearhead whose butt has been trimmed and, indeed, the technical term for such a tool is a 'butt-trimmed flake' (Ill. 1-29). It should be noted that although these tools are quite common in Antrim they are by no means limited to the Bann valley and they have been discovered throughout Ireland. Nevertheless, they are most often discovered along river banks or on the sea coast. Although the shape of the flake resembles that of a spear, the butts are often too thick to have been easily attached to anything as slender as a spearshaft or an arrowshaft. Rather, some archaeologists suspect that they were mounted in a wooden handle and that they served as all purpose hunting and fishing knives, something like the modern Boy Scout knife. It is also possible that what appear to us to be the same tool type was actually utilized in many different ways, and microscopic analysis of the use marks on the flakes should provide some evidence whether this is true.

In addition to flint tools, there were also axes made out of schist or mud stone (Ill. 1-30). These axes were made by first flaking the axe into shape

1-29. Bann or butt-trimmed flake (l. 9 cm).

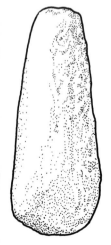

1-30. Mudstone axe (l. 12 cm).

and then grinding down the surface by rubbing it against an abrasive stone such as sandstone. The mudstone axes are especially interesting since this stone tends to be found only along a belt of territory stretching from Co. Down to Co. Longford. This presents us with a curious puzzle concerning both exchange and the distribution of these Later Mesolithic communities.

When we consider the flint tools that occur along the Bann, we generally assume that the flint used in making them came from coastal sites in Antrim up to 30 kilometres away. Unlike the coastal sites which have an abundance of waste material, the inland sites such as Newferry show almost exclusively finished tools. All of this makes perfectly good sense. We might imagine that groups of people moved from one season to the next between the coastal sites which provided not only sea resources but also the raw material for making their flint tools and the inland river sites. Naturally, they did not lug bags of flint nodules from the coast to the inland sites but prepared their flakes at source by the sea and then carried inland only the finished or nearly finished tools. While this pattern may be observed in northeast Ulster, the same cannot be said, however, for southern Ulster where we believe the mudstone axes originated. Here we really do not have good evidence for Mesolithic sites of any sort. It is possible that the same people who occupied the rivers of northern Ulster also made seasonal visits to Fermanagh and Tyrone where they collected the right sort of stone for making their axes. Or perhaps these western counties may have been better settled than our evidence so far indicates and that they exchanged their stone axes for something like better supplies of flint. Indeed, if we regard fishing as a primary focus of the Mesolithic economy, it is astonishing that we have so little evidence so far for Mesolithic sites from western Ulster where the rivers of Donegal or the Erne system, for example, should have attracted abundant Mesolithic settlement. A thorough picture of Ulster's early colonists is unlikely to emerge until professional and especially amateur archaeologists operating in Fermanagh, Donegal, Monaghan and Cavan undertake surveys in areas where we may well expect to find evidence of Mesolithic communities.

Other than the Bann flakes and mudstone axes there are few really distinctive tools used by these Later Mesolithic peoples. We do find a few scrapers for cleaning hides and burins for working bone and antler, but there is nothing of the diversity of tools known from the Early Mesolithic nor is their anything really similar to the type of toolkits used at the same time in Britain. Across the Irish Sea Mesolithic tool kits show abundant use of scrapers, presumably for cleaning the hides of red deer and wild cattle. The former seems to have played only a small part in the Later Mesolithic economy of Ulster and the latter was absent from Ireland. It is quite possible that we are missing a vast range of bone and wooden tools that have simply not survived.

There is one final object that should probably be attributed to the Later Mesolithic although archaeologists have been reluctant to discuss it for

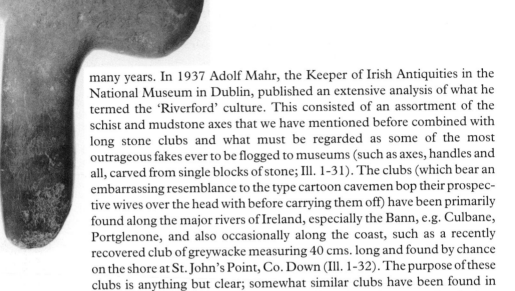

many years. In 1937 Adolf Mahr, the Keeper of Irish Antiquities in the National Museum in Dublin, published an extensive analysis of what he termed the 'Riverford' culture. This consisted of an assortment of the schist and mudstone axes that we have mentioned before combined with long stone clubs and what must be regarded as some of the most outrageous fakes ever to be flogged to museums (such as axes, handles and all, carved from single blocks of stone; Ill. 1-31). The clubs (which bear an embarrassing resemblance to the type cartoon cavemen bop their prospective wives over the head with before carrying them off) have been primarily found along the major rivers of Ireland, especially the Bann, e.g. Culbane, Portglenone, and also occasionally along the coast, such as a recently recovered club of greywacke measuring 40 cms. long and found by chance on the shore at St. John's Point, Co. Down (Ill. 1-32). The purpose of these clubs is anything but clear; somewhat similar clubs have been found in other European fishing communities and have been interpreted as devices for stunning or killing very large fish.

The Later Mesolithic sites are very much concentrated on coasts and in the flood-plains of rivers such as the Bann and we may well expect that fish was one of their primary sources of food. Perhaps the poor flint tools we find were primarily for manufacturing such things as fish-weirs and bone and wooden harpoons. Surely the discovery of several hundred axes at Culbane indicates considerable effort in woodworking along the Bann. We get a slight hint of what we are missing in the archaeological record from Toome Bay, Co. Londonderry, where the Bann joins Lough Neagh. Later Mesolithic material was recovered from the peat here in 1930 by Claude Blake Whelan, a lawyer who became one of the foremost amateur archaeologists in Ulster. In 1950 Frank Mitchell of Trinity College, Dublin, undertook an excavation at the site and uncovered the remains of several wooden implements of hazel and pine, some of which may have served as shafts for fishing or hunting weapons (Ill. 1-33).

Whatever the reasons, we should not imagine that the culture of these Later Mesolithic people had necessarily degenerated, but rather that it had simply changed, possibly from one primarily dependent on stone tools to one where most tools were fashioned from wood or bone. Once the change had taken place at the beginning of the Later Mesolithic, there is only slight evidence for further evolution and none whatsoever for contacts with Great Britain. This may summon up an image of a culturally stagnant society but we should also recall that it was a remarkably successful society since the culture of the Later Mesolithic inhabitants of Ulster survived for nearly 2000 years.

Although we can examine the stone tools of Later Mesolithic societies we have very little concrete evidence for any other aspect of their existence and, curiously enough, seem to know more about life in the Early Mesolithic than in the more recent period. We do have some economic evidence drawn from coastal sites found round Ireland. Most include shellfish, and a few include the remains of whale, wild boar, birds, fish and red deer. Some claim that the earliest evidence for red deer comes from the discovery of its bones at two sites in Belfast - near the Ormeau Bridge and at Sydenham Station - both reputed to date around 7000 years ago. It raises the question of whether settlement patterns in the Later Mesolithic differed much from those of the earlier period. As yet we have no evidence of a base camp such as Mount Sandel and Peter Woodman has suggested that life in the Later Mesolithic may have become even less sedentary than it was earlier. He has proposed that the tens of thousands of artifacts found at sites such as Culbane on the flood plain of the Bann points to short forays to the river system perhaps to establish and maintain fixed fishing stations rather than any form of longer term settlement. This would mean that families or very small groups of families moved about the landscape quite frequently, not even making use of base camps such as Mount Sandel to see them through several seasons. Indeed, where Later Mesolithic peoples settled during the winter is still a complete mystery. We can only note that the evidence of Bann flakes suggests that they not only exploited the coastal and river systems but they occasionally moved into the upland regions of County Antrim, possibly in pursuit of red deer.

What was the size of the Mesolithic population in Ireland? This is not an easy question to answer but at least we can make an educated guess. Peter Woodman carried out rough calculations on the various resources available to Mesolithic man in Ireland and estimated that the land could have supported anywhere from 1 person for every 100 sq. km to 1 person per 10 sq. km. If these broad limits are essentially accurate, then the Mesolithic population of Ulster may have been somewhere between several hundred to several thousand people at any one time.

We are still baffled by why there was such a dramatic change in technology between the Early and Later Mesolithic? Several ideas present themselves but none are particularly convincing. Was it because man now began to hunt red deer and required a different tool kit? This seems unlikely since the weapons used in the Early Mesolithic to bring down a wild boar could certainly have handled deer as well. Indeed, it is not easy to see what tool was specifically employed in hunting during the Later Mesolithic. The paucity of scrapers in the Later Mesolithic also indicates that red deer was never particularly important. It would seem that the economy remained largely the same between the Early and Later Mesolithic; it was the methods of procurement that changed.

Could the change in tool types have had something to do with flint resources? Those groups occupying the Antrim region would have had access to abundant flint supplies and could have used as much as they

wished in making their tools. They could have been quite wasteful in their production of tools and not required the more sophisticated and economical techniques used in the Early Mesolithic. But this too seems unlikely since we find the heavy bladed industries everywhere in the Later Mesolithic, even in areas where there is only chert or where the flint resources are extremely poor.

We are thrown back on suggesting that there was some 'cultural' reason why the population of Ireland changed its technology so much. Certainly, Ireland's isolation from Britain and the Continent during the Later Mesolithic meant that it was free to drift off to develop its own industries. But this is not a very satisfying answer and we may not know the real explanation unless we are able to discover Mesolithic sites that date somewhere between about 6000 BC when we see the last microliths and about 5500 BC when the Later Mesolithic industries appear.

Finally, we should return to the site of Newferry and see what was eroding out of the topmost layers of the site. Whilst all the lower layers were full of material typical of the Later Mesolithic, the uppermost layer yields something quite new - sherds from clay pots and a leaf-shaped arrowhead. New colonists had arrived to change the entire face of the Ulster landscape.

2   The First Farmers
4000 - 2500 BC

Introduction

The second major colonization of Ireland began about 4000 BC with the arrival of new people who not only introduced a wholly new culture but also changed the face of the Ulster landscape. Thousands of years earlier in southwest Asia, communities had begun to abandon a life based solely on hunting and gathering and gradually developed an economy involving agriculture and the keeping of domestic animals. Such a settled way of life permitted the growth of villages and an increase in the population which probably impelled some of these first farmers to cross into southeastern Europe. Over successive generations, these farmers either pushed slowly across Europe or influenced the local hunter-gathering populations to adopt the new economy (Ill. 2-1). By about 4500 BC farming communities existed along the Atlantic coast and soon afterwards they began to appear in Britain and Ireland.

What was so new about these colonists? To begin with, their economy was no longer based on seasonal movements but with greater control over

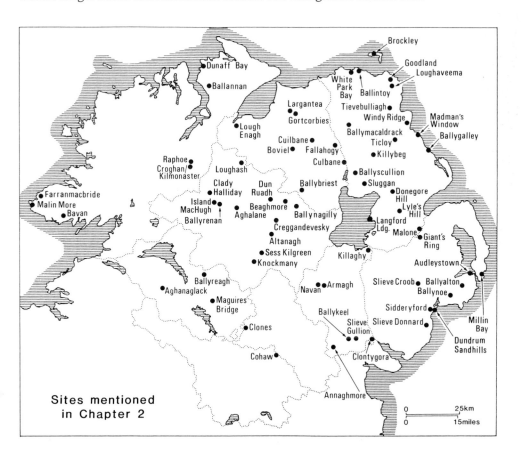

Sites mentioned
in Chapter 2

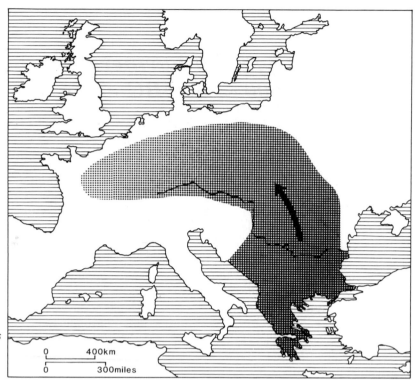

2-1. *The spread of agriculture across Europe.*

0 ⊢——————⊣ 400km

0 ⊢——————⊣ 300miles

their food sources, they were able to live in permanent settlements all year round. They introduced into Ireland a series of domestic animals - cattle, sheep, goat and pig. Except for the pig, all of these species were new to Ireland, at least since the end of the Ice Age, and we can well imagine how they might have impressed the earlier population of hunter-gatherers who occupied Ireland during the Mesolithic. To people accustomed to hunting wild pig and red deer, the appearance of domestic cattle must have been a shock and certainly nothing could have prepared a Mesolithic hunter for his first sighting of a sheep or goat. In addition, the earlier plant diet, such as hazel nuts or water lily seeds, was vastly increased by the addition of cereals such as wheat and barley. And there was also a new technology that had been especially developed for this new agricultural economy. The first farmer colonists introduced their own variety of polished stone axes for clearing away forests, flint tools for harvesting their crops, grinding stones for processing the cereal, and pots made from clay to assist in cooking and serve as containers. Even the type of tools used for hunting changed as these early farmers brought their own type of flint arrowheads and javelins, and now that there was easy access to animals whose hides were particularly useful to man, we begin to find abundant evidence for flint scrapers. Finally, they buried at least some of their dead and held their religious ceremonies in and about large stone monuments that still dot the Ulster landscape.

Now all of these changes suggest a radically different way of life from the earlier Mesolithic and, consequently, archaeologists term this new period

30

the Neolithic ('new stone' age). There has recently been some debate among archaeologists whether the introduction of the Neolithic way of life in Ireland was brought about by new colonists or whether the local Mesolithic population simply picked up new ideas that were spreading through the Continent and Britain at this time. Most would agree that the evidence strongly supports the idea of an actual colonization by new people crossing from Britain (or less likely directly from the Continent) in boats. It is one thing to say that ideas have wings but it is something else to attribute wings to the new animals such as cattle, sheep and goats. These domesticated animals had to be transported across the sea into Ireland and this would have required people to do it. The same is true of the cereals which first appear in Ireland during the Neolithic.

Some have still argued that the new economy might have been introduced by local Mesolithic populations rather than farmer colonists. According to this hypothesis, local Mesolithic peoples in Ireland may have come into contact with farming communities on the other side of the Irish Sea, and they themselves may have obtained the new livestock and cereals from there. But all the evidence we have seen so far suggests that the Later Mesolithic populations of Ireland remained culturally isolated from developments in Britain and it is most unliklely that seasonal hunter-fishers would immediately adopt the complicated and radically new techniques of agriculture and a settled way of life. Moreover, the new economy appears in Ireland at the same time as in Britain which suggests that it spread relatively rapidly through the British Isles rather than percolated gradually across the Irish Sea. In short, the Neolithic does appear to represent the occupation of this island by a new people, who probably introduced a new language, new religion and a totally new way of life.

Neolithic settlement

One of the earliest Neolithic farmsteads discovered in the British Isles is found in Ulster. This is the site of Ballynagilly, Co. Tyrone, where a Neolithic farmer sought out a small hill of gravel (today the only dry spot in the area) to establish a settlement which was occupied both in the Neolithic and then again later in the Early Bronze Age. Here Arthur ApSimon excavated a house measuring about 6.5 x 6 metres (Ill. 2-2). Since it was part of a permanent year round settlement, the building was constructed more substantially than the huts at Mount Sandel. The longer sides of the house were marked by trenches dug into the ground to receive upright oak planks that served as walls (Ill. 2-3). There were postholes not only around the edges of the house to help support the walls but also within the building. These interior posts held up the centre of a pitched roof. Such a roof was necessary and typical across temperate Europe to permit the rain to run off. Also within the house were traces of both a hearth and possibly an oven. The house had been burnt and charcoal from the walls yielded a radiocarbon date of about 3700 BC. In addition to the house, the excavators also uncovered many pits and hearths which dated to the Neolithic period.

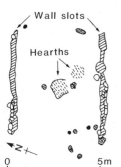

2-2. *Ballynagilly house plan.*   2-3. *Reconstruction of Ballynagilly house.*

Ballynagilly is but a single site and we are far less certain about assuming that it was typical for the Early Neolithic than we were about using Mount Sandel to represent the Early Mesolithic. We do know that there are other farmsteads similar to Ballynagilly outside Ulster. Archaeologists discovered a house at Ballyglass, Co. Mayo, during their excavation of a Neolithic tomb. It measured 13 x 6 metres and recently two Neolithic houses have been excavated near Tankardstown, Co. Limerick. One of these was elongated like the Ballyglass house and measured 13 x 7 metres in size while a short distance away stood a smaller house 7.4 x 6.4 metres. A number of other houses have been reported from other regions of Ireland. All of this type of evidence suggests a pattern of Neolithic settlement not far removed from that which we can still see today all across rural Ireland. Normally, rural families live in their own small farms which are scattered across the countryside in a pattern which is often called dispersed settlement (Ill. 2-4). This seems quite natural in Ireland but it does contrast with much of the rest of Europe at this same time where farmers generally lived together in villages rather than in isolated farmsteads. This pattern of settlement which involves clusters of families living together is called nucleated. Recent evidence from Ireland suggests that while people may have lived primarily in dispersed settlements, the range of settlement types may have varied more than previously imagined.

At one extreme we find what appear to be possible camp sites that were not as stable or as large as Ballynagilly. In the sand-dunes of Dundrum, Co. Down, for example, Pat Collins uncovered Neolithic pottery and flint tools that suggest that some groups of Neolithic people settled near or on the sea coast, although we have no idea how permanent their settlements were. Simarly, Neolithic pottery has also been recovered from the sand dunes of Whitepark Bay, Co. Antrim. What may have been small Neolithic camp sites have also been discovered at Mad Man's Window, near Glenarm, Co. Antrim, which Neolithic farmers like their Mesolithic predecessors visited in order to obtain flint for their tools, and quite recently Derek Simpson

4. Modern dispersed settlement in Ulster.

has been excavating a Neolithic camp at Ballygalley, Co. Antrim. Inland lakes also served as areas for Neolithic settlement as is shown by the remains of Neolithic pottery recovered by Oliver Davies in his excavations at both Island MacHugh in Co. Tyrone and Lough Enagh, Co. Londonderry. At Carnlough, Co. Antrim, there are traces of small Neolithic camps or farmsteads both in the lowlands along the coastal plain at Bay Farm II and also in the uplands at Windy Ridge near Lough-na-Trosk. These upland sites may have been associated with the seasonal movement of livestock to higher pastures, a practice known in Ireland throughout its history. This seems to represent a significant change in the settlement patterns of Ulster since almost all previous settlement was largely confined to the sea coasts and the river valleys. With domestic animals, Neolithic Ulstermen were able to penetrate and settle areas that had apparently been left alone during the Mesolithic.

Not all of our evidence points to such small sites and in Ulster we find the two largest enclosed Neolithic settlements in Ireland. Both of these are situated in Co. Antrim, near Templepatrick, on either side of the Six Mile Water. The larger of the sites is Lyles Hill which was excavated by Estyn Evans of Queen's University. As its name indicates, the site is located on top of a large hill measuring about 385 x 210 metres (Ill. 2-5). The entire top of the hill was surrounded by an earthen bank which Evans believed to

33

2-5. Lyles Hill.

date to the Neolithic. Recently, Derek Simpson of Queen's University re-excavated the bank and discovered that it had actually been built in the Bronze and Iron Ages and not earlier in the Neolithic as was previously supposed. At first this seemed to suggest that there were no surrounding defences to the site, however, he also discovered fortifications that Evans' excavation had missed. The top of the hill was defended by two lines of palisades - an inner palisade built about 3000 BC and an outer defence erected between 2800 and 2400 BC (Ill. 2-6).

During his excavations on Lyles Hill, Estyn Evans discovered pits, hearths, vast quantities of Neolithic pottery, stone tools and small stone ornaments. Much of the material was recovered from an area of ash and burnt bone which had been covered by a stone cairn. Some have suggested that the heaps of pottery, flint, ash and bones may therefore have been

2-6. Palisade trench on Lyles Hill.

2-7. Crop marks of ditches on Donegore Hill.

deposited as part of some form of ceremony. While this may have been so, excavations elsewhere on the hilltop and outside the area of the cairn also uncovered much pottery and flint all of which would suggest that there was a substantial settlement on Lyles Hill.

A few miles north of Lyles Hill stretches the longer Donegore Hill on whose summit another enclosed Neolithic site has been recently discovered and partly excavated. Here we do not talk merely of an enclosure but of defense since the site was surrounded not only by two timber palisades but also two ditches although they were probably not all contemporary with one another. The site is second after Lyles Hill in size and measures about 200 x 150 metres.

The ditches at Donegore were discovered by Barrie Hartwell of Queen's University who photographed the site from the air (Ill. 2-7). Aerial photography is a technique of archaeological exploration that is widely used throughout Ireland and Lyles Hill was one of the first sites ever to be discovered through aerial photography. Donegore Hill, however, offers a better example since without the aerial photographs the ditches that surround the site are invisible to anyone on the ground. The ditches themselves were excavated to a depth of 1 to 2 metres deep and about 3 metres across. When they filled up with soil, this meant that the soil in the ditches was looser and better able to retain water than the surrounding natural ground. During a particularly dry summer when the grass or barley would turn yellow-brown, the crop growing directly over the ditches would have a little better access to moisture and remain somewhat greener. The colour difference is not visible to anyone simply walking across the site, but from the air one can make out the 'cropmarks' produced by the ditches.

One of the remarkable aspects of the Donegore ditches is that they were dug through glacial till and solid basalt without benefit of metal tools. The excavation of such ditches is a topic which archaeologists in the British Isles

2-8. Antler pick.

are quite familiar with since we find in southern Britain many large circular ditched enclosures that are popularly known as 'causewayed camps'. Many of these lie on the chalk of southern England and there we find clear evidence that the ditches were dug with antler picks (Ill. 2-8). Although animal bone did not survive at Donegore, we suspect that a very similar technique was used here as well and the excavator carried out some experiments with red deer antler that showed that even an inexperienced 'Neolithic workman' could break up the solid basalt and remove a large bucketfull of basalt within about ten minutes.

Within the site were discovered even more remains of flint and pottery than at Lyles Hill. In addition, what would appear to have been the destroyed remains of several houses were also discovered. Radiocarbon dates indicate that this site was occupied for a considerable period of the Neolithic from about 4000 to 2700 BC. On the basis of the radiocarbon dates so far obtained, Donegore may have begun earlier than Lyles Hill but by c. 3000 BC both sites may have not only been contemporary with one another but possibly also at war.

That Neolithic communities employing such enclosures did engage in war is eloquently demonstrated by Crickley Hill, one of the causewayed enclosures of southern England. Here there is clear evidence of an assault both by archers (numerous arrowheads found about the entrance) and fire (burnt palisades). The evidence from the Six-Mile-Water sites is not so clear although less than 5% of each site has yet been excavated. We might note that the Donegore defences do not appear to have been particularly impressive - a schoolboy could have leapt across - and they may have posed more of a psychological barrier than a physical one (Ill. 2-9). Ditches have been used throughout the world to mark the extremity of a settlement and their excavation has often been associated with some form of divine sanction. Hence the would-be attacker not only must leap across a man-made barrier but may have regarded the ditch as under some form of sacred protection (Romulus is reputed to have executed his brother Remus for jumping across the walls that defined early Rome). Although hardly sanctioned by divinities, the grafitti which covers certain public areas of modern day Northern Ireland offers a similar form of psychological barrier to would-be intruders.

Beyond these particular settlements there are very few others offering clear traces of some form of architecture. Pits are found on a number of sites as well as the occasional hearth but our evidence for actual Neolithic

2-9. Neolithic 'attack' on Donegore Hill; men and ditches are drawn to scale.

settlement is far poorer than for most of Continental Europe at this same time. It has even been suggested that Neolithic people deliberately destroyed their settlements as part of their religious ceremonies. At Goodland, Co. Antrim, Humphrey Case excavated a Neolithic settlement that had been sealed under blanket peat. The site consisted of a small ditch and over 170 pits of various sizes (Ill. 2-10). Both the ditch and the pits had been frequently filled with stone cobbles, charcoal, broken sherds of pottery and flints. Case suggested that these pits had not been filled by natural processes such as erosion but rather deliberately and soon after they had been dug. In order to explain this he suggested that in Neolithic Ireland people may have performed fertility ceremonies wherein they dug up the debris from their own habitation sites and reburied it in pits. This would have been something like returning to the gods what man had made of the soil in order to insure that fertility was restored to it. Some archaeologists have accepted Case's hypothesis while others argue that the pits on these Neolithic sites may have filled up with rubbish quite easily and that there is no real proof that they came from a religious ceremony. Nevertheless, there are other Neolithic sites known associated with small ditches. On the shores of Lough Neagh, Dudley Waterman of the Archaeological Survey discovered traces of a Neolithic settlement associated with a ditch and Chris Lynn, excavating on Scotch Street in the heart of Armagh, found a circular ditched enclosure measuring about 12 metres across and one metre deep (Ill. 2-11). The ditch contained sherds of Neolithic pottery dating from around 2800 BC. There was no evidence what the ditch was for and Chris Lynn suggested that some form of 'ritual' explanation might have to suffice until we have a better idea what Neolithic

10. *Portions of the ditch and pits at Goodland.*

ditch

pit

0   5m

2-11. Circular enclosure at Scotch Street, Armagh.

societies were up to. This explanation is to some extent supported by the nature of some of the pottery found on the site - Carrowkeel Ware - which is normally confined to megalithic tombs or other presumably ritual structures.

Finally, one other Neolithic settlement in Armagh deserves some mention. On the summit of a drumlin situated about 2 miles west of Armagh, Dudley Waterman uncovered traces of Neolithic settlement - pits, sherds from about twenty pots and several hundred flints. The evidence for Neolithic occupation was not particularly abundant, however, this very site eventually developed into Navan, the Emain Macha of early Irish literature and tradition and the ancient capital of Ulster.

Neolithic economy and environment

The direct evidence for the Neolithic economy in Ireland is quite poor. The small number of sites and the fact that many of them are on acid soils which have long destroyed the remains of animal bones conspires to deny us most of the type of evidence that one often encounters on Neolithic settlements elsewhere. Preservation, as we have already seen at Mount Sandel, is often limited to organic remains that have been carbonized or charred since this alters the chemical composition in such a way to make them impervious to further decay. Hence charred remains of wheat and barley indicate that these crops were raised on Neolithic settlements in Ireland (Ill. 2-12). We also have evidence for such cereals from the surfaces of Neolithic pots in the form of impressions where people making pots have accidentally or possibly intentionally pressed seeds into the wet clay while making a vessel. A Neolithic bowl recovered from Dooey's Cairn, a megalithic tomb in Co. Antrim, exhibited the impressions of 13 spikelets of wheat.

2-12. Charred grain of prehistoric barley.

The domestic animals that are attested include cattle, sheep, goat and pig as well as the dog. The faunal remains from Ulster are so poor that it is nearly impossible to say much more about our earliest livestock. But if we take into consideration the evidence from Britain, than we may imagine that our Neolithic cattle would have stood about 125 cm. high at the withers (comparatively shorter than modern breeds). In addition, some argue that cattle during the Irish Neolithic may have been primarily if not exclusively raised for meat and that it was not until the Iron Age that we may expect the beginnings of the dairy economy in Ulster.

The earliest farmers were the first inhabitants of Ulster to make a substantial impact on the landscape. In order to grow their crops or provide pasture for their livestock, it was necessary to clear what had been largely virgin forests. Although these cleared forests may have later reverted back to forest or devolved into bogland, there is one scientific technique that allows us to recapture man's first impact on the Ulster landscape - pollen analysis or palynology.

The pollen that torments people who suffer from hay fever is both remarkably durable and varies according to each type of plant or tree (Ill. 2-13). As it rains over the landscape each year, it settles in lakes and bogs layer after layer, thus providing an indication of the changing vegetation through time (Ill. 2-14). The pollen can then be extracted from material such as peat and the different pollen grains can be counted to provide us with a picture of the landscape at a particular time. It is pollen analysis that indicates when the various species of trees entered the Ulster landscape

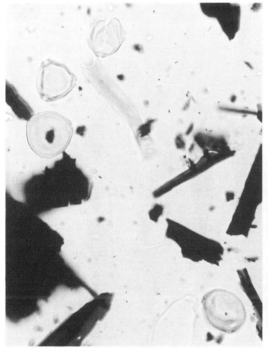

2-13. Pollen grains (hazel and birch) and charcoal from Island McHugh.

2-14. Coring through lake sediments for pollen.

after the last glaciation and the same technique can be used to indicate changes in the environment brought about by human activity. This has provided a major source of information about Ulster's past environment.

A study of pollen from the Neolithic sites of Ballynagilly, and Beaghmore, Co. Tyrone, and from bogs such as Fallahogy, Co. Londonderry and Ballyscullion, Co. Antrim, all indicate a similar phenomenon. At some time around 3800 BC there appears a marked drop in tree pollen such as that of oak, pine, hazel and especially elm (although many now regard the elm-decline to have been the result of disease). At the same time there is also a rise in grass pollen and not infrequently we also find charcoal flecks in the pollen profiles for this period (Ill. 2-15). All of this can be readily interpreted as a result of land clearance - Neolithic farmers moved into virgin forest and cut down the trees (hence the drop in the amount of tree pollen), burnt out the stumps (hence the charcoal) and planted their crops (from which we find both cereal pollen and certain weeds that we normally associate with cultivated fields). This new opening of the land is known as a *landnam* after the Danish word for 'land-taking'. It is with this *landnam* that we first mark man's impact on the Irish landscape as he began to clear its forests in order to create fields and open pastures. So far the evidence throughout Ireland indicates that land clearances were beginning by about 4000 BC, a date somewhat earlier than traditional Irish history which credited the first forest clearance to Partholon who supposedly settled in Ireland c. 2600 BC.

How forested was Ulster during the Neolithic? We can gain a hint of this by comparing the amount of tree pollen as compared with grass pollen. In recent experiments we find that the present relatively treeless landscape of Ulster yields only about 15% tree pollen in contemporary surface samples. In the Neolithic, however, the tree pollen amounted to as much as 80-90% of the total pollen. About a thousand years ago it had fallen to about 30%.

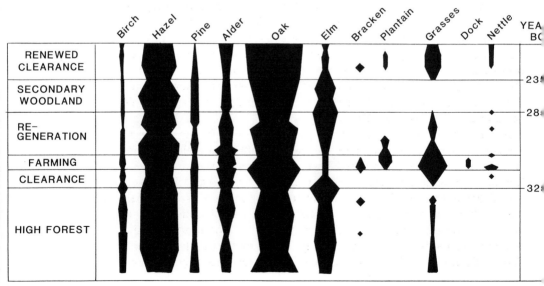

2-15. *Simplified diagram of land clearance at Fallahogy. As the amount of tree pollen declines, grasses, including cereals, increase.*

40

Hence we can see that over the past 5000 years, the Ulster forests have been continually diminishing, and that the period of their most dramatic reduction was during the prehistoric period. The modern Ulster landscape is to a considerable degree the legacy of its prehistoric inhabitants.

Some even suggest that the pollen record not only provides us with evidence of man's initial impact on the Irish landscape, but it also indicates the very pattern of farming settlement. For example, Jonathan Pilcher, working in the Palaeoecology Laboratory at Queen's University, undertook a comparative study of the three sites that showed clear evidence of a *landnam* (today there are many more and they provide a consistent picture). All three of these sites exhibited the same pattern. After the initial *landnam* and evidence for cereal cultivation, this was followed by several centuries of open landscape but without evidence for cereals. Pilcher suggested that this revealed a shift from a primarily agricultural economy to a primarily pastoral phase. Then towards the later Neolithic the forest regenerated around these various sites as farmers apparently abandoned their earlier areas of settlement and moved on.

Another source of evidence for settlement in the Neolithic are the tombs erected by Neolithic communities. Under the logical assumption that wherever we find a tomb, it is likely that the settlement of their builders must be in the same vicinity, we can plot the probable areas of Neolithic settlement in Ulster. Indeed, Gabriel Cooney has carried out a similar exercise in Co. Leitrim where we find a very good correlation between megalithic tombs and rockland soils, the best agricultural soils in the county (Ill. 2-16). In general, megalithic tombs are found primarily on well-drained soils between 120 and 240 metres above sea level. The governing factor appears to be the nature of the soils, but as we can see from the altitude of the tombs, these often appear far above where we normally find cereal cultivation today. Indeed, many of the tombs are situated in areas covered by heaths or outright blanket bog. The evidence suggests, however, that during the Neolithic the soils of these regions were well-drained and the easiest worked. To give an extreme example of high-altitude cereal growing, Sally Kirk discovered what would appear to have been cereal pollen in peat at an altitude of 485 metres on Slieve Croob, Co. Down, dated to c. 3600-3200 BC. As we will also see in the next chapter, this pattern of settlement of mixed agriculture in upland regions would begin to change during the Bronze Age.

In addition to the subtle evidence of pollen or the distribution of tombs, we also have some more concrete evidence for Neolithic agriculture. These are field walls, built of stone, which have recently become of great interest. But how can we date the erection of a prehistoric stone wall? These very early field walls are usually buried under peat. One then needs only to date the peat lying immediately above the base of the wall by radiocarbon to know by what time the wall must have been built. The most extensive system in Ireland is located in north Mayo where for the past twenty years Seamus Caulfield of University College, Dublin, has been investigating a

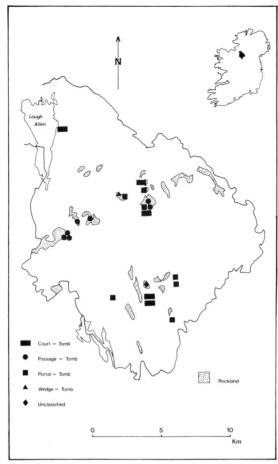

2-16. Megalithic tombs and
rockland soils in
Co. Leitrim.

Court – Tomb
Passage – Tomb
Portal – Tomb
Wedge – Tomb
Unclassified

Rockland

0   5   10
Km

series of field walls that extend for kilometres and date to the Neolithic period. The Mayo fieldstudy area extends over 250 square kilometres along the North Mayo coast. Within the area, field boundaries of stone but also of earthen banks have been found in many locations. Céide Fields, formerly known as the Behy/Glenulra system, is a 1000 hectare monument of parallel field boundaries which extends over the hills and valleys of many townlands (Ill. 2-17). The walls were used to divide the landscape into fields not to enclose one field after another in a haphazard fashion. The long walls in the valley bottom follow the contours closely but walls higher up the slopes ignore the terrain in order to remain parallel to those lower down. According to Seamus Caulfield, the field walls were most likely built to enclose cattle. He estimates that the entire area may have comprised some 50 or 60 families, something on the order of 300 people. While there is no evidence whatsoever for villages, it is difficult to see this planned network of field-systems as anything other than the product of a well-organized society and not the creation of individual farmsteads isolated from one another by thick forests.

Was the Ulster landscape similarly parcelled out into strips of land divided by fieldwalls? It is still much too early to answer this question since field-wall research in Ulster has not progressed as far as it has in north

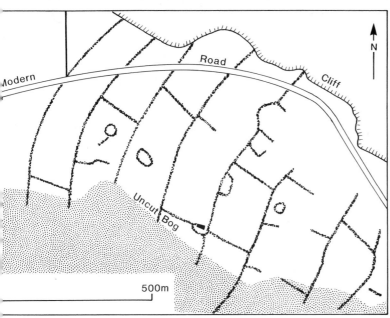

2-17. A portion of the extensive Céide Fields of north Mayo.

Mayo where a Neolithic landscape has been preserved under a bog for the past four thousand years. But we may at least have some evidence that field walls in Ulster also began in the Neolithic since a field wall possibly dating to the later Neolithic has been discovered on the Galboly plateau near Carnlough, Co. Antrim, and we are aware of other field walls that have been dated to later periods elsewhere in Ulster (Ill. 2-18). But we still have barely begun our field-wall surveys in Ulster although we have good reason to be optimistic. For many years, field-walls in mid-Ulster, especially County Tyrone, have been recorded disappearing beneath bogs and like north Mayo we may also some day find a Neolithic landscape preserved under the blanket bog of the Ulster uplands.

Neolithic technology

Museum cases straining under the weight of heaps of flint flakes and broken (and somewhat grotty) pots is generally the form in which we encounter the evidence for Neolithic technology. It is far easier to fill a

2-18. Field systems of various periods near Carnlough.

museum display with Neolithic artifacts than material from almost any other period because Neolithic flint tools and waste material as well as broken pieces of pottery were not only quite durable but apparently very expendable. While such material is hardly as romantic as a megalithic tomb framed against a sunset, it does provide anyone in Ulster with an opportunity to 'do' prehistoric archaeology. The flint flakes that litter a farmer's field are the tangible reminders of Ulster's prehistoric colonists and as archaeologists know, it takes no great amount of effort and time to discover for oneself 5000 year old relics of Ulster's first agricultural communities. For this reason we will spend a little time getting acquainted with both the objects and the society that they might represent.

Axes

Unlike the Ulster of today, the early Neolithic farmers confronted a heavily wooded landscape. In order to prepare fields for planting and establish pastures for their livestock, these forests had to be cleared and the primary tool employed in forest clearance would have been the polished stone axe although, for a time, they apparently also used flint axes. In Ulster the axes used during the Neolithic are often made from a special stone known as porcellanite. This is a volcanic stone that occurs in two places in Ulster - Brockley on Rathlin Island and the more famous site of Tievebulliagh near Cushendall, Co. Antrim. We'll consider first how these axes were made.

The manufacture of a polished stone axe such as one made from porcellanite involves several different processes. The first of these is extraction. At Tievebulliagh, Neolithic people must have discovered the outcrops of slightly bluish porcellanite weathering out of the face of the mountain, a dolerite plug (Ill. 2-19). Broken pieces of porcellanite probably lay about the area but we believe that Neolithic miners also worked the face of the outcrops, perhaps by building fires against the stone and then applying water to cause it to fracture and break off (Ill. 2-20). They would break the clumps of porcellanite into suitable sizes and then begin

2-19. Tievebulliagh.

2-21. Axe roughout.

2-20. Porcellanite outcrop at Tievebulliagh.

flaking them into the general shape of an axe, probably with quartzite hammerstones that can still be found around Tievebulliagh or perhaps antler hammers (Ill. 2-21). These half-finished axes are known as rough-outs and William Knowles, the Ballymena estate agent who discovered the Tievebulliagh axe factory, is reputed to have carried off cartloads of these roughouts at the turn of the century (he claims to have found about 4000 roughouts!). Such roughouts are still occasionally found in the area of Tievebulliagh and attest the workings of a sizeable industry. But it is exclusively rough-outs that are found here, not completed axes, which indicates that the final working of these axes occurred elsewhere.

After the roughouts had been formed, the second stage involved the polishing of the axe. The Neolithic axe-maker would find a suitably abrasive stone such as sandstone and then rub the roughout against this until the surface was smoothed and polished. At Culbane, Co. Londonderry, six porcellanite axes and a sandstone grinding block were found indicating a work station for this final part of the axe-making process. The time required to make a polished axe would be on the order of several hours to a day or more.

When you see polished stone axes on display in a museum you may ask how they were used and whether they were a particularly effective tool (Ill. 2-22). The Neolithic axe-maker almost invariably polished the entire

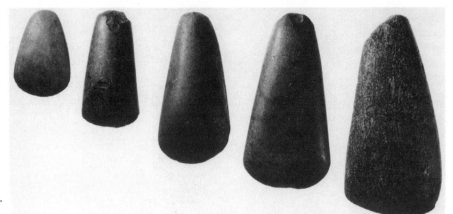

2-22. Polished stone axes.

surface of the axe and not simply the working edge. Such a smooth axe-shaped object is sometimes imagined to have thus served as a hand-axe. This, however, was the not the case and we know that they were inserted into a wooden handle and employed just like an axe is today. Although such wooden handles seldom survive, we know of similar polished stone axes recovered from water-logged sites on the Continent that still retained their wooden handles. Even in Ulster there have been several finds of such complete axes with handles. One was discovered at Maguire's Bridge, Co. Fermanagh (Ill. 2-23), and at least one other was recovered long ago somewhere in County Monaghan.

The only way to determine the effectiveness of a polished stone axe is to use it to chop down trees. Experiments have been carried out using polished stone axes by a number of archaeologists. For example, three Danish archaeologists, armed with polished stone axes, were capable of clearing about 500 square metres of birch forest in four hours while a Russian archaeologist chopped down a pine tree measuring 25 centimetres in diameter in about twenty minutes. Highly effective at clearing the virgin forests of Ireland, these axes were one of the primary tools of the earliest farming colonists.

The porcellanite axes are not only useful but their wide distribution indicates that they were important items of exchange. Porcellanite axes, originally manufactured at Tievebulliagh or on Rathlin, were exported all over Ireland and Alison Sheridan of the National Museum in Edinburgh has managed to catalogue something on the order of 1400 such axes. Moreover, 160 porcellanite axes are known from Scotland, Wales and England (Ill. 2-24). In return, we occasionally find in Ulster axes that were made in one of the great axe factories in Britain. In County Antrim, for example, axes manufactured in the Great Langdale Factory of Cumbria have been found at Cushendall, Portglenone and elsewhere and an axe from the Graig Llwyd factory in North Wales was recovered from Lyles Hill.

We are uncertain what form of exchange these axes took but archaeologists would regard the idea that they were simply traded to where they were needed as far too simple. If we examine the density of axe finds, we note that while County Antrim seems almost saturated with porcellanite axes,

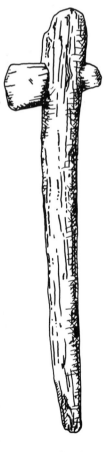

2-23. Axe from Maguire's Bridge.

46

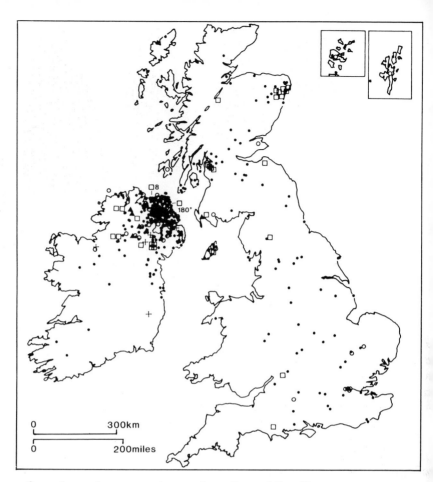

24. *Distribution of porcellanite axes.*

once one moves away from the main source, the number of axes falls off dramatically. Archaeologists speak of 'supply zones' to describe the area where one could go directly to the source of raw material and exploit it and this would seem to fit the situation in County Antrim. Beyond this, however, we move into the 'contact zone' where we suspect that the axes were obtained through some form of exchange. Alison Sheridan suggests a fairly simple form of trade which is popularly known as 'down the line' exchange where one community obtains a certain proportion of the axes and then passes them down the line to increasingly distant communities.

In addition to the exchange of the typical porcellanite axes, there was also the movement of some axes that were probably never intended for use. Anyone who has looked at the great Malone hoard of axes in the Ulster Museum can see that these porcellanite axes were far too large to be used by Neolithic man. These giant axes, measuring from 20 to 38 cm. long, would have required the likes of Finn McCool to wield them (Ill. 2-25). Consequently, we suspect that the function of these very large axes would have been more symbolic than practical; they would have expressed wealth or power and possibly served in religious ceremonies.

The same may be said of the more than forty stone maceheads that are known from Ireland of which nearly half have been recovered in Ulster.

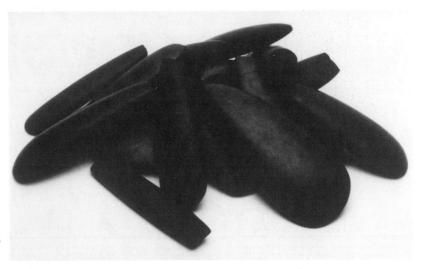

2-25.
The Malone hoard.

These maces were manufactured out of stone such as gneiss and amphibolite and were clearly made as fine works of craftsmanship (Ill. 2-26). They were perforated to be mounted on a wooden shaft and on a few occasions, such as their discovery in the passage tomb at Knowth, Co. Meath, they would appear to symbolize high status, much in the same way that maces are used today to indicate a position of authority. In a recent survey of the Irish maceheads, Derek Simpson has emphasized that they are primarily known from northern and eastern Ireland and that they are comparable to those from northern Britain, especially the Orkneys. All of this hints at some form of contacts between what we presume to have been the higher elements of later Neolithic society in both Britain and Ireland.

It can be seen then that exchange, such as that in polished stone axes, was not simply a commercial affair. Anthropologists have had opportunities to study people who still employed stone axes and exchanged them. The exchange of such axes is more than a business transaction; it is an extremely important social act that tends to bind different peoples together. The exchange of axes may have been carried out periodically at communal meetings and have been associated with other activities such as engagements, dowry exchanges, and trade in other commodities. The person or community receiving axes may have been placed under an obligation to return various favours to those offering the axes for exchange.

Finally, we might observe that as with flint artifacts, turning a penny by producing fake polished stone axes and flogging them to tourists was already a local Ulster enterprise during the last century. In a letter to the *Ulster Journal of Archaeology* published in 1857, a correspondent noted that one of the guides at the Giant's Causeway had been caught red-handed polishing up a basalt axe. The writer also claimed that there was a local industrial base for such production since weavers often employed smooth stones for flattening or beetling linen threads and when natural stones were not available the weaver would make his own, 'so perfectly like an ancient specimen that the most skilful antiquary would be deceived by the imitation'.

2-26. Stone macehead.

Flint tools

The most abundant artifact that we might recover from a Neolithic site are normally flint tools. During the Neolithic many of the same flint sources as we saw in the Mesolithic, especially those along the Antrim coast, continued to be exploited. Again we find major industrial sites where the raw flint nodules would be shaped into cores and then flakes would be struck off of them which would be formed into tools. Possibly the greater population of the Neolithic period prompted a still greater demand for flint such that we find evidence for open-cast quarrying of flint at Black Mountain above Belfast and Ballygalley on the Antrim coast. Beyond those areas where flint occurred naturally, it was probably imported. For example, already by the Late Mesolithic we may presume some form of coastal trade in flint to account for the find of flint pebbles at Dunaff Bay on the Inishowen peninsula in Co. Donegal. Moreover, Laurence Flanagan has commented several times on the discovery of rich flint industries elsewhere in Donegal (near Raphoe and in the court tomb at Bavan) which could not have been products of the drift but would seem to imply trade over a considerable distance. And, as with our stone axe trade, we occasionally find foreign 'substitutes' on Ulster sites. Pitchstone, derived from the island of Arran in western Scotland, has turned up at Lyles Hill and Ballygalley for reasons that defy explanation as it is inferior to the local flint sources. As some of the Antrim flint was being traded to Scotland (hoards of Antrim flint have been found near Portpatrick and Campbeltown), these occasional Scottish novelties may have been carried into Antrim by people involved in such exchange.

In reviewing some of the basic implements one discovers on a Neolithic site, we begin with the points - the general term for anything resembling an arrowhead or spearhead. The arrowheads at this time tend to be lozenge or leaf-shaped and were probably the main hunting weapon as well as occasionally employed in warfare (Ill. 2-27). The surface of the arrowheads were made thin and sharp by the technique of pressure flaking.

Even more technically impressive are the flint javelin heads known from Neolithic Ireland (Ill. 2-28). These are distinguished from the arrowheads by being at least five centimetres long and they may have been up to 25

2-28. Javelin head (l. 9 cm).

49

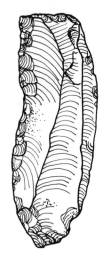

centimetres in length. In cross section they are also more robust than the arrowheads. According to Pat Collins, who has made a special study of these artifacts, they were probably designed to be used as javelin heads attached to a shaft for throwing rather than spears which might also serve as thrusting weapons. Their distribution in Ireland is primarily confined to Ulster, especially the northeast, and here again we see how the predominance of Ulster flint sources has probably affected their distribution. They have been found both on settlement sites and in court tombs, apparently as grave goods for the deceased. Outside of Ireland their closest parallels are found in the Neolithic ditched enclosures of southern Britain.

As a basic tool, the flint knife was quite popular in Neolithic Ireland. It was normally flat on one side and arched on the other thus giving it its technical name - the plano-convex (flat-curved) knife (Ill. 2-29). It also occurs on both settlements and in tombs.

There were other tools which we have already seen in the Mesolithic. End scrapers, for example, are probably the most abundant implement that one encounters on Neolithic sites (Ill. 2-30). We can well imagine their increased importance with the importation and raising of cattle and to a lesser extent sheep, both of which offer useful hides. In the Neolithic period, we also see the introduction or development of a new form of scraper where the end of the flake has been retouched into a curved shape (Ill. 2-31). This is called the hollow scraper and its function remains a mystery. While most scrapers are clearly designed for such things as cleaning animal hides, there is no transparent function for the hollow scraper. Some archaeologists have seen them as part of an archer's tool-kit where they would have been employed for preparing the shafts of arrows or perhaps fletching, i.e., inserting feathers into the ends of the arrowshaft. Others have argued that they may have served as sickles for reaping knives or saws for cutting bone. That they were a popular tool is undoubted since they have been found in considerable numbers on archaeological sites. At Island MacHugh in Co. Tyrone, 120 hollow scrapers were discovered during excavations while another 30 are known from Lyles Hill (yet only one is known from neighbouring Donegore Hill). They are not only found on settlements but also occasionally in hoards which suggests that they were being exported from one area to another. At Killybeg, Co. Antrim, for example, a hoard of 65 hollow scrapers and blanks for their manufacture were discovered. Their sheer number in various hoards prompted Laurence Flanagan to ask whether they may not have served a purpose somewhat similar to a set of ring-spanners that a mechanic might carry around. He measured a series of their diameters and the widths of their apertures but the results were still ambiguous and he could only conclude that they may have been made in various sizes for reasons that we can no longer discern.

When we find flint tools together in a single hoard we may suspect that they were being transported as part of a system of flint trade. We have already seen that such trade in stone existed in the Mesolithic and in this

2-30. Scraper.

2-31. Hollow scraper.

sense conditions were little different in the Neolithic when good flint sources were still to be valued. It is clear from the distribution of some flint implements, such as flint javelin heads in areas where there were no adequate flint sources, that flint was being traded in Neolithic Ulster in a fashion similar to that of the polished stone axes.

Ceramics
One of the main items of technology introduced into Ulster by the first farmers was pottery. For the archaeologists, pottery has always held a special place since it can provide us not only with information about how people lived but also their relations with other peoples and the dating of sites. As you well know, the pottery that you have in your house is probably different from that which your grandparents used. The reason for this is that the styles of pottery have changed over the years and new styles have replaced old ones. This was also so during the Neolithic although we believe that the change in styles then was very much slower than it is today. Before examining some of the Neolithic styles of pottery found in Ulster, it is useful to consider briefly the technology and manufacture of ceramic pots (Ill. 2-32).

Although we cannot be certain, it is probable that the manufacture of pots in Neolithic Ireland was the work of women. In general, when we examine societies that still make pottery by hand, pot making is a woman's task. Here we are talking of basically a domestic craft, the woman of a household making pots perhaps once or twice a year. A source of clay near to the settlement would first have to be discovered and the clay would then be brought on site and prepared for use. This would involve cleaning it of major impurities such as larger stones and also tempering it with some filler such as sand or crushed stone which would help prevent it from shrinking and breaking when it was fired. The vessel would be formed by making coils of clay and then building them up like a basket, pinching the coils together to make a uniform surface and then smoothing the inside and outside of the vessel. A smooth stone or bone might be rubbed against the outer surface of the pot in order to burnish it which would give it a polished appearance. The wet pot would then be allowed to dry naturally before it was fired. The type of Neolithic pots we find in Ireland would not have required a sophisticated kiln but were rather fired in some form of bonfire. The colours of the pots vary from dark black or brown where the pots were fired without access to oxygen, e.g. completely buried in the ash of a fire, or orange where they were exposed to the air during firing and their surfaces turned orange through oxidation.

We have no idea whether the making of pots was the task of every family or whether certain women were regarded as better at the job and hence made pots for their neighbours. One of the features of increasingly more complex societies is the development of craft specialists who are primarily engaged in making some item for exchange throughout their community. From our understanding of the cultural level of early Neolithic society

2-32. The manufacture of a Neolithic pot.

51

in Ireland, it is probably unlikely that there were full-time potters at this time.

Unlike flint which has been collected since the 19th century, our knowledge of Neolithic pottery in Ireland begins remarkably late. As late as 1927 R.A.S. Macalister could write that only two pieces of Neolithic pottery were known in the collections of the Royal Irish Academy - a bowl from Clones, Co. Monaghan, and another from Donegore, Co. Antrim. In actual fact, there were some other finds of Neolithic pottery but they simply weren't identified as such. Today, the quantity of Neolithic pottery is vast although our understanding of how the various styles changed through time and related to one another is still far from satisfactory.

The earliest style of pottery in Ireland is generally termed Western Neolithic or Lyles Hill ware. The first name derives from the fact that there are certain broad similarities in the Neolithic pottery all over the Atlantic fringe of western Europe. More often the earliest Neolithic pottery in Ulster takes its name from Lyles Hill where, up until the excavation at Donegore, the largest collection of early Neolithic pottery had been discovered. That the pottery first appears with the beginning of the Neolithic also provides it with yet another, now somewhat obsolete name, of Neolithic A ware.

Lyles Hill pottery is generally a simple though well-made ware. The pots have round bottoms and a generally rounded shape (Ill. 2-33). The only exception to this occurs at the shoulder of the pots where we often find a marked break in angle where the pot either splays outward at the mouth or is closed inward. The pottery is undecorated; occasionally small knobs or lugs, probably for handling the pots, are found. The Lyles Hill ware finds its greatest similarities with Grimston Ware which is the typical early Neolithic pottery of northern England. This provides us with some evidence that the earliest Neolithic colonists in Ulster came from northern Britain.

The later Neolithic sees the appearance of different styles of pottery (Neolithic B) which are often decorated. According to Michael Herity of University College, Dublin, there are three basic types of pottery from this period plus a number of more exotic forms. The first of these are necked vessels (Ill. 2-34) or Ballyalton bowls after pottery found in a tomb at

2-33. Lyles Hill ware.

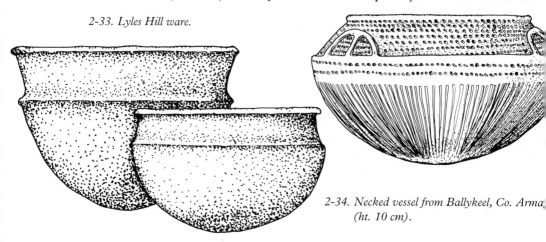

2-34. Necked vessel from Ballykeel, Co. Armagh (ht. 10 cm).

Ballyalton, Co. Down. These bowls are characterized by a small neck converging on a very wide shoulder and the surfaces are decorated with incisions or cord impressions. Of the 30 or so sites which have produced necked vessels, somewhat over half of them are in Ulster.

The second major type comprises a series of broad-rimmed vessels which may be decorated with small channels, cord impressions or small dots (Ill. 2-35). Because of the discovery of such pots in coastal sandhills, especially near Newcastle, Co. Down, this type of pottery has also been called Sandhills Ware. It was suggested that this type of pottery, somewhat cruder in manufacture than the Lyles Hill ware, was made by the descendants of the local Mesolithic populations who still occupied the coasts after the arrival of the first farmers. Such an idea holds much less attraction today since most believe that Mesolithic populations had long ceased to exist by the time that Sandhills Ware first appeared. Of the approximately 25 sites that have produced such ware, nearly 70% lie in Ulster.

The third type of pots are small globular bowls, again decorated with cord impressions and incisions. As a very good collection of these type of vessels was discovered at Goodland, Co. Antrim, they have also been called Goodland Bowls (Ill. 2-36). There are about 30 sites that have produced globular bowls and all but two of them are in Ulster.

Besides a number of more exotic forms we should also mention a type of pottery which is known as Carrowkeel ware as it takes its name from the passage-tomb cemetery of Carrowkeel, Co. Sligo. These pots appear primarily in passage tombs and they are characterized by a simple globular shape and decoration made with long grooves across the surface of the clay (Ill. 2-37).

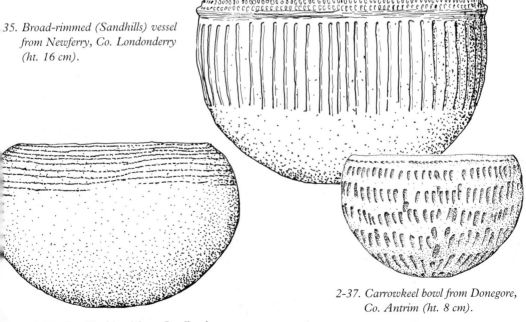

35. Broad-rimmed (Sandhills) vessel from Newferry, Co. Londonderry (ht. 16 cm).

2-37. Carrowkeel bowl from Donegore, Co. Antrim (ht. 8 cm).

2-36. Goodland bowl from Goodland, Co. Antrim (ht. 11 cm).

53

What do the different pot styles mean? To some extent they indicate changes through time in that the earliest vessels were the plain, unornamented Lyles Hill ware. The plain styles were gradually augmented or replaced by the decorated pots. In Britain, where there is a generically similar sequence of ceramic development, a variety of different interpretations have been placed on the various ceramic styles. One of the more interesting is the idea that they evolved socially. The decorated wares were introduced originally as high status markers and are generally found earliest in burials. But as people began to copy them, the social significance of the vessels was debased and styles of decorated wares became the common pottery found on settlements which forced the upper levels of society to develop and adopt yet newer exclusive styles to represent their status in society. Exact parallels from modern society are elusive but we might get a hint of this process if we were to pull into a filling station and find that we could obtain a Belleek vase for every £6 of petrol. Whether this was the pattern in Ulster or not we are hardly able to say since we have neither enough sites nor sufficient control of the dates of the various sites to demonstrate such an evolution. We can only note than over half of the sites are from tombs. The Carrowkeel vessels are normally found in tombs or on ritual sites and may have occupied a particular social role in societies whose own domestic wares are to be found among our other ceramic types. The similarity between Ballyalton bowls and the elaborately decorated bowls found in certain high-status individual burials (Linkardstown cists) outside of Ulster may also have occupied a particularly high social role at one time. But while some sites produce only a single type of pot, others such as Ballykeel, Co. Armagh, produce examples of nearly every form of Neolithic pot. It is clear then that we are still a long way from understanding one of our most abundant survivals from the Neolithic period.

Ornament and Dress
Decency forbids us reconstructing the appearance of a Neolithic man or woman since the hard archaeological evidence suggests even less clothing than one might find on page 3 of an English tabloid. There are no textile remains from Ulster during this period and the only probable traces of attire are a number of greenstone beads and pendants recovered both from megalithic tombs and settlements such as Lyles Hill and Donegore Hill. Some of these appeared to have derived from local stones (W.J. Knowles had over 50, largely of saussurite from the northwest) while some of the beads from Lyles Hill were identified as serpentine or jadeite and were suspected as imports from abroad. In addition, long antler pins, presumably to fasten cloaks or shrouds, are encountered in passage tombs.

The more important question of what people actually wore is not directly answerable although some obvious materials seem to be excluded. For example, woolly sheep did not appear until the end of the Neolithic in eastern Europe and they would not have arrived in Ireland until after the end of the Neolithic. This is further emphasized by the lack of spindle-whorls and other weaving equipment from our few settlement sites. Finally, in terms of faunal remains sheep seem to have played a very marginal part in the Irish economy until long after the prehistoric period.

There is no evidence for the most obvious alternative to wool, plant-derived textiles. In Switzerland where Neolithic villages have been preserved under lakes, textiles are well known, especially of flax, and it would seem that throughout much of Neolithic Europe, before the introduction of woolly sheep, flax was the major source of textiles. However, the Irish pollen record shows no evidence of flax being grown in Neolithic Ireland and the absence of weaving equipment is every much as applicable to linen as it is to wool. This leaves animal skins as the most likely material for clothing during the Neolithic and the abundance of scrapers suggests the preparation of hides, some of which were presumably worn. But it will take a spectacular find from an Irish bog before we can actually discuss fashion in Ulster dress from 4000 to 2500 BC.

Neolithic tombs and ritual

By far the most common and spectacular monuments of the Neolithic period are its tombs. As these were constructed from large stones, archaeologists use the word megalith (Greek *megas* 'large' and *lithos* 'stone') to describe them. They were a very common form of burial structure in Neolithic Europe all along the Atlantic coast from Spain and Portugal in the south as far north as Denmark and southern Sweden. In the British Isles they are primarily found in the north and west where they occur in Wales, Scotland and Ireland. Of the total number of megalithic tombs known from the British Isles, about half of them are found in Ireland. Why people employed large stone structures for burying their dead still eludes us although there is a considerable body of opinion that regards the tombs as linked somehow with marking out territories. In the Mesolithic, hunter-fishers would have had little or no concept of personal ownership of the land. Agricultural societies, however, depend on regular control of certain parcels of land. Hence, many see these tombs as indicators of social territories. The tombs house the remains of the ancestors of a local group which signals to their neighbours their right to possess the surrounding land.

Archaeologists studying the megalithic tombs of Ireland have discerned basic varieties of monuments which seem to date from different periods. To what extent they represent different societies not to speak of different peoples is a hotly disputed topic. Unfortunately, the precise dating of these tombs is still not securely settled and there are some major problems even concerning which of the tombs was the earliest. Here we briefly examine the four major types and then, at the end of this chapter, try to explore their significance.

Court tombs

Traditionally, archaeologists begin their discussion of Irish megalithic tombs with the type known as court tombs. These tombs generally contain three basic elements:

1) a stone gallery for the burials which is divided into various chambers. The number of chambers generally varies from two to five and they are often separated from each other by jambs or a single flat stone forming a sill.

2) The second element is a forecourt at the entrance to the gallery which is formed by erecting a series of stones in an arc. It is this fore-court that gives the tombs their present name - court tombs, or, as they were called in the past - court cairns or horned cairns (because in plan they looked like projecting horns). The stones that form the court are normally set standing upright and are called orthostats (Greek 'straight' and 'standing'). In some instances only a few orthostats are set up at intervals and the space between them is filled with dry stone walling which produced the 'post and panel' type of construction.

3) The entire area behind the court, including the gallery, is then enclosed in either an earthen mound or more commonly with stones (cairn) which normally has a trapezoidal shape, the wide end at the court side with the narrow end beyond the end of the gallery. Court tombs were generally erected with their entrances facing the east.

There are over 391 court tombs known from Ireland and these occur almost exclusively in the northern half of the island, north of a line drawn between Carlingford and Sligo (Ill. 2-38). Tombs of a somewhat similar

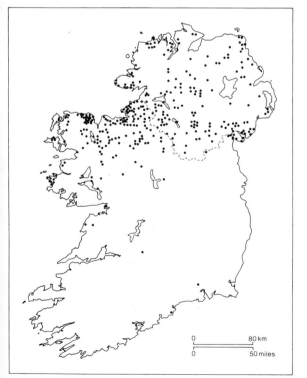

2-38. Distribution of court tombs.

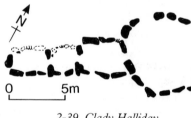

2-39. Clady Halliday.

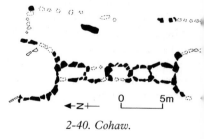

2-40. Cohaw.

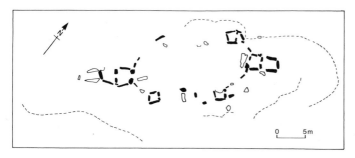

2-41. Farranmacbride.

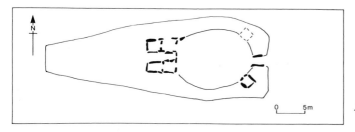

2-42. Malin More.

shape are also known in western Scotland and some archaeologists have lumped both the Irish and Scottish tombs into a single Clyde-Carlingford type. We might add that much of our knowledge of the Irish tombs is derived from the work of Estyn Evans and Oliver Davies who began a systematic programme of research into Ulster's Neolithic tombs in the 1930s and 1940s. Armed with budgets of about £10 and a handful of volunteers and workmen (on bicycle), these pioneers of Ulster archaeology began to put the analysis of these structures on a scientific basis.

Although archaeologists can discern certain basic elements in the court tomb style, the actual form of the tombs may vary considerably. There are tombs that were constructed exactly according to the above description such as the one from Clady Halliday, Co. Tyrone (Ill. 2-39). But at Cohaw, Co. Cavan (Ill. 2-40), and Audleystown, Co. Down, we find double court tombs built back to back. Conversely, at Farranmacbride, Co. Donegal (Ill. 2-41), and other sites we find two tombs facing each other and forming a common central court. This type may be further complicated by other features as seen in a tomb at Malin More, Co. Donegal (Ill. 2-42), where there were two galleries facing a fully enclosed court and then two small separate chambers set into the eastern side of the cairn.

What do we find inside the tombs? Generally, there may be remains of pottery, especially the undecorated Western Neolithic bowls. This, of course, is the same type and style of pottery that we find on large Neolithic settlements such as Lyles Hill and Donegore Hill or on smaller Neolithic farmsteads such as Ballynagilly. But we also find a considerable number of decorated bowls that we would normally associate with a somewhat later phase of the Neolithic. In addition, tools such as hollow scrapers, end scrapers, javelins, arrowheads, polished stone axes of porcellanite and occasionally polished stone beads are found in court tombs. This makes it certain that the tombs were originally constructed and used during the earlier part of the Neolithic period but continued in use for a considerably longer period. Radiocarbon dates from the tombs also supports the notion that they began to be erected c. 3800 BC but continued in use for perhaps a thousand years.

We normally regard the objects that we find in these tombs as offerings placed in the tomb for the dead, grave goods as they are commonly called. This means that when someone died, certain objects were selected by those burying the deceased and placed in the grave for some reason. We can never be certain precisely why these objects were placed in the grave since many people who practice this custom have very different beliefs. Some people deposit grave goods as useful objects to assist the deceased in the after-life; others place objects belonging to the dead person in the grave so that they will not be contaminated by using a dead person's tools or other property. We can see here how archaeologists can often reconstruct the ritual behaviour of a prehistoric people, e.g. that they place objects in their tombs, but that they cannot reconstruct with any certainty the beliefs of a prehistoric people, e.g. the precise reason why people placed objects in tombs. Keeping in mind that it is 'ritual behaviour' and not necessarily 'belief' that we are reconstructing, we can take a more detailed look at the actual burial of the dead in the court tombs.

After the actual erection of the tomb, we find occasional evidence that a fire had been set in one or more of the tomb's chambers (which some have assumed to be a purification fire). The burial might then be deposited directly on the ground or, as is the case in a number of tombs, on a stone pavement, especially prepared on the bottom of the chamber. In addition, the burial might then be covered with flat stones that formed a sealing layer. One tomb proved an important exception to this pattern. In 1935 Estyn Evans excavated what he dubbed 'Dooey's Cairn' at Ballymacaldrack, Co. Antrim (Ill. 2-43). Here, instead of the various stone chambers was a cremation trench below which were three substantial pits, one filled with charcoal and the remains of five or six individuals. All of these seemed to predate the actual erection of the stone tomb.

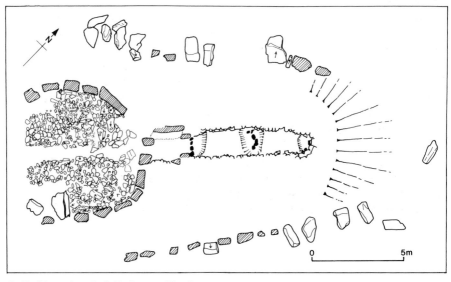

2-43. 'Dooey's cairn', Ballymacaldrack.

'Dooey's Cairn' was not only different from most other court tombs but it also shared a number of similarities with tombs in both England and Scotland. The problems raised by Evan's excavations were enough to entice Pat Collins of the Archaeological Survey to re-excavate part of the tomb forty years later when it passed into state ownership. While it still proved impossible to resolve some of the problems posed by the earlier excavation, the technique of radiocarbon dating was well known by 1975 and Pat Collins was able to demonstrate that the cremation trench had been fired c. 3800 B.C. The three pits have been interpreted as post-pits to receive the uprights of either a mortuary structure that covered the deceased or perhaps to support a platform upon which the bodies of the deceased were exposed before cremation. In any event, the evidence suggests that there were probably two cremation episodes, at least one of which involved a timber structure.

As for the burial itself, the most frequent way of disposing of the deceased in the court tombs was cremation. The body of the deceased was apparently placed on a pyre, presumably near to the court tomb, and burnt. The bones would then be picked or scooped out of the pyre (frequently charcoal and clay were scooped up with the burnt bones) and placed in one of the chambers of the gallery. The discovery of burnt flint tools accompanying a number of burials suggests that either the grave goods were sometimes burnt deliberately on the pyre or that the deceased may have had the flint arrowheads or scrapers on them (or in them?), probably in a leather bag, and these had been burnt in the cremation fire. In a number of tombs such as Audleystown and Ballyalton, Co. Down, there are also a number of simple burials (inhumations). There is some evidence that most of these were not the primary burials in the tombs and may be secondary interments, in some cases coming towards the later part of the Neolithic.

Besides the remains of the deceased, animal bones have been recovered from a number of tombs, generally from the chambers of the galleries. In a few instances they appear to have been placed along with the primary burial, for example, split bones at Ballyalton have been interpreted as the remains of a funeral feast. In many other instances, the animal bones appear to have been later insertions or offerings in the tombs.

The actual objects found with the graves include pottery and here we find that there are slightly more plain shouldered bowls of the Lyles Hill and other plain vessels than there were of the somewhat later decorated bowls. There have also been found 46 projectile heads, 80 hollow (concave) scrapers, 14 knives, 27 rounded scrapers, 3 polished stone axes, 10 beads and a variety of other flint tools and waste.

One of the more interesting aspects of the court tombs is trying to puzzle out what precisely they were for and why they were constructed in the form that we find them. One example should be enough to emphasize how much we don't know about these monuments.

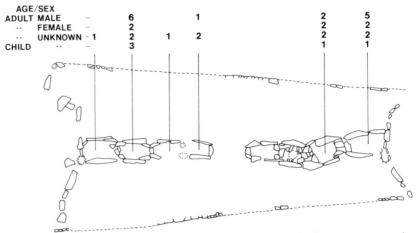

2-44. Location of burials in Audleystown court tomb.

The tomb with the largest number of burials is in the double court tomb of Audleystown, Co. Down, which was excavated in the 1950s by Pat Collins of the Archaeological Survey. Here over 30 people were buried in the various chambers. A closer look at the excavation report suggests that interpreting this tomb is by no means so simple as the actual plan of the tomb might suggest (Ill. 2-44). For example, we might assume that each person or family should have been buried in their own special chamber but this is clearly not the case. In the northeast gallery at Audleystown, the remains of ten individuals were found in the first chamber and another seven in the second chamber. This might mean that whole families were buried in their proper chamber and that these stone chambers served the same function as a family vault in a mausoleum. But there were no bones or grave goods in chambers 3 and 4. If each chamber was for an individual family, then why weren't any bodies found in chambers 3 and 4? If each chamber was not for an individual family, why were all the burials crowded into the first two chambers and others were left apparently empty? Moreover, some of the burials had not been burnt but seem to have been buried somewhere else until their flesh had decomposed and then they were reburied in the court tomb. The evidence for this is that these burials were neither laid out in their proper position nor were all the parts of the body found in the chamber. There is considerable archaeological evidence from both Ireland (Dudley Waterman found similar secondary burials in the court tomb at Annaghmare, Co. Armagh) and Britain for exposing the deceased to the elements or decay and then reburying at least part of their bones elsewhere in a stone or, in Britain, a timber built tomb. Such a practice has been known from many places of the world - a number of American Indian tribes did the same thing - and it raises the entire question of what the court tombs were really built for?

Some archaeologists such as Humphrey Case have suggested that court tombs were not primarily tombs. The absence of burials in some, the small number in others, and the practice of secondary burial suggested that other rituals may have been at work. Case has argued that the same type of dumping of earth and settlement debris known from under the Lyles Hill cairn and at the Goodland site can also be found in the chambers of court tombs. All of this, he argues, points to the possibility that the court tombs were not originally built as tombs but rather as shrines or ritual meeting places of some type. Almost all archaeologists would agree that the courts of the tombs were probably constructed to provide a small area for special rituals. The presence of burials in the court tomb may have been a deliberate part of some of these rituals, like depositing the relics of a saint in a church, or it may have been a widespread folk custom, possibly after the court tombs had ceased to function as important ceremonial structures. Recall here how abandoned churches have often been used up to this very day as a special place for burying the dead.

Why multiple chambers? As we have seen from Audleystown, not all chambers appeared to contain burials while others were filled with the remains of various individuals. This pattern is well known among the court tombs where we most often find the burial remains in the first or first two chambers or, as at Creggandevesky, Co. Tyrone (Ill. 2-45), where many burials were found at the entrance of the tomb. Oliver Davies once suggested that the bodies were placed in the first chamber and the entrails, as in Egyptian tombs, were deposited in the inner chambers. There is not only no evidence for this notion but we do find a number of tombs where burials have been found in an inner chamber and not in the first (outer) chamber.

The pattern of burials and goods in the various chambers probably offers us important clues concerning the function of the court tombs. Unfortunately, the combination of the activity of Neolithic people who apparently cleared chambers of their contents and more recent destruction - when Oliver Davies arrived to excavate Ballyreagh, Co. Tyrone, he found that it had been turned into a pig sty - conspire to deny us the type of information we need to understand why the numbers of chambers might vary and why we find such differences in fill between them. They most certainly pose an intriguing problem when we consider that nearly half of the chambers with grave goods lack any evidence for human burial. We will return to the mystery of the multiple chambers later after we have reviewed the evidence for some of the other tombs.

2-45. Creggandeveskey court tomb.

Besides their function, the precise origins of the court tombs has also been a matter of lively debate. Oliver Davies, for example, argued that the court tombs of Ulster originated in Sardinia. More importantly, Ruaidhrí De Valera championed the case for what archaeologists popularly know as the 'western entry'. He argued that the earliest court tombs appeared in the west of Ireland, in the area of Co. Sligo-Mayo-south Donegal, and that these tombs represented a colonization of Ireland by farmers arriving directly from the Continent, presumably Brittany. The evidence for this 'western entry' involves several lines of argument. The court tombs appear to be clustered most densely in this area which suggests that they had arrived and developed here the longest. It is also in the west that we find the largest and most elaborate of the tombs. Some of the basic characteristics of the tombs - their east-west orientation and the presence of two chambers (rather than more) - is best 'preserved' in the west. Hence, DeValera, believed that the earliest farmers came to Ireland from the Continent and settled in the west where they constructed their tombs. They then pushed eastward and northward across Ireland. As they moved further away from their original homes, the tombs became more scattered across the landscape and they began to deviate from the type of orthodox burial form that we find in the west. Finally, DeValera argued that the court tombs bear certain similarities with some of the early Neolithic megalithic tombs known from Brittany.

There is also a very substantial number of archaeologists who argue that the court tombs first appeared on the east coast of Ulster. They find it implausible that Neolithic colonists from the Continent would sail all the way round the entire southern and much of the western coast of Ireland before landing or establishing their communities. If the tombs in the west are larger than those of the east, this is hardly unexpected if the first settlers came from the east. The eastern tombs which seem to be scattered across the landscape and are smaller than those of the west could be regarded as more representative of the colonizing phase. Only later might we expect to see much more substantial monuments as occur in the far west. Once the idea of such tombs took root in the west, it might be seen to have particularly flourished so that is why we have so many tombs densely clustered in that area. As a salutory reminder how archaeologists, provided with precisely the same evidence, may come to totally opposite conclusions, Oliver Davies argued that the pure court tomb originally had three chambers and that these degenerated into two chambered tombs, which is clearly the reverse of what DeValera had argued. As for a source, those who do not believe in a 'western entry' look to southern Britain and the region of the Severn-Cotswold tombs. Here were also constructed tombs employing stone chambers, slight facades that might have been ancestral to the fully developed Irish courts, and a trapezoidal mound. Hence, colonists would have journeyed up along the Irish Sea and spread the idea of the court tombs both to the east coast of Ulster and western Scotland.

Questions of tomb origins have since become passé and they are certainly less amenable to the simple answers proposed decades ago. Since court tombs may have existed for many centuries, it is difficult to trace their dispersal from a single point of origin; regional peculiarities may have grown up over long periods of time and bear little if anything on the problem of the ultimate origins of the tombs. Most archaeologists are now more interested in their social function, a topic to which we will return at the end of this chapter.

Portal tombs

The simplest of the Neolithic tombs, and probably the one that comes first to mind, is the portal tomb, or, as it was formerly known, the portal dolmen. These tombs have a very simple structure - a single chamber constructed from orthostats. The two largest of these upright stones stood on either side of the entrance hence archaeologists use the term portal, i.e. 'door-like' to characterize these monuments. The truly spectacular aspect of these tombs, however, is normally the capstone that is set on top of the orthostats since it may weigh many tonnes. When remains of a cairn are found covering one of these tombs, it tends to be elongated like those covering court tombs. Altogether there are 174 portal tombs known from Ireland (Ill. 2-46).

Like court tombs there is a also a variety of individual forms for the portal tombs although their fundamentally simple plan does limit somewhat the scope of these differences. Generally, the plan of the tombs is quite simple as can be seen from examples such as Ballyannan, Co. Donegal (Ill. 2-47),

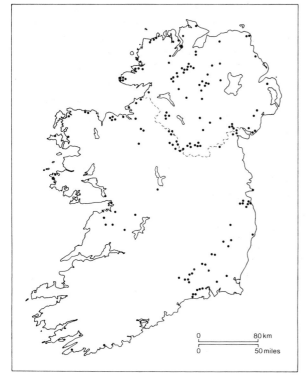

2-46. Distribution of portal tombs.

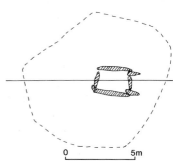

2-47. Ballyannan portal tomb.

63

2-48. Slidderyford portal tomb.

or Slidderyford, Co. Down (Ill. 2-48). But there are also examples that look half-way between a portal and a court tomb. A very good example of this occurs at Ticloy, Co. Antrim, which has the usual single small chamber of the portal tomb but also a low court-like façade more typical of a court tomb (Ill. 2-49). This, as we will soon see, may bear on the question of their origins.

Although the portal tombs are much more open to the elements than court tombs, excavations of their chambers have produced much the same evidence that we find in court tombs - Neolithic pottery, flint tools and stone beads. One of the richer tombs, Ballykeel, Co. Armagh, yielded a number of fine decorated bowls and flint tools. As is often the case in the acidic Ulster soils, there was no trace of a burial. However, from other sites such as Ballyrenan, Co. Tyrone, cremated remains have been uncovered while at other sites there have been traces of inhumations.

When we look at the distribution of the portal tombs, we see that like the court tombs, they are largely confined to the northern half of Ireland. There are other similarities. Both types of tombs normally face east, they have much the same type of grave goods inside them, and the form of the tombs is somewhat similar. The portal tomb from Ticloy, for example, was almost a miniature court tomb. This raises the question which type of tomb was the earliest?

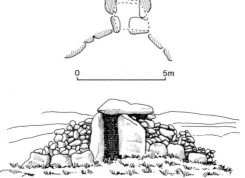

0   5m

2-49. Plan and sketch of Ticloy.

Traditionally, archaeologists have argued that court tombs probably came first and that portal tombs were derived from the earlier court tombs. When we say derived, we mean that after a long time, presumably many centuries, the tradition of building large tombs with many chambers and impressive ceremonial façades gradually died out and people decided to build simpler tombs. The building of façades was abandoned and the number of chambers was reduced to only one. Some would argue that even when people were building the larger court tombs, the idea of single chambered tombs already existed as is occasionally seen where we find a single chamber inserted into the cairn of a court tomb. According to this line of reasoning, portal tombs may be seen as degenerate court tombs.

Others have argued that the evolution of tombs was quite the reverse and that the smaller and simpler tombs must have been earliest. The simplest type of tomb would have been a box like structure and this best approaches the type we find in portal tombs. Later, the argument runs, the rituals of burying the dead or holding ceremonies became more elaborate and so people began adding new features, here more chambers, to the structure much as one might add a garage or extra room to a house. Not only did the numbers of chambers increase, but also the need for a more spectacular area for the ritual, hence the addition of façades to the entrances of the tombs.

It is not easy to evaluate these two theories. The same type of Western Neolithic ware as we find in court tombs has also been recovered from some of the portal tombs such as Clontygora Small Cairn, Co. Armagh. On the other hand, we also have later Neolithic decorated pottery from such tombs. Whatever way one wishes to read the evolution of these monuments, few dispute that their builders and the society that they represent are related and the periods of their existence may well have overlapped.

Passage tombs

The most spectacular tombs of the first farmers in Ireland are undoubtedly the passage tombs. They are found not only in Ireland but also in western Wales and Scotland, especially in the Orkneys. They are also well known on the Continent in Iberia, Britanny and southern Scandinavia. In all there are 229 passage tombs known in Ireland, over half of which are located in five great cemeteries such as the Bend of the Boyne, Co. Meath, or Carrowmore, Co. Sligo (Ill. 2-50). Passage tomb cemeteries are both few and small in Ulster with the largest at Croaghan/Kilmonaster in County Donegal where about twelve tombs have been recorded although almost all have long since been destroyed or 'excavated' around 1840. Nevertheless, there are still abundant examples of individual passage tombs in the province.

The basic characteristics of a passage tomb is that the part of the tomb concerned with burial is divided into two parts - a chamber which may stand alone or be divided into several different smaller chambers off a central area, and a passage that leads one from outside the monument into

2-50. *Distribution of passage tombs.*

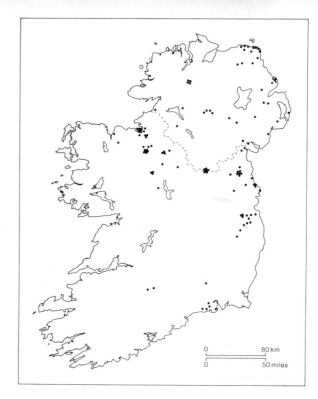

2-51. *Typical passage tomb from Loughcrew, Co. Meath.*

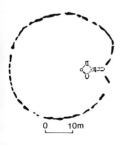

0   10m

the central burial chamber (Ill. 2-51). There is also a mound or stone cairn that covers the entire tomb. Unlike the other tomb types, the mound covering a passage tomb tends to be circular. The edges of the mound were held in place by a surrounding ring of stones which are known as kerb stones. Although it is this passage that gives this type of tomb its name, it is ironic that in so far as defining a megalith as a passage tomb, the passage is optional, and there are a considerable number of examples without passages both in Ulster and in County Sligo. These are sometimes termed 'simple passage tombs' (Ill. 2-52).

The type of pottery found in passage tombs is known as Carrowkeel ware which takes its name from a passage tomb cemetery in Sligo. This type of pottery is poorly made but highly decorated with deep grooves made with the end of a stick or bird bone. In the richer passage tombs archaeologists have discovered pins of bone or antler, stone balls, pendants and flint tools. Some of the cemeteries also include art work, usually found decorating the orthostats of the tombs.

The Irish passage tomb that normally comes to mind is New Grange which is located in the great cemetery at the Bend of the Boyne and which also includes the equally spectacular tomb at Knowth surrounded by 17 smaller satellite tombs. New Grange was covered by a mound that measured over 80 metres across and 11 metres high. One enters the tomb by a long passage formed from orthostats that had been decorated by Neolithic man in the form of spirals, circles and other motifs. At the end of the passage is a central chamber with a corbelled roof and three smaller chambers. Inside these were found large stone basins on which the

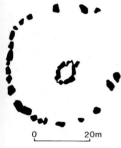

0   20m

2-52. *Simple passage tomb from Ballintoy, Co. Antrim.*

66

2-53. *Slieve Gullion passage tomb.*

cremated remains of the dead were presumably deposited. At New Grange a roof box above the entrance permitted sunlight to pass down the entire length of the passage to the main chamber at midwinter sunrise.

When we turn to Ulster we do not find anything so spectacular. The majority of passage tombs in Ulster are unexcavated, a number have been destroyed and many of them are identified as passage tombs largely on the basis of descriptions preserved in the Ordance Survey Memoirs of the 1830s. Among the better known passage tombs of Ulster is one situated on top of Slieve Gullion, Co. Armagh (Ill. 2-53). Here we see the typical round shape of the mound, the passage and the main chamber. But unlike many passage tombs, the walls here were not constructed out of orthostats but the same type of dry stone walling that a farmer might employ to build a field wall (Ill. 2-54). The tomb had been robbed many years before Pat

2-54. *Dry stone walling in Slieve Gullion.*

Collins and Basil Wilson could excavate it (an unfortunately all too familiar story) and other than a few pieces of burnt bone from a cremation burial, all that was discovered were three basin stones, an arrowhead and some pieces of flint and chert. The location of the tomb, high on a mountain, is by no means rare in Ulster and other passage tombs are known on Slieve Donard and Slieve Croob, Co. Down. At Knockmany, Co. Tyrone, Dudley Waterman and Pat Collins excavated a simple passage tomb which yielded some cremated bone, a few flints and a sherd of pottery. It also provided one of the few Ulster examples of megalithic art, the type of ornament characteristic of the Boyne valley tombs. Another Tyrone passage tomb, Sess Kilgreen, is probably the best ornamented tomb known in Ulster with its patterns of spirals and lozenges (Ill. 2-55). Possibly related in time are the rock engravings known from north Donegal which provide us with our most abundant evidence for later Neolithic (or possibly Early Bronze Age) art (Ill. 2-56). No passage tombs are known from counties Cavan and Monaghan and only a few are known from Fermanagh.

The origins of the passage tombs in Ireland is a hotly disputed topic. Michael Herity of University College, Dublin, for example, has argued that the passage tombs were introduced into Ireland by colonists from Brittany where there are a number of similarities with the Irish passage tombs. He has suggested that they came to Ireland, landing in the vicinity of the Boyne, and from there gradually spread both west and north into Ulster. In this way, the Boyne tombs with their passages would be regarded

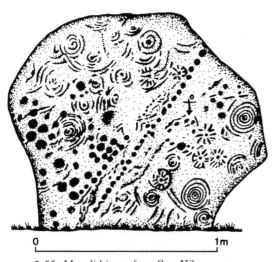

0   1m

2-55. Megalithic art from Sess Kilgreen.

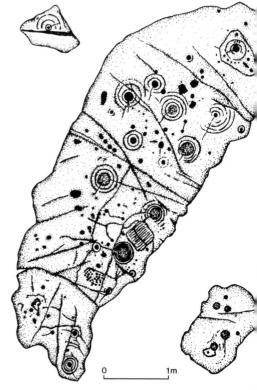

2-56. Rock art from Donegal.

0   1m

2-57. Ballynahatty.

as the earliest and the series of ten simple passage tombs in County Antrim such as the Druid's Stone in Ballintoy or the tomb at Ballynahatty, Co. Down (Ill. 2-57), that stands in the centre of the Giant's Ring near Belfast, are all degenerate tombs reflecting the decline in the passage tomb tradition. Alternatively, the Swedish excavator at the Carrowmore cemtery in County Sligo, Göran Burenhult, and others have argued that the tombs evolved in the opposite direction - the earliest are the simple ones and the great Boyne passage tombs are the latest. There is some radiocarbon and stratigraphic evidence to support this hypothesis since even at Knowth, one of the three great Boyne tombs, simple passage tombs preceded the construction of the larger central tomb. Alison Sheridan has argued a detailed six stage sequence of passage tomb development which would find the earliest concentrated in Sligo and Antrim. But while both areas are on or close to the coast they defy anyone to come up with a coherent common origin - be it from France or southern Britain - to explain why the earliest tombs should appear in these two fairly distant areas.

Wedge tombs

The last major type of megalithic tomb is commonly termed the wedge tomb. It takes its name from its wedge-like shape, i.e., the tomb tends to narrow at its far end. There is a central gallery for the burials which one enters via a short antechamber that may be blocked by a stone slab. The burial chamber is usually roofed over with flat stone slabs. Around the whole gallery is placed another wall of stones that retains the cairn. Unlike other tombs, the wedge tombs normally face the south-west rather than the east.

There are 465 wedge tombs known in Ireland and these constitute the largest single class of megalithic tombs. The wedge tombs are distributed primarily in the south and west of the island and the number known from Ulster is not great and primarily concentrated in Donegal, Tyrone and Londonderry with a few outliers reaching east Antrim (Ill. 2-58). Only about 20 of these tombs have been excavated so far and their date and origins are still very much disputed.

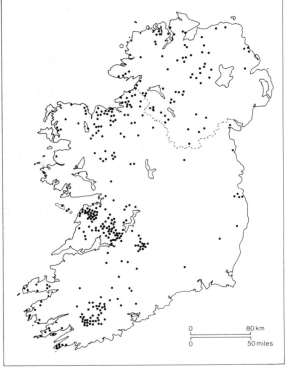

2-58. *Distribution of wedge tombs.*

A good example of an Ulster wedge tomb can be seen at Cloghnagalla, Boviel, Co. Londonderry (Ill. 2-59). Here we find the classic gallery which is divided in front by several stones that form an antechamber. There are also kerb stones that define the outer boundary of the tomb. Associated with the tomb were remains of late Neolithic Sandhills ware and tools such as flint scrapers and a polished stone axe. The burial consisted of the cremated remains of one individual who was identified as an adult female which brought some delight to the anatomist who related it to the local name of the tomb, Cloghnagalla, that is, 'the stone of the hag'. This tomb is rather unusual in that it offers clear evidence of having been constructed in the Neolithic period. Most wedge tombs have yielded remains which are better associated with the beginnings of the Bronze Age and there is a considerable number of archaeologists who would date the wedge tombs to a later period. At Loughash, Co. Tyrone, Oliver Davies discovered a mould for casting a bronze palstave (axe), a bronze blade and Early Bronze Age pottery. Indeed, at eight of the wedge tombs excavated in Ireland Beaker pottery of the Early Bronze Age has been discovered. In general, there is no one who would argue that the tombs were not utilized later in the Early Bronze Age but there is still some evidence that they were first erected in the later Neolithic although they may well have continued to be constructed and were most certainly re-used during the later period.

As for their origins, like a number of other tombs so far discussed, the wedge tombs have been compared to similar structures on the Continent, the *allées couvertes* of France, and Ruaidhrí De Valera once argued for yet more French colonists, this time setting ashore in Cork and Kerry and then

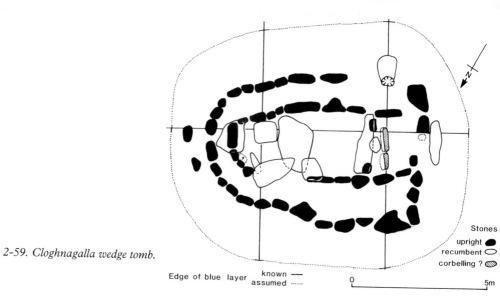

2-59. Cloghnagalla wedge tomb.

Stones
upright ●
recumbent ◯
corbelling ? ▨

Edge of blue layer
known ——
assumed ⋯⋯

0   5m

spreading their new tomb type northwards through the west of Ireland. In a recent review of this problem, Arthur ApSimon has indicated that he would support the architectural connections with the French tombs and that both the French evidence and the material recovered from some of the Irish wedge tombs could accommodate their appearance in Ireland during the later Neolithic. Whether we are actually dealing with new immigrants, however, is a more disputed matter and many archaeologists today emphasize the possibility of ideas moving from the Continent or Britain to Ireland without recourse to full scale movements of people. And, of course, others would find enough similarities between these megalithic tombs and the earlier types to propose a local development.

Stone circles

In addition to megalithic tombs, there are other stone monuments which we believe to have been erected towards the end of the Neolithic and on into the succeeding Early Bronze Age. One of the most impressive are the stone circles which number about 900 in the British Isles as a whole. In Ireland there are two main concentrations of these circles - one in south Munster and the other in mid-Ulster although some stone circles are also known outside these clusters (Ill. 2-60). Altogether there are over a hundred stone circles known from Ulster.

The stone circles are generally composed of a ring of stones that may include orthostats or recumbent, i.e. lying, stones. The numbers vary although over half of the circles known have more than 20 stones. The size of the rings averages about 11 metres but they may range from only 3.7 metres (Ballybriest, Co. Londonderry) to the larger circles of Aghalane, Tyrone (35 metres) and Ballynoe, Co. Down (33 metres). The stones themselves are hardly the spectacular type we find at Stonehenge and very few are more than a half metre in height. However, not all stones in a ring will be of uniform height and there is an obvious tendency among many of

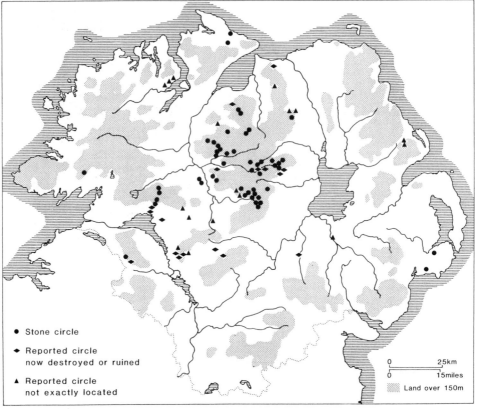

- Stone circle

◆ Reported circle
  now destroyed or ruined

▲ Reported circle
  not exactly located

0   25km
0   15miles

Land over 150m

2-60. Stone circles in Ulster.

the circles to have one taller standing stone up to one metre or more in height. Intuitively, this might prompt us to consider the orientation of these taller stones - for example, were they aligned toward the position of the rising or setting sun? A careful examination of the location of these taller stones has not yet revealed any particular alignment and it remains a mystery why they erected one stone larger than the rest.

The dating of the stone circles also remains very problematic. We introduce them here since there is some evidence that at least some of them were erected during the Neolithic. At Cuilbane, Co. Londonderry, a cache of Neolithic flint implements was found in the packing of one of the stones of the circle. They had been inserted there after the raising of the stone, consequently, we would date the erection of the circle also to the Neolithic. On a number of occasions a few artifacts or graves may be found near a stone circle and these have been used to provide approximate dates for their construction. Normally, the objects date to the later Neolithic or the Bronze Age.

One of the most impressive of the Ulster stone circles lies outside the mid-Ulster cluster at Ballynoe, Co. Down (Ill. 2-61). The site was originally excavated in 1937 and 1938 by the famous Dutch archaeologst A. E. van Giffen who unfortunately died before publishing his own examination of an extremely complicated monument. At Ballynoe a large stone circle encloses a smaller oval alignment of stones and a cairn which

2-61. Ballynoe stone circle.

included chambers on both ends (Ill. 2-62). The presence of a cairn in itself is not odd since we also know of other stone circles throughout the British Isles that include some evidence for burials. However, the actual sequence of events that led to the final appearance of the Ballynoe circle has so far defied all attempts at reconstruction and we seem to have a monument spanning several different building phases, beginning in the Neolithic and continuing on into the Early Bronze Age. Evidence for stone circles in the east of the province is fairly rare and Aubrey Burl has noted that a number of the characteristic features of the Ballynoe circle - its diameter, outlying stones, and North-South alignment - are closely paralleled in Cumbria.

Also in Co. Down is another enigmatic site, Millin Bay, situated on the Ards peninsula. Here Pat Collins and Dudley Waterman excavated another multi-period site that began with a dry stone wall several feet high (Ill. 2-63). Next to it was constructed a stone cist nearly 6 metres long and less than a metre wide which contained the remains of at least 15 people.

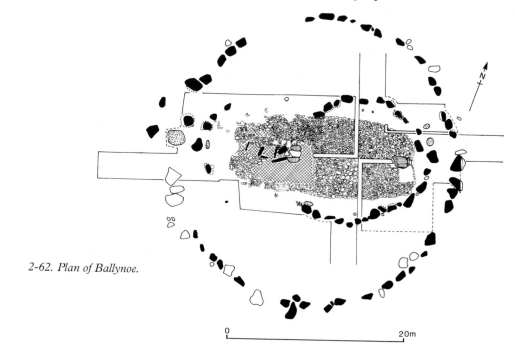

2-62. Plan of Ballynoe.

0   20m

2-63. Millin Bay.

Their bodies were disarticulated and the skulls and long bones had been collected together and placed in orderly groups (Ill. 2-64). A series of flag stones enclosed the long cist and many of these had been decorated with patterns reminiscent of those found on passage tombs. In addition, the remains of a Carrowkeel bowl also typical of passage tombs was found nearby. Beyond the central setting was another roughly oval enclosure of stone uprights. While we have yet to find other sites particularly analogous to Millin Bay, the disarticulated burials from the site are a forceful reminder of the practice of secondary deposition of remains in the tombs. Presumably, the dead may have been placed in mortuary houses or exposed to the elements until the flesh had decomposed before being placed within the tomb, a practice we would also associate with some of the court tombs. Moreover, the communal nature of the deposition perhaps emphasizes that what was ultimately buried in the tomb may not have been so many individuals but rather 'the ancestors' whose remains were all gathered together at one time for their final interment.

Henges

Although most would associate the word 'henge' with Stonehenge, an actual henge monument generally does not involve any stone structures. Rather, a henge is typically a large circular enclosure with one or more

74

2-64. Burials at Millin Bay.

entrances and where an earthen bank forms the outer perimeter of the monument while a ditch is found to the inside. Henges are known throughout both Britain and Ireland, although the number excavated in Ireland is exceedingly few. On what little evidence is available to us, they would appear to be ceremonial enclosures erected towards the end of the Neolithic period. Regarding the British henges, it has been suggested that they stood in the same relationship to the stone circles as cathedrals stand to smaller parish churches.

There are very few sites in Ulster that one can confidently identify as henges. Dun Ruadh, Co. Tyrone, may have been a henge in that it matches the configuration described above with its outer bank and inner ditch (Ill. 3-17). This appeared to have been erected on the site of an earlier Neolithic settlement and, presumably later, a large cairn with a number of Early Bronze Age burials was inserted into the centre, and recently, Derek Simpson discovered an Early Bronze Age burial placed within the earthen bank itself.

A more spectacular henge candidate is the Giant's Ring just south of Belfast (Ill. 2-65). This magnificent monument consists of a circular bank about 200 metres in diameter which stands about 4 metres high today. The bank was formed by scraping earth up from inside the ring and possibly also

2-65. The Giant's Ring.

from outside. Towards the centre of the ring is a small megalithic tomb which may be a partly destroyed passage tomb. The tomb was excavated many years ago but it had obviously been plundered (porter and lemonade bottles were found four feet below the tomb). There had been some traces of burnt bone and burning around the tomb but nothing of any importance has ever been found associated with the earthen bank. A section through the bank was cut by Pat Collins who recovered evidence that it had been scooped up from inside the ring and piled against low stone revetments. As to which came first - the megalith or the bank - archaeologists have generally assumed the tomb was earlier. This is because the circular earthen bank is very like the classic henge monuments which are well known in southern Britain and which tend to date from the end of the Neolithic or the Early Bronze Age. Recent research carried out on the Giant's Ring by Barrie Hartwell of Queen's University has revealed several new aspects concerning this monument.

Hartwell has analysed the plans of the monument and it would appear that the ring was laid out essentially centred on the megalith, perhaps by a cord, measuring c. 200 metres long. However, the hill on which the monument stands was not large enough to permit the late Neolithic architects to make a full circle centred on the tomb and they had to continually adjust its position in accordance with the terrain of the hill top. Aerial photography has also revealed that the Giant's Ring is not alone and that there seem to be traces of other circular enclosures in its immediate vicinity and the entire area may have once represented a sizeable ritual complex. Indeed, in the last century there were a number of reports of a considerable number of burials recovered in the fields adjacent to the monument. All of this helps substantiate the widely held theory that these henge monuments represented major ritual and social centres. Situated as it is near one of the few fords over the Lagan, the Giant's Ring may have served as a major tribal centre for people occupying south Antrim and north Down at the end of the Neolithic.

Society in Neolithic Ulster

Before examining the nature of society in Ulster during the Neolithic we might ask whether there was a Neolithic Ulster? While there certainly is abundant evidence for Neolithic occupation of Ulster, it is an altogether different thing to propose the existence of a distinct Ulster cultural entity at this time. There is certainly very little if any support for such a concept.

If we assume, for example, that the megalithic tombs would be the most distinctive ethnic markers at this time, we can only note that there is no tomb type found exclusively in Ulster. While court tombs, passage tombs and portal tombs all have a northerly distribution, so many of the tombs lie outside the borders of Ulster no matter how defined that we can hardly speak of an Ulster 'culture'. Moreover, when we examine the peculiarities of some of the tombs we can see that Donegal tombs are more easily compared with those of Sligo than with those of the rest of Ulster while the court tombs of south Down and Armagh are clearly part of the Carlingford group that also appears in Co. Louth. Indeed, when we look more closely at the peculiarites of the court tombs, we see that differences within Ulster often seem stronger than Ulster's contrast with the rest of Ireland. For example, those court tombs possessing four or more chambers are almost entirely confined to the east of the province while tombs with full courts are almost exclusively a western phenomenon in Ulster. Similarly, the typologically earliest passage tombs are confined to north and east Antrim. Only the Goodland bowls tend to be virtually confined to Ulster and even then they are primarily limited to the east. In general then, we can speak of regional groups within Ulster or across the borders of Ulster but not yet of a distinct Ulster cultural region.

If we turn now to the question of how society was organized in the Neolithic, we have several lines of possible evidence. The first and, perhaps, most straightforward involves estimating the degree to which society was organized by the labour required to construct the settlements and ritual sites that we have so far discussed.

We can best gain our footing in this area by observing how much effort was required of a Neolithic farmer to build his own house. D.W.A. Startin has estimated that a house such as Ballynagilly required something in the order of 550 man hours for its construction. Unfortunately, we do not know to what extent fieldwalls were constructed in Ulster during the

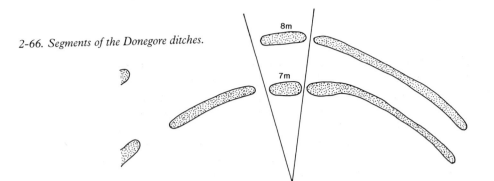

2-66. *Segments of the Donegore ditches.*

Neolithic, but the labour that might be involved in them could be quite substantial. Indeed, Seamus Caulfield has argued that as much labour went into the construction of the fieldwalls of north Mayo as went into the erection of the great passage tombs of the Boyne.

The best evidence for settlements larger than a single farmstead in Ulster are the enclosures at Lyles Hill and Donegore Hill. The ditches at Donegore provides us with the most substantial evidence for Neolithic settlement engineering in Ulster so far and the site is comparable with respect to both date and dimensions to the 'causewayed camps' of southern Britain and is amenable to the same type of analysis.

There are three aspects of the Donegore site that interests us from the perspective of social structure - was it a village settlement? How much effort was required in its construction? And how was the labour organized? We can at least offer some thoughts about each of these three issues, starting with the last.

One of the sections of the ditches excavated at Donegore is very similar to that of a causewayed camp. The ditches were not excavated continuously but rather in segments, the whole ditch resembling a chain of longish sausages. These 'sausages' are by no means uniform; they differ according to width and depth, which suggests that they were excavated on different occasions, possibly by different work gangs. We can see two such segments, one about eight metres long and the inner segment about seven, both beginning and terminating at the same point (Ill. 2-66). Rough experiments with an antler pick and a bucket suggest that the eight metre segment could have been excavated by a team of 12 in about 12 man-hours. And if we extrapolated this to the entire circumference of the site, the same team of about 12 could have excavated out the ditches in about 1500 hours, i.e. it would have required something on the order of 18,000 man hours to construct the two ditches. Notionally, a total population of about thirty people could have produced the work gang required to have built the ditches of Donegore Hill over a period of several seasons. Donegore seems to suggest a work force larger than a single family (and the quantity of debris from the site seems to indicate this as well) although it need not have entailed more than five or six families living either within the enclosure or in the vicinity to have built the site. These figures are, of course, hypothetical but probably of the right general order of magnitude. We may imagine then that various teams of workers assembled at Donegore on particular occasions in order to fulfill some form of work levy, indicated by the length of a particular ditch segment. They were probably divided into pickers/ shovellers and basket carriers for maximum efficiency. The next work team would then begin their own segment just beyond so as not to confuse the work order and perhaps to leave a visible reminder of their own effort.

The megalithic tombs would have obviously required some effort as well although the size of tombs in Ulster are never of the order of the great Boyne passage tombs. But there is one substantial monument that was probably erected toward the end of the Neolithic - the Giant's Ring. This would represent the extraction and piling up of something in the order of 30,000 cubic metres of soil. This might come to about 50 to 70,000 man hours and would have obviously required considerable manpower from the surrounding countryside. The development of large-scale labour projects, which presupposes considerable degree of social organization, is well documented for southern England where Colin Renfrew observed how the earlier Neolithic ditched enclosures ultimately gave way to substantial henge monuments. What is particularly intriguing about the Giant's Ring is that it is a very sizeable henge but it exists in an area which is almost devoid of earlier megalithic building other than the very simple passage tomb within the henge itself. The future work in this area by Barrie Hartwell may well shed further light on this problem.

The evidence of the monuments then points to a society that may have varied both through time and by region. It would have consisted primarily of individual farming families but in some areas there would have been larger social entities, perhaps co-operative units, who worked together to construct field-walls or the ditched enclosures. By the end of the Neolithic some regions such as the lower Lagan saw the emergence of social entities sufficiently large to draw on extensive manpower to erect what we presume to have been a large ceremonial enclosure.

Megaliths and society

A second route to understanding Neolithic society are its megalithic tombs, particularly the distribution and nature of the court tombs and passage tombs.

The court tombs, as we have already seen, are distributed primarily over the northern third of Ireland. They are generally situated on or adjacent to good soils. Although the actual evidence for Neolithic settlement is quite meagre, archaeologists normally assume that Neolithic settlements did exist in the general vicinity of these tombs. But what was the nature of settlement about these tombs? So far we have only been able to speculate that Neolithic farmers may have been dispersed across the Ulster land-scape in a fashion not substantially different from today's settlement patterns. Do the tombs provide any further information?

Some years ago Tim Darvill examined the distribution of the tombs as a method for ascertaining the structure of society behind them. He noted, for example, that although court tombs are more densely distributed across

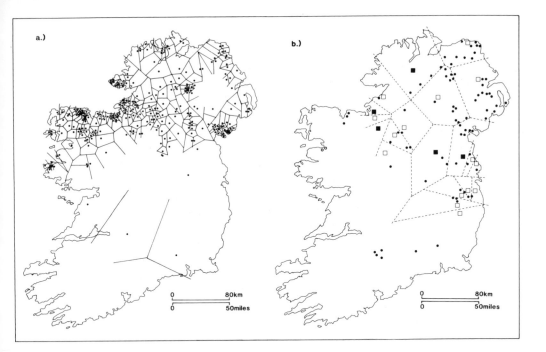

a.)

b.)

| 0 | 80km |
| 0 | 50miles |

2-67. Court tomb and passage tomb 'territories'.

the landscape in some areas such as north Mayo, where he presumes the carrying capacity of the land would have been better, they are all spaced at an average of about 4.5 kilometres from each other. This spacing or dispersal of the tombs suggests different court tomb groups, each holding its own territory (Ill. 2-67A). These court tomb territories range from about one to six hundred square kilometres in size, the minimum sized territories probably being the lower limit for the survival of a court tomb social group. There is no evidence for a hierarchy of settlement sizes that might indicate that some court tomb territories were more important than others. All of this, according to Darvill, is consistent with identifying the court tomb builders as members of segmentary societies.

The segmentary society is a form of social organization well studied by anthropologists, especially in Africa. They tend to be small social units, numbering between 50 and 500 people. Each segmentary group of people is autonomous and independent both economically and politically from their neighbour. Darvill imagines that the court tombs served as the ceremonial centres of such small groups. When we look at rural Ulster today we find analogous 'ritual' structures - chapels, churches, Orange lodges, pubs - that frequently appear to be standing in the middle of nowhere but which attend to the spiritual and social needs of the farms dispersed about them.

Some also see in the architecture of the court tombs an indication of the type of society that built them. Some claim that the court tombs with their multiple chambers mirrored in stone the segmented nature of what many suppose to have been the structure of early Neolithic society, i.e. just as the social bonds in society were built up of segments that might be linked together, so also were the galleries divided up into their individual

80

segments or chambers. This would mean that when we find two, three or four chambered galleries, these might represent either the reality of the various segments or family groups that made up the society that built the tombs or it was somehow related to ideologies that we will remain forever powerless to recover. It is generally assumed that the court area served for more theatrical ritual performances which the entire community might attend. The nature of the grave goods - pottery, flint tools - is precisely the type of artifacts that we find on settlements and they suggest grave gifts that all members of society might aspire to.

Where we have been able to ascertain the age and sex of the deceased, they appear to represent both adults and children and both sexes. Whether everyone belonging to a 'court tomb society' had the right to be buried in such a monument is difficult to say. The average numbers recovered during the course of excavations is not very large and most Ulster court tombs average between two and three burials with the exception of Audleystown and Creggandeveskey. The presumption that only the most important people were buried in the tombs is difficult to support on the basis of the available evidence. At Aghanaglack, Co. Fermanagh, for example, a dual court tomb yielded but two burials - a child and a juvenile - and our reading of Neolithic social structure hardly presupposes the existence of young princes. It is, of course, presumed that between earlier tomb robbings and the acidic soils that completely dissolve inhumations, the actual number of burials in most tombs might have been a good deal higher than we normally find. But even if we assumed both that there were originally at least ten or twenty burials in each tomb and that there were quite a few more tombs than we know today, we would still come up with not much more than several thousand people in Ulster over a period of centuries. This suggests that not all people of the court tomb societies were likely to have been buried in the tombs.

There is some evidence to support the contention that many if not the majority of the Ulster Neolithic population were not buried in megaliths. We do have a number of occasions where apparently Neolithic burials have been recovered from simple pits. Estyn Evans recorded such a possibility when one, possibly, two pits in a gravel quarry at Killaghy, Co. Armagh, yielded cremated bones and Neolithic pottery. More recently, Brian Williams of the Archaeological Survey uncovered four simple pit burials at Altanagh, Co. Tyrone, which he assigned to the Neolithic. Perhaps more persuasive evidence comes from the fact that there are very few Early Neolithic megalithic tombs known in the entire province of Munster yet there is increasing evidence that this region was settled throughout the Neolithic. This would naturally suggest that there was a substantial Neolithic population in this island who did not employ megalithic tombs for their burials.

Darvill extended his analysis to the passage tombs and argued that the earlier segmentary society later changed and that this can be seen in the erection of the passage tombs (Ill. 2-67B). Here we find evidence that conflicts with the idea of the segmentary society. These tombs are part of the great passage tomb tradition that is also seen on the Continent and may imply ritual practices spread over a much larger region. The passage tombs are clearly for burials (Darvill argues that the court tombs were not erected primarily for burial but to serve as ritual centres). Anthropologists have noted that tombs, as opposed to ceremonial centres, tend to be erected on the borders of territories rather than at their centre. However, important tombs may attract greater ritual activity and still more tombs to enlarge a cemetery. This may well have happened among the passage tomb builders since we now find full cemeteries of passage tombs. These cemeteries are dispersed on an average of 10.4 kilometres from one another, over twice the distance of separation seen in the court tombs. More importantly, we have the dense clusters of tombs together in major cemeteries such as the Boyne and Carrowmore. These, it is argued, point to centres of population and probably also indicate centres of political importance such that we no longer have autonomous groups of farming communities scattered across the landscape but rather hierarchies in some regions where certain people are of greater status and are able to call upon the labour and goods of substantial areas of the countryside.

The architectural form of the passage tombs is also contrasted with that of the court tombs. No longer is there an open court area for the public to witness ritual displays but now ceremonies may well have been performed within the interior of the tombs where very few people could assemble and which required one to pass through the long narrow entrance. This type of architecture, it is argued, suggests that the normal members of society might be excluded from rituals which would be more exclusively in the hands of priests - a phenomenon that we might expect of a more complex, socially stratified society. Moreover, the grave goods that one encounters in many of the passage tombs - stone balls, large antler pins - and the abundance of megalithic art and the large stone basins all speak of more esoteric practices. By this we mean the management of passage tombs by special, possibly secret, societies with their own sets of symbols and rituals.

The hypothesis that Irish Neolithic society was becoming more structured by the time of the great passage tombs of the Boyne is an interesting idea. Alison Sheridan argues that the increasingly larger and more elaborate tombs may have been the product of different passage tomb societies in active competition with one another, each attempting to display its superiority by increasingly more grandiose tombs, something not far different from some American tele-evangelists who compete to build increasingly greater 'spiritual' empires. With the erection of the greatest of the tombs, New Grange and Knowth, this competition appears to have collapsed.

If one accepts these ideas, it suggests an interesting contrast between developments in Ulster and immediately south of its border where the great cemetery complexes existed. According to Sheridan's classification, the majority of Ulster passage tombs belonged to the initial most primitive phase and there are only eight tombs that are assigned to the later, more developed, periods. If passage tombs are the tangible expression of social organization, then Ulster would have appeared to have remained largely outside the drive for greater communal tomb building efforts and chiefly control seen elsewhere in the passage tomb territory. It is unfortunate that we do not have better dates for both the court and passage tombs since there are a number of obvious questions that we might be in a better position to answer. Were both tombs built at the same time or does one follow on after the other ceased to exist? The evidence of the radiocarbon dates is not yet clear - the court tombs probably began earlier but there is good reason to suspect that there was some, perhaps a considerable, overlap in the use of court, portal and passage tombs.

If court and passage tombs existed at the same time, do they represent two different religions in Ulster in the Neolithic? One archaeologist has already made comparisons between 'Low Church' court tomb builders with their open courts and more public services in contrast with 'High Church' passage tomb people with their priests limiting access to the holy of holies, their religious art and their esoteric burial goods. However, if one wishes to pursue such modern analogies and trace Ulster's sectarianism back some 5000 years, then it must be admitted that Ulster passage tombs could hardly be regarded as 'High Church'. It may be that Neolithic communities in Ulster either were never so large as to encourage the growth of chiefs able to organize large labour projects or that they simply were uninterested in investing their time and effort in such ritual display.

In the end we cannot offer a simple picture of life in Ulster in the Neolithic. It does appear that individual farmsteads were probably part of somewhat greater communities and there is certainly evidence for distant exchange systems and the flow of ideas from the Continent and Britain as well as the rest of Ireland into Ulster. The Neolithic colonists also introduced the concept of wealth and status and we may find these ideas lurking behind the stone maceheads or large porcellanite axes of the Malone type. But we should not be too mesmerized by individual wealth and we may be dealing rather with communal wealth just as much of our megaliths suggest communal burial. The Giant's Ring, standing tentatively at the end of the Neolithic and symbolising the movement toward greater social entities may still not have required particularly important individuals or social structures that guaranteed the presence of chiefs. For this, we should perhaps look further to the developments of the Bronze Age.

3   Metal and Wealth
2500 - 1200 B.C.

Three Ages

In 1836 Christian Thomsen published a guide to the artifacts in the
National Museum of Denmark in Copenhagen. In his guide, he arranged
the various finds into three ages - stone, bronze and iron. By this time it was
becoming increasingly clear to the earliest archaeologists that this was the
order in which the early people of Europe and Asia had adopted these
materials in their technologies. It should be noted that this plausible
scheme was also resisted and in 1857 the Rev. James O'Laverty (among
others) was arguing that such a scheme was inapplicable to Ireland. One
of his reasons for rejecting the sequence of these three ages was the fact that
he was able to collect both stone and bronze implements, which he thought
dated from the same period, along the Bann near Portglenone. The
fundamental scheme, however, is still very much in place, however, we will
have very good reason to return to the subject of how bronze daggers and
spearheads found their way into the Bann.

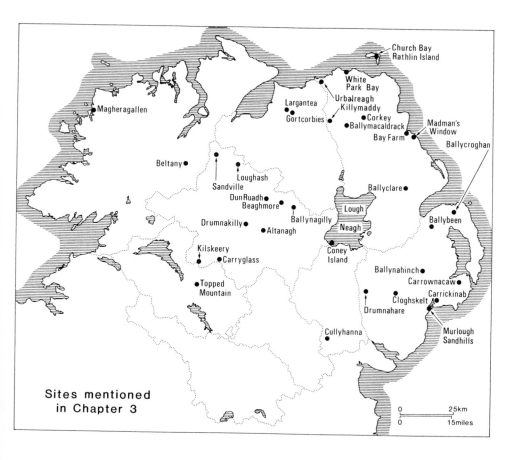

Sites mentioned
in Chapter 3

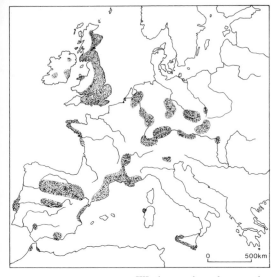

3-1. *Distribution of European beakers.*

We have already seen how the earliest tools known in Ulster during the Mesolithic and Neolithic were made out of stone. This was followed by a period during which metal tools and weapons were first added to their stone technologies and eventually replaced most stone tools altogether. The earliest metal to be regularly used for fashioning tools was copper since native copper could be beaten into shape comparatively easily. However, copper is not normally found in its metallic state but is generally combined with many other elements in a rock-like ore. In order to extract the copper metal from the ore it had to be heated and eventually people were able to melt the copper and pour it into a mould rather than having to beat it into shape. But copper axes and other tools cast in this way are not very strong without the addition of another element such as tin. The addition of a small amount of tin to molten copper produced bronze, a metal which was much harder than copper on its own. With the production of bronze tools, weapons and ornaments we begin the Bronze Age.

The Bronze Age in Ulster lasted from about 2500 to 300 BC. This is a period in which we see the gradual development of wealth in society. This wealth was displayed in public by those who had the power or prestige to obtain ornaments of bronze or gold, bronze weapons and tools. We are uncertain to what extent the general population had access to bronze and gold since these are quite rare materials that frequently had to be transported over considerable distances. Some classes of utilitarian tools such as axes may have been widely available while bronze weapons and ornaments of bronze and gold were probably possessed largely by the chiefs of society and their families. Even the Irish annals give a hint of this process when they suggest that gold working began in Ireland in the year 1544 BC and the different ranks of society were marked out according to dress only eight years later. The Bronze Age then is a period which many archaeologists see not just as a revolution in technology - a shift from stone to bronze tools - but also a social revolution where increasingly wealthier elements of society developed and used the new metal technology to reflect their status.

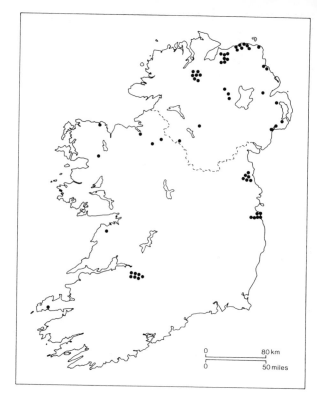

3-2. Beakers in Ireland.

New people?

In Ireland we traditionally begin the Bronze Age about 2500-2000 BC. At this time a particular type of pot began to appear over much of Europe. This pot is called a beaker since it is shaped like a drinking vessel without any handles. Although these beakers differ from region to region in detail, they are still remarkably similar in shape and type of ornamentation. They are also generally much better made pots than are found at the end of the Neolithic. On the Continent and Britain, beakers are normally found in graves along with a number of other items which suggest that at least some of their owners were archers. We know this because Beaker graves also contain bracers to protect the wrist from the bow-string, barbed and tanged arrowheads of flint, and even in some instances small bone pendants carved in the shape of bows. We also find in Beaker graves ornaments and small tools of metal, generally copper or gold but also occasionally bronze.

The Beaker burials are found over much of western and central Europe (Ill. 3-1). They are known as far east as Hungary and Czechoslovakia, as far north as Scandinavia and as far south as Sicily. The western limit of these beakers is, naturally, Ireland with the greatest majority of them known from the northern half of the island although there are some dense clusters of finds in Co. Dublin and Co. Limerick (Ill. 3-2). But what can such a wide distribution of beakers mean? Do we have a single people who spread over all Europe at about the same time? Many archaeologists once accepted this idea and imagined that the people buried in Beaker graves were very much like gypsies. The distribution of the finds indicated that they travelled widely, the retention of the same ceramic type indicated that they were conservative in maintaining their own culture, and like the traditional Irish tinker, they dealt in metals. Believing this, they talked of a 'Beaker folk' who migrated from the Continent to Britain and Ireland at the beginning of the Bronze Age.

Today, many archaeologists do not accept the spread of beakers as the result of the movements of a single people. Rather, they argue, the beaker is the only thing that unites all of these areas together and we should not confuse the spread of a pot with the spread of a people. They propose that beakers spread only among the wealthier members of society who were buried with these vessels along with their metal goods. The beakers themselves, it is argued, may have had a special role in ritual. There are parallels for all this in the later prehistory of Europe when the wealthier members of Celtic society were often buried with special wine serving sets imported from the Mediterranean. Those who follow this line of thinking regard the concept of a special 'Beaker folk' as nonsense, something like talking today of a 'Guinness folk' or a 'Coca-cola people'.

Archaeologists are still not agreed as to whether the discovery of beakers means the movement of a people or merely contacts between different peoples who adopted the special beaker 'cult package'. It does appear that the earliest beakers in western Europe began in Holland and spread from there toward the British Isles. Archaeologists suspect that beakers may have entered Ireland by several different routes. There may have been direct contacts between western Ireland and the Continent to account for the clusters of beakers in Limerick or even on Dalkey Island, Co. Dublin. But the concentration of beaker finds in Ulster, especially along the north coast, suggests that they entered Ulster from Scotland. We cannot be certain about whether 'they' means a new people or a just a new pot but the existence of substantial Beaker settlements in the Western Isles of Scotland does suggest the possibility that there was some movement of people.

Beaker settlement

Evidence for Beaker settlements in Ireland is even poorer than that for Neolithic settlements. And although there are traces of beaker huts (interpreted as 'squatters') known from around the great passage tombs of New Grange and Knowth, Co. Meath, and possible Beaker structures at Lough Gur, Co. Limerick, there is not a single Beaker house known in Ulster. This does not mean that we have no evidence for their settlement, however, since Ballynagilly, Co. Tyrone, which provided us with one of our few Neolithic houses was also the scene of later Beaker occupation. Here there were found concentrations of beaker pottery, tools, charcoal-filled pits and hearths over an area of about 600 square metres. The site dates to about 2500-2200 BC.

The bog that surrounds Ballynagilly and whose pollen provided us with a picture of the first Neolithic forest clearance in the area also gives us a hint

3-3. Beaker from Largantea (ht. 13 cm).

of what was happening to the landscape in the Early Bronze Age. After the land had been originally cleared of forest by Neolithic colonists, it was later abandoned and the forest regenerated about the site. However, in the Early Bronze Age the forest was cleared again and so we may suspect that the Beaker settlers at Ballynagilly were farmers like their Neolithic predecessors. Indeed, this is the type of evidence we find at other Beaker sites in both Ireland and Britain. We know that the people who used beakers raised wheat and barley, cattle, sheep and pig. From New Grange, Co. Meath, archaeologists have discovered that it was also in the Beaker period that the domestic horse was introduced into Ireland. In addition to Ballynagilly, there are other traces of Beaker settlement, generally found in the form of scatters of beaker sherds, found in the sandhills of White Park Bay, Co. Antrim, and Murlough (Dundrum), Co. Down, by the earlier Neolithic hearths at Gortcorbies, Co. Londonderry, or the maddening (at least to their excavator) occurrences of single beaker sherds in the otherwise Neolithic settlement at Mad Man's Window, Co. Antrim, or the Bronze Age settlement at Bay Farm, Co. Antrim.

Beaker burials

Beaker burials, as opposed to chance finds of beaker sherds, are not at all common in Ulster. While on the Continent and southern Britain, the people depositing beakers in their graves erected their own tombs, Ireland follows the tradition of western Scotland where Beaker burials were simply inserted into earlier monuments. A good example of this practice was discovered at Well Glass Spring, Largantea, Co. Londonderry, which Ivor Herring excavated in the late 1930s. Here the remains of several beakers were discovered in the first chamber of a wedge tomb (Ill. 3-3). We have already seen that the dating of the wedge tomb poses some serious problems for archaeologists concerning their date of construction. Some have argued that they were originally erected in the Beaker period while others have seen them as Late Neolithic tombs that were subsequently re-used by people who used beakers. This is perfectly possible since we know that these tombs were used over a long period and that even Later Bronze Age material has been found inside them. The Largantea tomb, for example, also contained somewhat later funerary pottery - Food Vessel and Cordoned Urn, and at another wedge tomb, Loughash, Co. Tyrone, Oliver Davies uncovered four beakers, a later Encrusted Urn, and part of a mould from a still later bronze axe. We might imagine then that once these tombs were erected, the people living about them would always regard them as sacred structures and even many generations later they

3-4. Re-use of abandoned church as graveyard at Arboe, Co. Tyrone.

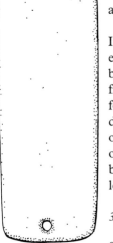

would be used for burials - in the same way that people have been burying their dead in the ruins of old churches in rural Ireland up into this century (Ill. 3-4).

Beaker technology

The Beakers are far better known by the traces of their technology than either their settlements or their burials. We ascribe to the Beaker period a special set of artifacts that is common elsewhere where we find more abundant evidence for the beaker-using societies (although none of them are exclusively associated with beakers). An archer's kit consisting of a barbed and tanged arrowhead and a stone wrist bracer (guard) is typical of the Beakers (Ill. 3-5). In Ulster there are special concentrations of both the arrowheads and especially the bracers in Co. Antrim (Ill. 3-6). The characteristic Beaker pottery is known from both the north Antrim coast as well as Co. Londonderry along the Foyle.

The relationship between the Beakers and the earliest metallurgy in Ireland is another one of those topics that has seen far more debate than evidence. It has been variously proposed that metallurgy entered Ireland by way of Beakers (either immigration or simply trade contacts) directly from Iberia, Brittany, or from the Continent through Britain. The reasons for identifying so many different sources is that nowhere on the Continent do we find the same type of beakers associated with precisely the same type of metal tools that are found in Ireland. Moreover, the most primitive type of copper axes in Ireland, which are also presumably the earliest, tend to be largely concentrated in Munster, precisely the region where we have the least evidence for Beakers. In Ulster where Beaker material is much more

3-5. Wrist-bracer and barbed and tanged arrowhead.

90

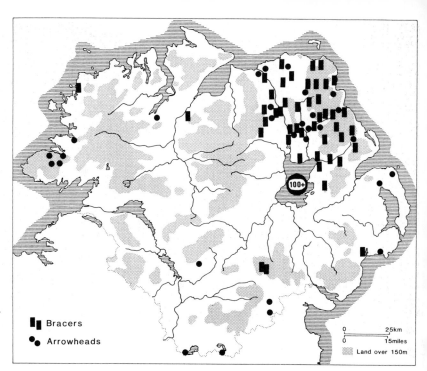

-6. Distribution of Beaker archery kits in Ulster.

Bracers

Arrowheads

0   25km
0   15miles
Land over 150m

abundant we find scant traces of the earliest copper axes. Moreover, sources of copper are far richer in Munster than they are in Ulster. In the south we have excellent evidence for Bronze Age copper mining. On the other hand, although Ulster has some native metallic copper that could have been exploited by early metallurgists, there is no evidence that they did.

Food vessels and urns

Although the beaker was the earliest and most characteristic type of pot at the very beginning of the Bronze Age, they are relatively rare in Ulster. But following the Beaker period there appeared a number of different ceramic styles that are all very well represented here. These normally provide us with our basic evidence for the occupation of Ulster from about 2000 to 1400 BC. These new pots are divided into a number of different types but they have several things in common. We seldom find them on settlements but rather in graves so that we regard them as essentially a special type of funerary ware. They occur sometimes in megalithic tombs but much more often in tombs that were only erected in the Bronze Age. These tombs may involve only a pit in the ground but quite often we find instead a well prepared grave whose walls are constructed from stones to form a stone box. Archaeologists call such structures cists (from a Welsh word for 'chest' that was borrowed from Latin *cista* 'basket'). Although they may be found to accompany inhumation burials, the great majority are found in cremation graves. Finally, all of these new types of pottery are generally in form and decoration closely related or derived from similar wares in Britain. Here again we have the problem of determining whether such

3-7. Irish bowl from Mt. Stewart, Co. Down (ht. 10 cm), vase Food Vessel, and Food Vessel 'Encrusted' Urn from Toberagnee, Co. Antrim (ht. 33 cm).

pottery accompanied new colonists to Ireland or were merely the result of trading contacts.

One of the major types of pottery is known as the Food Vessel which, depending on one's authority, may take up to three different forms. They derive their name from the fact that they are normally found in graves next to the remains of the deceased and it was suspected that they served as containers for food offerings for the dead (stylistically, they are related to a very late form of beaker). Food Vessels are frequently well decorated and may be divided into two or three basic forms - small round sided bowls (Bowl Food Vessels or Irish Bowls), more angular vessels with a pronounced neck (Vase Food Vessels) and large decorated urn shaped vessels (Food Vessel Urns) (Ill. 3-7). In addition to Food Vessels we also find several series of urns. These comprise large flower-pot shaped containers with a collar around the upper part of the vessel which gives them their name of Collared Urn (Ill. 3-8). They were used for holding the cremated remains of the dead. Cordoned Urns take their name from the fact that they are divided into various zones or cordons (Ill. 3-9). In addition, there is also a series of vases and urns that belonging to a Hiberno-Scottish tradition (or Drumnakilly series after a cemetery in Co. Tyrone). Finally, there are also some very small rounded bowls which archaeologists term Pygmy Cups (Ill. 3-10).

All of these different types of pots pose many problems of interpretation for the archaeologist. They are not all found in the same regions or in the same quantity. In his survey of the Early Bronze Age, Arthur ApSimon notes that Bowl Food Vessels, for example, are known from about 100 sites in Ulster and may be found almost anywhere. The more than forty Vase

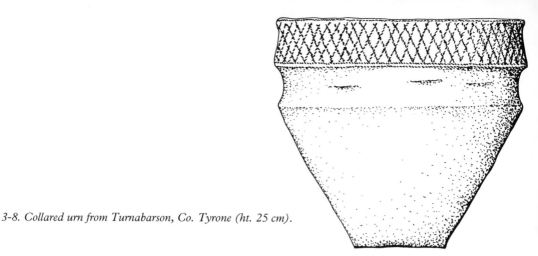

3-8. *Collared urn from Turnabarson, Co. Tyrone (ht. 25 cm).*

Food Vessels, on the other hand, are not only more sparsely spread across the landscape but appear in regional groups, many concentrated in east Donegal and the Foyle basin or north Down (Ill. 3-11). The Food Vessel Urns, on the other hand, are primarily an east Ulster phenomenon. Of these, over twenty have a distinctive relief-decoration and are often termed 'Encrusted Urns' and are largely confined to Antrim and Down. The Collared Urns, which presumably provided the inspiration for the Food Vessel Urns, are similarly confined to Antrim and Down with but a few found west of the Bann (Ill. 3-12). The Hiberno-Scottish series offers the most perverse distribution in that the approximately forty examples of this ware are largely confined to counties Antrim and Tyrone.

On the basis of all this evidence, some argue that Ulster may have been colonized by successive waves of immigrants from northern Britain, each employing different types of pottery for the burial of their dead. They not only speak of a Beaker Folk but also a Food Vessel Folk and an Urn Folk. As we might already anticipate, others claim that these different pots are only the result of contacts between Ulster and Britain throughout the Early Bronze Age and have more to do with the exchange of ideas than population movements. Moreover, some British archaeologists have argued that the difference between the various pot types was social rather than chronological. In Yorkshire, for example, the fact that Collared Urns

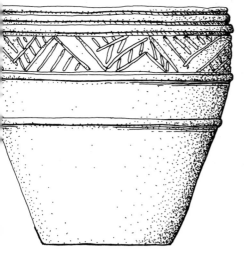

3-9. *Cordoned urn from Killinchy, Co. Down (ht. 25 cm).*

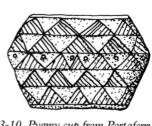

3-10. *Pygmy cup from Portaferry, Co. Down (ht. 6 cm).*

93

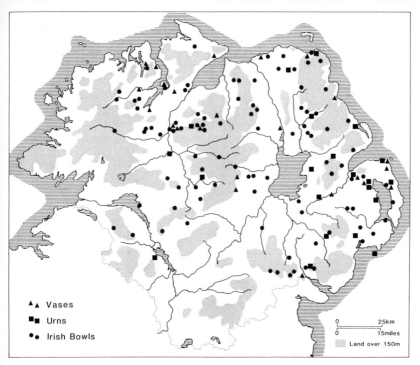

▲▲ Vases
■■ Urns
●● Irish Bowls

3-11. *Food Vessels types in Ulster.*

0   25km
0   15miles
▨ Land over 150m

tend to be secondary to Food Vessels, the main burials in a mound, has suggested that those who were buried under the urns were socially inferior to the primary Food Vessel burial. No one has really made such a case for the Ulster evidence where distinctions between primary and secondary burials are more difficult. What we can say is that certain forms are far more likely to be found together than others. For example, at Kilskeery, Co. Tyrone, an 'Encrusted Urn' contained a Pygmy Cup and was accompanied by two Vase Food Vessels, while on Lyles Hill, Estyn Evans uncovered

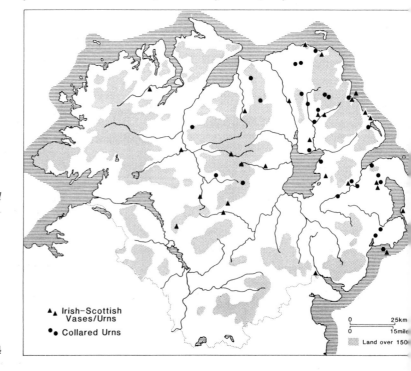

3-12. *Collared Urns and Hiberno-Scottish vessels in Ulster.*

▲▲ Irish–Scottish
    Vases/Urns
●● Collared Urns

0   25km
0   15mile
▨ Land over 150

94

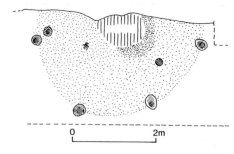

3-13. Bronze Age house from Downpatrick.

0   2m

both a Bowl Food Vessel, a Vase Food Vessel, a Food Vessel Urn and possibly a Cordoned Urn altogether.

One of the main problems preventing a better understanding of this kaleidoscope of funerary ware is that we have very few settlements from this period that might tell us what type of people actually lived in Ulster at this time. Instead, we find ourselves trying to discuss a whole people only on the evidence of what type of pot they left with their dead. The one thing all of these pots do emphasize is the pattern of regionalism which we first encountered in the Neolithic persisted very much into the Early Bronze Age and while we may certainly talk of regional groups within Ulster, we still cannot yet speak of an Ulster region markedly distinct from the rest of Ireland.

Early Bronze Age settlement

Although the great majority of evidence for the Early Bronze Age comes from graves, we do have a few hints at how people actually lived during the period after the Beakers. On Coney Island in southwest Lough Neagh, Peter Addyman discovered traces of two rectangular houses which appeared to have been constructed with post supports and sod walls. A hearth was found in one of the houses and Bowl Food Vessel ware was found lying about the site. This suggests that the site was probably a small farmstead dating to the Early Bronze Age. One of our best sites comes from the town of Downpatrick on the Meadowlands Housing estate. Here archaeologists excavated two round houses. One of them measured over four metres in diameter and contained a hearth in the centre (Ill. 3-13). The other round house was larger, over seven metres across. The pottery found all around the site belonged to Cordoned Urns. Donegore Hill, the site of the large Neolithic ditched enclosure, was occupied again during the Early Bronze Age, when a stockade was constructed about 2000 BC. Other evidence for settlement frequently comes from sherds of Bronze Age pottery found lying in the sandhills along the Ulster coast. A good example is Magheragallan, near Gweedore, Co. Donegal, where remains of a Bowl Food Vessel were found alongside shellfish, dog, sheep, ox, red deer, pig, and horse bones.

If the actual hard evidence of settlement is sparse, we do have yet other sources of information. Our main Early Bronze Age site is either single graves or small cemeteries, all of which were presumably situated close to the actual settlements. The pattern of these tends to differ somewhat from the earlier Neolithic tombs and various writers such as William Knowles and Edward Watson have observed that our Early Bronze Age funerary pottery is often found on sands and gravels, especially in Co. Antrim. These areas, often situated in valley bottoms which are devoid of earlier megalithic monuments, indicate the expansion of farmers into environments which had previously shown little evidence of exploitation. A number of reasons can be suggested for such movements. Population increase may have impelled Early Bronze Age communities to exploit new territories, a task made easier by the introduction of the plough by this time. But another factor in this movement may have been a degradation in the upland landscape of Ulster.

Following the secondary clearance of the land around Ballynagilly during Beaker times, Jon Pilcher and Alan Smith observed traces of slightly later clearances followed by an increase of heath. This pattern is also encountered in numerous other pollen samples from Ulster and here we see strong evidence for the shaping of the modern Ulster landscape. At about 2000 BC blanket bog either begins to appear in the upland regions or begins its relentless expansion over the landscape. The cause of this is still uncertain; climatic change may have had something to do with it but palynologists have also emphasized that this could be a result of periodic clearances from the Neolithic into the Bronze Age. Continuous forest clearance in the upland regions ultimately brought about an apparently irreversible degradation of the soil and heath and bog began to dominate, removing many areas that had previously served for cereal growing. This may also have resulted in the shift to the best drained soils of the lowland regions, the sands and gravels, upon which we often find evidence of Early Bronze Age burial. With the gradual collapse of one of the primary areas for cereal cultivation, many suspect that the Early Bronze Age economy relied increasingly on stockbreeding from this period onwards. A consequence of all these changes is still recognizable today throughout the Ulster uplands covered with their blanket peat and the primacy of the pastoral rather than arable in the Ulster economy.

Early Bronze Age burial

Although we occasionally find the remains of Early Bronze Age burials in earlier megalithic tombs - there was a Food Vessel and horse bone in one of the chambers of the Audleystown court tomb - most of our evidence comes from graves that were built or dug in the Bronze Age itself. The Early Bronze Age cemeteries may have been totally flat with no obvious covering or marker for the graves but we do know of some cases where burials were placed under or within stone cairns and at Urbalreagh, Co. Antrim, Dudley Waterman excavated an adult and child who had been buried in Cordoned Urns which were surrounded by a ring ditch (Ill. 3-14).

Often the body of the deceased was burnt and the cremated remains were placed in a pit, urn or a stone cist. Although the stone cist was normally built to hold a single individual (Ill. 3-15), on occasion we find more and at Church Bay on Rathlin Island no less than five people were

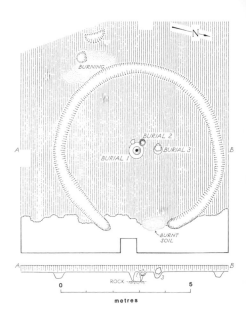

3-14. Urbalreagh burials.

recovered from a single cist. Usually the objects accompanying the dead were limited to one or two pots and there are a great many instances where we have pits or cists with cremated bones but no pottery whatsoever. Occasionally metal objects are found in the graves. A very good example of this type of burial was Carrickinab near Downpatrick, Co. Down, where a stone cist contained the burnt remains of an individual accompanied by a Food Vessel, a bronze knife or dagger, a bronze awl and two flint scrapers. Another bronze knife or dagger comes from the Bowl burial at Corkey, Co. Antrim. At Bay Farm, Carnlough, Co. Antrim, there was discovered a Collared Urn that was placed upside down over the cremated remains of an individual. Inside the urn was found a bronze dagger (Ill. 3-16), a shell button and a curiously carved piece of chalk. There are also many instances

3-15. Stone cist.

3-16. Bronze dagger (l. 9 cm)
and piece of chalk from
Bay Farm.

of actual burial or inhumation without any burning of the body. A very interesting example comes from Straid, Claudy, Co. Londonderry. Here Nick Brannon of the Archaeological Survey discovered a young man buried with a Food Vessel. He stood about six feet two inches tall and it was noticed that his right arm was much more robustly developed than his left. The anatomist examining the bones suggested that this may have been due to the greater use of the right side in such pursuits such as carpentry.

Burials were not only carried out in individual plots but we also know of a number of instances of small cemeteries of several burials found together and a few instances of larger cemeteries. One of the largest of these known in Ireland is Cloughskelt, Co. Down, where Laurence Flanagan of the Ulster Museum uncovered over twenty graves accompanied by Food Vessels and Encrusted Urns. Here some people were buried in simple pits, others had a few stones to form a box-like structure, others had a complete stone cist. At Carryglass, Co. Tyrone, eight cist burials were covered with a stone cairn. More elaborate was Dun Ruadh, Co. Tyrone, where an Early Bronze cemetery was inserted into what would appear to have been an earlier henge monument. The cemetery consisted of a large stone cairn the centre of which included of a pear-shaped cobbled area approached by an entrance way (Ill. 3-17). Upright stones and dry stone walling held back the interior of the cairn from what was presumably an area for rituals. About a dozen cists had been inserted into the cairn, most of which were accompanied by Food Vessels. Burial also existed outside the cairn as Derek Simpson recently discovered an Early Bronze Age cremation inserted into the earthen bank of the 'henge'.

The burials themselves tell us something of life in the Early Bronze Age. At Altanagh, Co. Tyrone, Brian Williams uncovered eight burials, some in cists, some in Cordoned Urns (one inverted, one right-side up), and simple pits. One of the cists included an elderly male suffering from arthritis and a young female while a Cordoned Urn covered a young man about 16 to 18 years old who was accompanied by bones of both pig and cattle,

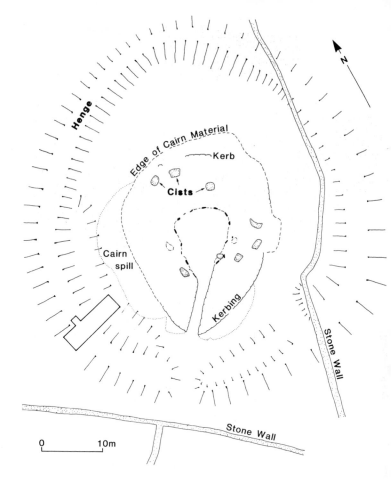

-17. Dun Ruadh Bronze Age cists and earlier henge.

0   10m

probably the remains of a funeral feast. In another Cordoned Urn were the remains of a woman of about 25 to 30 years old who was buried with a set of beads, a bronze ornament and several other objects. A striking reminder of the level of mortality prevalent in prehistoric Ulster is that of the 13 burials found at Altanagh, both Neolithic and Early Bronze Age, all but about two had died before the age of 35.

Early Bronze Age technology

The introduction of copper and bronze tools in the Early Bronze Age effected both a revolution in technology and an even more profound change in society itself. We can get a hint of these changes if we reflect on the nature of Early Bronze Age metalworking.

First, there is the problem of acquiring the necessary metals - copper, tin and gold. Today, the only mines known in Ireland certainly dating back to the Bronze Age are at Mount Gabriel, Co. Cork. These and possibly other mines in the same area may have provided much of the copper that we find in the Bronze Age. Tin is much rarer than copper and so far as we know, it was probably acquired from Cornwall which has long been famous for its tin mines. Gold on the other hand could have been found in Ireland,

99

3-18. Single-piece mould from Ballynahinch.

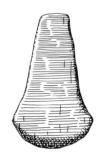

especially in Co. Wicklow. Now if this were the prehistoric situation, then all the basic metals known in Ulster would have to have been acquired from outside the province. This would have entailed long distant trading systems and the great effort required just to obtain the raw materials would have made all metals reasonably precious to Early Bronze Age communities. However, we cannot be certain that people in Ulster were not exploiting their own local resources. Copper, for example, could have been obtained from a number of places especially in Tyrone while tin deposits exist at Slieve-na-miskan in the Mournes. Gold also is to be found in Ulster in the sands of the Moyola river, the Sperrins or at Slieve-an-orra in Co. Antrim. These are all places where these metals occur naturally but, unfortunately, we have no evidence that these sources were either known to prehistoric man in Ulster much less exploited by them. The irony here is that County Antrim has produced more bronzes than any other county in Ireland which alerts us to the same problem we encountered in the Mesolithic - do the bronzes indicate the density of prehistoric settlement or the disproportionate effect of the Northern Collectors on the distribution of prehistoric objects? We have, for example, accounts from the mid-19th century of ragmen such as William Arthurs who worked the Glens looking for chance finds of bronze objects that he might sell to collectors.

After acquiring the raw metals Bronze Age smiths cast them into the shape of tools, weapons and ornaments. We know at least that it involved local smiths since we find the moulds used for casting in Ulster. The simplest form of casting involved the use of the open stone mould. This was merely a block of stone in which the shapes of an axe or some other tool had been hollowed out. As soon as molten metal was poured into such a mould, it cooled almost instantly and the smith could then remove it and

3-19. Flat axe (l. 16 cm) and decorated axe (l. 20 cm) from Co. Antrim.

100

hammer its edges sharp or give it any additional shape. A sandstone mould for casting four axes has been recovered from near Ballynahinch, Co. Down (Ill. 3-18).

As the Bronze Age progressed, increasingly more complicated objects came to be made where a simple open mould would not have served. Take, for example, the socketed spearhead which not only requires the shape of an actual spear but also a hollow socket into which one inserts a wooden shaft. In order to make such a weapon, the smith would have to employ a two-piece (bi-valve) mould, often of steatite (soapstone) or chlorite schist. Here the two valves would be hollowed out to cast both sides of the spearhead and a small clay core would have to be inserted in the centre part of the socket mould to keep out the molten bronze so that it could be cleaned out to form a hollow (Ill. 3-41).

The metal artifacts that we find in Ireland show a definite progression from very simple forms to increasingly more complex tools and weapons. Among the earliest metal tools in Ireland, the simple flat axes are the best known. These were made out of copper rather than bronze and were simply cast in open moulds. We know of about 500 of these tools from Ireland while only about 80 are known from the whole of Great Britain. Although they are found in Ulster, their greatest concentration lies in Munster and some archaeologists suspect that the inspiration for the manufacture of these axes came to southern Ireland directly from the Continent. After this initial phase of axe production, the smiths adopted the use of bronze and began casting axes with curving sides and decoration was added to the surface of the axe (Ill. 3-19). Experiments suggest that these Early Bronze Age axes were about twice as efficient as polished stone axes. But although the bronze axes could clearly serve as tools, this may not have been their only purpose. Clearly those that are covered with decoration may have also served other functions. The care that went into their finishing suggests that they may have had more of a social value than purely utilitarian, carrying out in bronze a similar function to the earlier Malone-type porcellanite axes. This becomes all the more plausible when one reflects on Greer Ramsey's observation that the decoration on a number of the axes continues all the way to the butt which should have been covered by a wooden handle. Moreover, some have argued that the large size of some of the axes suggests that they may have not been particularly practical tools but may have served as weapons. Here we have in mind special instruments of combat employed by the upper strata of society in what we may presume to have been fairly ritualized combat.

One of the great problems with manufacturing axes was fastening them to their wooden hafts and the smiths began to improve the grip of the axe on its handle. Simple flat axes might wobble on the end of a wooden shaft so in order to prevent this, the smiths both cast and hammered up a small flange that gave the axe a bit firmer seat in its handle (Ill. 3-20).

Those items more certainly identified as weapons also developed through time. The people employing beakers appeared to be primarily

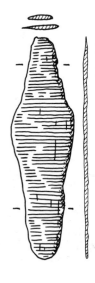

3-21. Tanged dagger from Clontymore, Co. Fermanagh (l. 11 cm).

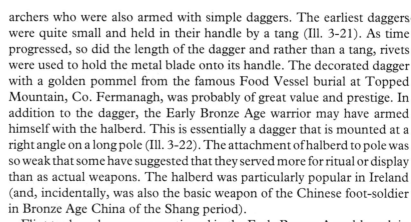

archers who were also armed with simple daggers. The earliest daggers were quite small and held in their handle by a tang (Ill. 3-21). As time progressed, so did the length of the dagger and rather than a tang, rivets were used to hold the metal blade onto its handle. The decorated dagger with a golden pommel from the famous Food Vessel burial at Topped Mountain, Co. Fermanagh, was probably of great value and prestige. In addition to the dagger, the Early Bronze Age warrior may have armed himself with the halberd. This is essentially a dagger that is mounted at a right angle on a long pole (Ill. 3-22). The attachment of halberd to pole was so weak that some have suggested that they served more for ritual or display than as actual weapons. The halberd was particularly popular in Ireland (and, incidentally, was also the basic weapon of the Chinese foot-soldier in Bronze Age China of the Shang period).

Flint tools and weapons continued in the Early Bronze Age although in some cases we see distinct changes. During the Neolithic, for example, the arrowheads were typically leaf-shaped, lozenge or hollow based. In the Early Bronze Age, however, we find a new type of flint arrowhead with both barbs and tang which may have made it more easy to fasten to an arrowshaft (Ill. 3-23). These required considerable craftsmanship and may have been exchanged as suggested by a hoard of 22 arrowheads and another 17 'blanks' for manufacturing arrowheads discovered at Ballyclare, Co. Antrim. The long javelin head also continued into the Early Bronze Age although by the end of this period smiths in Ireland were casting metal spearheads with hollow sockets using bi-valve moulds (Ill. 3-24).

3-23. Barbed and tanged arrowhead.

Other flint tools that continued included scrapers which were not easily replaced by metal tools. Simple flint knives also were manufactured but some metal tools such as awls and chisels were introduced.

To the tools and weapons we must add ornaments of bronze and gold. These included bronze and gold rings and bracelets, small gold discs which may have served as pendants or decoration for clothes, and finally the famous Irish lunulae. A lunula ('small moon') takes its name from its crescent like shape (Ill. 3-25). They were made of gold and beaten very thin and then often covered with the same type of ornament that we sometimes find on Beaker pottery. They were probably to be worn about the neck like some precious collar or symbol of office (today the President of the Royal Society of Antiquaries of Ireland wears such a miniature lunula). Altogether there are about 80 lunulae known distributed not only over Ireland but also in Britain and on the Continent. Unfortunately, in Ireland they have never been discovered during an actual excavation but only as chance finds so it is difficult to discuss either their precise date or their role in society. On the basis of their ornament which is also present on beakers, Joan Taylor has placed them within the later part of the Beaker period and since we have abundant evidence for burials and none have been discovered as a grave gift, she has suggested that they may never have been intended as personal property like a dagger or a pot. Rather, they may have been

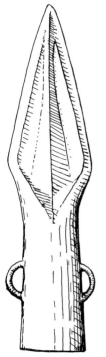

3-24. Socketed spearhead (l. 14 cm).

3-25. Lunula.

employed as a sign of lineage or in some form of ritual activity and buried for some reason which we still do not understand.

Stone monuments

As we saw in the last chapter, the erection of stone monuments such as circles seems to have begun as early as the later Neolithic. The main period of their erection, however, would seem to be the Early Bronze Age when we find a number of different types of stone monument.

The simplest monument that we can ascribe to the Early Bronze Age would be the standing stone. This is a simple upright stone which might be seen in many a farmer's field. A few of them have been excavated and may provide some hint as to their purpose (those erected in modern times normally serve as scratching posts for cattle). At Drumnahare, Loughbrickland, Co. Down, Pat Collins discovered cremated human bone at the base of a standing stone and, similarly, he excavated a possible Early Bronze Age burial at the foot of a stone at Carrownacaw, also in Co. Down. The only other excavated stone was the 'Longstone' on the Ballybeen Housing Estate near Dundonald, Co. Down (Ill. 3-26), where the only evidence for burial was the recent interment of a dog wrapped in a hessian bag and what appeared to be the burial of a pet rabbit, also quite modern. Rather than the type of treasure one often hears associated with these stones, the 'Longstone' yielded only an Edward VIIth halfpenny. A burial was found about 50 metres away but this dated to the end of the Bronze Age. This raises an interesting problem about the reason for the stones. Some have suggested that they were erected as grave markers since we do have some slight evidence for burials at the foot of these stones. But it is also quite possible that they were erected for other reasons and that Early Bronze Age and later burials were deposited close to them since they had always appeared to mark a sacred place. Some have even suggested that the stones marked ancient pathways although it must certainly be

3-26. The 'Longstone', Ballybeen.

admitted that one can hardly see from one stone to the next. The only thing that is clear is that their real function still seems to remain a mystery.

Stone circles, which we have already seen probably began in the Neolithic, continued through the Bronze Age, and with very few exceptions it is a brave archaeologist who assigns such monuments specifically to one period rather than another. This alone should emphasize to some extent the degree of continuity between the later Neolithic and the Early Bronze Age and although cultural changes most certainly happened we should be wary of assuming that our three 'ages' mark culturally distinct epochs in Ulster prehistory.

Ulster boasts several impressive and interesting circles. The great majority are concentrated in mid-Ulster, especially Co. Tyrone, but we can hardly omit such spectacular examples as the Beltany Stone Circle in Donegal that once may have consisted of about 80 stones and marks out

3-27. Beltany Stone Circle.

8. The Beaghmore
complex.

one of the largest circles in Ireland (Ill. 3-27). The most extensive circle complex is that at Beaghmore, Co. Tyrone, which consists of three pairs of stone circles, a series of stone alignments, several circular 'rockeries' of upright stones and a dozen small stone cairns, usually covering a cremation burial (Ill. 3-28). Radiocarbon dates from both the site and the surrounding bog indicate occupation of the area since the Neolithic through the Bronze Age.

Some archaeologists and astronomers have argued that the stone circles were laid out according to a specific set of geometric principles employing a basic standard of length which they call the 'megalithic yard', a unit of measurement of 2.72 feet. Circles and egg-shaped patterns such as are found at Beaghmore were constructed along these lines. Also, it has been argued that in some instances we can discern an alignment of stones that provides a line of sight related to the rising of the sun at the solstice. Alexander Thom, for example, suggested that two of the stone alignments at Beaghmore site on the summer solstice and we have already mentioned how the Neolithic passage tomb at New Grange is aligned to catch the light of the mid-winter sunrise. So here we have three possible functions for the stone circles - burials, public rituals and astronomical observations, all of which may have been related.

Middle Bronze Age

Some archaeologists recognize the division of the Bronze Age into three periods - Early, Middle and Late. While attributing items to the Early and Late is not too difficult, the Middle Bronze Age, which is notionally dated

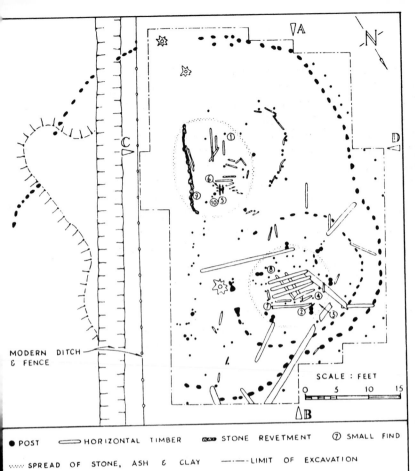

3-29. Plan of Cullyhanna structures.

POST　　⊂⊃ HORIZONTAL TIMBER　　STONE REVETMENT　　⑦ SMALL FIND

SPREAD OF STONE, ASH & CLAY　　—·—LIMIT OF EXCAVATION

MODERN DITCH
& FENCE

SCALE : FEET
0　　5　　10　　15

H·W·M·H·

3-30. Reconstruction of Cullyhanna
'hunting lodge'.

to about 1500 to 1200 BC, is not such an easy period to deal with since there is no distinctive pottery known from this period other than coarse bucket-shaped pottery, sometimes known as 'flat-rimmed' ware, and we cannot talk of a distinctly Middle Bronze Age type of settlement.

One possible candidate for a Middle Bronze Age settlement is a small camp site excavated by Henry Hodges on the present shore of Cullyhanna Lough, Co. Armagh. The architectural remains consisted of an outer enclosure, constructed of upright oak stakes, and measuring about 20 metres across (Ill. 3-29). Within the enclosure were two smaller structures - a timber built hut about 6 metres across with a central hearth and a much flimsier semi-circular structure that could have served as a wind-break for a hearth. There were very few finds and nothing that offered certain evidence of dating, however, the excavator suggested that it may have served as a temporary hunting lodge and compared the way of life suggested by the architecture with the literary descriptions of Finn McCool and his *fianna* bands who were reputed to have survived only by hunting from May through October (Ill. 3-30). He could only guess at the date of the site and suggested that it may have been built sometime between 500 and 1300 AD.

The story of Cullyhanna does not end here since both the oak posts that defined the enclosure and the stakes which were used in the construction of the hut were preserved and later examined by the Palaeoecology Laboratory at Queen's University. Since 1968 researchers such as Mike Baillie, Jon Pilcher and Jennifer Hillam have been attempting to establish the technique of tree-ring dating (dendrochronology) in Ireland. This is a technique that had been well-known elsewhere, especially in the American Southwest where it was intially developed, but many were dubious that trees growing in the generally wet Irish climate would be sensitive enough to permit its use here.

As any school child knows, a tree such as an oak puts on a ring each year and one can tell the age of an oak stump by counting its rings (Ill. 3-31). The width of the rings varies from one year to the next primarily because of the climatic conditions of the region they grow in. This means that oaks

31. Growth rings from oak tree.

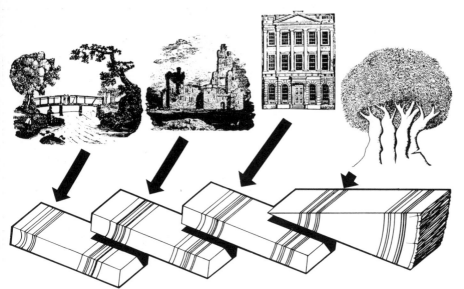

3-32. Building ring patte[rn]

from Ulster or indeed from Ireland as a whole tend to reproduce the same pattern of ring widths over time, that is, oaks growing at the same time will develop similar patterns of wide or narrow rings. By recording ring patterns from living trees and then examining successively older timbers, whose ring patterns overlap, one can build long patterns (Ill. 3-32). Once you have the master pattern you can date individual timbers from archaeological sites against the master. The Belfast master chronology now extends back to about 5400 BC (most of the prehistoric dates derive from bog oaks) and it is one of the longest in the world. When the samples from Cullyhanna hunting lodge were obtained in the mid 1970s, the master had not yet been completed and a precise date could not be assigned to the site. Nevertheless, the ring patterns from the various samples did indicate that the stakes used to build the outer enclosure and the hut were taken from trees cut down in the same year. Two radiocarbon dates were obtained from one of the samples and they point up rather well the limitations of this technique of dating. Generally, radiocarbon dates can only yield a range, never an absolute date (all of our dates so far have been only vague approximations). For example, one of the dates obtained from Cullyhanna can only be expressed as follows: there is a 95% chance that the actual date of the wood lies between the years 2030 and 1620 BC. The other date, taken from the same sample of wood, yielded a range of 1740 to 1460 BC. In neither case do these specify the actual date of the site. Fortunately, with the completion of the master tree-ring chronology we now know precisely in what year the trees that produced the stakes at Cullyhanna were cut. The year is 1526 BC which firmly places Cullyhanna in the period between the Early and so-called Middle Bronze Age (and certainly not the time of Finn McCool and his warrior bands). This date is still the earliest tree-ring date from an actual archaeological site in Ulster.

Henry Hodges dated another site that may possibly be roughly con-temporary with Cullyhanna. During the Bronze Age there is abundant

108

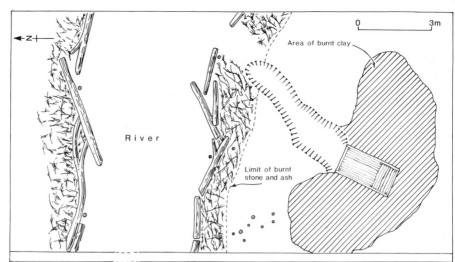

*33. Ballycroghan
fulachta fian.*

Area of burnt clay

River

Limit of burnt
stone and ash

0   3m

evidence for special outdoor cooking places which are known in the archaeological literature as *fulachta fian*. These involved the construction of wooden troughs built into the ground which are filled partly with water which is then heated by dropping hot stones into the water. This was sufficient to bring the water up to boiling and can cook a ten pound leg of mutton in about four hours. The evidence from some of these cooking places indicates that they were used hundreds of times. Such sites are known in great numbers in the south but they are very rare in Ulster and the site excavated by Henry Hodges at Ballycroghan, Co. Down, is our best example. Here several such cooking places were found. One of these had a trough, lined with oak logs, and measured about two by one metres in size (Ill. 3-33). Adjacent to it was a mound of the burnt stones and masses of charcoal employed in heating the water. Unfortunately, we do not have a dendro-date for the oak logs nor a radiocarbon date for the site. However, in a study of the other radiocarbon-dated examples of these sites elsewhere in Ireland, Richard Warner has observed that their greatest period of construction would appear to have been during the Bronze Age, up until about 1200 BC, although there is evidence that they continued to be built all the way into the Middle Ages.

Industrial changes

The Middle Bronze Age is foremost an industrial division of the Bronze Age and our attempts to give it a few other sites merely reflect our embarassment at assigning several thousand bronze objects to a few centuries in which we have little or no evidence for the people who made them. It is the changes in bronze tools and weapons, the advancements on the Early Bronze Age flat and flanged axes, daggers and tanged and looped spearheads, that actually defines the Middle Bronze Age.

The Early Bronze Age axe, for example, was modified yet again in order to improve its grip in the handle. Flanges were made very large and hammered not only up but around the wooden shaft to hold the axe-head firm. Such axes are often termed winged or wing-flanged axes because of

3-34. Wing-flanged axe (l. 15 cm).

109

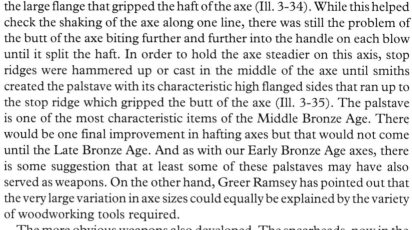

the large flange that gripped the haft of the axe (Ill. 3-34). While this helped check the shaking of the axe along one line, there was still the problem of the butt of the axe biting further and further into the handle on each blow until it split the haft. In order to hold the axe steadier on this axis, stop ridges were hammered up or cast in the middle of the axe until smiths created the palstave with its characteristic high flanged sides that ran up to the stop ridge which gripped the butt of the axe (Ill. 3-35). The palstave is one of the most characteristic items of the Middle Bronze Age. There would be one final improvement in hafting axes but that would not come until the Late Bronze Age. And as with our Early Bronze Age axes, there is some suggestion that at least some of these palstaves may have also served as weapons. On the other hand, Greer Ramsey has pointed out that the very large variation in axe sizes could equally be explained by the variety of woodworking tools required.

The more obvious weapons also developed. The spearheads, now in the distinctive kite-shaped form typical of Ireland or with the more general leaf-shaped blades, were provided with sturdier hafting. This was largely accomplished by extending the cavity within the spearhead so that the shaft might run all the way up through the blade, a considerable improvement on Early Bronze Age spearheads where the spearhead was liable to break loose from the rather shallow socket (Ill. 3-36). The presence of loops, for both fastening the spearhead tighter and possibly for decoration, was continued and now we find them in three basic locations: basal loops confined to the butt (Ill. 3-37), side (Ill. 3-38) or 'protected' within the blade itself (Ill. 3-39). These distinctions are not arbitrary but also correlate with the size of the weapon, the side-looped spearheads being much smaller and lighter than either the basal or protected. As Greer Ramsey has shown, the three styles also differ in the number of finds with about 650 side-looped, 1500 basal-looped but only about 40 protected-looped spearheads known from Ireland. As the basal and protected-looped varieties include some of the largest and most elaborate spearheads, some of these have been interpreted as parade weapons or objects of exceptional prestige. While there probably is a strong element of prestige assigning to some of the spears, we should also recall that the lighter weapons may have served primarily as javelins for throwing while the larger ones may have served as hand-held thrusting weapons. In any event we are certainly talking about actual weapons since in Britain similar spears have been found embedded in their victims.

In addition, as we have already seen, Early Bronze Age warriors were equipped with a dagger, bow and arrow. The daggers were gradually lengthened into longer weapons - dirks and rapiers. These served as thrusting weapons and the rapiers are also one of the most characteristic metal types attributed to the Middle Bronze Age. The most famous is reputed to have been found in a bog at Lissane, Co. Londonderry, and at nearly 80 cm. long, it is the longest rapier in western Europe (Ill. 3-40). Greer Ramsey has observed that although the Lissane blade may be a

3-36. The wooden shaft held firm in the head of a Middle Bronze Age spear.

paragon of craftsmanship, its short butt with its two rivets would hardly have secured the blade to its haft and it is hard to imagine how such a weapon might have served in combat. We should probably view these objects, as with some of the larger spearheads, more as parade weapons or prestige gifts than functional fighting tools. Indeed, the discovery of a considerable percentage of these Middle Bronze Age objects in either bogs or rivers raises the issue of whether they achieved their final resting place as ritual offerings.

Unfortunately, we have little or no idea as to the find-spot of over half of all the bronzes known from Ireland. From those objects where we do know their find location, Ramsey has assembled some instructive data. While axes of the Early and Middle Bronze Age would seem to have been generally recovered from dry-land sites, a little over 40% of the dirks and rapiers and about 35% of the Middle Bronze Age spears have been recovered from bogs or rivers. The dirks and rapiers are particularly associated with rivers and they have been recovered in sizable numbers from along the Bann, primarily as a result of 19th century drainage operations. The Rev. O'Laverty summoned up images of the Bann forming a natural boundary between warring tribes on either side of its banks and it is not impossible that some of the weapons recovered from it were the direct result of combat or were deposited as part of some riverine burial ritual. But many today would also argue that they may have achieved their final resting place as a deliberate act of ritual involving the conspicuous wastage (or offering) of certain metal objects to the gods. We have already seen that such a practice may have been current in the Early Bronze Age and we will have good cause to return to this theme in the next two chapters.

The technological changes of the Middle Bronze Age indicate not only improvements in the production of metal tools and weapons but also the gradual expansion of metal to more and more uses. There is no doubt that many of these artifacts were manufactured in Ulster since we find good evidence for local casting here. At Killymaddy, Co. Antrim, a whole series of two-piece stone moulds were found. These included moulds for casting socketed spearheads and dirks, and also simple razors and even sickles (Ill. 3-41).

Social changes

Many believe that the inception of metallurgy into Ireland stimulated major changes in society. The presence of valuable metals and objects fashioned from them required both extensive exchange relations and considerable effort to manufacture suggests the rise of stratified societies. Such societies would have involved some form of leaders who organized labour in their surrounding area and displayed their own wealth and prestige by their possession of metal weapons and ornaments. At first, metal tools may have served primarily as expressions of wealth for the upper classes but their increased production throughout the Early and

3-37. Basal-looped spear (l. 35 cm).

111

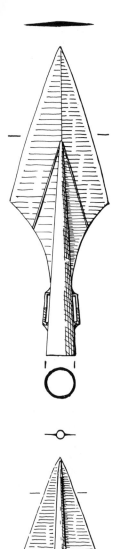

3-38. Side-looped spear (l. 15 cm).

Middle Bronze Age suggests that bronze was gradually replacing stone as the primary material for manufacturing tools. All of these changes are witnessed not only in Ireland but all over Europe where fashions of the new aristocracies may have spread from one country to another. This may, for example, help to explain the appearance of bronze razors in Ireland which are also well known across the rest of western Europe and suggests that your upper class Early Bronze Age Ulsterman kept himself shaven, following the latest European vogue (Ill. 3-42).

Metal, however, is only half the story of this chapter. Peter Harbison has emphasized that one of the fundamental differences between the Neolithic and the Early Bronze Age is the shift from communal to individual burial. Where co-operative effort erected the megalithic tombs and provided a repository for at least a segment of the community, in the Early Bronze Age we find individual burials where the accompanying grave goods, we presume, provide some indication of the status of the deceased. While the majority of graves are found singly there is a considerable number of Early Bronze Age cemeteries if we treat the term 'cemetery' in a fairly liberal fashion. There are nearly 50 sites with two burials and close to 40 others with three burials found together. After this, the numbers in Early Bronze Age cemeteries falls off dramatically, with 32% having between 4 and 10 graves and only 10% exhibiting still more burials. It is convenient to see these as small family cemeteries, however, the paucity of graves in so many of them leaves us wondering why so few graves are found together. Are they merely the graveyards of a family perhaps over a generation at most who then moved on to another site? And how do we explain the variety of mortuary wares in the same cemetery? At Ballymacaldrack, Co. Antrim, for example, five burials were uncovered which included a Vase Food Vessel, a Food Vessel Urn and three Collared Urns. Are we to take these as successive burials, the same community adopting new styles as time passed, or as John Waddell has suggested, possibly different communities with different funerary wares all burying their dead in the same cemetery. In this case, Waddell suggests the possibilty that our so-called Early Bronze Age cemeteries, like their megalithic predecessors, may have had more than strictly a mortuary function. They may also have marked out sacred areas for communal rituals in which the various different segments of society participated. These, as we have already discussed, may have been equals or, employing the Yorkshire model suggested earlier, they may have been socially distinct, although this model has never really been demonstrated for Ulster. Finally, we can only wonder why after such an abundance of burial evidence in the Early Bronze Age, the evidence for how communities buried their dead in Ulster virtually disappears by the Middle Bronze Age.

The prevalence of funerary wares and metal types in Ulster (and many other parts of Ireland) whose ancestry lay in Britain points to continuous contact between Britain and Ireland through the Early Bronze Age. That some of these involved exchange such as the importation of gold lunulae

3-39. Protected-looped spear (l. 21 cm).

3-40. The Lissane rapier (l. 80 cm).

3-42. Razor.

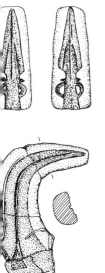

*3-41. Stone moulds from
Killymaddy, Co. Antrim.*

into Scotland, there can be little doubt. That such exchange may have taken place between people of considerable social status is also suggested by such finds as the bronze dagger from Topped Mountain, Co. Fermanagh, whose gold pommel is not only similar in style to others known from both Scotland and from the rich burials of Early Bronze Age Wessex, but would even seem to come from the same gold source. That contacts may have also involved some movement of people, a concept often regarded now as unfashionable, would still seem probable and it is difficult to regard all of the similarities in metal types and especially funerary wares as purely the result of an exchange of ideas.

One of the most striking aspects of the societies of the early metal age is the growing production and elaboration of weapons. This has normally suggested that the new upper classes were very much concerned with military display and warfare. This becomes even more evident in the succeeding period of the Late Bronze Age.

4 Arms and Aristocracy 1200 - 300 BC

The Late Bronze Age begins about 1200 BC but we cannot be certain when to end it: perhaps about 600 BC, when typically Late Bronze Age metal work appears to cease, or perhaps as late as 300 BC, when typically Iron Age metal work begins (yes! we do seem to have something of a 'Dark Age' in Irish prehistory). For our purposes we shall follow Late Bronze Age developments down to about the 3rd century BC.

The Late Bronze Age is the period of greatest wealth in Irish prehistory and our museums are filled with impressive quantities of bronze and gold objects. Yet it is also the period when we still know very little about how most people actually lived, and, even stranger for Irish archaeology, we know even less about how they buried their dead.

Whatever our lack of knowledge, most archaeologists would agree that this is a time marked by a more stratified society than had ever been seen before in Ulster and also one that begins to mark an increasing pre-occupation with warfare. This is evident in the settlements and weapons of the period which in some ways reflect the structure of Ulster society at

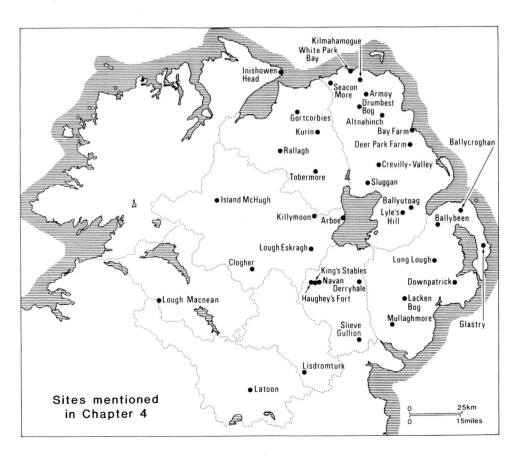

Sites mentioned in Chapter 4

this time. For this reason, we begin our survey at the top of the social pyramid, the archaeological complex centred on Navan Fort, Ulster's premier prehistoric site.

The Navan Complex

During the 1960s and early 1970s Dudley Waterman of the Archaeological Survey carried out excavations at Navan Fort, Co. Armagh. The visible remains of the site consist of a large circular earthwork nearly 290 metres across that encloses about 6.5 hectares of the top of a drumlin (Ill. 4-1). Within it are two other visible monuments: Site A, a low mound surrounded by traces of a ditch some 50 metres in diameter and Site B, a much larger mound occupying a similar area to Site A but standing some 6 metres high. Dudley Waterman excavated a portion of Site A and most of Site B.

On the original ground surface of Site B he found traces of Neolithic settlement, seen in the form of pits and pottery. Above this was a layer of soil that had been ploughed, presumably in the Bronze Age. The first substantial structure may have been created about 800 BC. It was a circular ditch that formed an enclosure about 45 metres across (Ill. 4-2). The ditch was not particularly deep, only about one metre, but it did measure five metres across at the top. Immediately inside it was a ring of pits that seemed to have served as post-holes for a palisade. The enclosure was entered via a causeway on its eastern side. The purpose of this enclosure remains a mystery although later this same area was clearly utilized for ritual purposes.

Sometime before 100 BC, either at the very end of our Late Bronze Age or possibly even in the succeeding Early Iron Age, the area inside the enclosure became the scene of intense activity. The inhabitants of Navan

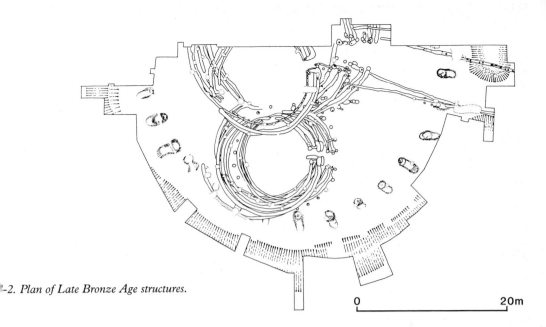

-2. *Plan of Late Bronze Age structures.*

0   20m

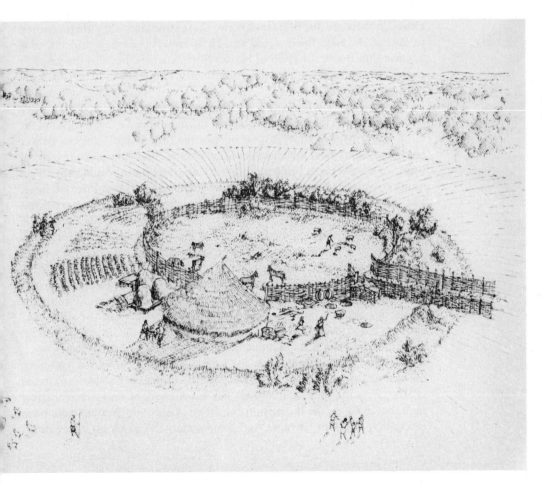

4-3. *A composite reconstruction of Site B; the ditch actually predated the houses by centuries.*

built a sequence of circular huts measuring about 10 to 13 metres across, apparently replacing each other regularly on the same spot. The entrances faced consistently to the east and the walls, indicated by slots dug into the ground, were built either of timber planks or wattling. If we interpret each wall-slot as the traces of an individual structure (and not part of a multi-walled building) then the original hut seems to have been replaced seven or eight times. How often this may have happened we cannot say for certain although evidence from Chris Lynn's Early Christian period site at Deer Park Farms in Co. Antrim suggests that wattle and daub houses were replaced at intervals of 20 years or less. Adjacent to these huts was a second series of structures, larger circular enclosures that measured about 18 to 20 metres across. These may have served as courtyards or animal pounds associated with the smaller residences (Ill. 4-3). Ultimately, the system of dual buildings was replaced by a series of three small circular huts.

Within this entire area there were found sherds of coarse bucket-shaped pottery and some objects of bronze, including a chape (the lower fitting on a sword scabbard), a sickle or reaping hook and possibly a spearhead. That the huts continued into the Iron Age, apparently without any marked break in continuity, is indicated by the presence of some iron objects.

Site A, a short distance away, also yielded traces of circular buildings and although there are no absolute dates for these structures, they are presumed to date to the Late Bronze Age and Early Iron Age as well. Indeed, they suggest that the occupation of Navan Fort extended beyond the areas of the visible monuments and more buildings may have existed on top of the hill.

The surrounding bank and ditch have never been excavated and they pose a number of interesting problems. For example, we find here an outer bank and an inner ditch, the same configuration that we have earlier recognized as typical for Late Neolithic henges. Now this is the reverse of what we should expect in a hillfort since an outer bank would provide an attacker with the opportunity to obtain higher ground than the defender. Recently Derek Simpson has suggested that Navan Fort may have origi-nally served as a henge monument, and that the enclosure itself may have long preceded the buildings described in this chapter. Without full excavation we cannot answer this question with confidence, however, we do have some evidence for its date. David Weir has sampled the ditch, which was originally two or three metres deeper than it appears today, in order to obtain pollen samples to reconstruct the prehistoric environment of Navan. From a pollen core he obtained evidence that the ditch was constructed at least before c. 750-400 BC, that is, by the Late Bronze Age. How much earlier still remains a mystery.

Since Navan later emerges as the Emain Macha of early Irish tradition, the seat of the ancient kings of Ulster and the Ulster capital depicted in the Ulster tales, this perhaps colours our assessment of the archaeological remains. Even so, the dimensions of the enclosure which must have been erected by the Late Bronze Age clearly mark it out as an exceedingly

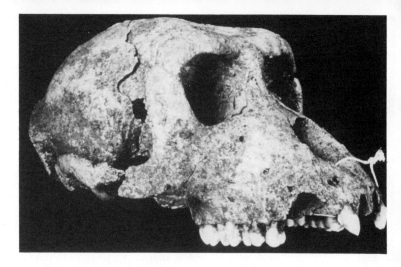

4. *Barbary ape from Navan.*

important site. We find similar enclosures at Knockaulin, Co. Kildare, which is identified with Dún Ailinne, the ancient capital of Leinster, and from the main enclosure at Tara, the Rath na Ríogh. All of this suggests that royal centres were being established in various regions of Ireland by about the Late Bronze Age and that they were demarcated by a henge-like enclosure, more appropriate to ceremonial than defensive use. We might also assume that the site was the scene of feasts and this is certainly not contradicted by the animal remains recovered from Site B. The most numerous animal recovered was the pig, which is surprising given that cattle is the predictable favorite on most prehistoric and later sites but perhaps not so odd when we recall from early Irish literature that pork was the preferred meat in royal feasts. That the residences of Navan included either a royal dynasty or at least a chieftain is further supported by the most exotic find from a prehistoric site in Ireland - the skull of a Barbary ape (Ill. 4-4). Clearly not native to Armagh, such an ape was probably a gift whose point of origin lay in North Africa and who was transported up the Atlantic seaways to Ulster. Rarer than any work of gold or bronze, exotic animals have always been regarded as regal presents. In the Middle Ages Harun al-Rashid sent the Emperor Charlemagne an elephant while a Norse tale recounts how an Icelander presented a polar bear to the King of Denmark.

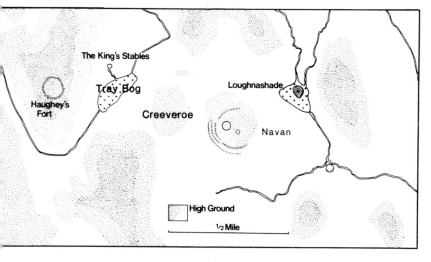

The King's Stables

Tray Bog

Loughnashade

Haughey's Fort

Creeveroe

Navan

High Ground

½ Mile

4-5. *The Navan complex.*

4-6. Three ditches surrou
Haughey's Fort.

Today we witness the same thing when heads of state return from China with a panda as a gift to their nations. One other aspect that we might expect of a royal site is further evidence of intense activity in the same vicinity. The evidence from Navan does not disappoint (Ill. 4-5).

Approximately three-quarters of a mile west of Navan Fort lies Haughey's Fort, a Late Bronze Age hill-fort, which was built and occupied about 1100 BC. The site was surrounded by three ditches, the outermost enclosing an area about 340 metres in diameter. Today there are no visible traces of the ditches left, however, their location can be clearly seen on aerial photographs (Ill 4-6). The ditches measure about 4 metres across at their top and were dug to a depth of approximately 2.5 metres. The innermost ditch was cut in the shape of a V, the classic form employed on defensive sites at this time (Ill. 4-7). Such a shape is too wide to leap at the top and any would-be attacker who tried to climb in and out of the ditch would have found himself in the precarious position of sliding back down the steep

4-7. Section of innermost ditch
at Haughey's Fort.

120

-8. Waterlogged wood and bone in inner ditch.

4-9. Wooden handle of axe or pick (l. 62 cm).

sides, especially if they were wet. Unlike the banks and ditch at Navan, Haughey's Fort was surely a defensive site.

The lower part of the inner ditch was waterlogged and very well preserved remains of animal bones, brushwood and some actual wooden implements were recovered (Ill. 4-8). These included the handle to some object such as an axe or pick (Ill. 4-9) and a bung (Ill. 4-10). Bones of all of the basic domestic animals - cattle, sheep, goat, pig, dog and horse were found, a number of which were quite large. Some of the cattle were among the largest known in prehistoric Ireland and the longest goat horn from a prehistoric site in Ireland was also recovered. More interesting, the ditch yielded two dog skulls, the largest known from a prehistoric site in the British Isles (Ill. 4-11). According to their skull measurements they would have been about the size of modern Alsatians. The size of some of these animals is consistent with one of the criteria that Richard Warner of the Ulster Museum has suggested as indicative of a royal site; larger animals should be expected from sites of the aristocracy, and indeed, we may recall here that the major tale of the Ulster Cycle, the 'Cattle-Raid of Cooley', begins with a dispute between the king and queen of Connacht as to who

4-11. One of the Haughey's Fort dog skulls compared with smaller medieval dog skull.

4-10. Wooden bung (l. 7.5 cm).

4-12. Post-holes (stock.
and large pits fro.
Haughey's Fort.

owned the best and largest bull. The ditch also yielded over 80 species of beetles and enough insect and chemical evidence to suggest that it possibly served as the latrine for the settlement (which may also have dampened the ardour of any potential attacker).

Inside the enclosed area there were found a large number of pits, apparently cooking pits with the remains of burnt stones, charcoal, sherds of pottery, burnt bones and the abundant remains of charred barley (the ditch yielded several saddle querns which were used for grinding the grain). Metal working was one of the activities on the site since traces of gold casting were found. No clear house structures have been found yet, but a long line of stake and post-holes attests the presence of some form of stockaded enclosure within the site itself (Ill. 4-12).

At the base of the hill upon which Haughey's Fort stands lies a totally unique archaeological site popularly known as the King's Stables (since

4-13. The King's
Stables.

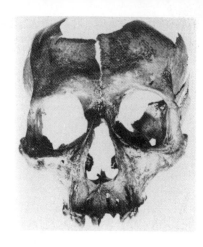

4-14. Skull from the King's Stables.

tradition held that this was where the early kings of Ulster stabled and watered their horses). In the 1970s Chris Lynn of the Archaeological Survey carried out a small test excavation on this peculiar monument whose radiocarbon dates indicate that it was contemporary with Haughey's Fort and in all likelihood built by the occupants of the hill-fort. The site is a roughly circular hollow about 25 metres across and 4 metres deep (Ill. 4-13). Examination indicated that it was filled with water (as it is still today) and would appear to have been a man-made pool, the water confined in the hollow and its surrounding earthen bank. On the bottom of the pool were found the remains of sword moulds, animal bones and part of a human skull. The animals included cow, red deer, dog, pig and sheep. These were not typical of an ordinary habitation site where they would have represented food remains. Sheep was present but only minimally, there was a strange abundance of stag antlers and dogs, and some animals were found in such a state that either the whole animal or at least part had been thrown in the water without having been butchered or cooked. Moreover, the remains of a young man were recovered (Ill. 4-14). This comprised the facial part of the skull which had apparently been cut away. All of this is suggestive of a ritual pool into which people deposited offerings to their gods. This practice is well known on the Continent from the Late Bronze and Iron Ages. The King's Stables, however, is the only prehistoric artificial pool yet known in the British Isles.

4-15. Timber and stone defences from Clogher.

123

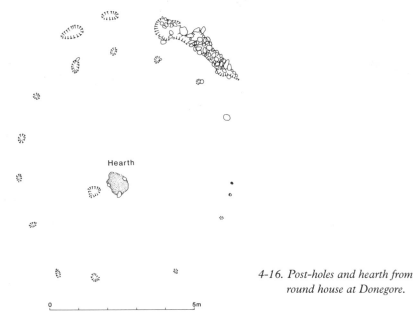

4-16. Post-holes and hearth from round house at Donegore.

Hearth

0   5m

Settlement

The Navan complex of sites clearly hints at a royal site or tribal centre although we cannot be certain as to the ethnic identity of its occupants. It is not the only royal site or, at least, major fortified settlement in Ulster at this time. Richard Warner excavated remains of a Late Bronze Age fortified settlement at Clogher, Co. Tyrone, a site that later served as the capital of the Airgialla, the successors to the ruling dynasty of Navan. The Bronze Age remains, like those at Navan, are situated on a hill-top and include traces of structures and coarse ware pottery as did Navan and Haughey's Fort. Of greatest interest here are the defenses which would appear to have been constructed out of timber and stone (Ill. 4-15), a technique of construction best known among the Iron Age Celts of Europe and Scotland. Traces of another timber-laced fort were observed by Richard Warner at Rallagh, Co. Londonderry, shortly before its destruction by a quarry. Warner believes that the timbers were deliberately fired by the builders to produce what is commonly known as a vitrified fort, a defensive construction well known in Scotland from the same period.

Lyles Hill, famous for its Neolithic settlement, also reveals evidence for Bronze Age occupation since the earthen bank that surrounds it appears to have been erected at sometime between the beginning of the Late Bronze Age and the Iron Age. Coincidentally, its earlier Neolithic neighbour, Donegore Hill, has also revealed Late Bronze Age occupation in the form of a circular post-built structure that measured about 8 metres across (Ill. 4-16).

Settlement in Ireland has never been limited to strictly dry-land sites. In the historic period we encounter crannogs, artificial islands, usually circular, constucted from brushwood, timbers, stones and other material enclosed within a ring of timber piles. These structures, set into lakes, were

124

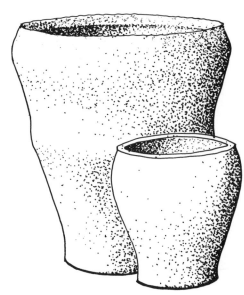

4-17. Late Bronze Age sites at Lough Eskragh.

4-18. Coarse ware pottery (h. 32 and 16 cm).

clearly defensive and apparently the residences of the more powerful members of society. When they began precisely is much disputed and Chris Lynn has suggested that the marked defensive nature of the mediaeval crannogs with their stout palisades or ring of piles does set them off from earlier lake-dwellings. No one would argue against the fact that lake-side dwellings or island habitation had already begun by the Neolithic as we have seen at Island MacHugh and Lough Enagh. By the Late Bronze Age we find some exceptionally good examples of such settlements in Ulster.

The level of Lough Eskragh, Co. Tyrone, dropped considerably in 1953 as water was drained off for use in a textile mill. The lowered water level provided an exceptional opportunity to investigate and recover substantial evidence for life in Late Bronze Age Ulster. Pat Collins and William Seaby examined several different areas of occupation. Then, twenty years later and under similar conditions the water level again dropped and Brian Williams had the opportunity to re-examine the site before it was once again inundated.

The largest part of the site exposed, Site A, consisted of some form of structures along the prehistoric shoreline and about 15 metres offshore what would appear to have been a crannog within the lake itself (Ill. 4-17). The crannog had been built from small birch pilings that had been rammed into the bottom of the lake. It consisted of a round platform, about ten metres across, constructed of timbers covered with brushwood. A tree-ring date from an oak plank from the crannog dated to about the 10th century BC while another sample of oak was radiocarbon dated to c. 920 - 790 BC. Within the crannog were two coarse ware pots (Ill. 4-18) plus other sherds

4-19. *Canoe with stumps of piles in background.*

4-20. *Wooden vessels from Lough Eskragh (larger ht. 27 cm).*

of coarse ware, seven saddle querns and a jet bracelet. Adjacent to it Collins and Seaby found two dug-out canoes, hollowed out of oak, and measuring over seven metres in length (Ill. 4-19). Within one of the canoes was a vessel carved from alder, and during Brian Williams' examination another alder vessel was recovered from the hut itself, which suggests that the canoes and the crannog were contemporary with one another (Ill. 4-20). The alder vessels provide a salutory reminder that much of the general household utensils in the prehistoric period were made of organic materials such as wood which we very rarely have the opportunity to recover.

The structure along the shoreline was composed of nearly 600 piles of birch and ash, the tips of which had been sharpened with a bronze axe, and then rammed into the mud. A total of seventeen saddle querns were recovered from this area and a radiocarbon sample from the piles indicated a date between 790 and 400 BC. Near Site A a bronze axe was also recovered.

A second site (Site B), about 120 metres from the Site A, also contained upright pilings and charcoal. But here there is a hint of something else. A large stone was found that had evidently been hammered and alongside were fragments from clay moulds used to cast bronze swords. This all points to the workshop of a bronze smith. A radiocarbon date of c. 1520 - 1140 BC was obtained. This date poses some difficulty since the type of bronze swords being cast on the site should not have appeared much before about 900 BC. Several other areas of settlement were also investigated.

Another site offering evidence of lakeside settlement is Island MacHugh, Co. Tyrone, which was excavated in the 1930s by Oliver Davies. Here he found remains of a brushwood platform and a quantity of Later Bronze

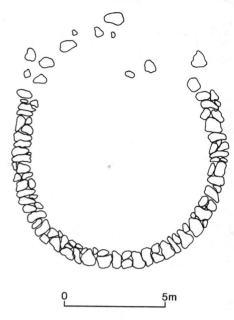

4-21. Hut of disputed date from White Park Bay.

0   5m

Age pottery. Derek Simpson's and Richard Ivens' more recent excavation of the same site has recovered evidence that it was occupied about 1200-800 BC (and much later) and a bronze sword was also recovered. Quite recently Brian Williams has uncovered further evidence for Late Bronze Age lake-settlement in Lough MacNean Lower in Co. Fermanagh.

While we most certainly have evidence for defended sites in the Late Bronze Age, we have no reason to assume that every Bronze Age Ulsterman felt constrained to live behind an earthen bank, ditch, timber palisade or surrounded by water. Traces of Late Bronze Age settlement have been discovered in upland regions such as at Ballyutoag, Co. Antrim, where a round house within a stone-built oval enclosure, first noticed by Oliver Davies, has yielded Late Bronze Age radiocarbon dates. Coastal settlement seen in earlier periods persisted also through the Late Bronze Age. For example, the north Antrim coast, particularly in the area of White Park Bay, was well settled if the quantity of coarse ware pottery recovered from its sand dunes is anything to go by. Here also were found twenty circular huts, many aligned along the shore and measuring about 6 metres in diameter which have been variously attributed to the Neolithic through the Late Bronze Age (Ill. 4-21). On a much less substantial scale and amidst the evidence for Early Bronze Age burials at Bay Farm III near Carnlough, Co. Antrim, there was also evidence for Late Bronze Age settlement on this rather exposed stretch of the coast.

Environment

Besides the meagre evidence for settlement, we do have another source of evidence for Late Bronze Age occupation - palynology. There is a considerable number of pollen diagrams that have been obtained from various Ulster sites such as Gortcorbies, Co. Londonderry, Sluggan and Altnahinch in Co. Antrim and Slieve Gallion, Co. Tyrone. They all appear

127

to tell a similar story. At about 1200-1000 BC there is a marked decrease in tree pollen and a rise in grasses and other indicators of forest clearance. This appears to have followed a long period of intermittent clearances and forest regeneration during the Early Bronze Age. In these later pollen profiles there also follows another brief period of forestation, perhaps as people abandoned different sites, but again there is a clearance phase around 900 BC. In short, there seems to be a general pattern of clearing the landscape for agriculture which should have provided the economic basis for the changes that we will soon see in industry, ornament and warfare.

Although the general trends of the environment can be seen in the pollen record, palynology may not be the appropriate tool for telling us about very sudden or short-lived change in the environment. Recently, some archaeologists and physical scientists have become interested in identifying short period climatic fluctuations that may have been too brief to influence the pollen record but may have had catastrophic effects on the societies who lived through them. Some have been bold enough to argue that one of these catastrophes may well have struck Ulster during the Late Bronze Age.

A glance at the map tells us that Mount Hekla in Iceland lies approximately 1300 kilometres north of Ulster, nevertheless, some suggest that this famous volcano may have affected life here over 3000 years ago. Volcanoes such as Hekla throw thousands of tonnes of dust into the atmosphere which can, among other things, severely alter both global and local climate. It has been suggested that during the period which we are now examining, Hekla experienced a major eruption which resulted in a mini-version of the dreaded nuclear winter. Dust reflecting sun light would have reduced warmth in the northern part of the British Isles and increased rainfall. This increased rainfall and accompanying cold would have rendered much of the uplands incapable of supporting crops and one might predict that much of upland settlement would collapse while communities were forced down into the lowlands, a pattern which historians have seen repeated during the later Middle Ages in Britain. John Barber has argued that a similar pattern occurred during the Late Bronze Age of Scotland where he cites the abandonment of about a thousand Late Bronze Age huts in Caithness and whole villages in north Uist during the 12th century, the approximate period assigned to Hekla 3 by various geophysical dating techniques. The abandonment of some areas, naturally, meant that populations were squeezed into the lowlands which produced a predictable response - increased warfare and the construction of defensive sites. Did the same happen in Ulster?

This question is still impossible to answer yet Ulster may shed some further light on this theory. The dates of archaeological sites are not the only story that our tree-rings tell us. Recalling that the basis for the variation in ring widths is very much tied up with the climate itself, scientists have been recently examining both the patterns and actual tree-

2. Narrowest rings may mark 12th century BC eruption of Hekla.

rings themselves to provide us with evidence of past climatic changes. At the simplest level, when the weather is extremely wet, then oaks growing about the edges of lakes (our future bog oaks) will be under severe stress and their rings will be quite narrow. Mike Baillie of the Queen's Palaeoecology Lab has observed that in the period 1159 to 1141 BC, Irish bog oaks experienced a period of quite severe stress and produced such extremely narrow rings that we can well suspect a rising of the water level, probably induced by increase rainfall (Ill. 4-22). These dates fit neatly into the period that other scientists would assign to the third great Hekla eruption (Hekla 3) and the periods of abandonment observed in Scotland. Our evidence for settlement in Ulster is nowhere as extensive as it is for Scotland and we would be pushing our evidence too far to say that the archaeological record for Ulster confirms a similar pattern here and we should not forget that both the implements for war and defensive architecture were advancing over Europe long before the Hekla eruption. What we can say is that a defensive site such as Haughey's Fort would appear to have been erected shortly after this 'event' (although not necessarily as a result of it) and, in an admittedly very speculative mood, several archaeologists have suggested that a ritual pond such as the King's Stables may have been an appropriate response by pagan Ulstermen desperate to appease their water deities. Whether this was so or not, we will have good cause to examine more closely the possible existence of gods who required watery offerings after we review the evidence for Late Bronze Age technology.

Technology

Major industrial changes were sweeping Europe by the twelfth century BC and they soon began appearing in Ireland. Here we find more sophisticated casting made possible by the use of the clay mould rather than the earlier stone mould, although the latter did continue in use. With clay, of course, it is much easier to form different shapes and cast decoration. The shape

4-23. Wooden spear model from Tobermore (l. 23 cm).

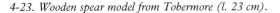

129

of the objects desired could be fashioned in wood and then each side could be impressed into a clay sheath. In 1911 a number of wooden models of bronze instruments was recovered from peat near the village of Tobermore, Co. Londonderry (Ill. 4-23). In addition to clay moulds, lead was occasionally added to the bronze to improve casting by retarding the speed at which the molten metal hardened during the casting process. Moreover, a whole new industry that specialized in beaten bronze work was developed to produce objects such as large buckets and cauldrons and shields. Furthermore, gold became increasingly abundant and Irish goldsmiths produced a vast quantity of ornaments not only for people in Ireland but also for export abroad.

Before we look at the types of objects made, we must consider our sources of information. Our bronze and gold objects are not normally discovered by archaeologists in the course of excavating a site but rather by the general public and by chance as we have already seen with regard to the Bann dredgings of nearly a century ago. Not all finds were limited to single objects; sometimes they were discovered grouped together into a hoard.

Hoards contain two or more metal objects and assist the archaeologists in dating various items since he can see which existed at the same time although sometimes metal working of different periods might be assembled together as scrap. But the hoards also present us with a mystery since they are not easily explained. Let's take a look at several examples.

At Crevilly-Valley, Co. Antrim, a hoard was discovered that contained an axe, chisel and a gouge (Ill. 4-24). Similarly, at Glastry, Co. Down, there was a hoard with two gouges and a chisel. In both these instances the objects found in the hoard appear to be associated with woodworking and so we might imagine them to have been carpenter's tool-kits which for some reason were either lost or hidden in the ground. On the other hand, from Killymoon, Co. Tyrone, comes a very famous hoard consisting of a gold dress fastener placed inside a wooden box. This was obviously a precious object that may have belonged to a wealthy member of the community. Why was it buried? It is very easy to say that people hid their precious objects in times of danger much in the same way that Early Christian monks might have hidden their gold vessels when they feared a Viking attack. But this may not have been the only reason. Often such hoards are found in bogs where we may well expect that it would have been very difficult to recover after it was hidden. Archaeologists in Scandinavia, where there are also many bogs, face a similar situation and many believe that the hoards found in bogs may not have been hidden there but rather placed in the bog as an offering to their gods, a theory that we will return to at the end of this chapter.

But not all hoards are obviously craftsmen kits or offerings. A bog near Dundrum, Co. Down, for example, produced a hoard with three spearheads, three axes, three rings and a pin. This would appear to be a very mixed bag of objects. In some instances the objects appear to have been

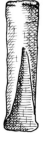

4-24. Hoard from Crevilly Valley.

130

broken. In these cases where the items of the hoard do not seem to come from a single tool kit nor appear to be particularly precious, we may suspect that the objects belonged to a smith and hence they are termed 'founder's hoards', that is raw and scrap materials one might associate with a foundry. These would be either the basic wares of a travelling smith or merely the scrap metal he collected in order to melt them down and cast new bronze objects from them. But again we must wonder why they were buried in the ground?

Now it is time to look at some of the advances in metallurgy that occurred in Ulster during the Later Bronze Age. The archaeologist normally discusses them period by period or by the evolution of a single object such as the shape of the axe. Thus, the Late Bronze Age begins with material of the Bishopsland phase, named after a hoard from Co. Kildare, which dates c. 1200 to 1000 BC and sees the introduction of socketed axes, hammers and a number of woodworking tools such as the saw, punch, graver and chisel as well as an 'ornament horizon' of gold bracelets, necklets, hair and earrings. The poorly known Roscommon phase from about 1000 BC sees the introduction of the first swords. By about 900 BC we find the full bloom of Late Bronze Age metalwork in the Dowris phase, named after a gigantic hoard recovered from Co. Offaly, and during which we find progressive developments of swords, and the introduction of buckets, cauldrons, horns and shields. Rather than taking on the different industrial types one by one, we'll confine our survey to looking briefly at the weapons of the warrior, the ornaments of the wealthy, and the tools of the craftsman.

The outfitting of a warrior

In the Middle Bronze Age an Ulster warrior was kitted out with a dirk or rapier and a spear which he either fought with or, at least, paraded about impressing his comrades and the lower orders. About 1000 BC a revolution in armament and warfare that had been sweeping across Europe finally reached Ireland. This involved the introduction of the sword, a weapon which was not used primarily for thrusting like the rapier but for slashing. This is clearly evident by the heavy leaf-shaped blades and the marked improvements in hafting the blade. Previously, the handles of dirks and rapiers had been wholly separate from the blade itself and attached to a small butt with a few rivets. With the introduction of the slashing sword, the warrior needed something he could grip with confidence and we now find that the blade is extended by a full metal hilt, which was then covered with wood, bone or ivory to form a handle (Ill. 4-25). The swords were apparently carried in scabbards made out of some perishable material. The bottom of the scabbard, however, was the chape which was sometimes made of bronze and hence we do find remains of chapes (Ill. 4-26). There are many bronze swords known throughout Ulster but the majority of finds comes from the Bann and Lough Erne. As with the hoards, we will return to possible explanations for this towards the end of the chapter.

Late Bronze Age spears saw the abandonment of loops, functional or

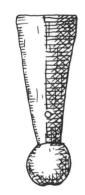

otherwise, and the adoption of rivetting for fastening the head to the shaft (Ill. 4-27). As in the Middle Bronze Age, the heads varied considerably in size and we may imagine that some were used as javelins while others for hand-to-hand combat.

A warrior facing an opponent with a slashing sword or large spear required some form of defence and hence we begin to find shields employed in the Late Bronze Age. The best evidence comes from outside Ulster where bronze, wooden and leather shields have been uncovered. It should be noted at the outset that although a bronze shield may appear far flashier than a leather shield, it did not provide superior defence. A bronze shield capable of withstanding the blow of a Late Bronze Age sword would need have been far thicker and heavier than any we find or that a Bronze Age warrior would be able to carry. John Coles has tested the quality of both types of shields and found that the point of a leaf-shaped sword could run through a metal shield and a slashing blow could cut right through the metal. The leather ones, on the other hand, proved perfectly adequate in deflecting severe sword blows. These shields were round and measured about 50 to 70 centimetres across. The only example from Ulster is a shield mould from Kilmahamogue, Co. Antrim, that was made of alder (Ill. 4-28). It measured about 45 centimetres across and was used to stretch and form leather into the shape of a shield.

There is one weapon that may well have disappeared by this time - the bow and arrow. While barbed and tanged arrowheads were exceedingly plentiful in the Early Bronze Age, they would appear to have disappeared by the Late Bronze Age and do not re-emerge again here until the Irish found themselves on the receiving end of Viking archers. Why they should have disappeared is a problem that admits several different solutions. The collapse of a good flint industry, and it should be remembered that the pressure-flaked arrowheads required great skill, in the face of an increasingly metal-based technology may have seen the abandonment of the very skills needed to fashion arrowheads. Alternatively, if warfare became increasingly the preserve of the upper classes, there may have been social pressures against the use of the bow in warfare (in Homer archers are regarded as second-rate, slightly cowardly fighters). No aristocrat, having invested considerable expense in his armament and expecting combat with

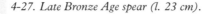

4-27. *Late Bronze Age spear (l. 23 cm).*

4-28. *Shield mould from Kilmahamogue,*
Co. Antrim.

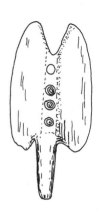

someone of comparable social status enjoys being taken out by a lower-class bowman well out of reach.

Dress and ornaments

What did an upper class man or woman dress like during the Later Bronze Age? This is what we will try to determine on the basis of the archaeological evidence, keeping in mind that like so many periods we will not be able to say much about how the average Ulsterman would have appeared. This is because our clues are largely bronze and gold ornaments that we suspect were restricted to the wealthier members of society.

The upper class Ulsterman of the Later Bronze Age may well have been shaven rather than bearded. We suspect this since one of the bronze objects that we find from this time is the razor. It's called a bifid razor since it has two edges (bifid means divided into two parts) and it is found widely over western Europe at this time (Ill. 4-29). All of this suggests that a fashion for clean shaven faces had been in vogue.

The actual clothes dating from this period have seldom survived and we have no certain idea as to the type of clothing worn. We do have, at least, some idea of the actual cloth since a piece has been recovered from Armoy, Co. Antrim. Here in a peat bog there was discovered a small hoard of bronze objects - a socketed axe, a pin, and a razor - all wrapped in a woollen cloth with a tassel made of horse hair. The technique of weaving was similar

4-30. *A man's costume from Late Bronze Age Denmark.*

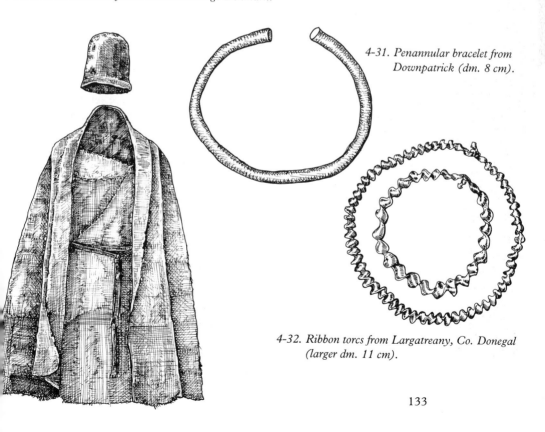

4-31. *Penannular bracelet from Downpatrick (dm. 8 cm).*

4-32. *Ribbon torcs from Largatreany, Co. Donegal (larger dm. 11 cm).*

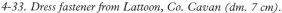

4-33. Dress fastener from Lattoon, Co. Cavan (dm. 7 cm).

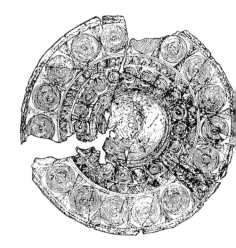

4-34. Sleeve fastener from Craighilly, Co. Antrim (dm. 2 cm).

4-35. Lattoon disc (dm. 12 cm).

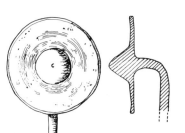

4-36. Sunflower pin from Derryhale, Co. Armagh (l. 19 cm).

to that sometimes found in Bronze Age sites in Denmark where entire suits of clothing have been found well preserved in burials. Whether a Bronze Age Ulsterman dressed in any way similar to a Bronze Age Dane, we cannot say, but at least the Danish evidence gives us some idea of how people elsewhere in northwest Europe may have dressed at this time (Ill. 4-30). The piece of cloth from Armoy is believed to have served as some form of belt. Other hints of Bronze Age dress comes to us from the ornaments that may have fastened them.

Among the most impressive objects known from the Later Bronze Age are the gold ornaments which give the impression that Ireland was extraordinarily rich in gold at this period. The ornaments took a variety of forms and many of them have been found in hoards. For example, fifteen simple penannular gold bracelets were recovered in two hoards discovered on Cathedral Hill in Downpatrick, Co. Down (Ill. 4-31), while twisted ribbon torcs of gold were recovered in considerable numbers from the Inishowen (14 torcs) and Largatreany (6 torcs) hoards in Donegal (Ill. 4-32). Some curious items include the dress and sleeve fasteners. The dress fastener (Ill. 4-33) is larger than the sleeve fastener (Ill. 4-34) and archaeologists suspect that it was worn to close the outer cloak. Fine examples of these were recovered from a bog in Lattoon, Co. Cavan, which also included an exquisitely decorated golden disc (Ill. 4-35). They are

4-37. Bronze ring from Seacon More, Co. Antrim (dm. 5 cm).

found all over Ireland. The smaller sleeve fastener, however, tends to be found primarily along the southern border of Ulster, for example, four were recovered from a hoard discovered near Arboe, Co. Tyrone. Another way of fastening one's cloak was with a pin and these are well attested in bronze. About a dozen disc-headed or sunflower pins of bronze are reputed to have been found together in a hoard from Derryhale, Co. Armagh (Ill. 4-36). Perhaps somewhat more enigmatic are the numerous small bronze rings, some clearly too small to have served as finger rings that have been uncovered (Ill. 4-37). Several of these were found in a pit at Haughey's Fort while they may also be encountered in hoards such as the 24 small bronze rings, out of a total of perhaps forty or fifty, that were discovered at Seacon More, Co. Antrim.

In addition to the gold neck ornaments, we also find necklaces made of amber beads which were certainly imported into Ulster, perhaps from as far away as Scandinavia. One of the most impressive of these necklaces came from Kurin, Co. Londonderry, which was composed of 421 beads.

Tools, vessels and musical instruments

We have already seen that tools are one of the types of objects one might discover in a hoard. One problem is knowing to what extent most people had metal tools or whether they were the property of only the wealthier members of society. What is important is the economic basis of the people since it was probably the surpluses gained in agriculture that provided the wealthier members of society with the ability to obtain the gold ornaments that we find.

The main tool encountered by the archaeologist is the socketed axe (Ill. 4-38). We have already recounted the various techniques that earlier Bronze Age smiths employed to improve fixing an axe to its handle. After flanges, wings, stop bars and palstaves, they finally developed the socketed axe, which often carried a small ring through which a cord could be passed to further secure it to its handle. Generally, we assume that these axes were used as tools for clearing forests or for a variety of other woodworking uses. Recall, for example, how we saw in the pollen diagrams a phase during which the amount of trees seemed to decrease in the Later Bronze Age as people opened new fields. The socketed axe may have been the main tool assisting man in expanding agricultural production.

Some have suggested that the axe may not have been purely or even primarily a tool but may have actually served as a weapon. The argument runs something like this. The majority of bronze objects that we find are weapons - swords and spears - of the upper classes. The basic occupation of such a class, as it was later in the Middle Ages, was probably warfare and so it is more likely that the socketed axes were to be used in combat rather than wasted in making tools. In addition, we know in other parts of Europe at a later date that similar axes were most certainly used as weapons, both by infantry and cavalry. This indicates that some axes may have served as weapons but this was probably not their primary function. Axes would

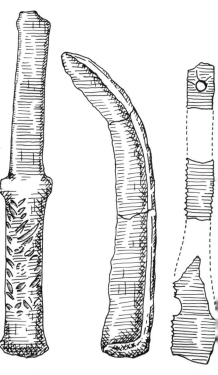

4-39. *Late Bronze Age tools.*

have been required to clear the forests as shown in the pollen analyses. It has been argued that the light-weight of many of the socketed axes shows that for forest clearance they would have been inferior to the Early and Middle Bronze Age axes. But we should also keep in mind the probability that a full range of axes of various sizes was required in the Late Bronze Age not just to clear the landscape but also to serve in an increasingly more sophisticated wood-working industry.

It is not only axes that we find but also other carpenter's tools. This, naturally, further supports the idea that some if not most of the axes were actually tools rather than weapons. We also find chisels, awls, gouges, saws, hammers and knives (Ill. 4-39). These implements indicate that bronze was becoming increasingly important in society at this time. The new bronze tools made it especially easier for craftsmen to work with wood and we have already encountered some evidence for this in the wooden dug-out canoes and vessels from Lough Eskragh or the wooden shield mould from Kilmahamogue. And although we lack any firm evidence, we should probably count the cart or wagon as one of the means of transportation, especially in light of the wooden trackways that have recently been discovered elsewhere in Ireland.

One of the main characteristics of the Later Bronze Age is the use of sheet bronze. Unlike other techniques required to turn out tools and weapons, sheet bronze involved the pounding out of bronze strips into thin plates and then moulding them into shape. The primary objects produced in this fashion were buckets and cauldrons. The buckets were probably large containers for some liquid. Since they were rare, they are thought to be associated with either the wealthier members of society or some form of

4-40. *Lisdromturk cauldron.*

ritual. The cauldrons were also expensive objects that could have been used in preparing feasts. A fine example comes from Lisdromturk in Co. Monaghan where one can clearly see how the bronze plates were riveted together with numerous staples (Ill. 4-40).

One more item of fine bronze craftsmanship can be seen in the bronze horns or trumpets. These horns appeared to have been blown in several different ways. Some were blown on the end and others on the side of the mouth section (Ill. 4-41). Up until recently it has proved very difficult to get much out of these superbly cast instruments, however, Siomon Ó Duibhir has recently carried out some experiments and revealed that one can really make music with these provided that they are blown like the didjerydoo of the Australian Aborigines. We often find both types of horns together, for example, a hoard was discovered in 1840 in Drumbest Bog, Co. Antrim, which contained two end-blow and two side blow horns. Ó Duibhir believes that the two different horns were meant to be played together, the end-blow providing the backing drone (in concert E) while the side-blow carried the melody (in concert G). Those horns found in Ulster tend to be decorated with incised ornament but those found in Munster are decorated with spikes. There are a number of other items that

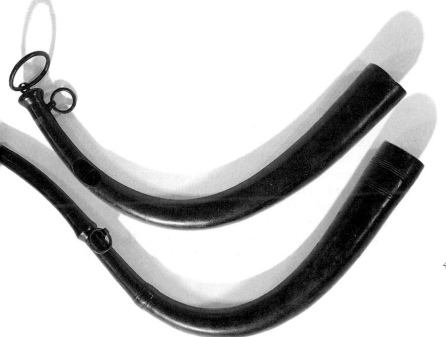

4-41. *Bronze horns.*

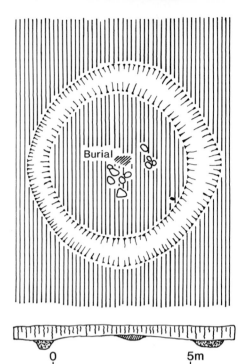

4-42. Ballybeen ring-ditch
and burial.

0   5m

are found either primarily in Munster or in Ulster which suggests that at this time Ulster was more closely oriented toward either Britain or Scandinavia while Munster may have drawn on other areas for its inspiration.

Burial

One of the most puzzling things about the Late Bronze Age is the lack of evidence for burials. Throughout the Early Bronze Age burials provided us with our main form of evidence but now we hardly find any at all or, at least, find it very difficult to ascribe any of the burials that we do find to the Late Bronze Age. Furthermore, when archaeologists discover other societies in Europe also rich in bronze and gold, they generally find extremely wealthy burials that belonged to the ruling classes. This was because the death of an important person was probably the occasion of a major funeral ceremony and the upper classes could take more wealth with them to their graves. But in all of Ireland there have been no more than about three or four burials assigned to the entire period of the Late Bronze Age. Two of these are known from Ulster. At Mullaghmore, Co. Down, archaeologists excavated a barrow (an earthen mound) that covered over a ring ditch. Within the mound were the remains of at least four people, cremated and found with sherds of pottery. Near the mound was yet another cremation placed in an upright pot. The style of the pottery suggests that it was of Later Bronze Age date.

The second site was found on the Ballybeen Housing Estate near Dundonald, Co. Down. Here the burial was very simple and consisted only of the cremated remains of an individual placed on the ground. Around the burial a small ring ditch had been dug and it was filled with charcoal, probably from the cremation fire (Ill. 4-42). The charcoal yielded a radiocarbon date of about 900 - 775 BC.

Later Bronze Age ritual

The stone monuments that were initiated in the Late Neolithic and flourished through the Early Bronze Age - standing stones and stone circles - appear to have ended before the Late Bronze Age, and, other than the presumably ritual pond of the King's Stables in the Navan complex (and perhaps the bank and ditch at Navan Fort), we lack overt evidence for places of public ritual. And, as we have just seen, we can say very little even about burial practices even though they have been one of the main forms of evidence up until the Late Bronze Age. But this lack of burial evidence, ironically enough, does suggest that we may have quite substantial evidence for ritual in the later prehistoric period.

In the previous chapter we already reviewed some of the evidence for depositing metal items in bogs and rivers, especially during the period of Middle Bronze Age metalwork where we also lack evidence for burials. These patterns persist through the Late Bronze Age. Nearly half of all swords, for example, have been found in rivers or bogs, and the situation in Britain is quite similar. There have been a variety of ways of explaining such a situation. One possibility is that swords were thrown into rivers or lakes as part of a ritual (recall the fate of King Arthur's sword Ex Calibur) or warriors may have been buried in rivers with their swords and, of course, the only thing that might survive such a burial would be the sword (although in the Thames there is also evidence for human remains). Another possibility is suggested by Dark Age literature. When we read the tales of CúChulainn or the Viking sagas, we often find that duels between warriors were traditionally fought at fords or islands within rivers. If the same were true of the Late Bronze Age, then the swords dredged from the Bann and the Erne may have been the remains of numerous prehistoric duels. But when we consider that well over half of all Late Bronze Age hoards have been recovered from wet environments, primarily bogs, and that many of these include no weapons, then it is hardly credible to presume that the discovery of weapons in bogs and rivers was regularly due to armed conflicts.

The deposit of wealth, especially metal objects, in bodies of water has been regarded as a widely observed ritual practice in many countries of Europe. In the early historical period we know from Posidonius that the Celts living around Toulouse about 100 BC deposited their treasures in sacred lakes. Colin Burgess has argued that one of the reasons for this behaviour earlier in the British Bronze Age may have been deteriorating weather conditions, especially more rain, in the first millennium BC, and we have already seen similar suggestions concerning the King's Stables and the proposed environmental impact of Hekla 3 on the Irish weather.

But of greater interest and credibility is the observation that we often find that the number of wet-land hoards tends to rise as the evidence of burial diminishes. From this, as Richard Bradley has proposed, we seem to find that the control and consumption of wealth may vary from one period to another or even from one area to another at the same time. The important factor is that surplus goods are being ritually destroyed by burial, either with individuals or, as in the case of our Irish Middle and Late Bronze Ages, in bogs and rivers. These, we presume, were not clandestine acts carried out by their owners but very public ritual performances designed to impress the neighbours and emphasize one's social position. This may appear like irrational behaviour but to some extent we still maintain such practices under the guise of philanthropy where a wealthy family may donate a substantial amount of wealth to renovating a church or building an extension to a hospital (with suitable plaques commemorating the gift), or endowing a lectureship in a university. This may even be associated with burial, in the same way we suspect may have been the case in the Late Bronze Age, since the occasion for such donation is often the death of a family member whose memory is to be perpetuated by the gift. In the absence of hospitals requiring extensions or chairs needing endowing, ritual offerings to the gods of gold and bronze on behalf of the whole (and presumably assembled) community may have been the behaviour expected of Late Bronze Age leaders.

Final Bronze Age collapse

Sometime after about 600 BC the great wealth of ornaments and weapons of the Late Bronze Age seems to disappear from the archaeological record and Ireland, at least from the viewpoint of the archaeologist, collapses into a Dark Age for several centuries. Why this should have happened we have no clear idea. Such a collapse could have been caused by natural catastrophes such as a worsening of the climate or it may have been brought on by man who could have overexploited his fields. Climatic deterioration has been observed elsewhere in northwest Europe and some Irish pollen evidence suggests that the earlier clearance phases that indicated farming activities seem to have been abandoned and the forest or bog began to expand. This may suggest some form of economic collapse since the failure of the agricultural basis of society would bring down the wealthy aristocracies who supported the rich bronze and gold industries. But we should beware of reading too much into pollen accounts from upland bogs since lowland sites such as Lacken Bog, Co. Down, indicate regular flunctuations between woodland and both pastoral and arable agriculture from the Late Bronze Age onwards. Perhaps we should imagine the continual and rather relentless removal of upland regions in Ulster from agriculture and increasing intensification of agricultural activities in lowland Ulster. For example, Valerie Hall of Queen's University has obtained a pollen core from Long Lough, Co. Down, which shows remarkably high tree pollen and some evidence for pastoral clearance during the Late Bronze Age but evidence for growing cereals does not begin to appear until about 100 AD.

One other factor that some might associate with the Bronze Age collapse is invasion. The evidence for a new people about 600 BC is very slender indeed but can hardly be avoided since it concerns the whole question of the arrival of the Celts in Ireland. Before 600 BC a new sword type begins to appear in Ireland (Ill. 4-43). This was called a Hallstatt C sword and it takes its name from a very important cultural horizon on the Continent that is often attributed to the Celtic peoples. In Central Europe these swords were made of iron and they mark the beginning of the Iron Age in western Europe. They have also been found in the British Isles, especially in the Thames river valley, eastern Scotland and Ireland. In Ulster they are mainly known from the Bann and here, as we have already seen, we find the particular association between swords and rivers. Some have suggested that these Hallstatt swords mark the path of Celtic chieftains who passed through Britain or Scotland on into Ireland. To support this argument further, they point out that we do not normally find these swords with typically Late Bronze Age goods so this may indicate that the people who used these swords were from outside the native population, in other words, invaders.

But there are serious problems tying these new swords to Bronze Age invaders. None of the fifty Hallstatt-type swords in Ireland are of iron but rather they are all of bronze. They do not, therefore, look like the weapons of invading warriors so much as copies of iron swords made by Irish bronze smiths. For this reason, most archaeologists suspect that the new swords represent little more than the spread of a new style to Ireland from Britain that did not require any movement of people. We must return to this whole problem in the next chapter since it concerns one major question of Irish prehistory: who was the first Irishman?

Finally, do we yet have an Ulster? Our traditional Irish history that ascribed the foundation of Ulster to Rudraighe of the Fir Bolg set this event to the Early Bronze Age. We have already seen that at the end of the Neolithic regional tendencies within Ulster itself appeared to be stronger than provincial traits that might have separated Ulster from the rest of Ireland. Now in the Bronze Age we find several different cultural patterns obtaining in Ireland. On the one hand, we can still see regional divisions within Ulster. The wrist bracers of presumably Beaker date are primarily found in Co. Antrim, with only occasional finds elswhere in Ireland; stone circles are clustered mainly in mid-Ulster; Collared Urns are primarily an east Ulster phenomenon while wedge tombs in Ulster are primarily found in the south and the west.

On the other hand, we can also perceive broader groupings of material across the entire island that distinguishes the 'north' from the 'south'. George Eogan, for example, has called attention to how certain types of cauldrons, buckets, horns, rings and the whole category of sleeve fasteners tend to be found almost exclusively in the north (Ill. 4-44) while other

141

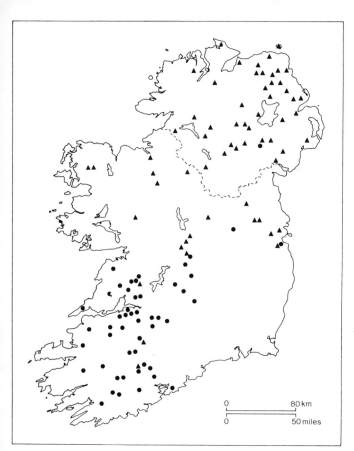

4-44. Northern versus southern metalwor
triangles = Class A cauldrons, buc
Class I horns, striated rings and
sleeve fasteners; circles = lock-rings
gorgets, Class II horns and bowls.

items such as lock rings, gorgets (large golden collars), other types of horns and bowl are found primarily in Munster. Such distinctions can be found all the way up to this century where the 'two sided' spade is typical of the north and the 'fish tailed' spade is characteristic for Munster. The geographical distinctions here, however, are very broad, the northern artifacts regularly cover parts of Leinster and Connacht and can hardly be regarded as specifically 'Ulster', even if one adopts the traditional defini- tion of Ulster as anything north of a line between the Boyne and the Drowse, the river that separates Leitrim from Donegal. Moreover, many categories of objects are the same both in the north and the south. Similar patterns will continue later as we will see but in the next chapter we will encounter, finally, some evidence for a prehistoric Ulster.

5 From Uluti to Ulster
300 BC - 400 AD

Ptolemy and Ulster

In the second century AD the geographer Ptolemy prepared a gazetteer of all the major places and peoples of the known world. In it he listed the names of rivers, promontories, peoples and towns and against each entry he gave its position according to his system of recording latitudes and longitudes. Ptolemy began his survey with the most western land known to the Ancient World, Ireland.

Ptolemy's gazetteer is among our earliest documentary evidence for Ireland and it gives us a vague picture of Ulster in the Iron Age. We must say vague since there are great difficulties in reading Ptolemy's map. He himself never visited Ireland but prepared his gazetteer in the library of Alexandria in Egypt. How he obtained his information would have been by a long and complicated route that would have introduced numerous inaccuracies. During the Iron Age, British and Continental merchantmen were in contact with Ireland and would have known where rivers discharged into the sea, the location of the larger tribes, and some of the major

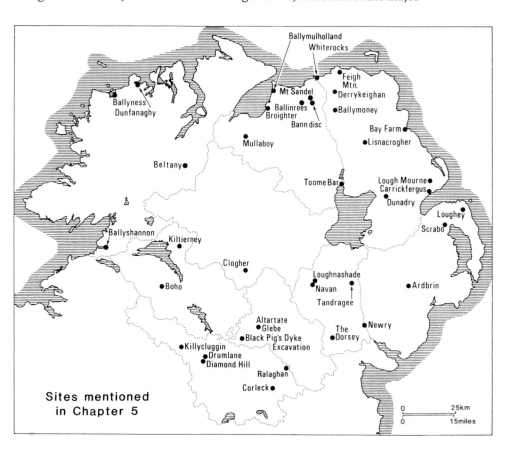

Sites mentioned
in Chapter 5

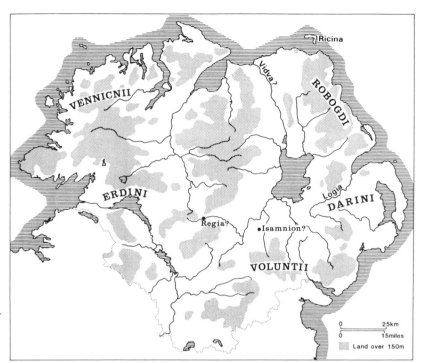

5-1. *Ptolemy's map of Ulster.*

places of settlement. This information could then be passed on to the Romans who had effectively conquered Britain in the first century AD. The Romans would have transmitted the information on to Rome and other centres of learning such as the library of Alexandria where scholars spoke Greek. From this we can see that the original names of peoples and places in Ireland may have been first conveyed by people speaking the ancient British languages, then they would have to be written in Latin and finally in Greek (Ptolemy's own book is in Greek). So here we have a whole series of people copying down the sounds of words from a language that they didn't know, a situation that could only lead to confusion. To add to the problem, we have no manuscripts from Ptolemy's time (the library at Alexandria was burnt down in AD 642) and so we must depend on mediaeval copies many times removed from the original manuscript of Ptolemy. Despite all these problems, we can still capture a glimpse of Ulster during this period.

The names on Ptolemy's map are, of course, very unlike those that we know today since they not only have suffered great distortion but they are also in a very archaic form of the Celtic language which is both older and very different even from our earliest Irish manuscripts. For example, at a grid reference which would indicate some place along the Antrim or Down coast, we find that a river known as the Logia discharges into the sea (Ill. 5-1). From medieval manuscripts we know that Belfast harbour was called Loch Loigh, i.e. 'the lough of the calf'. The naming of a river or lough after a cow or bull is not rare and on Ptolemy's map we find the river Buvinda which literally means 'white cow' and survives today as the Boyne. It is possible to determine the identities of some of the other names in Ulster.

144

Ptolemy mentions an island off the north coast of Ireland which is called Ricina. This seems to be close enough to Rechrann, the Irish name for Rathlin, that we can be confident about identifying it. Beyond this we sail into much more disputed waters. The Ravios, for example, equates linguistically with the Roe, but appears to be misplaced as Ptolemy puts in roughly where the Erne should be. Other than dead-reckoning there are no solid linguistic grounds although there are various linguistic arguments for associating the other rivers on the north coast (the Vidva and the Argita) with the Foyle, Bann or the Bush.

Ptolemy also mentions the names of tribes occupying the north. In the southwest were the Erdini which some such as Liam Gogan would associate with the Erne while Julius Pokorny denies such a link. To their north in Donegal were the Vennicnii whose name Gogan relates to the Venicones who occupied southeast Scotland. In Antrim we have the Robogdii. Julius Pokorny took this fairly peculiar name at face value and suggested that it equates with Old Irish *Ro-bochti* which would mean 'very poor', which he assumed appropriate as he imagined that during the Iron Age the Antrim coast was settled by the impoverished remnants of Neolithic fishermen! Others have assumed that the name has been horribly mutilated either before reaching Ptolemy or in manuscripts. For example, Thomas O'Rahilly suggested that the name may have originally been something like *Redodios* which would later emerge as Riata, the mythical founder of the Dál Riata, the major north Antrim tribe of Early Christian Ulster. Liam Gogan, on the other hand, suggested that the original name may have been *Gobordii* related to Old Irish *gobor* 'horse'. Opposite in Kintyre were the Epidii whose name unquestionably means horsemen and so he suggests that we may have had two similarly named tribes on either side of the Irish Sea. The Darini of south Antrim and north Down were explained by O'Rahilly as decendants of Darios, later Dáire, a traditional ancestor of both the Dál Riata and the Dál Fiatach who occupied west Down.

Probably the most important of Ptolemy's tribes seems to have occupied Louth, south Down and Armagh which in its Latin form was named the Voluntii. The primitive Celtic form of this word was probably *Uluti* which gave *Ulaid* in Old Irish. *Ulaid* means Ulsterman (the *Ul-* of Ulster is from *Ulaid*) and from this we can see that the whole province gains its name from one of the Iron Age tribes occupying the north by the second century AD. This may have been due to the preeminence of this particular tribe in the north.

In the area of the Uluti there existed a place called Isamnion. There is debate among scholars as to what Isamnion was precisely. Our copies of Ptolemy indicate that it was a promontory but some believe that this was the result of the confusion caused by centuries of copying out the original Greek manuscripts. They suspect that it referred to a town or at least a settlement since they believe the word survives to this very day although in greatly changed form. Linguists such as Thomas O'Rahilly and Julius Pokorny were agreed that Ptolemy's Isamnion was probably a slightly garbled version of *Isamonis*, a word which by the time of the earliest Irish manuscripts would have been shortened to Emain (usually pronounced Evin). This Emain or Emain Macha, the name of the ancient capital of Ulster, then passed into English at a time when the Irish article 'the' was regularly put in front of it, i.e. An Ehmain (pronounced uh-neven) which was anglicized by the 17th century as Navan. Ulster's other 'town' was simply listed as Regia, that is, royal place, and some have suggested that this is the name that should have been assigned to Navan. For those who equate Isamnion with Navan, then Regia should be a royal centre to its west. The site most closely matching this description is probably Clogher in Co. Tyrone which we have already seen emerged as a major centre in the Late Bronze Age.

Emain Macha

In the 7th or 8th centuries AD, Irish monks began to record the ancient legends of the peoples of Ulster. They wrote of the great events and battles between the Ulstermen and their traditional enemies, the people of Connacht. These are the stories of CúChulainn, Conchobor (Conor) Mac Nessa, Fergus Mac Roech (Roy) and, of course, Deirdre (of the Sorrows). In these tales Emain Macha is portrayed as the great capital of Ulster where King Conchobor holds court and feasts his warriors, and where the youth of Ulster organized into the *macrad*, the boy troop or boys brigade, played their early form of hurling and learned the techniques of warfare. It was where the severed heads of the enemies of Ulster were placed on display. And where poets and druids recounted the glories of Ulster warriors and their ladies. If King Arthur and his early Britons had their Camelot, the Ulstermen had their Knights of the 'Red Branch' at Emain Macha. But while the location of Camelot, if indeed it ever existed, is a topic of eternal scholarly debate, there is little doubt that the Emain Macha of Irish literature is to be identified with Navan Fort.

We have already seen in the last chapter that by the Late Bronze Age, a major complex of sites had begun to develop at Navan - the round houses and compounds at Navan Fort (which might very well be of Iron Age date), the ritual pool at the King's Stables and the hill-fort known as Haughey's Fort. The discovery of a Barbary ape skull at Navan Fort plus other important objects suggests that it had already become a place of great importance and may well have served as the seat of a local chief during the Late Bronze Age or Early Iron Age. By the first century BC it seems to have become the capital of the Uluti, the 'original' Ulstermen.

About 100 BC the people at Navan cleared away the remains of the round house-compounds to erect an enormous circular structure (Ill. 5-2). It measured about 40 metres across and was built from 275 posts arranged in six concentric rings. At the centre of the structure was a large central post of oak. In order to raise this massive post a ramp 6 metres long was built so that it might be tipped into its pit.

What did this structure look like when completed? Today we only have

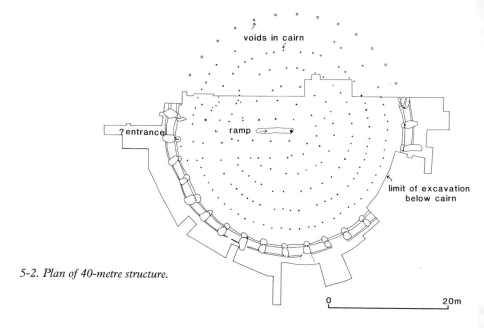

voids in cairn

?entrance

ramp

limit of excavation
below cairn

5-2. Plan of 40-metre structure.

0   20m

the post holes and the bottom stumps of some of the posts. Was it, for example, roofed? Some archaeologists suspect that indeed it was. When we look at the outer ring of posts we note that each post was augmented with another by its side. In addition, if the ramp for the central post was 6 metres long, we might expect that the post could have been twice as long, i.e. about 12 metres. The central post seems to have been the last of the posts erected and so we might imagine that it stood like some great totem pole. This great timber, incidentally, was dated by Mike Baillie at Queen's and appears to have been cut down in 95 BC. We are left then with a giant structure, at least 12 metres or more in height, built of timber posts and perhaps with a thatched roof (Ill. 5-3). Alternatively, the structure may

*5-3. Reconstruction of
40-metre structure.*

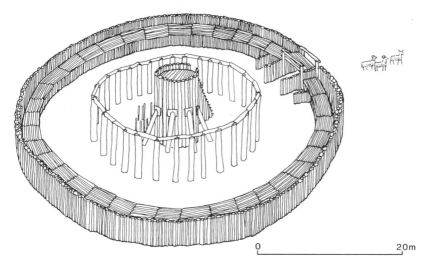

5-4. *Reconstruction of Knockaulin structure.*

have been open and recently Bernard Wailes who excavated a somewhat similar structure at Knockaulin, Co. Kildare, has reconstructed such a building as something like a timbered amphitheatre surrounding a series of free-standing posts with a nine-metre high tower in the centre (Ill. 5-4).

Nothing at all was found on the floor of this great structure which would appear to have been a large Celtic temple or hall. It is interesting to compare it with the descriptions of the 'Red Branch' Hall in the Ulster tales: "There was the Croebruad (Red Branch) of Conchobhor, after the likeness of the house of Tara's Midbrain. Nine compartments were in it from fire to the wall. Thirty feet was the height of each bronze front that was in the house. Carvings of red yew therein. A board beneath and a roof of tiles above. The compartment of Conchobhor was in the forefront of the house, with boards of silver with pillars of bronze. Their headpieces glittering with gold and set with carbuncles...with its plate of silver above the king to the rooftree of the king's house." This is, of course, a fantasy description which any reader of the Ulster tales knows is also applied to other great palaces in the stories. How closely the Ulster tales reflect the life and times of the Ulster Iron Age will be considered in more detail later on.

5-5. *Loughnashade horn (128 cm across).*

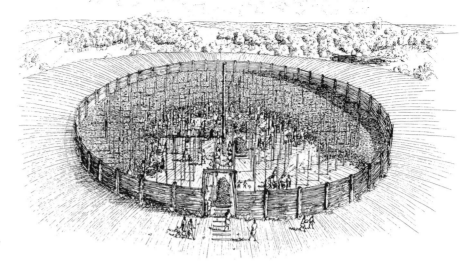

*Building the
limestone cairn.*

Immediately downslope of Navan Fort is Loughnashade. Today at less than half a hectare it is only a shadow of its previous size. In the Iron Age it was probably at least 2 hectares in extent and possibly much larger (its maximum size in prehistory was 8 to 10 hectares). At the end of the 18th century, men digging drains nearby discovered four great bronze horns which had apparently been deposited in the lake as some form of offering (Ill. 5-5). They were decorated in the traditional Celtic style and would probably date to about the first century BC when the great temple was still standing. Just as sacrifices were made in the King's Stables during the Later Bronze Age, so also it seems that sacrifices were made into Loughnashade (lake of the treasure) during the Iron Age. According to the original accounts of the discovery, not only horns but also animal bones and some human skulls were uncovered during the digging.

The end of the forty-metre ritual structure on top of the hill was even stranger than its original erection. Sometime, probably during the 1st century BC, the people ritually destroyed their great temple. First they filled the inside with limestone boulders up to over 2 metres in height (Ill. 5-6). They did this when the posts were still standing since Dudley Waterman could discern the voids in the stone cairn where the posts had once stood. Then they set fire to the outer wall of the structure which encased the stone cairn. Finally, they cut sods and covered the entire structure to form the earthen mound that one sees today when one visits the site (Ill. 5-7).

Why destroy the structure? We can have no certain idea as to the reasons for its destruction (here again we see the distinction between reconstructing ritual as opposed to belief). That it was carefully planned we can have little doubt and that it was done by the local inhabitants also seems to be reasonable. It is difficult to imagine why enemies of Ulster, attacking the site, would go to all the effort of piling up the limestone cairn and the earthen mound just to destroy the temple. Rather, the whole affair would

149

appear to have been part of a ceremony. Why there should have been a ritual destruction of the building is pure guesswork. A king may have died who was closely connected with the building and it may have been destroyed as part of his funeral. Another idea involves the decommissioning of the temple in this world to place it in the next. Early Irish literature indicates a belief that the way to the Otherworld was gained by entering a large mound. Therefore, ancient Ulstermen may have thought to remove the temple from the world of the living where it might rot or be destroyed and ritually preserve it under a cairn of stones and earth in the Otherworld. They may have even built the temple itself as a palace for a god who would dwell in it after it was encased in the mound. Finally, we know from the Early Christian period that Irish kings were traditionally inaugurated on mounds and thus even after its destruction the mound itself may have continued to serve as the place where the kings of Ulster were crowned.

Iron Age settlements

It is all too easy to become so mesmerized by Navan that we ignore the evidence for other Iron Age settlements in Ulster although this hardly amounts to much. A number of Iron Age radiocarbon dates indicates a certain amount of activity going on at Clogher, our other royal site, in Co. Tyrone, and there are also Iron Age dates for the top of the earthen bank at Lyles Hill. Excavations of one of the huts on Scrabo hill in Co. Down uncovered charcoal of Iron Age date while a pit and a hearth from Mount Sandel, Co. Londonderry, produced Iron Age dates and some Iron Age material. Generally, our evidence is confined to the odd hearth or pit without further supporting evidence of occupation. That the coast was one area of settlement is indicated by Iron Age hearths from Bay Farm II, Carnlough and Whiterocks, both in Co. Antrim, and an Iron Age shell-midden of Ballymulholland I on Magilligan strand in Co. Londonderry.

The linear earthworks of Ulster

Along the southern borders of ancient Ulster are a series of earthworks that bear such names as the Dorsey, the Dane's Cast, and most famous of all, the Black Pig's Dyke (Ill. 5-8). The first of these, the Dorsey, is situated in south Armagh. It takes its names from the Irish *doirse* 'doors' and has

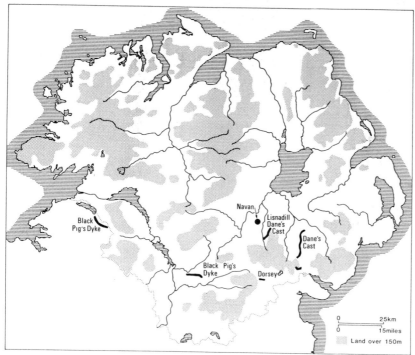

5-8. The linear earthworks of Ulster.

traditionally been interpreted as a gateway into Ulster (the old coach road between Dublin and Armagh is reputed to have run through the Dorsey). In form it is an enormous enclosure measuring about 4 kilometres (Ill. 5-9). The defences consist of a series of banks, ditches and timber palisades (Ill. 5-10). Today it encloses nothing more than a bog and its function has always remained a mystery. Although some people have imagined that it was an enormous cattle enclosure, it is a perverse farmer indeed who mires his cattle in a bog. Recently, Chris Lynn has suggested that it may not have been an enclosure at all but rather two lines of defensive earthworks, built at different periods, that only appear to be joined up because the second line of defence was required to plug the same hole as the first. Confirming evidence for this has come from Mike Baillie's tree-ring work which

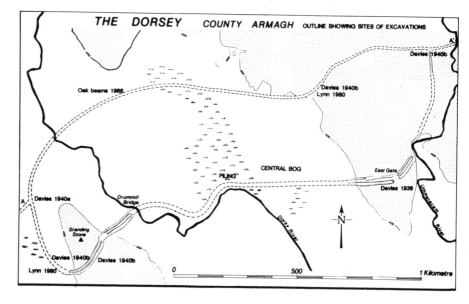

Plan of the Dorsey.

5-10. The Dorsey marked by double hed...

indicates that an earlier defensive line was built on the northern side of the Dorsey about 150 BC and then, as Lynn suspected, the entire line of defence was augmented about fifty years later when a southern line was constructed about 95 BC. The reason for this is only speculative but Lynn calls our attention to evidence for burning along the northern palisade which may have been the result of attacks. The other smaller earthworks which are popularly known as the Dane's Cast remain undated but not devoid of speculation. The Lisnadill Dane's Cast has been sometimes regarded as a second or third line of defence, Emain Macha being the site most likely to require defending. The Clanrye Dane's Cast, on the other hand, as it runs north-south and along what was to become the border of the greatly reduced territory of the Ulaid (Ulstermen) after the fall of Emain Macha, has been interpreted as a later defence, raised up by the Ulster dynasty occupying Co. Down, in the centuries around 500 AD.

The Black Pig's Dyke is the most famous of the linear earthworks in Ireland. It takes its name from a folktale that relates how a schoolteacher-magician was tricked into turning himself into a black pig and was then harried across the southern border of Ulster where it rooted up the ground leaving the ditch and banks that one can still see today. The name is applied to linear earthworks that appear in south Armagh, Monaghan and south Donegal. The best investigated is a stretch of the earthworks near Scotshouse in Co. Monaghan where Aidan Walsh of the Monaghan County Museum carried out a small test excavation. Here he discovered two earthen banks and remains of a timber palisade which had been burnt down (Ill. 5-11). The charcoal from the palisade dates to sometime between about 400 and 100 BC.

What was the purpose of these earthworks? They are clearly defensive and they are built in such a way as to impede an attacker moving from south to north. They are, however, not continuous across the entire southern border of Ulster but rather appear where the terrain does not offer natural protection such as the lakes of Fermanagh or the high ground of south

Armagh. We do not imagine that they served as a manned defensive line like Hadrian's Wall (Oliver Davies thought they had been modelled on the Antonine Wall of Scotland which we now know they predate) or the Great Wall of China, but rather as an impediment, probably to cattle-raiders. Early Irish literature suggests that the main preoccupation of society was cattle-raiding, especially between Ulster and Connacht. The Connachta were reputed to have had their capital at Crúachain, the modern Rath Croghan, Co. Roscommon, where King Ailill and Queen Medb (Maeve) ruled. These may have been characters out of fiction but a society concerned with cattle-raiding may have been quite real and so archaeologists have generally regarded the linear earthworks of Ulster as defensive measures taken by early Ulstermen against their neighbours to the south. It should perhaps be emphasized that the linear earthworks are built on rising ground with south-facing slopes and that they were clearly intended to protect Ulster from the outside and not, as some wags might suppose, to keep Ulstermen penned in!

Economy and industry

The remains of the Iron Age economy in Ulster or indeed anywhere else in Ireland are meagre in the extreme because there is so little evidence for settlement. We have seen in the last chapter the range of basic domestic animals from Navan. But since this site seems to have been a royal or ritual site, the diet obtained from Navan may hardly be typical for most Ulster. Ballymulholland I, an Iron Age shell-midden in north County Londonderry, is probably not at all typical either and only yielded evidence for a few cows, pigs and sheep plus a vertebra from a whale. Since this is a period often characterized as a time of constant cattle-raiding, we might note that on the basis of the only substantial Iron Age faunal remains in Ireland, Knockaulin, Co. Kildare, Iron Age cattle were still very small with an average withers (shoulder) height of only 107 to 115 cm. Although the cattle may have been small on modern standards, Ireland was seen as a paradise for cattle raising during the Iron Age. Pomponius Mela wrote

. *The Black Pig's Dyke under excavation.*

around A.D. 43 that the pastures of Ireland were so 'nutritious and savoury, that the cattle eat their fill in a small part of the day, and, if they were not restrained from feeding, would, by eating too long, burst.'

We have seen that there is some suggestion that there was a collapse in agriculture towards the end of Bronze Age. Later in the Iron Age there is indirect evidence that agriculture was well on its way to recovering, and indeed, cereal production seems to have intensified, at least in some areas. This can be seen in the discovery of well over two hundred querns in Ireland, many of which are found in Ulster. These are called bee-hive querns because of their distinctive shape and they are very different from the earlier saddle querns where one had rubbed one stone across the face of the quern (Ill. 5-12). Now, however, one could rotate the upper stone on the surface of the lower which was vastly more efficient. Better technology for processing grain suggests that agriculture itself may have been on the upswing and possibly, population as well. Seamus Caulfield has suggested that these new rotary querns indicate a new population in Ireland since they are also found in Scotland and northern England. We will return to the subject of migrations later in this chapter.

One further line of indirect evidence for the economy is a wooden comb, possibly used for extracting wool from sheep, which was discovered at Navan Fort. Such combs are quite typical of the Iron Age hill-forts of southern England, however, all of our evidence so far suggests that sheep remained of very secondary importance in prehistoric Ireland. Naturally, it cannot be ruled out that the comb may have been intended for grooming Iron Age Ulstermen or women instead. The existence of Iron Age fieldwalls is suggested by a collapsed wall discovered at Mullaboy, Co. Londonderry, which lay on blanket peat of Iron Age date.

Metal tools no doubt played an important role in the economy. The introduction of iron tools to Ireland is a major problem for Irish prehistorians. Elsewhere in Europe by the first centuries BC, iron had replaced bronze as the basic material for tools. Although bronze makes an effective tool, its constituent elements - copper and tin - were never so abundant that one can imagine that everyone would have easy access to it. When iron was discovered in the Near East and the Caucasus mountains, this provided a new way forward since iron could not only be shaped into a great variety

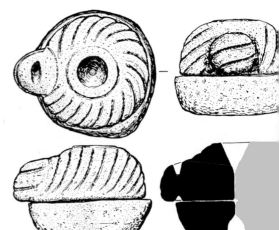

5-12. Beehive quern (dm. 26 cm).

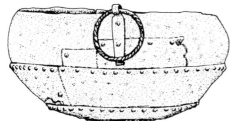

5-13. Drumlane cauldron (dm. 36 cm).

of tools but it was vastly more plentiful in nature than either copper or tin. But in order to extract iron from its ore, this required the development of new technologies, and still it was quite laborious to make. For these reasons, iron did not suddenly sweep across Europe to replace bronze but crept along slowly replacing earlier bronze tools. Our earliest iron tools tend to be crude copies of bronze implements. This can be seen on some sites in Ulster. At Toome Bar and Lough Mourne, both in Co. Antrim, there were found iron socketed axes in the same general shape as earlier bronze axes. This alone is curious since at this time, iron was forged rather than cast like bronze and this required the smith to beat the iron into the shape of a socketed axe rather than pour molten iron into a clay mould as one might have done with bronze. But in general our evidence for iron tends to be quite poor. This is probably due to at least three different reasons. Iron technology may have come slow and late to Ireland; we have very few settlements from which we might expect to find iron objects; and, finally, iron oxidizes (rusts) very quickly and is not so well preserved as bronze.

We have some evidence for cooking and serving food. Meals may have been boiled or simmered in large cauldrons such as the iron cauldron from Drumlane, Co. Cavan, or the bronze cauldron from Ballymoney, Co. Antrim, both of which have been assigned to the Iron Age (Ill. 5-13). There are even the remains of a cauldron fashioned out of poplar discovered at Altartate Glebe, Co. Monaghan. And for drinking, there were wooden tankards, one of the finest of which was discovered at Carrickfergus, Co. Antrim, which some archaeologists suspect was imported from Britain.

The Iron Age warrior

Probably the most prized weapon of the Iron Age warrior in Ireland was his sword and there are over twenty of these known from the whole of Ireland (Ill. 5-14). They are all iron except for a few instances of wooden 'toy' swords. These swords are generally quite short, the longest blade measures only 46 centimetres and most are nothing more than large daggers. This short sword is typical of Ireland and contrasts with the evidence from southern Britain where we find very large swords at this time. Nevertheless, both the British and Irish swords are similar in style. They are of the La Tène type, the major art style of the Celts during the Iron Age when they dominated western and central Europe. The Irish swords were probably used like a dagger or dirk rather than the heavy slashing sword we found in the Late Bronze Age. Their handles were made of some organic material such as bone, tusk or wood (Ill. 5-15). Some late interpolator inserted into the 3rd century AD writings of Solinus that

5-14. Sword from Lisnacrogher (l. 50 cm).

155

5-15. Sword hilt of bone and antler.

5-18. Boho spearhead (l. 15 cm).

5-16. Ballyshannon hilt.

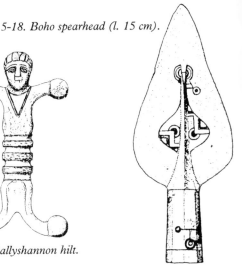

'Those [of the Irish] who cultivate elegance adorn the hilts of their swords with the teeth of great sea-animals'. Only one sword, from Ballyshannon in Co. Donegal, has a metal hilt (Ill. 5-16). It is in the shape of a man and is very different from all other Irish swords but does find parallels from western Gaul (France) and so archaeologists suspect that it was imported into Ireland about the 1st century BC.

In addition to swords we also have the remains of scabbards and chapes, the metal end piece to a scabbard. By far the most famous of these in Ireland come from Lisnacrogher, Co. Antrim, where a collection of scabbards and other Iron Age weapons was found (Ill. 5-17). The other major area of scabbard finds is the River Bann. What makes these scabbards so important is that they are covered in decoration which it is possible to compare with other La Tène objects in both Britain and the Continent, especially central Europe. So also are some of the chapes covered with decoration. All of this indicates warriors who were probably of very high social status and who used the most expensive and spectacular of Irish weapons. That so many swords and scabbards have been found in Co. Antrim also suggests the possibility that there may have been an armoury there during the Iron Age although, as we shall see, we may again be dealing with a votive deposit.

The basic weapon of the rank and file warrior was probably the spear. We suspect that spears were much less expensive to produce than swords (they used up far less metal and were technologically much easier to make). We might note that several hundred years later during the Early Christian period the Old Irish name for a warrior was a *gaisced*. This word is a compound of the Irish word for spear *gae* and shield *sciath*, so we might imagine that the spear and shield either represented the basic equipment of a warrior or were at least the traditional weapons presented when a young man came of age. Despite all this, the number of spearheads demonstrated to date to the Iron Age is extremely few. Perhaps this is because so many were made of iron and they have rusted away or else

5-17. Lisnacrogher scabbard (l. 55 cm).

156

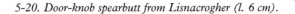

5-19. Tubular spearbutt from the Bann (l. 20 cm).

because it is very difficult to distinguish between a spearhead made in the Iron Age and one made at a later period. From Ulster comes a particularly elegant bronze spearhead from Boho, Co. Fermanagh, which is decorated (Ill. 5-18). There were also one or two large spearheads found at Lisnacrogher.

Curiously enough, while we may be missing the spearheads we have an abundance of spear butts. There are over 65 of these known from Ireland and they are generally regarded as having served to protect the end of the spear or provide it with better balance, and several of these have been found attached to the remains of long spearshafts. The spearbutts were of several different and very distinctive shapes - some are long tubular shafts (Ill. 5-19) while others resemble door-knobs (Ill. 5-20). Some suggest that they were not so much for the protection of the bottom of the spear as for display and that they may have been used for public demonstrations and parades rather than in warfare.

The other half of the definition of the *gaisced* is his shield and there are no more than two known from Iron Age Ireland. One of these is from Navan Fort. All that remains of this shield was a part of a binding strip. On the basis of comparable evidence from Britain, we may imagine that the Iron Age warrior was defended with a shield of either oval or rectangular shape and that there may have been a small metal boss in the centre of the shield behind which the man held it by a small handle.

Finally, we must mention one further item that some have assumed was employed by the Iron Age Irish in battle - the chariot. We do not have any complete evidence for chariots in Iron Age Ireland although there is ample evidence from Britain at this same time. However, about one quarter of all the La Tène objects known in Ireland are either bronze horse bits or objects that may have served as pendants for horses (Ill. 5-21). Since a few of the bits have been found in pairs, some suggest that they belonged to paired teams, that is, two horses drawing a cart or a chariot although the paucity of such finds, as Martyn Jope observed, may well indicate that there is really very little evidence on which to propose the use of the two-horse chariot. Sometimes associated with these bits is a somewhat mysterious item shaped like a Y which has encouraged archaeologists to suggest that they probably had something to do with horses and that they may have served as a leader or pendant (Ill. 5-22). Wooden yokes have also been discovered and one of these, a bog find from near Dungannon, is at least similar to yokes recovered from La Tène sites on the Continent although there is no certain evidence for its date (Ill. 5-23). The yoke can be used for two types of animals, horses or cattle. One further object more certainly associated with chariots is a terret, a device for holding the reins of a chariot which is commonly found in Britain. There are over 140 of these known in Britain but only one in Ireland which was discovered in Co. Antrim and seems to have been imported from Scotland or northern England (Ill. 5-24). This alone suggests that the Iron Age Ulstermen were not driving around in the same type of vehicles as their British counterparts. It seems likely that our

5-20. Door-knob spearbutt from Lisnacrogher (l. 6 cm).

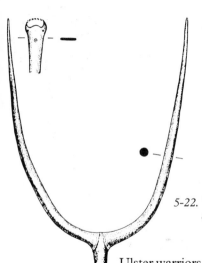

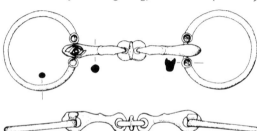

5-21. Horse bit from Lough Beg, Co. Antrim (l. 33 cm).

5-22. Y-shaped pendant from Coleraine,
Co. Londonderry (l. 31 cm).

Ulster warriors had to make do with a small cart rather than a full-fledged war chariot. As for the condition of the roads we can say nothing concerning Ulster but on the basis of Barry Raftery's excavations at Corlea, Co. Longford (Ill. 5-25), we may presume the existence of extensive wooden trackways through boggy areas.

Iron Age clothes and ornaments

Although there is evidence for bog-burials in Ireland, only one from Galway is demonstrably Iron Age and we can say very little of the Ulster evidence since so much of it was recovered many years ago. Our evidence for how people dressed then must come almost exclusively from metal ornaments and occasional toilette articles. The latter would include such objects as mirrors. We have the remains of the handle of a mirror from Ballybogey Bog, Co. Antrim, decorated in the La Tène style (Ill. 5-26). In addition, we have tweezers from Loughey near Donaghadee, Co. Down,

5-23. Wooden yoke
(l. 118 cm).

5-24. Chariot terret
(8 cm across).

5-25. Corlea trackway.

although, as we will see below, this burial cannot be used to typify native behaviour in Ulster.

By far the commonest ornament in the Iron Age was the fibula, the large metal safety pin which was used both to fasten clothes together and to serve as an ornament. It may seem strange that archaeologists specializing in the Iron Age are particularly interested in these oversized safety pins. The reason for this is fairly simple - there is no other object from the Iron Age which was both reasonably common and liable to change in style so frequently. Just as today, Iron Age people followed the latest fashions and hence they would wear the most modern styles of fibulae. These objects then might provide us with more precise dates than any other Iron Age object which was not so given to stylistic change and fashion. But while there are thousands of fibulae known from the Continent, there are only a little more than 25 examples known from Ireland so we find it difficult to use this evidence for precise dating. And although we can compare the Irish styles with those found abroad, almost all Irish fibulae were clearly manufactured locally and employed native elements of design. There are three basic types of fibulae, the simple rod-bow (Ill. 5-27), the somewhat broader leaf-bow which offerred greater scope for ornament (Ill. 5-28), and the wholly Irish Navan-type brooches employing an ingenious ball-socket mechanism which seems so far to be unparalleled anywhere else (Ill. 5-29). Although Navan gives its name to the final type because several such brooches were reputed to have been found near or at Navan, finds of the other types of brooches have also been ascribed to the Navan area. They are nearly all chance finds except one leaf-bow fibula receovered from an Iron Age grave at Kiltierney, Co. Fermanagh. In addition to fibulae, clothes were also fastened with the help of ring-headed pins, some of which were well decorated (Ill. 5-30).

The most spectacular sorts of ornament in the Iron Age were of gold and these included bracelets and neck rings. By far the most famous of these comes from the great Broighter hoard, found near the river Roe in County Londonderry. It included a very large torc, two gold necklaces, a golden bowl and a small golden model of a boat, complete with oars (Ill. 5-31).

5-30. Ring-headed pin (l. 18 cm).

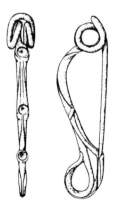

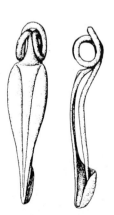

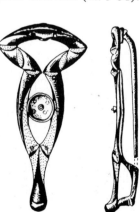

5-27. Rod-bow fibula, Dundrum, Co. Down (l. 9 cm).

5-28. Leaf-bow fibula, Bondville, Co. Armagh (l. 9 cm).

5-29. Navan fibula, Navan Fort, Co. Armagh (l. 8 cm).

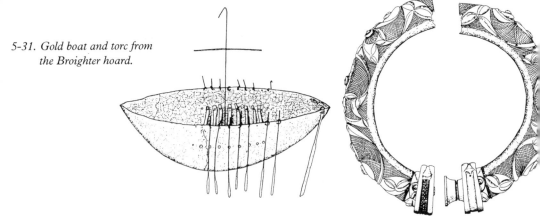

5-31. *Gold boat and torc from the Broighter hoard.*

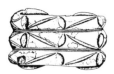

5-32. *Newry bracelet (dm. 13 cm).*

The Broighter hoard does not look like the personal property of a single individual but rather the type of ornaments that might have been worn during a religious ceremony. Richard Warner has argued that the hoard was deposited in water as an offering to a god, possibly the Celtic sea god Mannanan who gives his name to the Isle of Man. Bronze bracelets are also known, a massive one having been found near Newry, Co. Down, which may have been imported from Scotland (Ill. 5-32). Glass beads were also strung together as a necklace and worn during the Iron Age.

Religion and art

In the Iron Age religion and art go together. We have already seen how all of the gold objects of the Broighter hoard may have been a religious deposit. Similarly, another watery offering seems to have involved the placing of the four bronze horns in the waters of Loughnashade in the Navan complex. Other horns have been found in Ulster. The longest (and still blowable) example was discovered at Ardbrin, Co. Down (Ill. 5-33). It consisted of two tubes that joined together to form a horn measuring over 1.40 metre in length and requiring nearly 1100 rivets to seal. We also have some evidence for wooden horns which may date from the Iron Age. One was found near Clogher, Co. Tyrone, and another at Diamond Hill, Killeshandra, Co. Cavan.

From a more strictly artistic viewpoint the Iron Age metalwork of Ulster has been divided into two main categories by Richard Warner following on

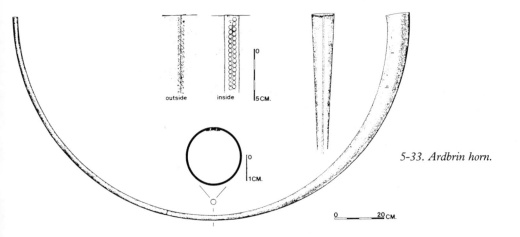

outside   inside

5CM.

1CM.

5-33. *Ardbrin horn.*

0 _____ 20 CM.

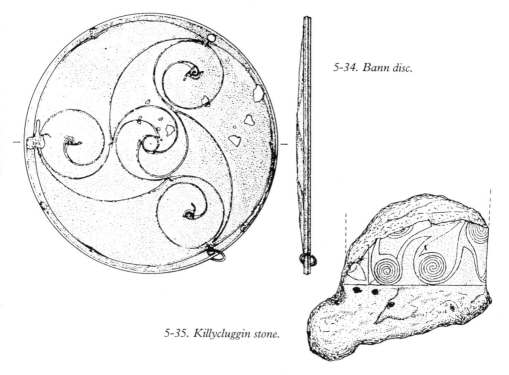

5-34. Bann disc.

5-35. Killycluggin stone.

from the pioneering work of Martyn Jope of Queen's University. The earlier art work, which Warner assigns to his Early Iron Age I phase, can be seen in the decorated scabbards from Lisnacrogher where we find a series of S-shaped motifs arranged symmetrically to fill out the scabbard plates. The later Early Iron Age II style is to be seen in the three-dimensional style of ornament, often assuming such motifs as 'trumpets' and oval bosses, that we find on the collar from the Broighter hoard and on the Bann disc (Ill. 5-34). This last item is generally regarded as one of the finest artistic creations of Iron Age craftsmen in Ireland. It consists of a circular bronze plate about 10.5 cm in diameter. The ornament, a triple whirly-gig, spiraling out from a central circle, was accomplished by tooling down the entire plate to leave the design itself standing up in relief. The only clue to its use are three holes on its edge which indicate that it could have been suspended. Martyn Jope and Basil Wilson suggested that it may have either been worn on the breast or even been employed as the centre-piece in some form of headress, an idea not entirely to be excluded since its closest parallels are ornaments on a bronze head-dress known as the Petrie Crown.

Iron Age art is not only found on metal objects but also may occur on stones. The finest examples lie outside of Ulster, especially the famous Turoe stone in Co. Galway, but there are good examples from Killycluggin, Co. Cavan (Ill. 5-35), and Derrykeighan, Co. Antrim (Ill. 5-36). The ornament on these stones is very similar to that found on La Tène metal work and other Iron Age stonework and Barry Raftery suggests that both of these stones date to about the 1st century BC or AD. The locations of both stones are interesting. The Killycluggin stone had apparently been

5-36. Derrykeighan stone.

tipped into a hole and defaced, perhaps by an enterprising Christian missionary bent on obliterating a monument to a rival deity. On the other hand, the Derrykeighan stone was 'discovered' in the gable wall of a ruined church.

Our most graphic confrontation with pagan Ulster comes in the form of stone and wood figures, the best examples of which are to be found in Ulster. From Corleck, Co. Cavan, comes a stone figure displaying three heads (Ill. 5-37), an absolutely classic 'pagan Celtic' pose and we know parallels across western Europe that suggests that this is the head of a Celtic god. Another stone head from Cavan town itself also belongs to the Iron Age and a similar claim has been made for a carved wooden figure found at Ralaghan, Co. Cavan. This figure is complete and was probably part of

5-37. Corleck head.

5-38. Ralaghan figure (ht. 115 cm).

5-39. Tandragee idol.

a fertility cult (Ill. 5-38). To the north, another figure is known from Boa Island and it, along with another crude stone head from Beltany, Co. Donegal, may date to the Iron Age. Finally, we may mention the so-called Tandragee idol (probably found near Newry), now tucked away in the vestry of St Patrick's (Church of Ireland) Cathedral in Armagh (Ill. 5-39). Here, we see what seems to be a horned or helmeted figure clutching his shoulder.

As for Iron Age ritual itself, we can only speculate. The discovery of so much fine metal work such as the Broighter hoard at the mouth of the Roe, the Loughnashade trumpets, and the impressive quantities from the Bann all indicate the probability that offerings were made regularly into rivers, lakes and bogs. In some instances we presume votive offerings, in others, as Martyn Jope first suggested for the Thames, the formal burial of warriors in rivers with their parade weapons and ornaments. In addition, there is a hint that earlier ritual structures were also employed as both the Killycluggin stone and Beltany head were discovered in or adjacent to presumably earlier Bronze Age stone circles.

Burial

There are not a great many burials that demonstrably belong to the Iron Age in Ireland although we have no reason to believe the observation of the first century A.D. geographer Strabo that the Irish 'deem it commendable to devour their deceased fathers'. Of those burials positively assigned to the Iron Age, we recognize only three for Ulster. There may well be many more since we do have a number of typically Iron Age ring barrows in Ulster, however, these may also date to other periods.

At Dunadry, Co. Antrim, a large earthen mound was destroyed which seems to have covered a stone cist in which a body had been laid out. A few ornaments accompanied the burial such as bracelets of glass and jet all of which have since been lost. Nevertheless, this is regarded as a typical type of Iron Age burial.

Kiltierney, Co. Fermanagh, offers our only proven example of an Iron Age cemetery in Ulster and a very strange one at that. During the Iron Age a ditch was dug around a Neolithic passage tomb and then on the outer periphery nineteen smaller mounds were erected (Ill. 5-40). A number of excavations have been carried out on the site and during those of Laurence Flanagan in 1969 and more recently Claire Foley in 1983-84 clear traces of Iron Age burials were recovered. These were cremations which had been deposited into the earlier mound or on the outer edge of the ditch where they were covered by the small mounds. Grave goods for the dead or perhaps the clothes they wore included bronze brooches, glass beads and what would appear to be a bronze mirror. The objects indicate that the burials date to about the 1st century AD.

The dawn of Ulster

Up until the Iron Age every attempt at discerning a distinct Ulster entity in the archaeological record has failed both because the material culture

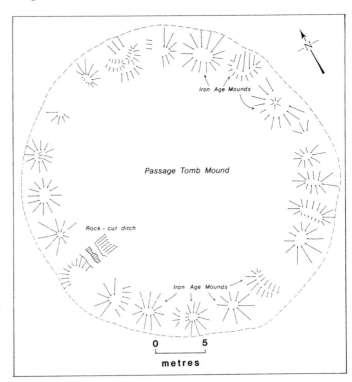

5-40. Kiltierney Iron Age cemetery around Neolithic passage tomb.

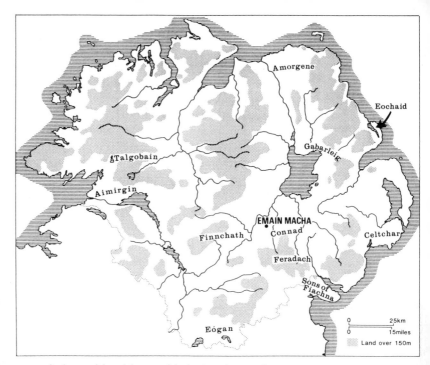

1. Ulster chieftains summoned to defend the province in the Táin.

found in Ulster also extended considerably outside its borders or because regional differences within Ulster itself were often more marked than those between Ulster and other parts of Ireland. That the entire island was not culturally uniform is continually emphasized by major cultural differences, seen in everything from megalithic tombs through Bronze Age metalwork, between the northern and southern halves of the island. Indeed, these differences would seem to fit far better with the traditional division of Ireland into Conn's half, the north, and Mug's, the south, than the more detailed provincial divisions.

During the Iron Age, however, we begin to get our first hints of political boundaries which can be seen both in terms of what we presume to be royal capitals such as Navan and Clogher and, more obviously, in the linear earthworks. The erection of defences across the Ulster border in both Monaghan and Armagh during the Iron Age suggests the development of a political frontier that separated Ulster from its southern neighbours. Whether this was a unified Ulster is another thing altogether and we have every reason to be suspicious of the political world depicted in the Ulster tales where Conchobor, king of Emain Macha, can summon his forces from Downpatrick to the Erne and as far north as Dunseverick on the north Antrim coast (Ill. 5-41). This is probably an idealization of a much more complicated state of affairs of local chiefs, divided as Ptolemy indicates, into tribes occupying territories comparable to two modern Irish counties. That Navan may have been the most important and, perhaps, the symbolic centre of Ulster, is arguable but whether it exercised coercive power over the rest of the province is doubtful.

While a political frontier may well have been erected between the 4th and 1st centuries BC, it is by no means clear that the Black Pig's Dyke and

165

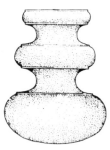

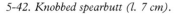
5-42. Knobbed spearbutt (l. 7 cm).

the Dorsey represented a cultural border. Our hard archaeological evidence for deciding this issue is primarily the distribution of metal objects and to a much lesser extent architectural remains. An examination of La Tène metalwork in Ireland indicates that they covered not only Ulster but also Connacht and north Leinster; only in Munster and south Leinster are La Tène objects exceedingly rare. If we examine the various categories of objects according to their individual styles, we can see that some, such as knobbed spearbutts (most of which were found at Lisnocrogher) are only found north of the border (Ill. 5-42) while one of the sword types is only found south of the Black Pig's Dyke. With other objects such as bee-hive querns many more of one type may be found in the north than in the south although both areas will possess at least some examples of each variety. In general, while we can talk of accumulations of particular types of material in certain areas, for example, much of the Early Iron Age I material tends to be found in Antrim, it is difficult to argue for any major cultural differences between the communities north and south of the border. Moreover, when we compare the ritual structures from Navan with those recovered at the Leinster capital at Knockaulin (Dún Ailinne), Co. Kildare, the similarities are too great to argue for major cultural differences. This is not to say that they might not have existed, but if major cultural differences did exist they don't really appear to be reflected in the type of evidence the archaeologist has at hand.

If there is no sharp break in culture between Ulster and the south, what about regionalism within Ulster itself? Here again, patterns seen in earlier prehistory persist. Antrim, for example, able to exploit iron in the Antrim basalts, would appear to have continued as a metallurgical centre with a major workshop either at Lisnacrogher or at least responsible for the

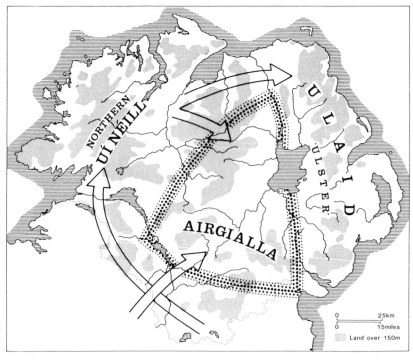

5-43. The collapse of the Ulaid to the Airgialla and Uí Néill.

quantity of material recovered from the site. It shows regional peculiarities since here we find many ring-headed pins but virtually no fibulae, the characteristic clothes-fastener especially well known in Armagh around Navan. The scabbards and swords of Antrim similarly point to a regional style not paralleled elsewhere. Barry Raftery has recognized two main regional groupings of material within Ulster, one in the Bann Valley and the other in south-central Ulster in the region from Navan to Clogher and south into Cavan. On the other hand, both the northwest and southeast are poorly represented by La Tène metalwork although both Down and Tyrone-Londonderry are very well represented with respect to the bee-hive querns. In general, patterns of regional traditions seem to have remained strong in Ulster right through the Iron Age.

Finally, if the linear earthworks ever did define the southern political limits of a greater Ulster, the province depicted in the Ulster tales, this may have been short lived. Irish tradition relates that about the year 331 or 332 A.D. (or perhaps as late as 450 A.D.), the last Ulster king of Emain Macha, Fergus Fogha, fell in the battle of Achad Leithderg in Co. Monaghan. The victors are known to legend as the Three Collas and they are reputed to have burnt Emain Macha and driven the Ulaid, the Ulstermen, eastwards. The Three Collas established the kingdom of Airgialla in central Ulster while the Uí Néill pushed up from the south to occupy all of west Ulster. By the Early Christian period, the Ulaid themselves had been driven east of the lower Bann and the Newry river (Ill. 5-43) and in our earliest native texts the terms Ulster and Ulsterman are confined largely to those who inhabited the present counties of Antrim and Down. But by the seventh and eight centuries Christian monks began recording or composing tales set in Ulster's 'Golden Age' which they presumed to have existed during what we today term the Iron Age.

The Ulster Cycle and the Iron Age

Among the greatest works of early Irish literature are the tales of the Ulster Cycle. They take their name from the fact that most of these tales concern one or more of the legendary heroes of Ulster, who were held up to early mediaeval society as the warriors par excellence. The tales depict the continual fighting that went on between the Ulstermen and the *fir n-hErenn* 'men of Ireland', especially their traditional adversaries, the men of Connacht. The centre-piece of these tales is the *Táin Bó Cúailgne*, the cattle-raid of Cooley, that describes how the armies of the rest of Ireland, led by Queen Medb of Connacht, attempted to invade Ulster in pursuit of a great bull. For the course of a winter they were held off single-handedly by CúChulainn until the rest of Ulster could muster its troops and defeat the invaders in a final battle.

The relevance of these tales to Iron Age society has often been asserted. Traditional Irish history as expressed in the early Irish annals would date the events of the Ulster Cycle to the first centuries BC and AD and so it is clear that the medieval Irish imagined that the heroes of these stories such as CúChulainn, Conchobor, Fergus, Conall Cernach and Deirdre all lived in what seemed to them to be the distant past and to us the Iron Age. Furthermore, the behaviour and some of the descriptions of the Ulster warriors seems to accord well with that of the early Celts. The Ulster heroes drive and fight from chariots, a fashion of warfare that had disappeared from the Celts on the Continent by the first century AD and continued in Britain to perhaps the second century AD. When a warrior killed a foe, he regularly cut off his head which would serve as a trophy, a practice well known among the Continental Celts where we find whole shrines of the severed heads of victims. The Ulster warriors enjoy feasts where they boast about their deeds and contest for the 'champion's portion' of meat, all of which is described as typical Celtic behaviour in Gaul during the first centuries BC. Furthermore, the religious belief of the Ulster heroes is pagan. They regularly swear by the gods of their tribes and they look to their druids for foretelling the future and advice. Finally, in the tales the Ulster capital is Emain Macha which is recorded as having fallen by the 4th or 5th centuries AD. After this collapse, the political entity of Ulster constricted to little more than counties Antrim, Down and north Louth, a small fraction of the area of Ulster regularly depicted in the Ulster tales. For all of these reasons, the Ulster tales have sometimes been described as a 'window on the Iron Age'.

The best way of testing whether the descriptions in the Ulster tales do indeed present life in Ireland during the Iron Age is to compare them with our actual evidence for the Iron Age. When we do this, we quickly see that the objects do not make such a good fit as some have suggested. CúChulainn, for example, regularly uses a great long sword that hacks people to bits or decapitates them. The swords described in literature are said to have hilts of gold and silver or ornamented stones. But when we recall our evidence of Iron Age swords, all we see are small swords which could hardly hack someone to pieces with the same *elan* as described in the Ulster tales. Furthermore, other than the metal hilt on the imported sword from Ballyshannon, Co. Donegal, the hilts on Irish Iron Age swords seemed to have been made of wood or bone. If we compare the swords described in the tales with later evidence from the Early Christian period and the Vikings, we often find perfect matches (Ill. 5-44).

Similarly, if we look at other evidence such as spears we find the same type of problems. The Ulster heroes sometimes carry spears with silver binding rings yet these did not appear on spears anywhere earlier than the Dark Ages. Moreover, despite full descriptions of the Ulster warriors in the tales, we nowhere find depictions of their spear-butts despite the fact that this is one item of parade work that we find in great abundance in Iron Age Ireland. Similarly, ornaments are regularly decorated with silver in the tales yet silver was not employed in such a way until the Early Christian period.

So the story goes for any object that can be matched against the various periods of Irish archaeology. In general, it will almost never fit well into the

5-44. Iron Age warrior (left) and warrior described in the Táin (right).

Iron Age but rather in the later period from about the 7th to 10th centuries AD. Now this is the very period in which the tales were written down. Because of this, we may imagine that the early Irish writers may have taken tales that were very ancient in structure but dressed them up in the clothes and weapons of their Early Christian contemporaries since they had no idea what Iron Age man looked like; that period had already passed long before.

What about Emain Macha, the Ulster capital, for which we have both literary and archaeological evidence? Here too the descriptions must be set aside since they do not portray Emain Macha as it was when it was flourishing in the first centuries BC. The Ulster Cycle depicts fabulous palaces there but the same description for Emain Macha is also used for other sites which indicates it was a stock description. There is, to be sure, some mention of the great mound at Emain Macha, and we can feel reasonably certain that this was the mound (Site B) that Dudley Waterman excavated. But this only means that they saw this mound the way it appears to us today - as a large grassy mound - and not the great circular wooden structure that archaeologists discovered (unless one believes that the descriptions of royal palaces in the Ulster tales harken back to this building). In many ways, early mediaeval Ulstermen had even less an idea of what Emain Macha looked like than we do today.

But if the Ulster tales reveal little about the archaeology of Iron Age Ulster, they along with our other sources for early Irish literature and tradition do provide us with some idea of what life may have been like during the Iron Age and even some hint of those beliefs that the archaeologist is generally powerless to recover. Our reasons for reconstructing these Iron Age practices does not rest solely on the evidence of later Christian monks who could hardly be trusted to give us a clear picture of Ulster's pagan past but because both some of the practices and words used to describe them are not only found among the mediaeval Irish but also their Celtic neighbours and other related peoples of Eurasia. This suggests that such beliefs and practices were introduced into Ireland with the arrival of the Celts.

The evidence of both literature and linguistics suggests that during the Iron Age (and possibly earlier) the population was organized politically into tribes, which in Old Irish was called a *túath*. The ruler of the *túath* was a king (Old Irish *rí*) and the prosperity of the *túath* seems to have been very much dependent on the integrity and the personal prosperity and health of the king. The king himself was possibly inaugurated during some ceremony that involved his ritual marriage with a mare and/or some form of horse sacrifice. This pattern of inauguration, which is also known in ancient India and Rome, continued in Ulster until at least the 13th century when the somewhat jaundiced writer of Irish affairs, the Norman Geraldus, recorded that:

There is in another and remote part of Ulster, among the Kenelcunil (Cenel Connel) [i.e. Donegal], a certain tribe which is wont to install a king over itself by an excessively savage and abominable ritual. In the presence of all the people of this land in one place, a white mare is brought into their midst. Thereupon he who is to be elevated…steps forward in beastly fashion and exhibits his beastiality. Right thereafter the mare is killed and boiled piecemeal in water, and in the same water a bath is prepared for him. He gets into the bath and eats of the flesh that is brought to him…when this is done right…his rule and sovereignty are consacrated.

Although this is only recorded during the Middle Ages, its resemblance to similar rituals of other Indo-European peoples of India and Rome suggests that this practice was carried to Ireland by the ancient Celts. This ceremony was the ritual enactment of a belief that the well-being of society sprang from a sacred marriage between the king (of the *túath*) and a goddess who seems to have borne the name 'mead', e.g. Queen Medb, after the ritual drink.

In addition to kings Iron Age society would also have had their priests, the druids. The mediaeval monks provide us with a considerable amount of information about the druids, none of which we can really trust. In terms of warfare, we also may suspect the existence of war-bands (Irish *cuire*) composed of young males who have come of age, perhaps about the age of 14 but not yet married or settled down formally within their *túath* (about 20), thus spinning out their teens in an existence somewhere between a football hooligan and a paramilitary. Frequently adopting the name or the behaviour of wolves, and occasionally going into battle virtually naked, they might serve as the shock troops in combat, the Irish equivalent of the Viking berserkers.

This image of Iron Age society and its beliefs, depicted in language and literature, goes far beyond what archaeologists have so far recovered from examining artifacts and the handful of Iron Age settlements that we know. It is also very much dependent on the assumption that the people who occupied Ulster during the Iron Age spoke a Celtic language, more specifically the language immediately ancestral to Irish or Gaelic. It is for this reason that we need to examine the origins of Gaelic Ulster.

The origins of Gaelic Ulster

The origins of the Irish is a problem which is about as difficult as one could imagine. It involves linguistics and archaeology with neither offering sufficient evidence for a firm conclusion on its own and, in some cases, each discipline appears to support a theory that is either contradicted or at least unsupported by other evidence.

For our purposes the only useful definition of Irish is a linguistic one, that is, Irish refers to a particular Celtic language. Moreover, by the time of our earliest native incriptions and written documents, Irish is the only language attested in Ireland north or south. When and by whom it was introduced is our main problem.

Our earliest serious source for the language(s) of Ireland is Ptolemy's gazetteer which mentions about 55 names. Many of these we recognize as being clearly Celtic, e.g. the rivers Buvinda (Boyne), and Logia (Lagan), but we cannot prove with certainty that any are necessarily Irish or even directly ancestral to Irish. We must remember that Irish is not the only Celtic language (Ill. 5-45). On the Continent the ancient Celtic languages included Gaulish, the language of the Celtic tribes who fought and lost to Julius Caesar in France; Lepontic, a Celtic language that was spoken in northern Italy near Milan before the Romans had dominated all of Italy; and Hispano-Celtic, the Celtic language of the northern two-thirds of Spain and Portugal. In the British Isles there were two basic groups of Celtic languages: Goidelic and Brittonic. Brittonic included the ancient languages of the Britons who occupied Britain when the Romans invaded. From these languages are descended Welsh, Cornish (now extinct but with some attempt at revival) and Breton which was transplanted to Brittany about the time of the Anglo-Saxon conquest of Britain. The Goidelic branch includes Irish and the two other languages of Gaelic origin that were spread by the Irish, i.e. Scots Gaelic and Manx (now extinct).

There are a number of differences between Goidelic and Brittonic but one of the most obvious is the way that they treat the primitive Celtic form of the 'Qu' sound. In Goidelic it was preserved as a Q, at least in the earliest Irish inscriptions, and then became a C in Old Irish and later forms of the language. In the Brittonic languages the Q sound regularly became a P-

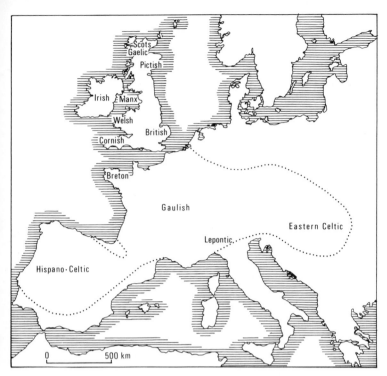

5-45. *Celtic languages of Europe*

sound. For this reason, some speak of Q-Celts and P-Celts. The differences can be seen clearly in this comparison between Irish and Welsh forms (and we list their corresponding forms in Latin which with all the other Indo-European languages is related to the Celtic languages):

	four	*five*	*horse*	*son*
Latin	*quattuor*	*quinque*	*equus*	-
Irish	*ceathair*	*coic*	*ech*	*mac*
Welsh	*pedwair*	*pump*	*ep-*	*map*

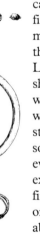

Ptolemy's map mentions names that are distinctly Celtic but most cannot be firmly assigned to either the Goidelic or Brittonic branches. At first any concern that we have British tribes in Ireland during the Iron Age might seem strange, however, Ptolemy's gazetteer does mention names that appear to be Brittonic or at least P-Celtic. For example, one of the Leinster tribes was called the Manapii. Had this been an Irish tribe it should have been called the Manaqii or Manacii instead. Because of this word and several others, Thomas O' Rahilly once proposed that Ireland was originally British (in the linguistic sense). The reason for this amazing statement was that Ptolemy's map showed an Ireland full of Celts and, in some instances, obviously British-speaking Celts but not a single trace of evidence for Irish speakers. O' Rahilly argued that this might be best explained by assuming that Ptolemy's map was not based on Ireland of the first centuries AD but had been drawn up on the basis of a much older map, originally prepared by the Greek explorer Pytheas who supposedly sailed about northwest Europe in the 4th century BC. Later during the period

5-46. *Grave goods from 'Loughey'.*

172

150 - 50 B.C., according to O' Rahilly, Celtic tribes speaking a language directly ancestral to Irish crossed directly from the Continent to conquer Ireland.

O' Rahilly's grand scheme has not won much acceptance. We should recall that in the first century AD the Goidelic and Brittonic languages were extremely similar and that the source of our Irish names was most likely someone whose own language was Brittonic, hence, if we find the Brittonic pronunciation for Irish names we should not be too suprised. On the other hand, the existence of British tribes within Ireland cannot be dismissed either. Both native tradition and some archaeological evidence, for example, would indicate that the Laigin, the people who gave their name to Leinster, were British and Gaulish in origin. The close contacts between Ulster and Scotland in the Iron Age also suggest enough coming and going to permit some movement of British populations into Ireland. Finally, we have fairly conclusive evidence of at least one person from Britain being buried in Iron Age Ulster. The remains of a burial were found about 1851 near a still unidentified place called 'Loughey' near Donaghadee, Co. Down. Although this was discovered a considerable time before any proper archaeological work in Ireland, we can make a fair guess as to what it involved. A woman was apparently cremated and her remains placed in a small pit. Along with her bones, there was also placed a bronze fibula, tweezers, ring, and other bronze objects, several glass bracelets, and about 150 glass beads (Ill. 5-46). All of the material would seem to have come from southern Britain about the first century AD. So here we have what appears to have been a rich woman, buried according to the rite of her native people, who had come from southern Britain to the shores of Co. Down. When Martyn Jope and Basil Wilson 're-discovered' the Loughey burial they suggested that she may have been either a refugee fleeing before the Roman Conquest or may have just been accompanying one of the British merchant ships trading along the Irish coast.

Ptolemy's map then only indicates evidence of one sort: by the second century AD there were unquestionably Celtic tribes in Ireland. Whether these tribes spoke a very early form of Irish or a Brittonic language or both we cannot say. The earliest positive examples of Irish do not occur until the erection of the ogham stones perhaps about the fourth or fifth centuries AD. These monuments, serving normally as commemorative stones on the occasion of someone's death, are written in a special script (Ill. 5-47) devised by the ancient Irish which involved cutting strokes onto the corner of a stone (or piece of wood). Generally the inscriptions record the names of people including whose son they were and they appear to have been largely confined to Munster although a number are known from Ulster.

Ptolemy's map does provide some indirect information regarding the origins of the Irish. The strong similarities between our earliest evidence for Celtic names in the British Isles coupled with the earliest linguistic evidence for both the Britons in Great Britain and the names of the Irish on ogham stones all indicates that it is unlikely that the Celts of any sort

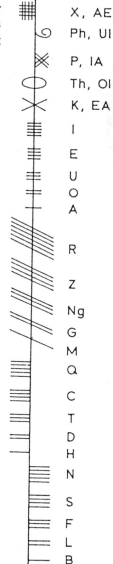

5-47. Ogham script.

had been in Ireland for a very great amount of time. If they had been, we would expect far greater differences in the languages of Britain and Ireland than we find. Moreover, both Goidelic and Brittonic and some of the Contiental Celtic languages share the same names for Late Bronze Age or Iron Age technological items that indicates that they either had not physically separated form one another when they gained them or, at least, had not been separate for long enough time for linguistic divisions to emerge between them. For this reason, recent attempts by Colin Renfrew to push back Irish origins all the way to the Neolithic or the occasional suggestion that we should look to the time of the Beakers holds little attraction for most linguists who, like David Greene, would look for our earliest Irishmen in the period sometime between the Late Bronze Age and the first century BC. Knowing when to look is almost as important as knowing what to look for.

If linguists can help narrow down the time when we may expect to find the earliest Irish, this still leaves plenty of problems for the archaeologist. Evidence for migrations during the period between about 1000 and 100 BC are very slight indeed. At about 700 BC we saw earlier that material, especially swords, of the Hallstatt style began to appear in Ireland. Are these traces of the first Irishmen? The evidence is hardly impressive since we are only talking of a particular sword style and instead of the iron swords typical of the Hallstatt culture on the Continent, we only find bronze copies presumably cast by local smiths. Generally, archaeologists have not been impressed with the evidence for a movement of new peoples into Ireland at about 700 BC although they cannot wholly exclude the possibility.

Our second major 'window' for an intrusion is normally set to about 300 BC when we find the first La Tène artifacts in Ireland, especially the northern half of the island. Here the evidence is somewhat more convincing. Most of the evidence comes from Ulster, it is primarily associated with warfare - swords, scabbards, and it seems to take its artistic inspiration directly from the Continent, possibly northern France. Consequently, Martin Jope and Richard Warner among others have sought in this appearance of La Tène material small bands of warriors, chiefs plus their retinue and craftsmen, who crossed into Ulster. Does this provide us with sufficient evidence to talk of an Irish invasion? Most archaeologists would again remain unconvinced. All of Ireland became Gaelic speakers, not just the northern province, and one can always argue that we are dealing with the spread of an art style, not of an actual people. Finally, about 100 AD there appears another phase of La Tène material that seems to relate more easily with styles in Britain. But this material is so sparse and its comparisons so diverse - from Scotland to eastern England - that few would regard it evidence for a major invasion.

When we draw all of this evidence together we find it difficult to make any firm statements on when Irish-speaking Celts first arrived in Ireland other than the fact that they must have arrived at some time before the 4th or 5th centuries AD (when ogham stones were probably erected) and it seems linguistically more plausible to have them come during the last millennium BC than a much earlier time. If our evidence seems to be quite poor, we should not be too surprised since there are many similar situations involving other colonizations. For example, history records how towards the end of the 5th century AD Ulstermen began conquering and colonizing southwestern Scotland to form the kingdom of Dál Riata (later Dál Riada) which spanned the northern region of the Irish Sea. From here, the Gaelic language expanded inland to eventually embrace almost all of Scotland by about 1000 AD. This colonization supposedly explains the origins of the Scots-Gaelic tongue since prior to this time the people of Scotland spoke Brittonic or Pictish, a combination of Brittonic and a perhaps a native non-Celtic language. This whole process may have taken nearly 600 years and so there was no sudden and obvious expansion across the face of Scotland. Indeed, despite the fact that we believe we know when all of this took place, there is really not a shred of archaeological evidence to prove that it did happen. Similar short term migrations between Ireland and Britain or perhaps directly from the Continent may have been regular features throughout this period and in the mass of apparent 'foreign influences' and contacts there may lie the actual traces of population movements.

We can learn several lessons from this example. We probably have no right to demand that the coming of the first Irishmen must be marked by obvious archaeological evidence and so we would be wrong to exclude the various possibilities suggested before. Possibly, Irish colonists drifted into Ireland over the course of many generations during the first millennium BC and gradually assimilated the local population. In addition, by the time the Irish did arrive, the basic population of Ireland was probably already well established and certainly much larger than the newcomers. The blood that runs through the veins of most people in Ireland was probably here long before the Irish arrived. What the Irish did manage to accomplish was to spread their language and culture over the whole population of Ireland. How did they do it?

People often imagine that invaders sweep into a country, swing their swords about a little and soon everyone is speaking their language. This doesn't really work as any former student who had the latin language beaten into him with a strap well knows. Normally, people will not give up their own language unless they have good reason and that reason normally concerns their advantage. For example, if today Irish were the language of the major corporate magnates and the wealthier members of society, then most people might well want to learn it in order to secure for themselves faster advancement in society and better access to goods. By learning Irish you would become bilingual and speak both Irish and English. If you persisted in this for a number of generations and found that the circle you moved in was better off, Irish speaking, that most of the people who represented your interests politically were Irish speaking and that your church was Irish speaking, you might abandon English altogether. Certainly, you might raise your children as Irish speakers (why teach them English if it is a language that leads nowhere socially?). Your children would then be only Irish speakers and gradually the whole of society would shift their language. Thus, the early Irish had something to offer the basic populations of Ireland to entice them away from their own native tongues. What that was, is still a mystery to us and we can only speculate. The apparent collapse of Late Bronze Age society may have seen the end of an old order and if bands of Irish speakers had entered between about 600 and 300 BC and offered greater opportunities to social and economic advancement among the population, then native peoples may have been gradually absorbed into Irish-speaking communities. If, for example, newcomers occupied Navan then they would have controlled a major ritual and presumably trade centre and the native population may have then learned Goidelic (Irish) in order to gain preferential access to both goods and public rituals. Or perhaps the native Late Bronze Age society found themselves primarily in a pastoral economy and an intrusive Goidelic population, armed with more efficient agricultural practices, including the rotary quern, were able to out-compete the native population as it was confined to the marginal uplands. Finally, it is just possible that the Irish came in during the Late Bronze Age itself when we find the establishment of hill-forts which would have provided society with political and perhaps economic centres. If the builders of the hill-forts had been Goidelic speakers, the local population may well have been attracted to learning the new language in order to achieve entry into the new aristocratic society. All of these ideas are, of course, mere speculations that future archaeological work may be in a position to dismiss or accept.

The Cruthin

In the preceeding section we limited our discussion of Irish origins to language and archaeology and have deliberately avoided a third body of evidence, the traditions of the mediaeval Irish about their own origins and the various ethnic groups they assigned to the period before the 'Gaelic conquest'. These essentially present us with a succession of invasions - Cessair, Partholon, Fir Bolg, Tuatha Dé Danann - that climax with the 'Sons of Mil', the Irish, occupying Ireland. The mixing of Irish traditional 'ethnography' with archaeology produces a brew much too strong for the stomach of most professional archaeologists. It is not just our inability to handle the sources but also because the traditional account of the coming of the Irish is widely recognized as a combination of various elements that include native traditions, a desire to depict the Irish as something akin to a lost tribe of Israel, and the mediaeval political aspirations of their creators. Scholars such as Thomas O' Rahilly have claimed to unravel the 'true' meaning of these accounts but invariably all such attempts to separate prehistoric wheat from mythological chaff can only be done by making a long string of assumptions, none of which demand acceptance.

Early Irish tradition also recognizes a number of 'ethnic' groups, one of which, the Cruthin, has received considerable popular attention in Ulster as they have been cast as the original stock of Ireland and at least Scotland - the Picts - if not all Great Britain. The name Cruthin is the Irish form for Priteni, from whence the Greeks coined the term 'Pretannic Isles', that is, the British Isles of today. Following the traditional accounts of invasions, the Cruthin in Ireland were later assimilated by the Goidelic (Irish) invaders. Some would then go on to argue that the Cruthin returned from Scotland to reclaim their ancient heritage in the Plantation. Other than providing an illuminating illustration of how mediaeval origin myths might still serve contemporary political aspirations, we might be tempted to avoid the Cruthin hypothesis if one of its major proponents, Ian Adamson, had not proposed an archaeological scheme wherein the Cruthin are seen to be the native population of the British Isles, presumably descended from the Neolithic colonists. The introduction of La Tène objects in the 3rd century BC (what we have termed Warner's Early Iron Age I) is regarded by him as marking the initial Celticization of Ireland and our Early Iron Age 2 material, presumably derived from Britain, is held responsible for 'Belgic' (Fir Bolg) intrusions that produced such Ptolemaic tribes as the Uluti. Finally, as in the mediaeval accounts, Adamson derives the Irish from Spain about the second century AD and sees them conquer the entire island, the Cruthin of the north holding out the longest.

Whether any of this is true or not is hardly discussable since the Cruthin as a distinct ethnic group are archaeologically invisible, that is, there is not a single object or site that an archaeologist can declare to be distinctly Cruthin. The only thing an archaeologist can do for those interested in Cruthin prehistory is make what few observations the archaeological evidence seems to warrant. First, if the Cruthin are imagined to have been early mediaeval descendants of the original Neolithic population in Ireland, than everything that we have seen so far suggests that attributing to them a common all-Irish much less an Irish-Scottish identity up until the arrival of the Celts is quite remarkable. The Later Mesolithic would appear to have been the last period where similarities across Ireland may have outweighed regional differences within it and it is questionable whether communities in Britain or Ireland ever saw themselves as a common related people at anytime since the Neolithic. From the archaeological standpoint one should begin with areas where the mediaeval texts tell us the Cruthin actually lived. In so far as Ulster is concerned, the main area ascribed to the Cruthin comprised much of Antrim and part of west Down, the territory of the Dál Fiatach of the Early Christian period. Now we have already seen that this is one of the areas that experienced close associations with Scotland and northern Britain. In other words, the area in Ulster where the Cruthin are deemed to have survived into the historic period has been as culturally mixed as any other and it would be extremely difficult to see them as 'pure' descendants of the earlier Neolithic settlement of Ireland. If one concentrates then on the usual association between the Cruthin and the Picts of Scotland, then one might suggest that our Ulster Cruthin may represent a later intrusion into parts of Ireland from Scotland by either pre-Celtic or even Celtic peoples. But we have already seen how difficult it is to sort the Celts out (the proposed second century AD Goidelic invasion from Spain has absolutely no archaeological support whatsoever) and about the only thing the Cruthin hypothesis does emphasize are the continuous interactions between Ulster and Scotland. We might add that whatever their actual origins and ultimate fate, when the Cruthin of Ulster emerge in our earliest texts they bear Irish names and there is not the slightest hint that they spoke anything other than Irish.

The Romans and Ulster

During the first century AD the Romans conquered Britain and brought it into the Roman Empire, a process that began with Julius Caesar a century before. This meant that Ireland gained a literate neighbour who could leave us written testimony, not always flattering, about Ireland before the establishment of native Irish records. For example, the first century A.D. geographer Strabo informs us that the 'natives are wholly savage and lead a wretched existence because of the cold' and that it is with Ireland 'that the limits of the habitable earth should be fixed'. Solinus, writing in the 3rd century AD puts the lie to the St. Patrick legend when he informs us that 'there are no snakes' in Ireland. The warlike nature of the Irish is emphasized when he tells us that 'the people are inhospitable and warlike' and that 'the victors in battle drink the blood of the slain and smear it on their faces'. He also tells us of the difficulties of crossing between Britain and Ireland and that the 'natives sail in boats of wickerwork covered with the hides of oxen'. Finally, we might mention the famous comments of Agricola, one of the great military leaders who was especially responsible for conquering northern Britain. We know a considerable amount about him since his son-in-law Tacitus wrote a short biography of his father-in-law. Tacitus recounts how the Romans had conquered all of Britain and then turned his attention to Ireland with these words:

> In soil and climate, in the disposition, temper, and habits of its population, it differs but little from Britain. We know most of its harbours and approaches, and that through the intercourse of commerce. . . I have often heard (Agricola) say that a single legion with a few auxiliaries could conquer and occupy Ireland. . .

Now as everyone knows, the Romans never did invade Ireland but were soon faced with enough problems holding on to Britain until they finally abandoned it. Archaeologists, however, do have some evidence for contacts between Ireland and Roman Britain.

What type of evidence do we have for Roman contacts? First, we have the finds of Roman coins in Ulster. Probably the most spectacular is a hoard of over 1500 silver coins discovered buried in the ground at Ballinrees, Co. Londonderry. In addition, there were over 200 ounces of other forms of silver treasure, generally silver bars and ingots, and the remains of silver plate, including such things as a bowl and two spoons. Another instance of such buried treasure was discovered by a farmer, James Quig, who was shovelling potatoes on Feigh Mountain, Co. Antrim, in 1831. He came down onto a flag stone and when he lifted it he found about 500 silver coins. Other sites have revealed different types of Roman material such as typical Roman or Romano-British brooches which were discovered at Ballyness and Dunfanaghy, Co. Donegal. Also, post-Roman pottery has occasionally been found on Ulster sites such as several sherds of an amphora, a jug for transporting wine, was found at Clogher, Co. Tyrone.

The traditional interpretation of these Roman objects in Ireland is to assume that they were either the results of trade between Britain and Ireland or perhaps spoils of piracy. We know, for example, that Irish pirates supposedly harried the coast of Roman Britain a few centuries later. Against this theory is the fact that we do not find native Irish material accompanying these goods nor do they seem to be in areas of demonstrable native Irish settlement.

Richard Warner has suggested that the location of many of these Roman finds is critical to understanding them. A number are known from the coastlines and sand dunes such as the two sites mentioned for Donegal. Here it is much easier to imagine shipwrecks that left Roman or Romano-British travellers stranded in Ulster. Moreover, the large coin hoards or burials such as the one from Donaghadee, might be better interpreted as evidence for refugees who fled Roman Britain for Ireland. When the Romans were expanding through Britain, there was much fighting and a considerable number of people may have fled the country for Ireland.

During the second century AD there were probably continual contacts between Roman Britain and Ireland that involved trade, shipwrecks and the actual flight of refugees. After this time, it was the Irish who began to expand toward Britain. Initially this took the form of raids where the Scotti, the major part presumably from Ulster, proved a periodic scourge to the northern frontier of Roman-Britain but also were, on occasion, hired as mercenaries in the Roman army. By the 4th century the Irish began full-scale colonization establishing settlements in Wales, the Isle of Man and then western Scotland. This coupled with trade may have encouraged the introduction of Roman practices such as inhumation cemeteries and Romano-British fashions in dress and ornament and weaponry. Latin loan words began appearing in Irish apparently associated with trade, weaponry and money, and it was perhaps at this time that an Irishman, acquainted with Latin, developed the ogam script. Ultimately, the Irish assimilated so many foreign influences that in terms of material culture they began to show greater resemblances with the collapsing world of Roman Britain than the La Tène. Although these changes were well under way before 432, the traditional date of the arrival of Patrick, it is with the subsequent Early Christian period that we mark the end of Ulster's prehistory and the emergence of a truly new society.

6 Kings, Christians and Vikings c. 400 - 1177 AD

Christianity, archaeology and the historical record

Saint Patrick was credited by later generations with bringing Christianity to Ireland. It is true that we know little about him now, neither the dates of his birth or death, nor where he came from or where he worked in Ireland, all this being overlaid by legends and speculation. Nor was he likely to have been the only Christian missionary from the Roman world, but now he stands for all of them. He and his fellow missionaries did more than change the personal beliefs of the Irish. Conversion to Christianity brought into Ireland an organised institution, the Church, which demanded a place throughout the structure of society, and the resources in land to support its role. The Irish Church was part of Western Christendom, so that there was from now in existence an organisation part of whose function was to maintain contacts, both in ideas and through individuals, between Ireland and the rest of Europe. The Church was a machine for literacy; its full-time officials, priests and monks, were trained to conduct their business through writing, so that later generations would know their opinions and information independent of the personal contact of an oral

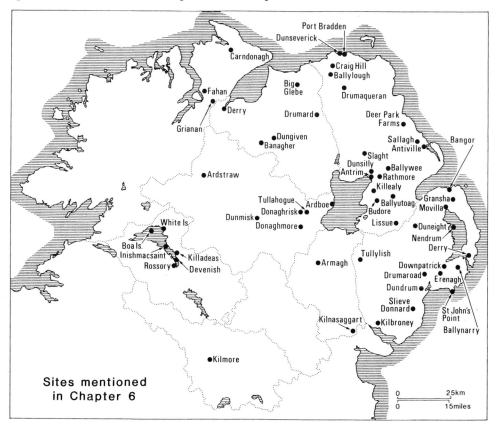

Sites mentioned
in Chapter 6

0   25km

0   15miles

tradition. These later generations include our own. The literacy of the past and the fact that it has come down to us must change our view of the past completely; we are now in a historical period.

The impact of the historical record on the way we use the physical, archaeological evidence needs some consideration as a theme by itself. The immediate reaction is to assume that the documentary record is so complete that there will be no need to look at the archaeological record. This ignores two things; firstly the historical record is neither complete nor entirely trustworthy, and secondly, that it often deals with different aspects of life than that shown by the archaeological evidence. Untrustworthiness may involve positive distortion of the facts for contemporary ends or the preservation, as though they were part of contemporary life, of laws that were long obsolete. Historical records were obviously normally written by the educated classes, and they note down what is of interest to their writers or readers; this may exclude much of life. The writers of any period are often not aware of underlying trends or slow-moving processes which mould their lives. Rarely do they feel the need to sit down and describe the familiar things of their own and others' lives directly.

Because historical and archaeological evidence are different does not mean that they should be seen to be opposed, or that they should be used independently of one another; they must be combined where it is appropriate, as long as neither is distorted to fit the other. For example, it is clearly unacceptable to identify an otherwise undated patch of burned debris on a site with an attack recorded which might not even be the same place, or to argue that some shift in craft tradition or practice must be explained by a military invasion of "new people". On the other hand it is equally ridiculous for the archaeologist to refuse to discuss an event known from history, such as the Black Death, simply because it is difficult to identify directly in the physical record. The written works tell us mostly about political activity and the formal stucture of society. We are no longer in the anonimity of prehistory; we know the names of individuals, the divisions of kingdoms and classes and the religious beliefs of the leaders of the period. To this archaeology makes us concentrate on the means of exploiting the land, the wealth of classes, the traditions of crafts and of communications both within a community and with the outside world.

Apart from the initial revolutions of religion and literacy which mark the opening of the historic period as a whole, it is punctuated by four major events: three are political, the invasions of the Vikings, the Anglo-Normans and the Tudor armies and the other a natural catastrophe, the Black Death and the subsequent population decline. Even the first three are not the same in nature at all, and it is indeed a moot point whether they are all invasions strictly speaking. However, all four were major upheavals, or were seen to be so at the time, and act as marker posts through the time we are considering. They give us divisions respectively at the 9th-10th centuries (the Vikings), the later 12th century (the Anglo-Normans), the 14th century (the Black Death) and the late 16th century (the Tudor

Wars). These are divisions which do not always fit the archaeological record, which is an interesting phenomenon in its own right, but they provide a basic framework of chronology for discussion.

The arrival of Christianity

E-ware pot from Gransha, Co. Down (ht. 13 cm).

6-2. Early penannular brooch (diam. 7 cms.).

From the 5th century, there is the impression of a quickening pace both in the amount and variety of evidence available to us. Initially, like the conversion to Christianity, this shows as an extension of links with the post-Roman world, mostly in Britain but also further afield. We can see the trends most clearly at first in objects rather than sites. Obviously these are portable things and some may not have been made in Ulster, but objects which were made to be worn, such as cloak pins, are in part ornamental and therefore respond to fashions; these fashions the archaeologist can then date. Direct imports of the 5th-6th centuries are very few, amounting to a number of pot sherds, the so-called A and B wares, of jars that probably contained wine, and table ware, derived from the Mediterranean (Ill. 6-1). Within Ulster, they have only been found at the royal site of Clogher, Co. Tyrone, but their significance may be gauged by the contrast with the earlier centuries, when we have found so few sherds in Ulster of pottery derived from Roman Britain, even though it was so close and producing so much pottery. In metalwork we encounter new types of objects and new skills used to decorate them. For the first we can instance the so-called penannular brooches, pins decorated with a nearly complete hoop at one end: the ends of the hoop were enlarged and decorated ever more elaborately in time (Ill. 6-2). The craft of enamelling was revived at the

183

same time and added colour to the basic yellow of the bronze objects. These small-scale beginnings of the 5th to 6th centuries led on to much more spectacular achievements in the next three hundred years.

As a whole it is clear that the arrival of Christianity in Ulster came at a time when much of society was changing rapidly as we know from scanty historical sources. It is disappointing that we cannot as yet point to or study sites of the period 450 to 550, but it is explicable. Without a number of places already identified it is difficult to know what to look for, and with none found we have no basis for any firm identification of objects of the period which would date the sites we are now used to ascribing to later centuries. The natural choice would be those of the new religion, whether erected on new sites or establshed on existing pagan ones. The church in Ireland as a whole, however, underwent a large scale re-organisation in the later 6th century, replacing its early bishoprics with a structure centred on monasteries. Kingship also changed greatly with the demise of the ritual aspects of the old order. Instead there was founded a network of smaller kingdoms based on a close alliance with the aristocracy in a system of patronage and support based on detailed agricultural rents and estates. The net result is that we can describe what the society of the 6th century developed into but not what it developed from or how, apart from the evidence noted above of the new contacts and new beginnings in craftsmanship.

There is one casualty of the arrival of Christianity. In the prehistoric periods, people were often buried with artifacts of the period and sometimes fully dressed. Christianity put a stop to this practice. As a result a Christian cemetery is a less helpful place to the archaeologist, a place of bodies alone. Clothing we know only from sculpture, drawings or literary description except for simple shoes. Dating is difficult, especially if later graves disturb the early ones. Add to this the acid soils of Ulster and the pickings are few. Analysis of skeletons - for stature, the age at death or disease - is best undertaken on a large number of skeletons. Ulster Christian graveyards were both small and the preservation poor. At one site, Dunmisk in Tyrone, Richard Ivens excavated over 400 graves. The average age at death was only about 25; only about one person in 40 lived beyond the age of forty. On the other hand their teeth were better than ours; no sugar meant no holes.

Types of sites

Secular society was divided by the lawyers of the 6th to 8th centuries into a great number of classes, but it is legitimate to assume that these minute subdivisions were hardly applied in daily life. Instead, we may lump some together and regard the people as belonging to one of four classes: royal kin, aristocrats, free farmers and bondmen. Beside this hierarchy was a parallel one for the men of skill, learning and religion: the craftsmen, lawyers, poets, priests, monks, bishops and abbots. Politically, Ireland was divided into many (perhaps up to 150) small units called kingdoms, which might be linked together by over-kings: each kingdom has its own social hierachy. It is in these terms that we may examine the evidence from the sites of the period in Ulster. These sites are many: Ireland as a whole is remarkable in Europe for having literally tens of thousands of sites probably occupied between 500 and 1000 A.D., more than in the rest of the Continent north of the Alps. A convenient approach to a summary of our knowlege is to classify them as far as possible according to a hierarchy, before describing the types individually and trying to see how they related to each other in time, space and social structure.

6-3. Island McHugh crannog.

The most easily defined site is the crannog, an artificial island constructed by driving a ring of strong timber piles into the bottom of a shallow lake and infilling the space with timbers, stones and brushwood. They often survive now as tree-covered islands in lakes, such as Island McHugh, in Tyrone, or the numerous examples in the lakes of Fermanagh. The result was a platform perhaps thirty metres or so across set in a lake, entirely surrounded by water, and reached only by boat or an underwater causeway (Ill. 6-3).

There are a few cases where sites have been chosen in this period which are marked out by nature for their difficulty of access: hilltops like Scrabo, Co. Down or rock stacks such as Dunseverick, Co. Antrim (Ill. 6-17). It is worth stressing the rarity of these last, hill or rock top sites in Ulster, compared for example, with the situation in Scotland or Wales at the same period. The great majority of sites known to us during the 6th to 9th centuries are enclosures which, even when set on hill tops, are hardly difficult of access or look as though they have been chosen for their defensibility.

These enclosures are produced in a number of different ways which give different appearances both then and now, and their subsequent history has varied, which also leads to variations in their forms. All are more or less strictly circular in plan, enclosing an area between twenty and forty metres across (Ill. 6-4). Modern academics refer to them as raths (more usual in

185

6-4. Univallate rath at Budore.

the North) or ringforts (more usual in the South of Ireland). One way of delimiting the enclosure was by digging a ditch and piling up the earth to form a bank on the inner side. Done once this gives us the simple univallate form. Some sites, however, have two or three banks and ditches around them, the bivallate and trivallate forms (Ill. 6-5). At Budore in Co. Antrim, there are two raths, one with a single bank and one with two banks, set in the same field: the triple-ringed Lisnagade in Co. Down is also close to a univallate rath. Another way of producing the enclosure is by steepening the perimeter of a naturally round hill (one of Ulster's many drumlins, for example) to give a sharp drop, as at Finner, Co. Donegal; this can be further emphasised by piling earth on the uphill side of the scarp to level up the interior: this gives us what is known as a platform rath. Especially where a platform rath has been constructed on a ridge rather than a hill, there is often part of the perimeter which is not cut off by the line of scarp, and which acts as a line of easy access; the interior is not normally raised above the exterior at that point. On occasions the interior of an enclosure was deliberately raised above the level of the land outside, as at Slaght Co. Antrim, normally in a series of layers laid down over time, to produce a raised rath (Ill. 6-6). Usually the raised interior has a distinct

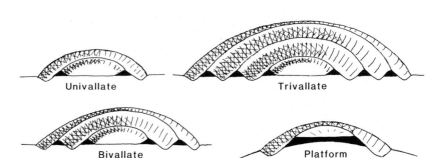

6-5. Types of rath.

Univallate

Trivallate

Bivallate

Platform

slope down to the entrance which may even appear as a ramp up into the enclosure. On at least one occasion, at Big Glebe in Co. Londonderry, the process of making a mound was not gradual but was achieved in one stage, although there was a clear line of access left to the top. Finally, the enclosure may be achieved not by a ditch and bank of earth, but by a dry stone wall, or a stone-faced bank, a variant known to modern scholars as a cashel, as at Altagore, Co. Antrim. (Ill. 6-7).

By their very nature, it is much less easy for archaeologists to detect the unenclosed sites, simply because they leave no upstanding features on the landscape to be noted by map makers or other surveyors. They appear in three ways. The first and rarest is when someone interested in archaeology notices the remains of one, the ash and charcoal of a hearth, pottery or the

6-7. Altagore cashel.

stones of a wall footing, perhaps in some process of earth moving, ploughing, farm improvements, ditch or foundation digging or the like. Another signal is the discovery of an underground passage and chambers, lined and roofed with stone, known in the country often as a cave, but to archaeologists as a souterrain. These passages which were often built beside unenclosed houses, can vary from simple linear passages to complex systems of several chambers linked by passages at one or two levels. Both these circumstances apply to the lower lands in Ulster, but recently archaeologists have been attempting to examine the uplands more carefully, notably in Co. Antrim. The result has been the discovery of a number of sites with fields and house sites still visible as upstanding remains in the grass and heather.

Farming and the appearance of the landscape

These are all rural sites now and they were then: it is only right to start with any discussion of them by looking at what we know of the landscape and the farming of the period, i.e. the 6th to 9th centuries. Our understanding of these problems derives from a number of sources, physical and documentary, ranging from pollen analysis and the study of preserved crops or animal bones to the laws written down in the 8th century. The first point to be made is that the environment was a very heavily managed and exploited one. To judge from the pollen from bogs or from the ditches of raths the countryside in the immediate vicinity was very open, with about as few trees in it as now (I11. 6-8). The trees were open land species, such

6-8. Pollen diagram from Crossnacreevy rath, Co. Down.

as ash and poplar rather than oak or elm. Woods clearly did exist, for we find the timber of them on sites and the laws treat of them as resources to be valued and exploited, but they must have been confined in extent, perhaps to strips between the kingdoms or marginal areas such as the shores of Lough Neagh.

The country was occupied by farms devoted to both arable and pastoral agriculture. This is to be expected, for it is only in a very market-oriented world of good communications that farmers can concentrate on one aspect alone. The farming system can be looked at two ways: what the farm units were and what they grew. Archaeology has little to tell us directly about the units and estates; for this we turn to documents. Land and farms were totally bound up with an individual's status and the hierarcharcical system of society. A man held land in conjunction with his family, which meant not just his own children but also his brothers, sisters and first or second cousins and their parents and children, and his status was derived at least in part from the hereditary position of them all as well as his own possessions. The classes were bound together by a system of clients and lords, which was maintained by the lord granting his client cattle in return for farm produce, both surplus beasts (cattle, pigs or sheep) and other food stuffs. In this way an aristocrat could extend his power over a much wider area than his own family lands, and in fact the system may have encouraged aristocrats to concentrate on cattle rearing, and rely on their clients for the results of arable farming.

6-9. Reconstruction of a horizontal mill.

The evidence for arable crops is always hard to assess. Nearly all excavated sites have produced quernstones for grinding. The development of tree-ring dating has led to our identifying a number of mills of the 7th to 10th centuries, which can only have been for the processing of corn (Ill. 6-9). A number of domestic sites have produced the remains of crops,

6-10. Reconstruction of a rath.

usually preserved by being charred in an accidental fire. These, if the sample is a true one, can tell us that barley was the commonest crop, followed by oats and wheat: flax seeds have also been found. What none of this tells us is how important arable farming was in the diet of individuals or in the farming system; all we can say is that it was clearly widespread.

The archaeological evidence for stock rearing rests on the evidence of the animal bones excavated from individual sites. The bones are dominated by the remains of cattle. Where a large enough sample has been found (and no site from Ulster yet has, so we depend on sites from the rest of Ireland), the pattern of the age and sex of the cattle whose bones we find shows that they were kept primarily for their milk rather than for beef. Very few calves were killed before they were six months old, because they were needed to encourage the cows to give milk. Contrary to one long held view there seems to have been no great pressure to slaughter beasts before the winter: the great majority were killed between six months and three years old at any time of the year. They were not killed because the farmers could not keep them through the winter but because they were surplus to the dairy herd and so were eaten. By contrast the next commonest animals, the pigs were mostly killed in autumn, when their main food source, the nuts found in the woods, was over. The pattern of sheep bones, with most being of mature animals, shows that they were kept primarily for their wool rather than for mutton, which might be a reason why they are less commonly found than the others.

The laws and the evidence from the bones agree that the farms were carefully run and managed. Hay does not seem to have been cut and stored, so that the farmers were forced to rely on careful management of all the available grazing lands to feed their stock throughout the year, moving them around from summer to winter lands. Combined with the evidence for arable fields in each farm, it is clear that, as the laws also show, the land was carefully fenced. The fences might be permanent banks and ditches or movable hurdles, and there is a distinction in the laws between beasts crossing the fences between fields within a family's lands and those between one family's land and another's. Many of the family farms were of some size: an aristocrat advanced up to twenty four cows to the richest grade of free farmer when he retained him as his client: the one must have had a sizeable herd to make such advances, while the other may well have had other beasts of his own. A final point about the intensity of management of the land is made by the scarcity on any excavated site of the bones of wild animals.

Buildings

All the monuments discussed were living places; we may start discussing the structures found within them by looking at the houses found. Our knowlege of these derives from excavations, and as a result is at the mercy of the level of preservation at each site. Most raths have been cultivated in recent times, with the consequent destruction of the traces of structures which had once been there. In places we have the bottom levels of walls, in others we can only deduce the plan of a house either from the gullies dug to carry water away from the base of its walls, or from the area not covered by the cobbling of the courtyard outside. Again, a tiny sample only of the sites has been excavated. These warnings dutifully given, we must make bricks with the straw we have, and try to give a general picture; exceptions will come at the end (Ill. 6-10).

6-11. Model of Deer Park Farms rath house.

The houses on the great majority of sites were not complex affairs, either in construction or plan. A single room was the norm, with very little evidence that it was sub-divided internally. Two basic plans are found, round and rectangular, usually almost square (Ill. 6-11, 6-13). Neither are large, the diameters of the round houses being around six metres or less, while a typical rectangular house might be some seven by six metres externally; the floor areas are therefore in the order of thirty to fifty square metres. The round houses were usually made with wicker walls supported by many quite small stakes, although walls of planks have been found. The rectangular planned houses frequently used stone, either laid dry or with a binding of clay or sods; no mortared wall has been found on a secular site. In terms of resisting the pressures of a roof to spread the walls apart and cause them to collapse the wicker houses may well have been stronger, but probably more vulnerable to other problems, particularly to casual fires. There is little evidence from the houses, either in the form of regular walls or of pairing of the supports, for substantial timber framed structures. Indeed, surprisingly few sites have evidence of substantial posts, set in deep post-holes; linked to this must be the lack of the substantial long rectangular halls of the rest of Europe at the period.

It has so far been impossible to distinguish classes of people from their houses. This is in part a question of the preservation of evidence, for we have no houses from such a clearly upper class site as a crannog. However, there was probably a change over time, from the earlier round houses to the rectangular or square ones which are found later. When this happened will be discussed later, along with other points of chronology. The reasons for the change are quite obscure, in the sense of seeing any advantage in it to the builders or occupiers. It does seem to reflect a shift away from the use of wicker for walling to stone, but this would have brought little structural advantage, because wicker walls are surprisingly strong and the stone was unmortared. It is difficult to believe that stones were significantly cheaper or more plentiful than the hazel rods used in the wicker walls. The rectangular houses were probably somewhat larger than the round ones, but it did not need a change of plan to make the difference. This is especially so because the walls of the rectangular houses were unlikely to have been able to support the roof if they were more than a metre or so high. The roof slope must have started low down in these houses, restricting the use of the floor space at the edges of the house.

Round houses had only single doors, while some of the rectangular ones had a second one. Some of the rectangular houses had stone-paved floors, but the majority had floors of beaten earth. Most had a central hearth, the owners of the exceptions presumably preferring to be cold or rely on portable braziers rather than live with the risk of fire. Given the construction of the houses it is difficult to envisage that they had windows at all in many cases, and if they did they were merely holes in the wall, blocked by shutters; there is no evidence of any transparent window material being used. Evidence for internal arrangements is scarce apart from the hearth,

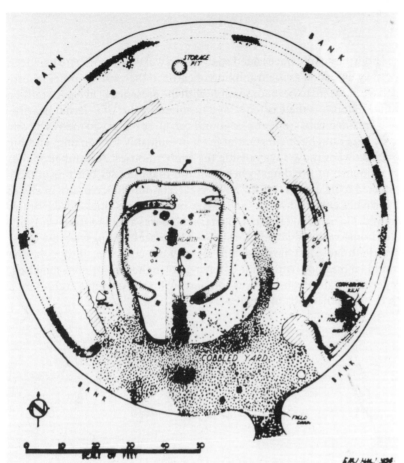

6-12. Ballymacash rath.

except for the massive collection of houses excavated by Chris Lynn at Deer Park Farms, in Co. Antrim (I11. 6-13). Dudley Waterman suggested that there was a bench around the wall of the square house which he excavated at Drumaroad, Co. Down, and there was a line of charcoal about thirty centimetres wide along the walls of the similar house at Dunsilly, Co. Antrim, that looked either like the remains of the dirt never cleaned from under a bench, or else that the roof-slope stopped people going close to the wall and cleaning it. Organic remains are best preserved on wet sites such as crannogs, which show that food bones at least were fairly common on the floors. In all, the houses were low, dark and dirty, unimpressive structures, at least when compared with the larger and better-built structures of contemporary Europe.

Outside the houses

The space outside the houses was usually covered with some sort of paving. Paving is usually the wrong word, as is cobbling, which is also used by excavators. The stones were never properly bedded in a layer of sand or other medium but were simply spread out on the soil, and in some cases the stones themselves were only five or ten centimetres across. It is difficult to see how they could have lasted at all well in wet weather if there had been any heavy use, such as the trampling of cattle in the yard. Another feature which would seem to be incompatible with the presence of livestock milling about the house is the existence at a number of sites of external hearths. These are lined with stones on edge and can be as big as two metres by one across; big enough for substantial fires, presumably for cooking, and big enough to want those fires outside the timber houses. A number of sites have evidence of buildings other than the main house, but presumably connected to its use (Ill. 6-12). The greatest number occur, not in any of the formally enclosed sites, but at the more or less unenclosed site at Ballywee, Co. Antrim (Ill. 6-13). Here there was a square stone and sod-walled house with the remains of some eight lesser buildings nearby. None were identifiable as having been for any specific use, although one rectangular building, with a line of paving down the middle of its long axis, was perhaps a storehouse; it was too narrow for the paving to represent a path between the stalls of a byre.

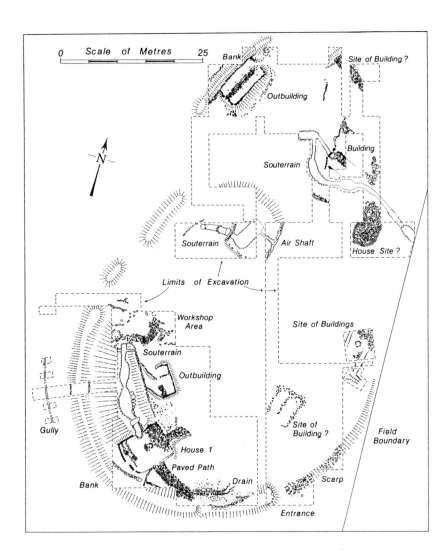

6-13. Ballywee.

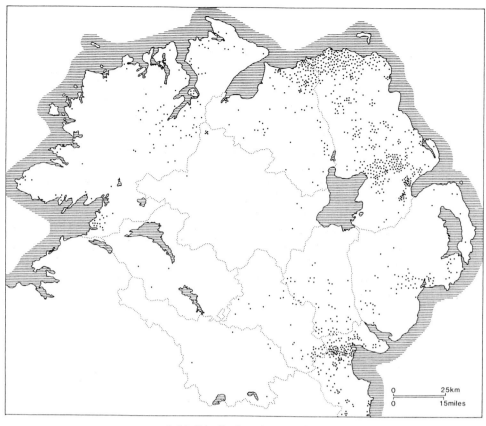

6-14. Distribution of souterrains.

Just outside Lisburn in Co. Antrim lies the site of the rath of Lissue, excavated shortly after the war by Gerhard Bersu. Here he found a series of concentric rows of posts, set about four metres apart, which filled the entire space enclosed by the rath bank. Bersu noted that the ground was stepped down from one ring to another towards the centre of the rath. From this he argued that the whole structure must have been roofed for otherwise rain would have collected in the centre where there was a hearth. Since then, such an arrangement has only been found at one other site, and neither it nor Lissue are yet fully published so it is difficult to be sure of the conclusion. If it was so, then the rath must have been most impressive, like a vast thatched mushroom set in the landscape, rather than the enclosed open yard with separate buildings that we think of for the rest of the sites.

One special group of structures needs particular comment, the souterrains. As already noted they are underground structures, lined and roofed normally with stone (one timber one has been found), and consisting of a passage or passages, which open out into chambers a little over a metre wide and a little under the height of a person. The passages between the chambers are narrower and lower, but there are also often deliberately contrived obstructions, in the form of low "creeps" or drops between two levels, which make accesss along the chambers difficult. The souterrains of Ulster have a variable distribution (Ill. 6-14): they are most frequent

195

along the coast of north Antrim and north-east Londonderry, in the Six Mile Water valley of south Antrim, and in Co. Louth. There are moderate numbers in Co. Down, Armagh, Donegal and Londonderry, but very few in Fermanagh or Tyrone. Within this distribution, the souterrains of Down are less elaborately constructed, in the numbers of chambers and in the difficulty of access to them, than those of Antrim.

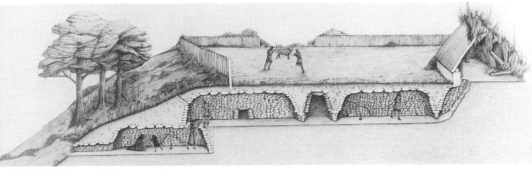

6-15. Souterrain in use as a refuge.

The use of souterrains has long been a cause of speculation, with the commonest explanations being that they were for storage or for refuge (Ill. 6-15). It has never been easy to accept these awkward structures, which were made deliberately difficult of access, as being places where people stored their everyday goods. Rather they must be seen as refuges, where people could retreat to if attacked. The main difficulty with this view has been that the souterrains could easily be approached by the attackers who could then proceed to dig down to the roof lintels and prise them up, or else light fires and burn out the refugees. This objection is valid if we accept that the attackers had ample time and intended to kill the refugees. If, however, we envisage their use as refuges from quick slave raids, where the object was to capture people as slaves before their friends could help, then they would have been effective. It would be a brave man to be the first into a dark tunnel on his hands and knees to tackle an unknown number of people inside who knew he was coming and had the advantage of knowing the plan of the souterrain better than him.

The purpose of enclosures

This brings us to the purpose of the enclosures themselves, which has been a matter of dispute. It is a question not only of why the banks and ditches were constructed, but also why multiple banks and ditches were built and why some houses were never enclosed. Had the banks a specialised function which we can assume was not always necessary or useful? Some of the popular reasons given for the enclosures are: for defence, to keep cattle in, to keep beasts out, or as a status symbol with no direct material use. Excluding beasts means either domestic or wild beasts. Domestic beasts cannot have been allowed to roam unrestrained across a countryside

196

which had fields of corn. Wild predators in Ireland must mean wolves, which have never anywhere shown an inclination to attack houses or cattle fenced in beside a house and are unlikely to have been common in a landscape which as we have seen was heavily cleared by man. Multiple banks in particular seem a curious response to wolves. If the enclosures were to pen cattle in, either as a matter of nightly routine or in an emergency, the form of the enclosure was a curious one. A fence or hedge would seem more effective for less effort than a bank with a ditch outside it, and again the multiple enclosures are hard to explain. As well as this, the structures within raths, neither the buildings nor the surface of the yards, seem capable of surviving a night with a herd of cattle milling around.

6-16. Causeway into Budore bivallate rath.

Defence has always seemed the likeliest reason for these enclosures, as shown by their common name of forts. As structures for war, however, the banks and ditches of raths are in several ways defective. The most obvious of these is at the entrances, which are the most vulnerable point of any defensive work. In raths, the ditches do not continue across the line of the gateway, with a bridge over (which might be removed in time of trouble); instead there is a causeway of undug earth (Ill. 6-16). The main problem of building a gate through a bank comes with the gate itself, hung usually from two substantial gate posts, and its relationship with the bank on either side. If the bank is unsupported by any revetment, it will slump to a slope with an angle of about thirty or forty degrees to the vertical (Ill. 6-10). If you erect two posts at the base of this slope, there will be a gap between the posts and the top of the bank which any intruder can use to go round the gate. Unlike earthworks of the Iron Age in Britain and Europe, or later military earthworks, the entrances of raths are simply marked by a pair of gate posts at best, with no revetments or other connection between them and the bank. If a bank is to be used to fight from, it needs a strong fence along the crest, and a platform behind on which the fighters can stand. Few decently long stretches of rath bank crests have been excavated, although forty or fifty have had narrow trenches excavated through them. No convincing evidence of a fighting platform or perimeter fence has come from excavated sites. The problem is that the evidence would be in the form of post-holes at regular intervals to support the main uprights; it is just possible that the excavations could all have been dug in the gaps between the posts but it is stretching the statistics of chance a long way.

The third problem for a defensive purpose is that in very few of the excavated examples has there been any evidence that the ditches were cleaned out after the inevitable silting of material into them, nor of the banks being maintained after any slumping. This implies not only that they were neglected, but also that the front slope of the bank and the sides of the ditch were constructed at quite shallow angles, not the steep sides that we expect for defences. Fourthly, the multiple enclosures are no stronger defensively than the single ones. To be effective, the inner ones should overlook the outer ones so that they do not obstruct the defenders' vision or fire; if they are to be used in succession, it has to be possible to fall back from the outer line to the inner. Neither of these things are present at the multiple enclosure raths. Finally, the perimeter of a rath thirty metres in diameter is about 100 metres long; this is a long line for the single family, who we think lived in a rath, to guard without help; if the idea was that their neighbours all rallied round to help defend what was in effect a communal fortress, we would expect fewer of them and that they would be in more impressive defensive sitings.

All this leaves us with the explanation that the raths were made not for a material purpose, or combination of them, but for a social one. This would account for the simple multiplication of the banks and ditches in the multivallate examples. It would mean that the unenclosed sites were not deprived of any essential part of life. Above all it would come some way to

6-17. Dunseverick.

explaining the unevenness of the distribution of raths in the countryside (Ill. 6-20). These gaps, such as the area of eastern Co. Down, or parts of south Co. Antrim, we would have to consider either as being relatively uninhabited, which we know to be untrue, or else not needing defence from people or beasts. It is only the vagaries of human institutions which give us reasonable grounds for having gaps.

There are two major exception to all this, the case of crannogs and the strongly sited promontory or rock stack forts (Ill. 6-17). Here the motivation for their construction must be defensive, for it is only this that would persuade someone either to live on a damp artificial island or on a hill top or cliff equally difficult for daily access. These sites, therefore stand at the other end of a spectrum from the unenclosed ones, which were, of course, totally undefensive in character. Given the historically attested association of the kings and aristocracy with the practice of war, we can assume that the military sites are of a higher status than the others. In between we have the range of enclosed sites.

Two kinds of sites do not fit well into the categories so far discussed, because they do not seem to be living sites, or if they are, they are only temporarily so. There is only one kind of secular site so far known to archaeologists other than habitations and that is the mill (Ill. 6-9). Remains of five mills have been found in Ulster to date, which have been shown by dendrochronology to date to the period. All are of the simple horizontal wheel type, in which the wheel is set horizontally in the stream bed; its shaft is then connected directly to the mill stone (which also turns horizontally) without any need for gearing. Apart from the mills, there are the more or less temporary sites. The first are the small but growing number of sites recorded from relatively high ground, i.e. above the 600

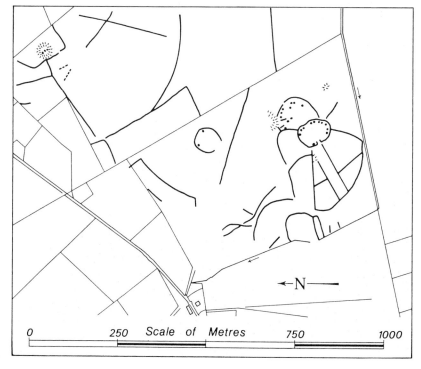

←—N—

0   250   Scale of Metres   750   1000

6-18. Ballyutoag.

feet or 200 metre contours. Houses such as those from the townland of Ballyutoag in the hills above Belfast were simple round examples of the sort we have already noted, set within the remains of a field system (Ill. 6-18). Because of their height, they were probably not occupied all the year round, but represent the houses and fields of people from further down the hill side, taking advantage of the summer pasturing. They came presumably from some way away in order to justify building a separate house and not simply running the herd from an existing house. Along the shoreline, either in caves, such as Port Bradden in Co. Antrim, or in sand dunes, as at Dundrum in Co. Down, have been found the debris of short-lived occupation, either hearths or the piles of discarded shellfish dateable to the period. These are presumably the remains of fishing or wild-fowling expeditions away from the main agricultural activity of the community.

Towards a framework of dates

Before we can discuss how these various sites might have related to each other, we must try and be clear as to their date; it is no good comparing one site with another which did not coexist with it but which replaced it. For our chronology we are forced to depend on those sites which have been excavated, a very small proportion of the whole, perhaps sixty or seventy sites investigated in Ulster out of ten thousand. This is a situation which we can do little to improve suddenly, so if we argue that the sample is unacceptably small or biassed we can say little more about them. That course leads nowhere except to an academic purity, gained by saying nothing. It is also sometimes implied that the period and its sites exhibit no signs of a chronology, that we cannot distinguish sites by their dates from the fifth to twelfth centuries. This is not so, for there are horizons visible within the material and techniques of examination which will give us more dates in the future. Like other archaeological dating, any chronology of this period must be based on the stylistic study of artifacts combined with radiocarbon and dendrochronolgy techniques.

The starting point must be with those sites dated by dendrochronology, because their dates are the most precise. The method has given us two sets of dates for sites either in Ulster or Ireland, crannogs and mills: raths have yet to produce more than the occasional substantial timber, let alone of oak. The dates from six crannogs all fell between 550 and 620 A.D. The dates of eleven mills from the whole of Ireland fell between 630 and 935 A.D. Dating of portable objects has also produced chronological landmarks. In the east of Ulster, pottery is found, which, while it may not be closely dateable, does show changes in time. There is imported pottery, successor to the earlier "A" and "B" wares; the so-called "E" ware from western France. This is difficult to define (indeed if there were other pots found in any quantity with it, it might be difficult to recognise it at all) but can be given a date for its use of the 7th or 8th centuries. It is not common but a few sherds at a time have been found at a number of Ulster rath and crannog sites.

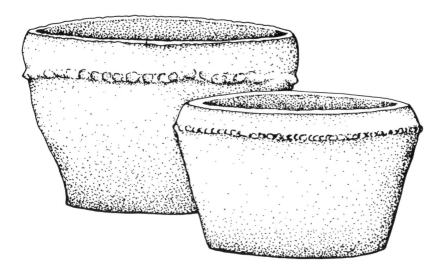

6-19. Souterrain ware pots.

Souterrain ware is the name of the pottery produced locally and used in eastern Ulster; it is found in large quantities on sites in counties Down and Antrim in particular (Ill. 6-19). It is remarkably uniform over time, but there does seem to be a progression from totally plain pots to those with attached cordons and some sort of decoration. Souterrain ware appears during the currency of "E" ware; there are sites where "E" ware is found alone in layers below souterrain ware, and sites where the two are found together, but none where souterrain ware has been found in undisturbed layers below "E" ware. Very occasionally elaborate metal objects which can be related to dateable fashions in art styles have been found on raths or crannogs. A final horizon is provided by the influx of English artifacts associated with the conquest of the late 12th century.

It is difficult to be at all precise about the dates we might attach to these horizons, apart from the beginning and end. Perhaps the key dates to concentrate on are those of the introduction and elaboration of souterrain ware. The first is likely to have taken place some time in the 8th century, some time after the first arrival in Ulster of "E" ware, but to have happened in time for a sherd to have apparently been dropped during the construction of a mill at Drumard, Co. Londonderry, in 782. The relative elaboration of souterrain ware is clearly later and may have come in the 9th century. The shift from round to square houses already noted appears to have happened at about the same time as the elaboration of souterrain ware. Neither of these last two statements is at all securely based on proof as yet, but if we follow the indications as they exist at the time of writing, we will be led to argue that the shift in house type took place in the 9th or 10th centuries.

None of this gives us precise chronologies for the use of the sites; the only precision comes from the dendrochronological dates for the beginnings of crannogs and mills. This is one of the hardest questions to assess: irrespective of absolute date, how many of the sites we have discussed were in existence at the same time, and did that number change in time, either through any type of site becoming more or less common, or indeed one or more types as a whole being earlier or later in date than another. Clearly, for example, from the set of dendrochronological dates we have, it would seem that the bulk of crannogs had been built before there were any mills in Ulster. This can be explained simply by the invention of the mill or its introduction into Ireland, an event before which there can have been no mills here. There is a considerable variation in the results of excavating sites in regard to the length of time that they appear to have been used. The irregular houses of the sites do not look as though they would have lasted for more than a quarter or half a century and a number of the simple, one-ringed raths have only one or two periods of occupation. It is difficult to think of these sites as being in use for more than about a hundred years. On the other hand the raised raths, made of successive layers, one on top of the other, must have been longer lived, as were at least some of the crannogs.

Some, if not all, crannogs had their origins in the 6th to 7th centuries. Some raths have their beginnings before the introduction of souterrain ware, while others start after that point. Some sites continue in use through the change from plain to more decorated pottery, and some also show the change, in successive periods, of round to square houses. Some at least of the single raths were apparently not occupied for more than about a century. When we take these statements together, it seems clear that some of the individual sites cannot have been contemporary with others. This is not to say that the types as a whole were not broadly contemporary, only that we cannot assume that any two particular monuments were in use together. Apart from mills, it is not easy to isolate out one set of sites as being earlier than any other, for example crannogs, which have the early dendrochronological dates attached, do not seem to go out of use before any other type. Open sites with souterrains attached do seem to have square houses, which might indicate that they are rather later, but this is the one type of site whose discovery is so dependent on chance that we can be sure that the excavated examples cannot be taken as a representative sample; still, the hint is there.

Patterns of the distribution of sites

This line of reasoning runs counter to the conclusions of the study of the distributions of the sites in the landscape. We have already mentioned that raths in particular are not found all over Ulster, where there is suitable land, as we might expect, if we think of them as the normal living place of the free farmers of the period. Clearly the distribution of crannogs depends to a large degree on the availability of lakes to site them in, but this does not apply to raths (Ill. 6-20). In Co. Down, for example, the Ards peninsula and the lands north of a line between Comber and Belfast have few raths. On the other hand in the west of the county, from Dromore to Newry, there are many more. This cannot be explained either by the soil in the western area being better, or by the farmers of the north and east destroying many more raths than their western counterparts; the difference is probably genuine, but not susceptible of a material explanation.

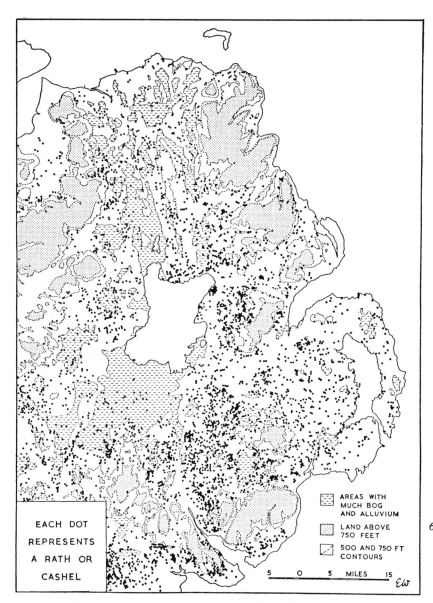

EACH DOT
REPRESENTS
A RATH OR
CASHEL

AREAS WITH
MUCH BOG
AND ALLUVIUM

LAND ABOVE
750 FEET

500 AND 750 FT
CONTOURS

5   0   5   MILES   15

6-20. *Distribution of raths in eastern Ulster.*

One argument derived from the pattern of rath distribution is that the areas which have a lesser density of raths lie in the east of Ireland occupied by the English in the late 12th century, and the reason for the lower density is because the English prevented any more raths being built in the areas which they controlled. This left the construction of raths to continue unrestricted in the rest of the country and so these parts accumulated relatively more sites. This ignores the fact that excavation of perhaps one hundred raths in Ireland has yet to uncover evidence from their artifacts of one constructed after 1200. As has been noted above, there are dating horizons within the period, which proponents of a late date for rath construction simply ignore. The argument is further complicated by the uncertainty as to whether the pattern is a product of destruction in the areas

203

of lower density or of increase in the other parts: if the former it is quite unclear when this destruction took place, and no reason has been advanced as to why the English of the 12th to 15th centuries should have been responsible. Thirdly, the argument ignores the complexities of the distribution patterns within the broad categories of dense and sparse; there are wide areas with a low density of raths where the English did not occupy. We must conclude that there are other forces at work here.

This leads to looking for patterns of distributions, not of single types of sites, but of all sites in relationship to each other. If we envisage many raths as being relatively short lived individually, but yet as a type to be found through two or three centuries at least, this should affect their distribution in the countryside. We should expect perhaps that the new sites would be sited close to the ones that they replaced. If that was the case, we should find clusters of raths at intervals, with some maybe showing the sequence of construction, either by overlapping sites, or by some being better preserved (because it is newer) than others. Equally, if the builders do not re-use more or less the same sites, the raths should become, with time, increasingly evenly distributed over the country. In fact, while some do occur, clusters of raths are rare, much rarer than replacement on the same site would lead us to expect. Conversely, raths are not evenly distributed, as we have seen, either across a whole county, nor are they evenly distributed in the areas where they are relatively common.

We have already seen that there is reason to believe that they can be arranged in a hierarchy of social order: can this be reflected in their distribution? What we might expect is that higher status sites would be fewer and that they might be seen to be in a set relationship to other sites, appearing to "control" them. Something of this sort of pattern can be seen in certain areas. These are questions to which we will return, but before we can we must look at the archaeology of the other hierarchy in society, that of the men of skills, learning and the Church.

The Early Christian Church in Ulster

We have seen that the historical sources make it clear that the Church underwent a considerable reorganisation in the middle and later part of the 6th century. Archaeology has little to say about this, for we have yet to identify more than a single site which we can with any degree of confidence attribute to that date. The site concerned is that of Armagh, where excavation, by Cynthia Warhurst, Alan Harper and Chris Lynn, in two places has produced remains which may go back to that time (I11. 6-21). The first is a ditch, which may have surrounded the top of the hill, now occupied by the mediaeval cathedral, the second on the site of what was later the church of "Na Ferta", down the hill in what is now Scotch Street. Neither site has produced evidence to tell us of the nature of the buildings or life in Armagh before 600, but they have confirmed the legendary antiquity of the site as a religious centre, and that there were, as later traditions said, two centres to it.

The later sixth century saw the foundation of a number of major monasteries, which succeeded in dominating the Church in Ulster and Ireland until the twelfth century: Derry, Bangor or Movilla, together with Armagh which exploited (or invented) its 5th century associations with Patrick to become the most powerful monastery of Ireland. We have literary descriptions which talk of large numbers of "monks" at these places, but they are not monks in the modern sense of full-time religious men spending their whole life within the monastery; instead these include the monastic tenants and craftsmen, often married, and indeed who held their positions through inheritance, and who might not live at the monastery but only on its land. We must not assume that the sites were large centres of population, although they may have been, and were certainly major centres of resources. The siting of the sites, especially those major ones that were famous then or now, has one important message. The early Irish church is sometimes described in terms which give prominence to the ascetic tradition which impelled some monks to retreat to sites remote from society both then and now; the classic example is the isolated rock of Skellig Michael off the Kerry coast, but in Ulster we might give the hermitage on the top of Slieve Donard in the Mournes. These are not typical sites, for by far the greatest number are sited at places which were positively chosen for their accessibility, like the ports of Bangor or Derry.

All physical traces of the major centres have now been lost, usually buried under later towns, or destroyed by later grave digging. The best example we have is of a second-rank site, Nendrum, which is sited on an

6-21. Air photograph of Armagh city.

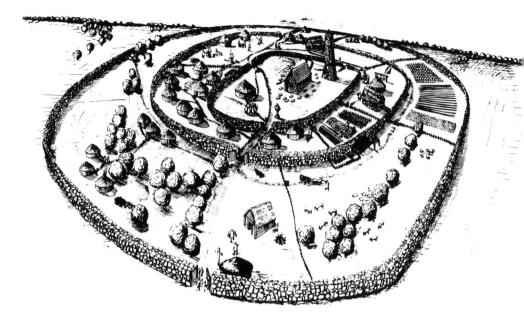

6-22. Reconstruction of Nendrum.

island in Strangford Lough, and which fortunately escaped both the usual fates (Ill. 6-22). It appears, to our modern land and road based world, to be sited in a remote spot, hard to reach across three islands and two causeways from the Co. Down shore, but to boats it was close to the harbour of Whiterock and well-placed for traffic up and down the Lough. It consisted of three stone enclosures: the inner one contained the church and graveyard; the middle one at least one row of round houses for the monks to live in, and a craft workshop; the use of the outer one is unknown. There is no sign of any regular planning of the enclosures, certainly no hint of the rectangular cloister which has dominated monastic planning in the rest of Europe since the ninth century. The actual buildings seem to have been unimpressive as architecture; the church was only some ten metres long by four wide. The tall and elegant round towers, which are the most distinguished features of Irish monasteries, belong to the centuries after 950. How much of the three enclosures was actually built up is unknown, but a large part of the outer one was probably given over to growing food.

Nendrum was badly excavated in the 1920s even by the standards of the time: the chronology of the buildings is quite unclear (although some of what we see today was probably in existence in the 8th or 9th centuries) and the techniques of digging prevented the excavators finding any traces of the wooden structures, which must have existed. Excavations at Armagh have uncovered the remains of craft workshops away from the main monastic centre on the top of the hill; burials and the circular enclosing ditch to the monastery have also been found at Downpatrick. Sites outside Ulster show that rather than building larger stone churches, the monks tended to build

206

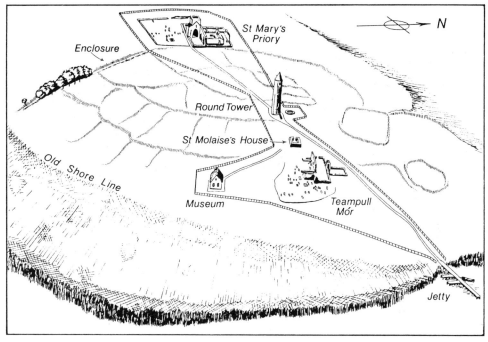

several small ones, presumably for different groups of worshippers, or for services at different times. At the present time, we know more about the large monasteries from written documents than from archaeology. It is from descriptions of sites that we hear of large wooden churches, separate guest houses, schools and barns, along with evidence for farming and diet. These are enough to give us a rather vague general idea of the larger monasteries, circular or oval enclosures containing a somewhat random collection of houses and workshops with a graveyard all set around one or more small churches (Ill. 6-23). Until we find a second Nendrum, and excavate it to recover evidence of timber structures and the remains of food and environment, this will remain the picture. On the other hand, there are many more church sites in the countryside, dating to the period than those we have discussed.

These are not large sites, and few have much or any documented history, and it is in this that their interest lies. Many now survive only as burial grounds, abandoned for all other uses when these were concentrated on parish churches in the twelfth century or later. Excavation has also demonstrated that later parish churches, like Tullylish, Co. Down, can also date back to churches of this period. Typically the main surviving feature is the circular enclosure, like that of the greater sites, but suitably smaller in diameter, but occasionally the churches themselves survive or have been excavated. The churches of Derry and St. John's Point, both in Co. Down, survive in part and have been excavated (Ill. 6-24). The earlier Derry church and the St. John's Point church were both very small, six by four metres internally or less. In both cases, these were preceded on the site by equally small timber or dry-stone buildings, associated with burials and so presumably also churches. The burials at Derry were of men, women and children, and not just the adult males that we might expect from a monastic community alone. The bodies must be those of the people living in the land around, and many other burial grounds, as has been shown at the extensive early cemetery of Dunmisk in Co. Tyrone, must have been for the local communities as well. The status of these sites in ecclesiastical terms is a matter to which we will return in discussing their relationships with the secular pattern of settlement. Before that, however, we should turn to the evidence of the men of skills.

Metalworking

The crafts of the metalworker, above all the bronze-smiths and the jewellers, straddle the secular and religious worlds. There is evidence of the making of ornaments, such as the elaborate cloak pins from both secular and religious sites, and the objects themselves, whether reliquaries for the churches or brooches for the aristocracy to wear, share the same motifs and techniques. We have seen the quickening impulses of the fifth century which were working in the metal-workers crafts, new forms of object and new techniques introduced from Britain. This trend continued steadily until the tenth century. During the seventh century come in new skills, like chip-carving where the surface of the bronze was cut up into sharply angled facets; this was linked to the widespread use of gilding of the bronze and to the "cloisonné" technique of setting coloured enamels, amber or glass,

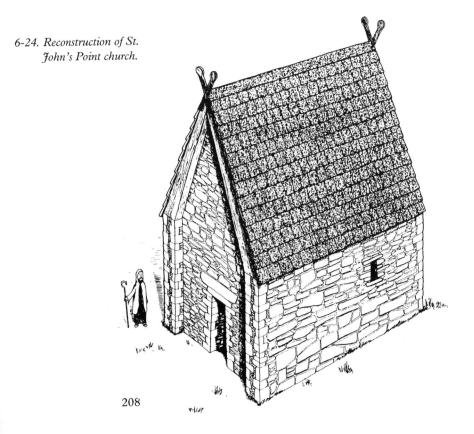

6-24. Reconstruction of St. John's Point church.

in cells raised above the surface of the object. These all combined to give a much more brilliant, even flashier, look to the jewellery. At the same time, came interlace designs, often animals intertwined with each other; their outlines were sometimes drawn in filigree, lines of minutely twisted gold wire soldered to the object, resembling lines of tiny balls of gold (Ill. 6-25).

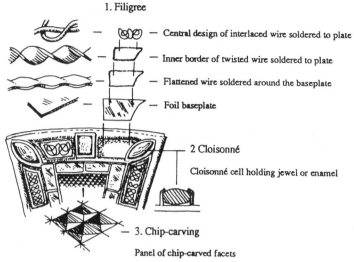

1. Filigree

— Central design of interlaced wire soldered to plate

— Inner border of twisted wire soldered to plate

— Flattened wire soldered around the baseplate

— Foil baseplate

2 Cloisonné

Cloisonné cell holding jewel or enamel

3. Chip-carving

Panel of chip-carved facets

6-25. Metal working techniques.

All these new techniques and designs were shared with the contemporary jewellers of Anglo-Saxon England. The actual objects produced, however, especially the penannular brooches, were traditionaly Irish, and from the clear evidence of moulds found on Ulster sites, made locally. This raises the question of the means of transmission of these techniques; they were hardly separately invented on both sides of the Irish Sea at the same time. The seventh century saw very close connections between England, particularly the North, and Ireland. The obvious part of this was the conversion of much of England to Christianity by Irish missionaries but links were maintained after the conversion through the Church. In the shared techniques of the metal-workers, we see another side of the same contact. That the similarities are to be found in the techniques of producing the objects is the key to the interpretation of it. If the shapes or designs were found in common, these could have been copied from objects brought from one area to the other, or even from descriptions of churchmen who had seen them in their travels. For techniques to travel, however, means that men who understand the craft must have talked to each other; descriptions by unskilled people will be of no use, and the objects themselves may show a craftsman what he should aim at, but not how he can do it. As a result, we can see that the contacts were not confined to churchmen alone, but involved other kinds of men, an indeed the two lines of communication may have been somewhat independent of each other.

6-26. Loughan brooch
(diam. 4.8 cms.).

6-27. Parts of
crozier shrines.

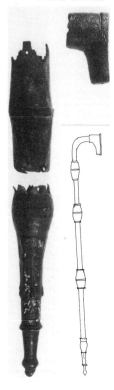

The achievements of the metal workers of the eighth and ninth centuries have long been justly famous. It produced the fine brooches, of which the Tara brooch (actually found at Bettystown, Co. Meath) is perhaps the best known, and reliquaries or ecclesiastical objects such as the chalices from Ardagh or (more recently discovered) Derrynaflan. From Ulster come counterparts of the Tara brooch, such as the splendid gold penannular brooch from Loughan, near Coleraine (Ill. 6-26). On the other hand, first-rate examples of ecclesiastical metal-work of the seventh to tenth centuries are missing from Ulster; indeed a high proportion of the ones we have comes from the south-west of Ireland. Given the relatively small number of objects known in total, it is difficult to know if there is any significance to this.

During the later ninth century, fashion seems to have moved away from the highly coloured metalwork of the preceding century, and a rather more monochrome style sets in. Instead of the glittering gold facets and glass or enamel insets, there is a trend towards silver, relieved with inlay of black niello (silver sulphide). The decoration is often organised by being divided up into little geometric fields, separated by raised borders, each of which contains a single motif, like a piece of abstract interlace or an animal. This is a style found on both secular and religious articles: large silver penannular brooches or the crosier shrines of saints. These latter, like the example from the River Bann at Toome, are made by covering the walking-stick - like wooden croziers of saints in metal sheets or lengths of tubing, held together by covering the junctions with raised knops; these knops lend themselves well to subdivisions around the circumference (Ill. 6-27). Again, like the earlier fashions, this represents ideas from the rest of Europe and England in particular. The shift to silver may be linked to the general move away from gold, always rare in Europe, to silver which was mined at a number of places, a shift which we can see in the coins of England and the Franks from the end of the eighth century. The division of the ornament into geometric cells is seen in the metalwork of the south of England, in the style named after a hoard of objects found at Trewhiddle in Cornwall, with coins

dateable to around 875. The context of this find is worth emphasis; from the ninth century, the dates of jewellery and precious metal objects can be tied to hoards containing coins which give dates for the deposit of the hoard.

In concentrating on the major objects, which are the most spectacular and are probably the ones which reflect or set the general fashions most closely, it is easy to overlook a second point. From the later seventh century, not only does the quality of metal objects increase but so does their quantitiy. This is partly a matter of simple numbers, but also of variety, so that there is a definite impression that there was a steady increase in output of the metal workers from the seventh to the tenth centuries.

If metal workers served both lay and religious customers, if they could afford the products, some crafts were specialised. Weaponry, for example was the preserve mainly of the secular aristocracy; the chief remains of this are the swords. They display two characteristics. Firstly, although the few swords that are known from Ireland are larger than their Iron Age predecessors (perhaps under the influence of late Roman swords) they still have blades only about fifty centimetres long, two thirds the length of tenth-century Viking blades (Ill. 6-28). The second point is that they do not display the complex smithing of the pattern-welded Frankish or Anglo-Saxon swords of the sixth and seventh centuries.

Metalwork cannot be confined to the expensive jewellery that we have noted above. At a humbler level, there was a continual need to produce cheaper dress ornaments or objects, such as the universal cloak pins, normally of bronze or brass, unornamented with any inlays or much decoration of any sort (Ill. 6-29). Tools of iron were even more of a necessity for the basic farming on which everyone depended. Remains of both crafts have been found at many of the excavated sites. Iron working was the more common, with many of the rath sites producing the slags resulting from working iron, apparently from smelting the ore as well as working the metal itself (Ill. 6-30). It is difficult to believe that the occupiers of the simpler univallate raths were able to work iron or bronze, any more than that the remains of metal-working found at higher status sites (e.g. the gold traces from Clogher, Co. Tyrone) were the results of a lord's handiwork. Presumably the craftsmen concerned were more or less itinerant, working for the rath farmers in a district or more permanently in an aristocratic or royal household or indeed in a monastery.

Manuscripts

The clearest examples of specialised crafts are those associated with the Church, notably the production and decoration of manuscripts and stone carvings. Some manuscripts, produced in the high cultural milieu of the British Isles during the seventh to ninth centuries have inscriptions on them referring to individuals whose dates are known from other sources, such as lists of abbots or annals which often note the deaths of prominent men. The known points in chronology are then combined with analysis of

6-29. Ringed pins.

6-30. Students reconstructing the smelting of iron.

the ornament that is found on their illustrated pages, to give a general typology of style for the period across the British Isles as a whole. It is a process which has obvious defects (are the identifications of the people in the two sources right? Can the history of ornament in one craft be applied to another?) but the basic result has been accepted by everyone as the best solution to the problem of chronology.

There is no space for considering the process of this chronology building here, apart from stating that that is the basis for analysis of the period's art work. Rather we can stress two other aspects: the connections implied in this process, and the resources involved. Major illuminated manuscripts were produced in more than one region. The Book of Lindisfarne was almost certainly written in Northumbria, but the place where the Book of Kells was produced is more controversial: Ireland, Iona in the western isles of Scotland, eastern Scotland or Northumbria have all been suggested. The fact that scholars can diverge so much is in part a reflection of their modern nationalism, but also that there was a basically uniform culture across the areas concerned; otherwise it would be clear what the answer was. The areas have regional tendencies and traditions, but there was so much sharing of designs that it is not easy to be sure about the place of origin of a single object form studying its motifs alone.

Illuminated manuscripts were very expensive items. The skins of about 150 calves were needed for the vellum on which the Book of Kells was written; the joint monasteries of Jarrow and Monkwearmouth in Northumbria produced three particularly massive copies of the Bible around 700, each copy of which needed the skins of 515 calves. Cattle herds which could satisfy such demands without being wiped out were not small; it has been calculated that it would have needed a thousand acres of land to produce the three Jarrow and Monkwearmouth manuscripts. We must add to this cost the pigments for the coloured paintings, some at least of which came from far away. This only covers the raw materials, but the men who produced them must have spent years not only on the production of the book in question, but also in training. Their lives must have been devoted to the work and to little else; throughout they must have been supported by others.

Monasteries which could support such activity were clearly few. The writing workshops (or *scriptoria*) produced, of course, not only the great luxury works but also less lavish works, books for daily use in the services, or else scholarly collections of new or old works. We can see something of such a workshop at work, in Armagh in the ninth and early tenth centuries. The Book of Armagh contains a complete New Testament, bound up with accounts of St. Patrick's life and his "Confession", all aimed at asserting Armagh's association with the saint and its pre-eminence as a church in Ireland. The book was writtren by Ferdomnach (described as "a wise and excellent scribe of Armagh" in the Annals of Ulster when they recorded his death in 846) under the direction of Torbach, abbot of Armagh for just one year, 807-8. It is a workmanlike production, written in a script which was both smaller and quicker to write than the script of the great books and much less ornamented. Two books of Priscian's Grammar were written in a similar style of script to the Book of Armagh: one is recorded as being the work of the scribe Dubtach in 838.

The Book of Mac Durnan is a book of the Gospels, recorded as being used by Maelbrigte Mac Tornian, or Mac Durnan, when he taught. He became abbot of Armagh in 888 and was then the head of the Columban monasteries in Ireland before his death in 927. The script is like that of Ferdomnach, but the style of the painted scenes is very different; it looks as though two men, a scribe and a painter were involved. These four manuscripts show the scriptorium at work, as a group maintaining a tradition. The abbots of Armagh are closely involved, as patrons of the work in general, or of individual books, and as users of them. There are both scribes and painters involved, sometimes on the same work, especially, obviously, a more elaborate piece. Perhaps the fact that Ferdomnach's death was noted in the Annals, unlike that of Dubtach, means that he was a more important man, maybe the head of the scriptorium. Finally, these manuscripts come just before a gap in production of such work which lasted for a hundred years after the early tenth century, in Ulster and in Ireland as a whole.

Stone carving

The pagan Irish had carved stone before the arrival of Christianity; figures such as the two-headed Boa Island statue from Fermanagh are probably pagan idols. There are a few examples in Ulster of stones with inscriptions carved in the clumsy Ogham script, which are relatively common in the southwest of Ireland. It is a script which represents each letter (based on the Latin alphabet) by up to five strokes cut on one or other side of a vertical line; most stones have room for a person's name alone. The date of Ogham stones is early in our period, probably from the fifth to eighth centuries. A

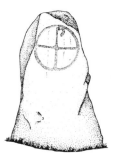

6-31. Drumaqueran stone (ht. 1 m).

similar date might be given to the carving of simple crosses on some natural boulders. A plain cross might be carved at any time from the introduction of Christianity down to the Penal times of the eighteenth century, but some designs, such as that on the stone at Drumaqueran, Co. Antrim, which has a design derived from a late Roman monogram of Christ's name, could well belong to the sixth or seventh century (Ill. 6-31).

The earliest secure date we have from Ulster for a stone carving in the period is the pillar stone with a number of crosses carved on it from Kilnasaggart in Co. Armagh, which also has an inscription in Latin, which records the dedication of the site by a man who died in 714 or 716 (Ill. 6-32). By this time at least, craftsmen were being trained in the cutting of stone, and in learning the sources of suitable stone in the countryside, the two essential skills needed to practice the craft. The result was the fine series of High Crosses, which, along with the jewellery and the manuscripts, are what has made this period famous. The Irish High Crosses are like those of Northumbria, for example, in being high stone crosses carved with figures and scenes on the shaft, but are distinct from them in their proportions, the ring around their heads, and in the treatment of the panels of sculpture. The Irish crosses are not uniform in their designs either; in both cases we can see a general idea being given particular local treatment, either in comparing Ireland with England, or regions within Ireland. Of these regions, one is Ulster, where the two best preserved of the crosses, Arboe and Donaghmore in Tyrone, both show the local characteristics of having tall shafts with rather small cross heads, and a systematic arrangement of narrative scenes on them (Ill. 6-33, 6-34). Their decoration is not as elaborate as the crosses of Monasterboice or Clonmacnois from the Midlands of Ireland, or as delicate as the abstract designs from Ahenny in Kilkenny or as naive as the granite crosses from the south Wicklow hills.

At Fahan and Carndonagh, in Co. Donegal, are two monuments which have been claimed by scholars in the past as the starting point of the whole series of Irish high crosses (Ill. 6-35). Both are slabs, however, with crosses and decoration carved on them, rather than true free-standing crosses; putting them at the start of the series requires that the crosses almost literally grew, of their own accord, into the later form. It also ignores the fact that there are more and less elaborate examples of crosses in the same area; Kilbroney in Co. Down has no figure scenes and Inishmacsaint in Co. Fermanagh, is a cross with no decoration at all (Ill. 6-36). The grand typological scheme for all the crosses in Ireland puts them in a series, beginning at Carndonagh or Fahan in the early eighth century or earlier and ending with Arboe or Donaghmore in the later tenth. In between the developments are supposed to have happened at intervals at different places in Ireland. Each stage is said to take place in a different area, the sequence passing over the whole island like a cloud, and leaving each area in turn with a different set of crosses; no area is allowed to continue with the carving after it has produced its number of examples in the overall scheme. It is much more likely that the regional differences are just that,

6-32. Kilnasaggart pillar (ht. 2.25 m).

214

6-33. Arboe.

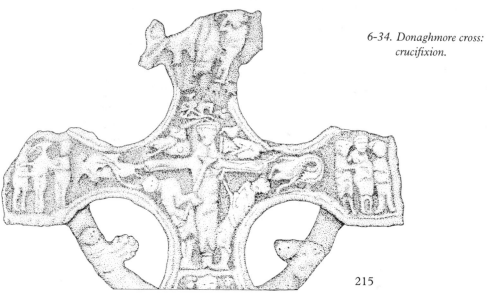

6-34. Donaghmore cross: crucifixion.

215

6-35. Fahan cross slab.

with no distinction of time; the craftsmen of each area working out their own versions of a common idea. Simple versions need neither be earlier nor the work of a different tradition, but simply because they were made with more limited resources.

The idea that most of the crosses in Ireland are roughly contemporary is reinforced by recent work which has shown that many of the motifs and schemes of iconography are common across Ireland. If we accept this view, there are two pointers as to when they might have been made. The crosses from Ahenny in particular are close in their use of ornament to the manuscripts of the eighth century. The monastery of Iona, itself founded by St. Columba from Derry, saw the erection of at least two crosses like those of Ireland. This presumably happened before the monastery was abandoned in the middle of the ninth century in the face of Viking attacks. Even allowing for a heavy rate of destruction of these crosses, and Ulster has seen as heavy damage as anywhere, they would have been produced in hundreds not thousands. With different regional groups of craftsmen at work, it seems difficult to believe that the period of their production lasted for more than a century and a half or so perhaps from the mid eighth to the early tenth.

6-36. Kilbroney cross.

This is also the period to which we should probably assign the remarkable sculptures from White Island in lower Lough Erne (Ill. 6-37, 6-38). They are not crosses or slabs but eight figures, carved, if not to be freestanding, at least to stand projecting from a wall or other background. Two carry croziers, and at least five were built into the church on the island; they are Christian and not, as is sometimes stated, pagan. They were built into the church probably because they were known to be sacred and therefore needed to be preserved, even if this meant using them as building stones, which seems to us disrespectful. This was not the mediaeval view, however, which was that that this was a sacred use; the same was frequently done to Anglo-Saxon crosses. The church itself has a 12th century door, as we shall see, so the carvings must be earlier than that. Two figures carry croziers of a shape resembling the crozier shrines of the 9th to 12th centuries; one wears a penannular brooch, a type of jewellery which was apparently not made after the 10th century. Their original use is unknown: six can be paired according to height, with two of 105 cm., two of 80 cm. and two of 60 cm.; all six have sockets in the top, apparently for wooden beams. The most attractive suggestion is that these six were made to be the supporters of three wooden steps, perhaps to a pulpit.

6-37. White Island: figure of a churchman.

If their use is in doubt, the skill of their carver is not, and can be appreciated all the better than that of the crosses because the figures are better preserved. They are beautifully modelled with smooth surfaces, whether curved or flat, contrasting with the crisply carved details of the faces, clothes and hair. Their eyes are round and stare fixedly ahead; their mouths are held in a stylised pout: there is no sign of movement or emotion. Two of the figures are churchmen, distinguished by each carrying a crozier and one a bell as well (Ill. 6-37); another is a noble, with his brooch, shield and sword (Ill. 6-38). The clothes are the same upper-class dress on both ecclesiastic and noble, and the same as the figures on the high crosses: a long tunic worn under a cloak. Similar figures in high relief, at Killadeas in Fermanagh, and Carndonagh in Donegal, may hint at a tradition of stone carving perhaps restricted to western Ulster. If so, it is a reminder of the possible regionalism of the craft at the highest level, just like the differing traditions of the crosses.

Pottery

One craft is peculiar, that of pottery, which has already been mentioned in terms of the chronology of sites; dating is only one of the problems that the souterrain ware pottery presents to the archaeologist. The pots are round and flat-bottomed with straight, nearly vertical sides, like flower pots but much wider in proportion to their height. The decoration which appears to be a later feature of the ware consists either of giving the rim a sort of pie-crust effect or else of sticking on to the side, near the top, a strip of clay which is either left as a plain band or else is pinched up at intervals. The means of its production pose the question of whether it was made as a sort of home industry by householders or whether it was a specialised craft. The

6-38. White Island: figure of a noble.

clay is usually well-sorted and prepared so that the body of the pot is quite thin and even, and the pots are reasonably skilfully shaped by making it from coils of clay rather than on a wheel, although they are so simple that this is hardly evidence of professional expertise (Ill. 6-19). They are poorly fired to a uniformly low temperature, not as high as would be indicated by putting them in a decent bonfire, let alone any sort of kiln. Analysis of minerals in the clay has not been done systematically yet, but such work as has been done indicates that the clay used was local, i.e. that the pots were produced at different places, not at one and then marketed across the country. This is perhaps best explained if we imagine that this was a cottage industry, part-time at best. The problem is that the pottery is uniform across its range, and seems to show signs of only the one change in either its shape or development from the end of the eighth to the twelfth century. It is difficult to see how such a pattern of uniformity could be maintained if it was being made in households up and down the country. Again we may be dealing with itinerant craftsmen.

6-39. Distribution of souterrain ware.

This becomes even more of a problem when we consider the geographical spread of its discovery (Ill. 6-39). It has been found in considerable quantities at many excavations, and chance discoveries in Counties Antrim and Down. Recently it has been found at a few sites further west but always in smaller quantities, even in prosperous places such as Armagh. The problem of its distribution is connected to that of its intended use. We normally think of pottery as for cooking over or in a fire, and souterrain ware pots often have carbon deposits baked on to them that look like the remains of cooking that went wrong. The pots have no handles and even the applied cordons seem very badly designed to hold a loop around them; it seems that they could not be suspended over the fire. Their poor firing would have meant that they were very weak to put directly into a hot fire, unsuspended, and if they had been, they would surely have become fired themselves in the process. Nor can they have been in any sense waterproof. Above all, why did the people in the east of Ulster apparently need the pottery in some quantities, but those in the west need it much less if at all, like the people in the rest of Ireland who used no pottery at this time? As an exercise in frustrating archaeological explanation processes, souterrain ware rates highly.

As such it serves to remind us of the crafts and material evidence of which we are ignorant, and the list is a formidable one. Wood working is represented by stray timbers which show that carpenters could at least make a mortice and tenon joint (which needs a good chisel for oak), and some turned bowls which must have been the commonest eating vessels. We have effectively no furniture, and virtually no direct knowlege of roof timbers. Evidence of food is also missing, apart from some inkling of the raw materials of meat and cereals, and literary descriptions of doubtful relevance to more than a tiny elite. It is a depressing list, like those of other periods. Simple leather shoes have survived; apart from them we derive our knowledge of clothing from literature and island sculpture, such as the White Island figures some shoes or literary descriptions of the rich..

Towards an overview of seventh to ninth century Ulster

There is one site which is going to alter our whole perspective on the period, in so far as a single site can, and that is the raised rath at Deer Park Farms, Co. Antrim (Ill. 6-11). It has been too recently excavated, by Chris Lynn, to be assessed and included in a general account such as this. The site was a succession of occupation periods, each adding layers on to the remains below, until the mound was formed. During the excavation the remains of at least thirty house were uncovered, almost doubling the number of houses known from Ulster. The lower, earlier houses were waterlogged and had been since they were built, so that they were in an excellent state of preservation, showing for the first time the actual wattle walls of the round house, as had been presumed but not found before. Inside the house were the remains of beds and the details of the interior uses and planning. Outside, the water-logging meant the preservation of a whole array of objects of organic materials, normally only preserved on crannogs. The chronology, based on dendrochronology (which gives the date 648 for the felling of one of the door jambs) and high-precision radio-carbon, of the structures will give precise dates to the sequence both of the buildings and of the artifacts associated with them; for example, the sequence sees the introduction of souterrain ware at one point. It is clear, from the elaborate details of the structure, particularly the monumental stone lined entrance to the rath at one phase, and the impressive facade added to the outside face of the bank at a later one, that this was a high-status site. Whether this site will prove to be so remarkable that we are never able to integrate it with others, much less well preserved and so much less well known, time will tell; until its publication, at least, we will have to reserve our judgement on Deer Park Farms.

So far we have been concerned with the state of factual knowlege about the archaeology of the period such as the basic types of sites and objects. It is time to attempt to draw up some sort of tentative picture as to how it all fitted together into a system of settlement and organisation. To do this we must repeat some general points in order to reinforce and expand on them. We may start with the social hierarchy whose principal classes were the kings (both of the small kingdoms and those who were more powerful so that they had kings beneath them), the nobility, the free farmers and the bondmen. These classes were held together by clientship, the formalisation of relations between a higher and a lower class individual. There were two kinds of clients, according to the Laws of the seventh or eighth centuries; free and base. Free clients received a stock of cattle from their lord (king or noble) and gave in return a rent in cattle and also their service, either in war or in his retinue, by giving general support, or by occupying an honourable and often hereditary position like steward of his household. Base clients also received cattle from their lord and returned a rent in the same, but as well they gave, not honourable service but food renders and manual labour; base clients were drawn from the ranks of the free farmers. The grants of stock and the rents or renders given in return all presume that both sides of the bargain had farm land; we hear little about the landless from the laws. The aristocrats in this system were freed from concerning themselves directly with arable farming, which was the business of the base clients, but took their share of the produce through renders. Cattle farming was the business of the aristocrat, leaving his time much freer for politics and war.

Men in this society were only individuals in part. Status was to a large extent based, not like modern society on a man's actions or work, but on his pedigree. The land he owned was not fully his, in the sense that he might dispose of it as he wanted without constraint. A man held land as part of his family, and he was expected to manage it as much as a trustee for the family, if he was the head of it, as if he was its owner in the modern sense. Family did not mean only himself, his wife and children; it included all the descendants of his grandfather or great-grandfather (there is a shift from the latter to the former at some time before the eighth century), i.e. his uncles, aunts, cousins and their children. These family groups each had a recognised head, just as the royal family and kingdom had a single king. Any member of a royal family whose grandfather (in earlier times great-grandfather) had been king could claim to succeed as king, so too a family was held together; when the Laws talk of a man, we must often see his kin beside him as well.

If society was based on a hierarchy, so too, as we have seen, is the archaeology. The secular sites must be seen as representing differing levels and status, just as the ecclesiastical ones must. It is not always easy to describe all the stages involved, although the extremes are clear enough. The crannogs with their military siting and the evidence of good jewellery are obviously at one end of the spectrum; great monasteries with high crosses and full *scriptoria* are a world apart from the small graveyards with a church served by a single priest. Raths with one bank should, however, be of lesser status than those with more, except that we know of at least one royal site, Rathmore near Antrim, which has only one bank. The problem is compounded by the existence of the long-lived, raised sites, which seem also to be of higher status. A second source of confusion is the refusal of the men of the period to express their status in their houses. A king might live on a crannog and wear the Tara Brooch in his cloak, but yet have a round house no bigger than a free farmer. This is not to deny that sites should be graded, however, only that we do not know all the rules.

From later sources, some as late as the 17th century, there have been attempts to reconstruct the patterns of landed estates, in the areas where the English settlements from the twelfth century onwards did not penetrate and affect the pattern of land holding. In western Ulster the basic unit seems to be a large one, the ballybetagh, which was divided into four quarters, each of which held four townlands, making sixteen townlands in the ballybetagh, a unit of at least a thousand acres. The subdivisions of this large unit were themselves more than would be needed by a single nuclear family as its farm, so that in units like the townland we may be seeing the land of an extended family, or a group of people, perhaps a number of men of the same status. Some land was set aside for the aristocrats' own personal farms, while some would be of his clients; a king had land, both of his own, which he had before he became king and which he would pass on to his son after his death, and also land attached to the office of king, which passed to his successor. The farming system implied in the Laws certainly seem to distinguish between the divisions between the fields of men of the same kin and the fields of those of different kin. In some cases we can see the large, ballybetagh, unit becoming equated with the parish, when this was introduced from England.

Attempts have been made to correlate the field monuments with such a pattern of land holding, with some success. It has long been noted that the larger monasteries were closely related to the royal families of the kingdoms in which they lay; for example Bangor abbey was associated with the Ulaid kingdoms of Dál nAraidhe and Dál Fiatach, while the personal status of the bishop of a kingdom was said to be equal to its king. Members of the ruling family normally provided the abbot of "their" monastery, and the choir monks, as opposed to the monastic tenants, the "*manaig*", were probably recruited from the aristocratic families. That works for documented sites, but the question is whether we can take this a step further. We want to be able to detect which sites belong to which class and then, by observing the relationships between the sites in the landscape, deduce how the settlement pattern worked. This means both appreciating the sort of land that was being exploited and how the differing sites, and therefore the people who lived in them, related to each other and their differing roles in the settlement system.

A map of County Down shows a good correlation between the higher status secular sites, crannogs, raised and multi-vallate raths, with the parishes; there is usually only one per parish, and the sites are nearly all located on the boundaries (Ill. 6-40). We can see elsewhere areas of land (about the size of a parish and sometimes equated with one) where single-banked "ordinary" raths occupy the central part, with a higher status site on the periphery. This would fit the system of clientship well; the aristocrats were less concerned with direct farming, other than with their cattle herds, but were involved with war. The free farmers were the reverse, concerned with arable farms rather than fighting. It makes environmental sense to put the warriors and their large cattle herds away from the core of good arable land, which was the concern of the base clients. It would be

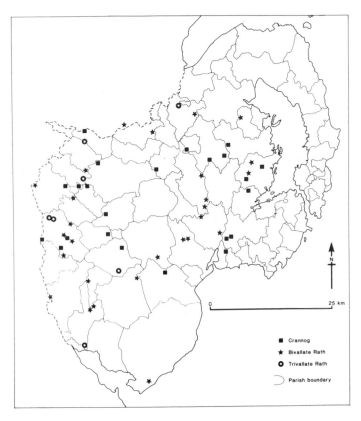

6-40. *Distribution of high status sites in Co. Down, with parish boundaries.*

these smaller communities, or estates, which the lesser church sites were founded to serve; in a few places, there is a correlation between the church sites and these small territories. In these cases the church may be in the core area or in the periphery, presumably depending on whose land it was founded on.

A second possibility is that land was held by groups of men of similar status. If we see rath construction as being confined to certain groups in society, this provides an explanation for the variations in the density of the monuments. This is not a sign of variations in the density of occupation of the land as such, but rather in the distribution of the rath-building class. Areas with few raths might, for example, be the lands farmed directly by the aristocracy or by monastic manaig. To this picture must be added the question of whether the sites stood alone in the countryside, or whether they may have been in some sense centres of population, not all of whom lived within the enclosure.

If the present distribution does come near to being the original one, and that most of the destruction, which has surely taken place, has been in relatively recent times, then the density is not great. There is no consistent equation of one rath to one townland, but in places there are hints of it, and the density is of that order. It is difficult to imagine that the country was occupied so thinly, if a rath were to represent a single family. Pollen analysis and the Laws both indicate a landscape heavily managed by man, with fields and individual holdings up against each other, and the trees that were present not those of dense forest cover, except in a few well-defined areas. The buildings uncovered within raths are inadequate for more than a single nuclear family, not the larger family group who, the Laws tell us, held and worked the land; it is likely that even a single farm would need more buildings, to store equipment and grain, than were provided within a rath. This gives a picture of the countryside where the individual sites that have left their traces above ground, the raths in particular, are the nuclei of a greater number of buildings. We must imagine houses and other buildings, both farm buildings and houses for the wider family circle of the man who lived in the rath.

The single raths in this scheme are the dwelling places of the free farmers in particular. They are gathered together in groups (occupying areas similar to that of the later parish) under the protection of an aristocrat, whose clients they would normally be. Other areas would be set aside for similar groupings of different classes, manaig or bondmen, who were not entitled to construct enclosures around their houses. These small landed groupings are those which continue to emerge in the later records as the ballybetagh estate units or the "tuoghs", small districts often occupied by a single kin group or sept.

A system such as this needs to be demonstrated in a number of places before we can accept whole-heartedly that it is not the result of some fortuitous set of circumstances. Study of the distribution patterns alone, after all, has produced the argument that many raths continued to be constructed long after the twelfth century, which is almost certainly wrong. Again, it is difficult to assess how far the destruction of some of the sites would affect our perception of any such complex pattern of relationships between them. Above all, there is the problem of chronology, which has already been discussed. We must be careful that we are not proposing a pattern of settlement which is made up of individual sites of differing dates, where some sites only came into existence after others were abandoned. As we have seen, the question of chronology is not clear-cut. There are horizons visible, which certainly show that some of the monuments concerned could be constructed at any time between the sixth century (crannogs, dated by dendrochronology) to the later eighth (raths with souterrain ware from the onset). Given that some of the sites appear relatively short lived, it is quite possible that not all the sites which we see today were in existence at the same time in the past.

While we must suspend judgement on this scheme put forward for the monuments of the period, the ideas are valuable for other reasons. The key argument, that the sites had different puposes, because they were built and lived in by different classes of people, is crucial. This gets away from the view, expressed in the 1960s and later, that the various types of secular sites were all versions of the same thing: "the normal single family form of settlement" of the period. Just as the society was arranged in a hierarchy, so too we must expect the sites to be differentiated. Secondly, we are confronted with questions as to the meaning of the presence of the sites; how they related to the farming life of the period, to the holding of land and to the structures of society. The sites are seen, not as isolated monuments in their own right, but as the tips of icebergs. Each one had lands attached which were farmed, and were probably also the focus of an estate. How big this estate or farm was, and how many people were involved in it are unclear, but the question is an important one if we are to understand what the presence of a site meant at the time it was being used.

The context of Ulster settlement

Recent work in Britain has tended to emphasise the difference between the larger villages, typically one per parish, which form the basis for the pattern of estates and settlements from the tenth century onwards, and the small hamlets of the eighth century and before. This has been aligned with a system, known as "extended estates", which is found underlying some of the eleventh century English arrangements, and which has also been found in Wales and Scotland. In this system, smaller units than the later parishes were occupied by groups of people who owed food renders and traditional services at the estate centre: the estate might include a large number of these smaller units (the vills) and cover a wide area, up to fifteen or twenty square miles. In Wales these vills were actually occupied by hereditary groups, some bond and some free, with traditional services, sometimes manual labour, sometimes skilled. It is not difficult to see parallels with the sort of scheme of settlement proposed above for Ulster, with the estates of the aristocracy composed of their own lands and those of their clients, which were not single farms but groups of kin, represented by the man living in the rath. Likewise, the idea of tracts of land devoted to different classes of people, some tied hereditarily to their vill, would fit well with the variations of density of monument types, if they represent different classes of people on the land. It is traditional to contrast the dispersed settlement patterns of the "Celtic" world with the nucleated pattern of the "Germanic" world; it may well be that there was not that much difference in the seventh or eighth centuries, any more than there was a great difference between their art styles.

This leads us to a consideration of the uniformity of culture of the period within Ulster, and to whether there are features in Ulster distinctive to the province as opposed to the rest of Ireland, the British Isles or Europe. The clearest evidence of an artifact which has a limited distribution and use within Ulster is pottery. Why souterrain ware should be restricted, and for so long, is a puzzle. In the absence of full mapping of sites, it is difficult to write with confidence about the possibility of differential distributions of sites, but there are some hints. The distribution of crannogs is obviously constrained to lakes, but within this constraint, they do not seem evenly distributed. Even allowing for its numerous lakes, Fermanagh seems to have more than its share of crannogs. Enclosures were also made of dry stone walls, of the same general size as raths, the so-called cashels: again, like crannogs, while they are are mainly found in areas of extensive stone outcropping, they are neither confined to those areas, nor have all such areas cashels rather than raths. Within the general category of raths, there are differences, which may also be regional; for example, the raths of north Antrim seem to be rather smaller in diameter than the norm.

It is not easy to point to features which are at the same time found throughout Ulster, but not in the rest of Ireland, or vice versa. Ogham stones are certainly rare in Ulster, but they are mainly confined to Munster rather than north Leinster or Connacht. The Ulster raised raths do not seem to be common in southern Leinster, but whether this is a feature of Ulster or Leinster is unclear. These phenomena must be put against the many features which are common to the whole island, the basic types of both artifacts and sites. There were no raths or crannogs in Anglo-Saxon England, just as the Anglo-Saxons did not wear any form of penannular brooch. There is a distinctly Irish material culture in the post-Roman period, which is closer to the cultures of Wales or Scotland than that of England, in spite of the connections which we have already noted. The differences within this Irish culture are probably not provincial in scale but local and regional, like the distribution of souterrain ware. It is significant that it is in the humbler sites and artifacts that we find these differences, as opposed to the culture of the elite. The more distant connections and borrowings, along with the wider cutural unity were more to be found among the kings, aristocrats and upper clergy than among the free farmers.

Ulster and the Vikings: invasions or colonization?

Our discussion has now taken us well into the 9th century. The 9th and 10th centuries, right across northern Europe are often known as the Age of the Vikings, and it is time to consider the impact of the Vikings on Ulster archaeology. Before we do we must summarise our historical knowlege of them, and perhaps clear up one or two common misconceptions. There was no such thing as a political unit, kingdom or tribe, of Vikings; this is the name, given by their enemies and later writers, to the bands of Scandinavians who roved across the seas during this period. The men who came to Ireland were in origin basically Norse, as opposed for example to the attackers of southern England and northern France, who were basically Danish; in neither case were the groups homogenous. In particular, the Vikings of Ireland may well have been born and raised in the western and northern Isles of Scotland rather than in Norway itself. The numbers of raiders was probably never large, groups of a few hundred at most would seem to have been the norm. Given their mobility, derived from their fine ships, they could attack swiftly and effectively before any superior force could be mustered against them; nor was a force of 500 men small by any standards in 9th century Europe.

The Viking attacks were not chronologically homogenous, but varied considerably in intensity over time. We may distinguish four periods of them. In the first, from the 790s to c. 835, there were purely coastal hit and run raids during the summer, at a rate of less than one per year somewhere in Ulster. From the mid 830s for some 50 years, the frequency of raids increased as did their nature: from 840-841, there were Viking forces spending the winter in Ulster at semi-permanent bases, and raiding deep inland. Towards the end of the 9th century, in the 30 or 40 years centered on 900, the attacks were few as men were drawn away from Ireland by the major land seizures in England and northern France, and the settlement of Iceland. A second period of intense warfare lasted from the 920s to the end of the 10th century.

One thing is clear: that the whole of Ulster was not subjected to a constant state of burning, rapine and pillage for the two hundred years of the Viking invasions. Nor was Ulster of the 9th century innocent of wars and violence from its own inhabitants without the teaching of the Vikings. Beyond this lies uncertainty. Historians are quite undecided on what story the documentary evidence tells about the effect of the Vikings on Ulster or Ireland. Did they seize land in Ulster as well as raid? Was the violence of these wars so destructive as to alter the nature of society as a whole? If not, might some part of it be particularly affected, such as the Church? Inevitably, there has been a tendency to appeal to the evidence of archaeology to help resolve these, and other, questions. In one sense this is wrong, for archaeological evidence does not usually bear well on questions about political events of the past; its strength lies with longer term processes of economic or social trends. Excavation of a church site may well show that it was destroyed by fire; it may with luck give a date to this event, let us say in the 9th century; there may be evidence that the fire was not an accident but was accompanied by a massacre or deliberate destruction. None of this tells us, of course, who was responsible or why, the two question which we must answer if we are to relate it to the work of Vikings, nor does a single site tell us if this was a common event, or if it had a lasting effect on society as a whole.

This is no reason for refusing to look at the archaeological evidence in the light of the known historical position. We might expect to find evidence of two kinds; either positive traces of intrusive material brought into Ulster by Vikings, or the sites they may have occupied, or else, negatively, in the disruption of traditions of crafts or sites of the period before the Viking raids. From these we may be able to suggest something of the nature of the period. In making any suggestions, we must be wary of distinguishing between the date of the sites, objects or events which we may observe, and attribute, to the relevant period and the involvement of actual Vikings in the explanation we give.

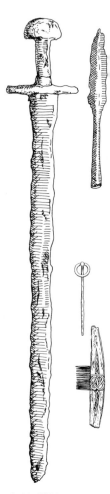

Direct evidence of Viking presence is rare. In spite of an annal which claims that in 866 there were Viking fortresses along the north coast of Ulster, there is no site yet found which looks like a Viking habitation. This is not because, as in England for example, the Viking houses were so like those of the Irish that we could not tell them apart, for the two are quite different. There are perhaps five recorded Viking burials recorded from Ulster, identifiable because of the pagan rite of burying grave goods with the body and from the nature of those goods themselves. They are all along the coasts, except for the least well-known, near Banagher in Co. Londonderry. The best known was uncovered in 1840 while workmen were building the railway along the shore near Larne (Ill. 6-41). It was the burial of a man around 900, put in a grave along with his sword and spear, of Viking type, but also with a bone comb and a cloak pin of Irish type, a ringed pin. The few burials in Ulster (and in Ireland in general outside Dublin) is in marked contrast with the western Isles of Scotland where a number of sites with Viking houses have been excavated, and some 40 graves discovered; the Isle of Man has also produced both sites and graves in larger numbers than Ulster. Neither of these two areas are particularly fertile, and neither has seen much more intensive archaeological work than Ulster. By the end of the 10th century there were Viking towns established elsewhere in Ireland, notably at Dublin which may also have generated the considerable 9th century cemetery up the Liffey at Islandbridge/Kilmainham, but there is no trace yet known of such a town in Ulster. The archaeological evidence for any sort of permanent Viking settlement in Ulster is very slim.

6-41. Viking grave goods from Larne.

Individual Viking objects are difficult to identify. Their weapons, iron axes and swords, were adopted by the Irish and used long after the Vikings were gone, so that their discovery tells us little about a Viking presence. The Viking battle-axe in particular became by the 12th century, something which all Irish fighting men carried about with them all the time. In the West Highlands of Scotland it continued to the 16th century as a principle weapon, used in Ireland by the Scots mercenaries. Mail body armour, however, the Irish did not adopt apparently, nor the bow and arrow, until the 13th century. Surprisingly few axes survive. We can deal with one myth here; the horned helmets attributed to Vikings, and so beloved of cartoonists and Tourist Boards. Very few Vikings could afford to wear any helmet, and none had horns on them. The idea goes back to 18th century discoveries of helmets with horns in both England and Denmark. Ignorant of the true date of the helmets (they are of the pre-Roman Iron Age), scholars at the time not unnaturally but quite wrongly jumped to the conclusion that an item of war-gear, found in both Denmark and England, must be Viking.

The impact of the Vikings

The negative aspects of the Vikings in archaeology, the interruption of traditions, are by their nature difficult either to identify or to attribute to the Vikings. In documentary sources, the 9th century sees the last of the production of Laws, either secular or ecclesiastical. In archaeology, this has its counterpart in the apparent end of the production of decorated manuscripts; after the Armagh works mentioned earlier (Maelbrigte Mac Durnan died in 927) comes a gap of some 150 years, until about 1070, before we have surviving decorated manuscripts again. By the early 12th century there are dated free-standing crosses elsewhere in Ireland, although not from Ulster. If the arguments we have outlined above on the dating of the high crosses of Ulster and the rest of Ireland are correct, there is a gap in this craft as well, from the end of the 9th century perhaps to the beginning of the 12th.

6-42. Silver bossed penannula
brooch (diam. 10.3 cms

The story of the upper class metalwork in the 9th and 10th centuries in Ulster is a complex one, with three basic components: objects continuing at least in part an Irish tradition, objects of a Viking one, and imported English coins which have both an economic dimension and are the basis of a chronology, for they are found in hoards with the other two types. The first consists of ecclesiastical objects, such as the croziers already noted above, and various forms of penannular brooch, normally of silver. The decoration of the croziers and the most notable of the forms of penannular brooch, the so-called bossed penannulars, is based on the division of the surface into geometric cells, each containing an animal or a simple piece of interlace (Ill. 6-42). This is related to the style of decoration in use during the later 9th century in the south of England, the so-called Trewhiddle style. The 10th century also sees the production of a few massive but rather plain silver brooches, the thistle brooches, named after the decoration at the ends of the ring of the penannular shape. The Viking objects are rings, usually from their size called armlets, of two main types: those of flat rectangular cross section like a watch strap, and those of more or less square cross section (Ill. 6-43). The decoration of both, if it exists, is relatively simple. None of these objects would seem to be produced after the middle or later part of the 10th centuries. Indeed there is then a gap in the record of fine metalwork until the beginning of the 11th century.

Both of these groups of material are interlinked, both by being of silver and by being found together in hoards, either with or without coins. About a dozen coin hoards of this date have been found in Ulster and a further eight without any coins, more than in Connacht, but a similar number to those from Munster; Leinster has produced many more, while the Irish ones belong to the whole series of contemporary hoards found right across northern Europe, with the same mixture of coins and silver objects. These hoards are clearly related to the Vikings, because of their distribution; bossed penannular brooches were probably made in Ireland but they have been found in hoards buried in northern England, the Viking parts of Scotland, Iceland and Norway. The pattern of Irish finds of hoards differs from that of England and Scotland. In England the hoards are predominantly of coins throughout the 9th and 10th centuries and their numbers correlate well over time with periods of intense fighting with the Vikings. In Scotland hoards are small in size and contain objects as well as coins through the period. In Ireland, the hoards are sometimes very large (the two largest associated with Irish Vikings contained in one case, forty kilos of silver or, in the other, five kilos of gold) and see a shift from the 9th century hoards of objects and coins to the 10th century when hoards purely of coins are more common. Within Ireland, however, this is a feature mainly of the many Leinster hoards, and is not so clear in Ulster.

These hoards obviously represented great wealth, and show that Ireland as a whole was drawing in silver on a scale previously unknown; silver from the late 8th century was the basic bullion metal of the whole of northern Europe. Much of this wealth was drawn to eastern Ireland, around the

6-43. Viking silver armlet from Roosky, Co. Donegal.

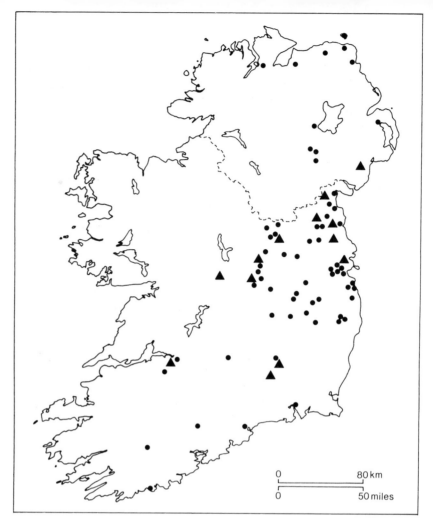

6-44. *Distribution of Viking period coin hoards in Ireland.*

Viking entrepot of Dublin, but some filtered north to Ulster (Ill. 6-44). It was not wealth confined to Vikings, however, even if they were the men who brought it into the country. The penannular brooches were an Irish style and most, if not all, were made in Ireland; some must have been made for Irishmen to wear: the croziers were made for Irish churches not for pagan Vikings. The ornamental style used relates to that of another kingdom attacked by Vikings, King Alfred's Wessex, not to Viking ornament. The silver wealth was drawn in presumably in exchange for an Irish export in demand in the rest of Europe. The only such product that Ireland had was people, exported as slaves, the capture of whom is a constant theme of the annalistic descriptions of Viking raids. This was a trade in which all of Ireland participated.

Of sites, the best dated are the mills, because of dendrochronology. Twenty four have now been dated from the whole of Ireland, all lying within the range of 630 to 940; five of these are from Ulster. These include one of the two latest examples, that from Rossory, Co. Fermanagh, dated to 926 +/- 9. It would appear that no more mills were constructed in Ulster or Ireland after the middle of the 10th century. Against this there are examples of individual sites which must have been occupied throught the 9th and 10th centuries. Ballynarry, Co. Down, excavated by Brian Davison, had a history of occupation which ran from a period with apparently only plain souterrain ware through ones with decorated ware, to the 13th century. Less clear examples are Gransha in Co. Down, excavated by Chris Lynn, or Sallagh and Killealy (or Tully) raths in Co. Antrim, excavated respectively by Oliver Davies and Alan Harper.

Allied to this one can cite examples of documentary continuity for individual sites through the period concerned. Dunseverick and Rathmore are both forts associated with minor kingdoms in the 7th or 8th centuries, which emerge as the centres of English estates in the 13th century; Ballylough in north Antrim has a crannog beside the centre of an estate in existence from the 13th century to the present day. These may be examples of an illusory continuity, that purely of the name of the place which lasted even if no-one was actually living there, but they are suggestive. By definition, the documented sites and those with lengthy occupation leading to the formation of a mound site are both likely to be upper class sites. It may be that continuity was confined to them or it may be that they are simply the only ones we can point to.

A number of souterrains survived long enough to be blocked by material which contained 13th century English pottery. Souterrains are also mentioned in accounts of the late 12th century English invasion as places of refuge or concealment of goods during the fighting. When unenclosed sites have been excavated, usually because of the souterrain that formed part of them and which was discovered by accident in recent times, the houses have been square and the pottery associated with them has been decorated souterrain ware: examples are Antiville, Ballywee or Craig Hill in Co. Antrim (excavated by Dudley Waterman and Chris Lynn). It is possible that these sites should be linked with the "normal" raths of the earlier period; that what we are seeing is a continuity of the type of house and much of the material culture of that class of site and person, but without the enclosure. If so this sets up a distinction between these lesser sites and the long-lived enclosed sites of the upper classes.

It might be expected that the church sites would show clear evidence of an interruption of construction and occupation during the period of the Viking raids. After all, it is from church sources that we have our most dramatic accounts of the ferocity of the invasions. In fact this is not so. There are no archaeologically dated churches earlier than the 12th century in Ulster or Ireland, although there are plenty of candidates, usually on the basis of "this is a simple or even crude structure, therefore it must be early", a well-known fallacy. However, from documentary evidence we know that there were stone churches from the late 8th century onwards in Ireland; one at Armagh is referred to in an annal of 788. Building in stone and mortar seems to have been continued from then on. The scale of the

6-45. Antrim round tower.

buildings was almost certainly small, to judge from examples from the rest of Ireland which may be 11th century; under 20 metres long for a cathedral. They were also apparently devoid of ornament, which is why they cannot be dated.

In contrast to the simplicity of the churches are the round towers. The first reference to one in the annals is to the example at Slane, a bell tower used as a refuge for monks and valuables when it was burned by Vikings in 948. The tower at Devenish, however was not built until the 12th century, so the type was long lived. The towers were free standing within the monastic enclosures. The two complete Ulster examples, at Antrim and Devenish, give a good idea of their appearance; 25 to 35 metres high, delicately tapering to a conical top, and with a succession of wooden floors inside (Ill. 6-45). The Irish name for these towers is to be translated as bell towers, and this was probably their main purpose; a hand bell could be rung from the top windows to summon monks for services, etc.; their use as a secure storage place and refuge was probably a secondary purpose.

The source of the inspiration to build them was probably the 9th century churches of Europe, which saw the development of high round towers at key points to act as stair turrets but also to emphasise the height of the building. Certainly the Irish towers must be seen as status symbols for the monasteries who erected them, meant to be seen from afar proclaiming the presence and wealth of the community. This would be curious if they were a response to the fear of a Viking raid, for a tower invites attention and the wooden floors inside a thin stone tower must have acted as a chimney when attacked, as indeed it did at Slane. The site of Nendrum makes the point well (Ill. 6-22). Here is a site of the 7th and 8th centuries set on an island in Strangford Lough which was used as a Viking base, yet it was able at some point in the 10th or 11th centuries to put up a round tower. Its stump led to the identification of the site in the 19th century; the complete tower would have attracted more unwelcome attention in the 10th. If any monastery should have been destroyed by the Vikings it should have been Nendrum.

Of the humbler crafts, archaeology informs us about pottery and about lower grade metal working. In the latter, the production of iron tools went on as far as we can see unchanged, as one would expect because it is difficult to change the design of iron tools. The humbler pins for cloaks, made from bronze or brass continued to be made, often decorated with a ring through the upper end (Ill. 6-28). These ringed pins are indeed frequent finds in Viking burials of the Irish Sea area, like the one at Larne, and up into the western Isles of Scotland. Again the distribution of an artefact crosses the political divide between Irish and Viking. The main problem of souterrain ware, as discussed above, is its stability of production and distribution. Apart from the small amount of decoration added at some point, perhaps the 9th century, it carries on unchanged from the 8th to late 12th centuries.

Does any of this shed light on the impact of the Vikings on Ulster? The paucity of burials is surely significant and allows us to see documentary references to Viking forts in Ulster as being at best short-lived and probably purely as raiding bases, not full settlements. The pattern of archaeological dislocation, if there is any, points much more to the 10th rather than the 9th century. The evidence for dislocation is very selective. Traditional ecclesiastical crafts decline, such as manuscript painting, and (less certainly) stone carving. But stone building produced the first real surviving stone architecture during the period, the round towers, significantly derived from Europe. There is no evidence here of a wholesale decline in the Church; some sites clearly prospered at least in the long term. Likewise some secular sites continued in use, and we can assume that their estates and owners did so too. The most intriguing evidence is that of the mills and the apparent abandonment of them in the 10th century after three hundred years of building them. It is interesting that this hiatus appears to coincide with the dislocation of the fine metal work.

The abandoning of mills must surely indicate a decline in the growing of corn. The only likely way that this would come about, other than the large-scale import of corn from elsewhere which was technologically impossible in the 10th century, is if the population declined. We can rule out any question of climatic change affecting corn growing, because the 10th century saw an increase in corn growing elsewhere in northern Europe, and weather patterns are not so discriminating. It is here that we must recall that the period between 850 and 1000 saw much silver come into Ireland, presumably in return for the export of slaves. While the Vikings may have been the medium for this trade, it is clear that the wealth also reached Irishmen, who must therefore have participated in the business. The section of society who would be involved would be the fighting men, kings and aristocrats, to whom the Viking network of trade and communications now offered the chance of selling many more slaves than they could have afforded to keep in their own kingdom. War was now profitable. The evidence is, however, that this profitability may not have been long lasting. Too much slaving may have reduced the population severely, enough to affect the pattern of agriculture. In such a world, the losers would be the lesser men without the ability to fight back, and who would have to seek protection from the lords, with a consequent loss of status. Lords' power grew at the expense of their clients; perhaps the "normal" univallate raths were victims of this period.

Craftsmanship after the Vikings

Whatever the dislocation of the Viking period, it is of course obvious that Irish society did not succumb to it; otherwise, the Vikings would have been able to take more land than they did. By the end of the 10th century, a new and more ruthlessly powerful form of kingship was being evolved in Ireland, typified by the career of Brian Boru, who died in 1014, or in Ulster by the kings of Cenel Eogain, who ruled from Inishowen to Armagh. One of the curious features of the 11th and 12th centuries, however, is a dearth of surviving objects of secular display which we would expect, especially the high class metal work such as jewellery. On the other hand we have a series of ecclesiastical items, showing that the skills and patronage were there. A high proportion of these are shrines, a number of which bear inscriptions recording the names of the donors or the abbots of the recipient monasteries. Some at least of the royal wealth was directed into these gifts, rather than into endowments which might have been expected to produce more ritual vessels such as chalices or other altar pieces. These inscriptions provide a reasonably secure chronological framework, all the more needed than usual for this is not a period when there was a single uniform style prevailing. Instead we are faced with craftsmen who were prepared to borrow features from a number of different traditions from outside Ireland, while at the same time apparently harking back to the achievements of the 8th and earlier 9th centuries. Interestingly one of the most common sources of ideas was the Viking world, at a period in which their main political influence was in decline.

The first way this shows in the rejection of the monochrome tradition of the 10th century with its heavy reliance on silver. The story begins with a shrine from one of the most prominent monasteries in the archaeology of the period, Devenish in Lough Erne. The shrine is for a Gospel, named after the patron saint and founder of the abbey, St. Molaise, the Soiscel Molaise, and an inscription on it records that it was made for Cenfaelad, abbot between 1001 and 1025 (Ill. 6-46). It preserves a fragment of an earlier shrine, while the 11th century decoration is of two types. On the one hand are panels of gold filigree and animal interlace, which surround the main figures. The design of the interlace and the execution of the filigree are both crude, particularly the thickness of the latter when it is compared with the fine work of the 8th century. Yet they appear to look consciously back to that period, and, however clumsily, seem to be a genuine attempt at revival. The main figures are quite different. They are in high relief and well modelled: their design is assured, effective and original.

In 1090 the annals record that relics of Columba were sent from the O'Donnell king of Cenel Connaill (now roughly represented by Co. Donegal) to Kells in Meath, along with 120 ounces of silver, presumably in order that they should be enshrined. A somewhat later text names three of the principal relics of Columba whose possession was said to be crucial to the success of the O'Donnells of Cenel Connaill: the Cathach (a 6th or 7th century Psalter), a bell and the 'Misach', which was presumably another manuscript. The shrine of the Cathach survives, with an inscription recording that it was made for Cathbar O'Donnell (king of Cenel Connaill, who died in 1106) and the abbot of Kells between 1062 and 1098: it is almost certain that this was one of the relics sent in 1090. It has been much damaged and repaired but some of its decoration is still visible. The 'Misach' shrine is also still in existence, although also much damaged. Both of the shrines have ornament in bronze and silver, in particular in plaques of silver with either open-work decoration or insets of black niello (silver sulphide). The designs are not in origin Irish, but Scandinavian, with an interlace of animals whose limbs and features dissolve into a pattern of foliage motifs, fronds and tendrils wrapping around themselves and the animals' bodies. This is a style known to modern scholars of Scandinavian art as Ringerike; it is in part an adaptation of 10th century English style to Viking taste. Its use in shrines of the 1090s here represents a rather out-dated use of the style.

6-46. Figure from the Soiscel Molaise.

The shrine of St. Patrick's bell from Armagh was made at much the same time (Ill. 6-47). It carries an inscription recording that it was made for Domnaill Mac Lochlainn, king of Cenel Eoghain from 1094 to 1121, for Domnaill Mac Amhalgadha (or Mac Auley) abbot of Armagh between 1091 and 1105, and Cathalan O'Maelchalland, steward of Armagh, by Cuduilg and his sons. It was therefore made between 1094 and 1105 or very soon after. Its survival is a remarkable story in its own right and one which sheds light on the sructure of an Irish monastery. The shrine continued to be guarded by the family of the steward named in the inscription; after the 17th century and the Dissolution of the monastery,

6-47. St. Patrick's bell shrine.

they still held on to it, although they changed their name to Mulholland. The last keeper was a schoolmaster, one of whose pupils was Adam McLean, a Protestant who became a merchant in Belfast. Mulholland was implicated in the rebellion of 1798, but McLean was able to intervene on his behalf and save his life. Mulholland died childless and in return on his deathbed told McLean where his most precious possession was buried in his garden. This was the bronze and silver gilt shrine of an iron bell.

Its design is superb, but the techniques for its production are also of interest. Part of the decoration is of small interlace panels, composed of lines of a remarkable sort of imitation filigree, made of gold foil wrapped around thick beaded brass wires, to give the appearance of the fine gold grains of filigree. The main decoration is of thin, elongated animals coiling in spirals around themselves and within the coils of even thinner, wiry snakes. The design is a combination of bold curves and diagonals, both usually composed of two or more lines each, which run in and out of each other, while the whole, panel by panel, is strictly organised and symmetrical. Technically, as shown by the filigree or the gilding, it may not be the equal of the masterpieces of the 8th or 9th centuries, but in the virtuosity of its design it is. The art style, like those of the Cathach or Misach shrines is Scandinavian in origin, but of the later so-called Urnes style rather than Ringerike.

The contrast between the Cathach and Misach shrines in their handling of the Ringerike ornament and the treatment of Urnes style on the St. Patrick's shrine is marked. The first are good straightforward examples of borrowing a foreign style; they were a little out of date perhaps but are capable reproductions both of the individual motifs and of the ideas behind them. When Cuduilg made the Armagh shrine, however, he took the

236

motifs of Urnes style, the great beast entangled in the coils of a wiry snake, and made something quite different out of them. In the 8th and 9th centuries, Irish art had been marked, at its best, by a great attention to discipline and symmetry in its designs. Viking art, by contrast, was barbaric and rejected both symmetry and blank spaces; every square centimetre of an object had to be covered with ornament. Urnes style is unique among the Scandinavian tradition in making some attempt to control this. Cuduilg picked this up but carried it much further and gave to the Viking style the control of the Irish art of the pre-Viking period. He was not alone in this. In Connacht, the craftsmen working for Turlough O'Connor produced the cross of Cong and St. Manchan's shrine in a similar symmetrical and disciplined Irish adaptation of Urnes style.

These three or four objects are hardly the sum total of surviving metal work from Ulster in the period. At least one other major shrine, the Breac Maodhóg, comes from Co. Cavan and may be a product of the same tradition of craftsmanship as the Soiscel Molaise from Devenish, although a hundred years later (Ill. 6-48). It has the same figures in high relief and the same skill shown in modelling their drapery and features. Yet ideas from outside Ireland have also been noted; the best parallels for some of the figures' stances and for the fronds they hold are from western France of the 11th century. It may be that in this we have a hint of at least two different traditions or groups of workers: Cuduilg of Armagh was certainly not using the style of the two shrines from the Erne. Whether these were coherently different traditions or simply random results of the chance that the two similar objects survive from nearby places, it is true that there was not a single line of the development of the craft. The craftsmen of Ulster were working to provide their patrons with objects which would be impressive, but were doing so without a clear idea of what such a thing should look like. They borrowed motifs from abroad and combined them with an attempt to revive the much older styles rather than the work of the 10th century.

The work of the great monastic craft of manuscript illumination tells a similar story. There is, as we have noted a clear gap not only in their style but even in their very production. From Ireland as a whole, about twenty manuscripts have survived from between 1070 and 1170; only two are known from the century before. We have two manuscripts from the Armagh scriptorium, both small Gospels of a type which goes back to the 9th century, one of which can be dated to 1138. There are also a number which appear to have been produced in the east of Ulster, possibly associated with the revival of Bangor under St. Malachy after 1124. In all we see a mixture of traditional forms of books and handwriting with new decorative motifs. These are principally found in the decoration of the capital letters, rather than in the full page pictures. They consist of beasts drawn to the shape of the actual letter, surrounded by foliage and interlace of Ringerike type.

6-48. Figure from the Breac Maodhog.

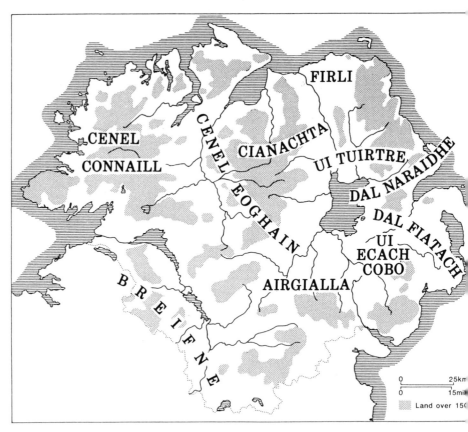

6-49. Political map of 12th century Ulster.

The new kings

The Viking raids and any attempts at colonisation were defeated by the kings of Ulster and Ireland of the 10th century. As has been pointed out, the 10th, 11th and 12th centuries saw the kings in Ireland acquire new powers. In several kingdoms the old customs of alternating succession between different families was suppressed by one of them excluding the others from the kingship. A whole series of provincial kings attempted to make themselves king of Ireland, in the teeth of opposition from the other provinces. Within Ulster, it was the kings of Cenel Eoghain (drawn from two lines of the larger family, known from the 11th century as O'Neills and Mac Lochlainns) who were the most powerful, controlling most of the present counties of Londonderry, Tyrone and Armagh. They alone of the Ulster kings contended for the high kingship of Ireland. They were normally opposed by the two next most powerful kingdoms, the Cenel Connaill (O'Donnell), covering approximately modern Co. Donegal, and the Ulaid of the east, roughly the modern counties of Antrim and Down (I11. 6-49). The battles were fiercer than they were in earlier centuries, and the wars were marked by a new feature, attempts to divide the kingdoms of enemies and to control the succession to the kingship, even replacing existing kings.

More powerful kings might be expected to produce new kinds of centres for their kingship. We have sites which can be linked to the kingdoms of Cenel Eoghain and Ulaid. The former were always termed the kings of Ailech. This has been identified since the 19th century at least with the hill-top fort known as the Grianán of Ailech just over the border from Derry in Co. Donegal. As it now stands this is a strong fort of dry-stone construction set in a larger circular enclosure, defined by very low banks. The fort in particular owes much of its present appearance to 19th century restoration work, although there is no reason to think that it was very different originally. As such it is a completely traditional form of site for the 10th and 11th centuries when Ailech appears as the royal fort. The identification of the Grianán with the royal centre of Ailech may not be correct; the name of Ailech is now represented by Elagh, a group of townlands at the foot of Grianán hill, centred on the site of Elaghmore. Here the ruins of a later (13th or 14th century) castle occupy a low rock outcrop or stack, which may be the real site of Ailech.

The association of the kings of Cenel Eoghain with the fort of Tullahogue in Co. Tyrone dates only from the 11th century, when they expanded their power south-eastwards over the Sperrins (Ill. 6-50). In the absence of excavation, it is impossible to say whether the existing structure was built by them or by the family whom they displaced in the area, the O'Flynns of Uí Tuirtre. It is set on a prominent local hill and has the superficial appearance of a rath: there are two banks of normal height, broken by an entrance, and the area enclosed is similar to that of a rath. The banks are set wide apart, with a flat area or wide, shallow ditch between them. It

6-50. *Tullahogue.*

appears in later documentation as the traditional crowning place for the kings of Cenel Eoghain, but the immediate land around was not directly farmed by them. Instead their main estates seem to have lain a little to the south while the site and lands of Tullahogue were occupied by one of their principal supporting families, the O'Hagans. Nearby lies the small enclosure of Donaghrisk, the traditional burial place of the O'Hagans. They played a prominent part in the inauguration ceremonies of the Cenel Eoghain and it is typical of this new kingship of the 12th century to have such a permanent relationship between the overking and such a family. In the seventh century, the O'Hagans would have considered themselves as kings in their own right, but now they were much more formally subordinate.

After 972 the kingship of eastern Ulster, the Ulaid who were the Ulstermen par excellance, was confined to the family of Dál Fiatach, whose lands lay in eastern and northern Co.Down. To the south they had a centre at what is now known as Downpatrick, where there are two monuments which are dated to the period before the English invasion of 1177. The first is the monastery on the hill-top now occupied by the Church of Ireland cathedral. It first appears specifically as a monastery in the 8th century, and excavation in the past few years has shown that the enclosure, formerly thought to be a prehistoric hillfort, dates from the time of the monastery; souterrain ware was found in its silting. North-east of the monastery hill lies a very strongly defended enclosure, known now as the English Mount, occupying a promontory which used to project out into the marshes of the River Quoile (Ill. 6-51). Historical sources of the 11th and 12th centuries show that there were two sites at Downpatrick, a monastery

6-51. English Mount, Downpatrick: defences.

and a secular centre of the kings of Dál Fiatach. The English Mount is a large site, an oval of 100 by 175 metres, with a massive bank and ditch especially on the line of the approach with no break for an entrance; this is no rath. It contains a motte castle which has every appearance of being inserted into the pre-existing enclosure at the end of the 12th century, after the English occupation. It is only reasonable to identify the strongly fortified original enclosure with the Dál Fiatach centre of the 11th and 12th centuries.

In the north of Co. Down lies the other main Dál Fiatach, and Ulaid, centre of the 11th or 12th centuries, Duneight. It is set on the highest point of the low bluff on the side of the Ravarnet river, cut off from the easiest line of approach by two ditches; the inner ditch at least was backed by a bank. This site, too, saw the addition of a motte, or castle mound, in the late 12th century, when the bank was apparently widened. The area enclosed was much smaller than that of the English Mount; if we assume that the motte was set within the enclosure, its dimensions would be roughly 45 by 30 metres within the bank. This is not much bigger than a rath; the main difference lies in the nature of the defences. The bank had been ploughed down severely in recent times, but the ditch survived, about four metres deep below the surface of the enclosure. The entrance was also carefully guarded by a palisade lining the gap in the bank. Both of these features, the depth of the ditch and the palisade set Duneight apart from any rath.

Duneight was attacked in 1010 by the king of Cenel Eoghain, and fighting between his predecessor and the Ulaid in 1003 took place beside it. The 1010 entry is interesting, not only because it identifies Duneight as the goal of a raid aimed at the Ulaid, but also because the Cenel Eoghain are said to have both burned the fort of Duneight and broken down its township. The fort clearly did not stand alone as an isolated settlement. The story of Duneight reflects the pressure applied right through the period by the kings of Cenel Eoghain eastwards on the Ulaid, which appears to have been reflected in their centres of power. While those of Cenel Eoghain appear to belong with the traditional idea of Irish royal places, the Ulaid ones are much more strongly fortified. In a different social scene, they might be termed castles. Most unfortunately the excavations at Duneight shed little light on the interior of the fort, either on the king's house, or on the number of people who lived in the fort with him, or on his economic resources.

The story of secular power in the 10th to 12th centuries is one of a concentration on fewer and more powerful kings; the religious world saw similar developments. From the 12th century come historical references to monasteries as the centres of more population than their own monks. In Armagh, fires destroyed three streets in 1112, the abbot's great house and twenty other houses in 1116, and four streets with several churches in 1166. At Derry a reforming abbot wished to make an enclosure around St. Columba's church in 1162; to do so he destroyed eighty houses. At no site

6-52. Kilmore door.

have such remains been identified in the ground, although excavation by Chris Lynn along the line of Scotch Street in Armagh has uncovered the debris of an extensive area of small scale industry outside the line of the inner monastic enclosure (Ill. 6-21). It stretched over an earlier graveyard and may date from the 10th or 11th century, representing, perhaps the sort of expansion of the settlement which led to the existence of streets and houses by the 12th century. It has been suggested that these large monastic settlements acted as the towns, anticipating the craft and commercial roles of those founded by the English after 1177.

The link of political and religious centres is also seen in the rise or decline of individual sites. Downpatrick was closely associated with the Dál Fiatach line of Ulaid kings as we have seen, and it profited by the association. So too, apparently did Nendrum, at least in the 10th and 11th centuries, to judge by the presence of the round tower. By contrast in Co. Down were the old famous sites of Bangor and Movilla. They lay to the north east of the county and had been associated with the rival line to the Dál Fiatach within Ulaid, the Dál nAraide. The period which saw the rise of Downpatrick saw their decline, so that in the 12th century, Bangor required to be re-founded by St. Malachy.

6-53. Head carved on Devenish round tower.

The reform of the Church and Irish Romanesque building

We have seen the prosperity of the monasteries of the Erne valley expressed in the production of metal work; it is also shown in buildings of stone from the 12th century. The Church of Ireland cathedral of Kilmore in Co. Cavan has built into a vestry on its north side the most complete example of an architectural feature of the period (Ill. 6-52). It is a door said to have come from the abbey on Trinity Island in nearby Lough Oughter. There are four arches set in diminishing size within each other, all four decorated and the outer three standing on stone shafts attached to the wall. The range of motifs used to decorate the arches, chevrons (zig-zag) aligned with the wall or set at right angles to it, pellets, human and animal heads are typical of the period. The only other contemporary door from Ulster, surviving complete, is the plain example of the church at White Island in lower Lough Erne; this is the church into which the remarkable figure sculptures were built. At Devenish are two buildings with decoration of the 12th century. Around the top of the round tower is a frieze with heads in high relief, their beards and hair running into interlacing patterns (Ill. 6-53). The little church known as St. Molaise's house has the bases of its angles carved with foliage designs. Away from south-west Ulster, there are only fragments of such work, loose carved stones at Downpatrick, Inch (Ill. 6-54) or Killyleagh in Co. Down or from Armagh.

The work is typical of the buildings of the Irish Romanesque style. This drew mainly on the early 12th century work from England, but with many changes; it is first seen in the remarkable Cormac's Chapel at Cashel, built between 1127 and 1135. The inspiration and some of the motifs may come from Norman England, notably the chevron, but Irish Romanesque is not a recreation of English work. The decoration is confined to individual elements, a door, chancel arch or windows, of what remained a small building. Aisles, transepts or tiers of arcades and galleries form no part of the Irish buildings, unlike the vast Romanesque churches of England or the Continent; they remain in essence small rectangular boxes without spatial or structural elaboration. What the Irish craftsmen did was to take some of the decorative ideas from England, with some from France and Germany as well, and apply them to their own structures; the resources, either of the numbers of skilled men or materials, apart from anything else precluded any other course of action.

Cormac MacCarthy, who gave the chapel at Cashel, was king of Munster; he was also involved in the movement which loomed large in 12th century Ireland, to reform the Irish church in line with the rest of Europe. In the 10th and 11th centuries the European church was reconstructed on the twin principles of uniformity of practice throughout and of freeing the church from what were seen as secular influences and entanglements. A clear chain of command was established from a strong Papacy through clearly defined bishoprics to the priests of a crucial new institution, the parish, a clearly defined parcel of land. Everyone was to know in whose parish or diocese he lived and who was responsible for his spiritual welfare or control. The monastic orders were reformed. The older monasteries belonged to the Benedictine Order; their practices were reformed along the new lines, either by individual abbots or by placing them under the control of the abbot of Cluny in France or Gorze in Germany; on occasions the local bishop might act. New Orders were founded, notably the Cistercian monks and the Augustinian Canons. The first aimed at a harshly ascetic regime based on the return to a rigidly simple observation of a Benedictine Rule. The Canons aimed at providing a regular framework of rules for the many communities of priests who had grown up over the years; they were not true monks although they held property in common, but were more involved in the wider community, often serving as parish priests.

6-54. Romanesque carved stone from Inch.

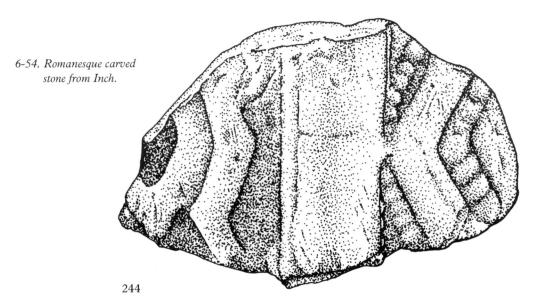

244

New monasteries and cathedrals

To all this the Irish church around 1100 was a glaring exception, and it is no surprise that a reform movement arose to bring Irish practice into line. This movement may have had its origins in Munster at the beginning of the 12th century, but Ulster quickly became crucial in its history. The abbots of Armagh had throughout the 11th century been recognised as the most senior churchmen of Ireland. They were typical of the unreformed Irish church, from 966 to 1129 all drawn from the one family, the Clan Sianach, and neither celibate nor necessarily ordained as priests. This did not prevent them being prominent as patrons of art and learning, nor of energetically defending the position of pre-eminence of the church of Armagh. One of their number, Cellach played an important part in the reforming Synod of Rath Bresail in 1111, which established territorial bishoprics throughout Ireland on the European model; Armagh was recognised as the seat of an archbishop. As his successor he chose in 1129, Malachy, who was a keen reformer and bishop of Down and Connor since 1124, but a man from outside the family of the Clann Sianach. Malachy never succeeded in ousting the Clann Sianach claimant from Armagh, but he did mange to exercise most of his duties as archbishop in spite of him, and in 1137 felt able to leave Armagh and return to being bishop of Down and Connor.

His career as a reformer was not only concerned with the establishing of bishoprics, but he was also the principal reformer of Irish monasticism of the 12th century. When he first became bishop of Down in 1124, he accepted the abbacy of Bangor, installed ten monks from Armagh and restored the buildings. In 1127 he persuaded the king of Ulaid, Niall MacDunleavy, to found a monastery at Erenagh near Downpatrick, which was the first monastery in Ireland to belong to a Continental Order, the Order of Savigny, which later joined the Cistercian order. It was probably through his influence that the abbey of St. Peter and St. Paul in Armagh, founded in 1126, accepted the rule of the Augustinian Canons soon after. After his return as Bishop in 1137, he re-organised Bangor abbey as a house for Augustinian Canons, building a new church in European style, according to his biography.

The 12th century reforms had a considerable physical impact. The new bishoprics were usually founded at existing monasteries but eventually their existence must have called for new buildings commensurate with their status. The new Continental Orders, of Savigny or the Cistercians, required their Irish churches to conform to their ideas not the Irish ones. The earliest Cistercian monastery in Ireland was founded in 1142 at Mellifont in Co. Louth. It had a church 57 metres long with transepts and a crossing, eastern chapels off the transepts, a choir projecting further to the east, and an aisled nave. To the south of the church was a rectangular cloister with regular ranges of buildings set around it according to a standard plan. Nothing like this had been seen in Ireland before. Cormac's chapel is a simple nave and chancel building a little under 17 metres long. The Irish monasteries, as far as we know, had never adopted the idea of a formal cloister, and remained a haphazard collection of buildings. The contrast was clear to contemporaries. When the locals saw Malachy's new church after 1137, one man objected, in the true voice of Ulster: "We are Irish not French men.....Where are you, a poor man without resources, going to get the money to finish this building ?"

It is a great pity that, as with the old monasteries of Armagh or elsewhere, the new churches of Malachy's tradition have vanished. Bangor is gone, while even the site of Erenagh is unknown, except that the name lives on in that of a townland. The first Cistercian abbey in Ulster was Newry, founded in 1154 by Muirchetach Mac Lochlainn, king of Cenel Eoghain and high-king of Ireland. Its only relic is the boundary of the barony of the Lordship of Newry, which preserves the boundary of its lands. These, incidentally, show that Muirchetach endowed his new foundation not with his own lands but those of the Ulaid.

It is clear that the history of the reform movement was as much involved with secular powers as with ecclesiastical ideals; at its most basic it took resources to found new monasteries or bishoprics and only the kings could provide them. The reformers needed support against the traditionalists, a support which again only kings could provide. Three churches in Co. Londonderry illustrate the complexities of the actual carrying out of the reforms in a locality. The churches of Banagher and Dungiven later looked back to two different families as founders in the 12th century, respectively the O'Heaneys and the O'Cahans. Their contemporaneity is indicated by the fact that the south window of the nave at Dungiven is identical to that at Banagher (Ill. 6-55). The nave at Dungiven is clearly earlier than the chancel built in the first half of the 13th century, and it has decorative shafts with capitals of 12th century type. The families of the O'Heaneys and the O'Cahans were rivals in the 12th century for the local kingdom of Ciannachta. The O'Cahans eventually prevailed thanks to Cenel Eoghain support; they occupied a position similar to that of the O'Hagans of Tullahogue as principal lords or kings within the Cenel Eoghain hegemony. Dungiven by the end of the 12th century belonged to one of the reformed orders, the Augustinian Canons.

The church of Banagher has a west door which is structurally identical to the west doorway of the church of Maghera; the latter is, however, elaborately carved while the Banagher door is plain. The carving is of a crucifixion across the lintel; the jambs are carved with interlace, one of them being related to the Irish Urnes style of contemporary metal work. The spectacular door at Maghera was probably built when it was selected as the site for a bishopric in 1152 (Ill. 6-56). The bishopric was not a new one but was the result of the moving of the diocese for the Cenel Eoghain from Ardstraw, where it had been sited in 1111. It was moved not for ecclesiastical reasons, but because the Ardstraw area had fallen away from the control of the Cenel Eoghain in the interval. The foundation of all three

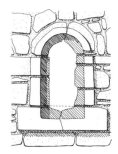

6-55. *Windows at Banagher (top) and Dungiven.*

6-56. Maghera west door.

churches was clearly closely connected with political events, and can only be explained in their light, either the families who were vying to control the region or the ambitions of the Cenel Eoghain over-king. Equally the cultural links shown in the three buildings are interesting. They are decorated but the decoration is not really that of the rest of 12th century Ireland; there is no chevron, for example, and the Maghera door is square to the outside, not arched. It is possible that they represent another line of inspiration in Ulster than the line ultimately dependent on Cormac's chapel. If so, whatever the inspiration, neither the Augustinians of Dungiven, nor the bishop of Maghera seem to have looked to the Cistercians either.

Ireland's churchmen associated themselves with the general European reform movement of the 10th and 11th century church. At the same time there was a similar reform (or indeed a revolution) in the structure of secular society in Europe. After the invasions of the 9th and 10th centuries by the Vikings, Hungarians and Saracens into western Europe, a new structure of power arose. It was based on a new form of lordship, based firmly on the control of relatively small tracts of land, which were all the more precisely defined because they were not large. These estates, or manors, were organised around both rights and duties, involving both the tenants of the manorial lord and his superior lord. The manorial lord owed specified services, usually as a mounted warrior in his lord's army, and exacted work from the men who farmed the land of the estate. These rights or duties were not personal but, once entered into were indissoluble for ever in theory; they passed automatically from each man on both sides of the contract, whether king, lord or peasant, to his heirs and the heirs of the other party. The estates often formed the basis for the church's new parishes, and in time formed the lands of a new class, the knights. In a warlike world the land and the rights over it were often held through fortification, building castles for the lord to live in and control the land.

This revolution, termed by later historians feudalism, passed Ireland by. We have seen how in the 7th or 8th century, Ulster might not have been so very different in its social structure from that of England and northern Europe in general. By the 12th century it was, at least as different as was the church. Just as the churchmen tried to reorganise the ecclesiastical structure in line with the rest of the church, so too did kings. They were involved intimately in the church reform and the links with England or France that it forged. As a result they could see the new feudal kingship in action, especially in England after the Norman Conquest of 1066. The power of Irish kings was not based on perpetual contracts linked to the control of land. It was based on personal loyalties alone, with no mechanism for continuing them beyond the death of either partner. Succession to kingdoms was unregulated and resulted in constant battles between rival claimants from within the royal family; at a lower level, land was held in common by a family, so that the chances of exerting control over it through one man were nil.

To the Irish kings who envied the feudal kings their power and stability there beckoned the example of Scotland. There a Gaelic king had, through the 12th century, systematically settled Anglo-Norman lords on lands granted to them under feudal conditions. The king of Scotland retained control while converting his lordship into one of the new kind, thanks to bringing in landless younger sons of the feudal nobility of England. Irish kings tried to reproduce this 12th century Scottish revolution. At the beginning of the century Muirchetach O'Brian formed alliances in Wales and Scotland, and had his daughter marry Arnulf de Montgomery, brother of the Norman Earl of Shrewsbury. Nothing came of this, for the Montgomery family rebelled against king Henry I of England and were crushed, but in 1169 a second such attempt was made. Dermot MacMurrough, king of Leinster, faced an overwhelmingly powerful combination of his enemies, led by the high king of Ireland. He decided to recruit mercenaries among the Anglo-Normans of south Wales, and gave his daughter in marriage to one of them, Strongbow, Earl of Chepstow and Pembroke.

7 *English Earls and Irish Lords 1177 - 1550 AD*

The establishing of the English Earldom of Ulster

The 12th century saw the population of Europe continue to grow as it had in the 11th. The increasing numbers of people needed more land for more food, and the lords and the peasants of the time found two solutions. One was to expand the area of land within northern Europe which could produce corn for bread; to drain the fens and cut down the forests. The other was to take other people's land; to conquer the lands of Slavs to the east or Moslems to the south. Ireland and Scotland lay between these two plans. The second saw mainly an internal expansion led by English immigrants. Dermot mac Murrough tried the same idea in Ireland, but it developed into a land taking exercise by the English. In Ulster, one John de Courcy was invited into the kingdom of Ulaid, which covered eastern Ulster, in 1177. He then proceeded to takeover the kingdom in spite of the men who had called him in, converting it into the Earldom of Ulster.

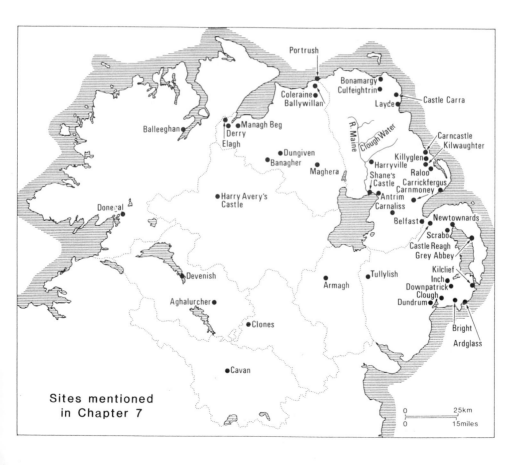

Sites mentioned in Chapter 7

7-1. *Political map of the British Isles in the late 12th century: the arrows show the lines of expansion of the feudal kingdoms of Scotland and England.*

The question which then faced such lords as John de Courcy and his successors as Earls of Ulster, was whether they could convert their new Irish lands into estates on the European model, which would then make money for them, based on producing corn for the market of the growing number of mouths in Europe, but especially England. In fact, they failed in this aim. On the one hand the area of Ulster actually seized by the English was barely a quarter of the province at most, nor was even that part transformed (Il1. 7-2), so that one result of the invasion was to be a society with elements drawn from both England and Gaelic Ireland. The 14th century saw the population of Europe as a whole reduced to about a half, as a result of plague and other factors. The basic reason for an influx of people from England into Ulster was gone; land was now relatively

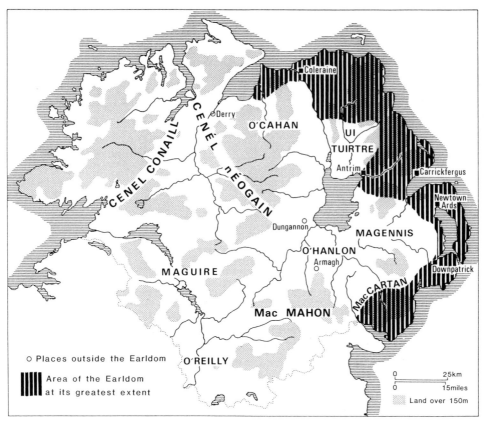

7-2. Ulster in the later 13th century, showing the maximum area of the Earldom.

plentiful and the urge to try and grow corn in Ulster for export disappeared. Politically, the English settlement was almost eliminated, replaced by a number of Irish lordships, such as that of the O'Neills of Clandeboy. A new order emerged, which during the later 16th century came into bitter conflict with England when the Tudor kings and queens, particularly Elizabeth I, determined to assert (or re-assert) English control tightly over Ireland. The resulting wars, in which Ulster figured largely, from the 1560s to 1603 bring this period to an end.

As always our knowledge of the past is partial, because the survival of evidence is incomplete. This period is dominated by the traces of the English Earldom of the east from the late 12th to 14th century. The Earldom may have been in effect a private estate, but the Earls were subjects of the king of England. As a result we have surveys of land holdings, records of court cases, and detailed land grants preserved. The society of the Earldom was partly modelled on the general pattern of English mediaeval society, so that the words and references of these records can be interpreted with reference to our knowledge of that society. We have economic information about the agriculture and trade of the Earldom. Within the Earldom, we may well know the actual occupier and builder of a site and we can almost certainly place it within a hierarchy of the period. The relative wealth of sites and information from the Earldom presents us with two areas of caution. It is biassed towards the holders of land and towards the townsmen; the peasantry are not nearly so visible in the record, either of sites or of documents. The Earldom's evidence must not lead us to neglect the lives of the Gaelic world, either of their lords or of their farmers. The study of the English Earldom is much more directly accessible than that of the Irish society, where chronology and the social position of sites is much less easy to state; we have seen the problems of interpretation which that creates.

There are still great gaps in the evidence, even of the best preserved areas. The houses of the bulk of the population have not yet been found. As with the earlier historic period, we have yet to see much work done on the physical anthropology of skeletons from graveyards excavated. Age profiles, stature and the incidence of disease are virtually unknown from archaeology. Clothes, either directly preserved or else portrayed in effigies are a similar blank. Clothes are sometimes preserved with bodies in bogs but they are by definition from a curious context. Neither their date nor whether they are typical is easy to assess. We know very little about the physical environment. We are still dealing with a period which we know from a number of relatively isolated sites or the objects found in them, not from a landscape as a whole. Equally the fact that we have so much more information from documentary sources changes the role of archaeology. Even more than the archaeology, the documents tell us of a number of individual places and events, randomly preserved; archaeology may help us to see the norm or the trend behind the event. Documents often present a picture which is very clear-cut; in the case of mediaeval Ireland, for example, of a land divided sharply both politically and culturally between English and Irish. This may be the result of the language used rather than being a true reflection of the state of affairs in all areas; the relative neutrality of archaeology may mediate between the blacks and whites of contemporary phrases. This said, the period is dominated by the existence of the Earldom which John de Courcy established and it is by looking at it that we must start. It was controlled by the Earl so it is the sites which he occupied, the castles of the Earldom, which must be our entry point.

The Earl's castles

The English Earldom of Ulster was governed by the Earl as his personal estate. He was expected to live like a lord, spending his wealth on his followers and on a splendid standard of living; careful husbanding of his resources or a modest way of life would have simply earned him the contempt of his men. The most obvious effect of this we can see in the great stone castles built by the different Earls. Each castle had to provide living accommodation not only for the Earl and his family, but also for his many officials from his senior councillors down to the grooms, huntsmen, cooks, or porters. At least two hundred people might be living in the castle when the Earl was there. He moved around continually not only within Ulster but in Ireland and Britain. Administration and justice were personal matters to be dealt with by the Earl so he went round his lands in Ulster to meet his men and settle their affairs: he kept in touch with his king and fellow lords in England or Ireland, outside Ulster, by visiting them. His life in a castle was a public one, therefore, administering justice to his men, seeking their advice and explaining his policy on public issues, and formally greeting visitors, whether English lords or Irish kings. This public life he carried on in the great hall. His more private life he led in his chamber or chambers, while his main officials would also have expected private rooms to sleep in. Add to this basic list of hall and chambers, the kitchen, storerooms, chapel and stables which would have been essential and it is easy to see how crowded the courtyards of castles could become. This complex of buildings had to be defended in a warlike age, which continually developed its method of attack and defence.

The stone castles of Ulster illustrate well both how the Earls defended their castles and how they lived in them. Throughout the mediaeval period Carrickfergus was the main centre of English Ulster, with its castle standing (as it still does) and dominating a group of mediaeval monuments: church, harbour and market place (Il1. 7-3). The building we see today illustrates well the changes in the way men defended castles from its start in 1178 to the 1250s (Il1. 7-4). The first castle, which is now the inner courtyard, relied on the massive tower-block, the keep, for defence: its height allowed the defenders to dominate any approach along the rock, while its massive walls and protected single door meant that they could use it as a final refuge point to hold out in if the attackers had captured the

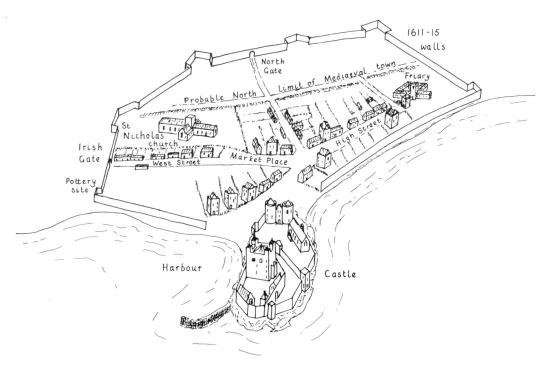

7-3. Carrickfergus: bird's eye diagram of the historic town.

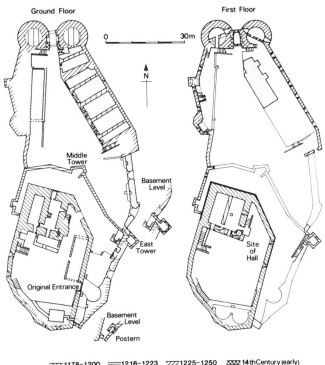

Ground Floor

First Floor

0   30m

N

Middle
Tower

Basement
Level

East
Tower

Site
of
Hall

Original Entrance

Basement
Level

Postern

1178–1200   1216–1223   1225–1250   14th Century (early)

16th Century   19 & 20th Centuries

7-4. *Carrickfergus castle: plan of the principal phases.*

courtyard. From the point of view of purely defensive effectiveness, military opinion from about 1200 in Europe generally moved against the building of keeps; they provided the attackers with a single target and yet, because they were a simple tower with only one door, they prevented the defenders from stopping their attackers approaching the base of the walls, either to undermine them or to put ladders against them. Leaning over the wall top to drop a rock on the attackers made you a wonderful subject for target practice for his archers. We can see the answer in the extension of the defences of Carrickfergus in 1216 to 1223, now the middle ward (Ill. 7-5). The castle wall itself was now to be the main defence, provided with towers at intervals; individual strong points from which archers could fire all around at the enemy in front of the wall. There was one obvious problem here however; the gateway into the castle. The next phase at Carrickfergus not only completed the castle as we see it now but built a great twin-towered gatehouse at the end of it (Ill. 7-6). Defence in the 1170s had been passive, relying on the simple massive keep, by 1250 it was aggressive, meeting any attack with towers which both covered the gate and provided platforms for archers to fire at the besieging forces before they even reached the castle walls.

There are two castles in Ulster called Greencastle, which were built before the middle of the 14th century; the one in Co. Down of the 1230s or 1240s, and the one in Donegal which was built as part of the English advance to the mouth of the Foyle in the first years of the 14th century.

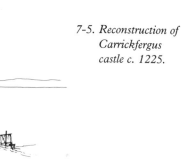
7-5. Reconstruction of Carrickfergus castle c. 1225.

Excavations along the outer wall of the Co. Down Greencastle showed that it was defended according to the fashion of the day, with a water-filled moat to prevent anyone coming up to the base of the wall. The excavations by Cynthia Warhurst and Chris Lynn uncovered not only the ditch but also the dam built to retain the water in it (Ill. 7-7). They also showed that Hugh de Lacy who probably ordered the work was swindled; the rock strata are porous and the ditch could never have held water, so he paid for an impossibility. The Donegal Greencastle is still dominated, in spite of its sadly neglected state, by the remains of its massive gate-house. Two towers flanked a gate passage nearly twenty metres long. The passage was vaulted and closed by at least two gates along its length, although it is now too ruined to detail all the means used to prevent anyone going down it without permission. At the same time as the Donegal Greencastle, the gate-house at Carrickfergus was rebuilt to extend and strengthen the gate passage. To get into the castle now by the gate meant crossing a pit, going under a slot

7-6. Model of Carrickfergus castle in the later 13th century.

7-7. Greencastle, Co. Down: dam and ditch.

projecting from the battlements from which missiles could be dropped, or water to put out a fire lit against the next obstacle, the first gate; behind this was a portcullis and then a vaulted (fireproof) passage with holes in the vault for more missiles to be dropped, which was closed at the inner end by another portcullis and a gate (Ill. 7-8). Edward Bruce's army spent a year blockading Carrickfergus in 1315 to 1316, rather than risk a direct assault.

The principles of attacking and defending castles are better known perhaps than how they were designed for their normal peace time use. To do this we must identify the various rooms listed before: the hall, chambers, chapel, kitchen, etc., from their surviving remains. In a draughty castle a fireplace in a chamber made all the difference to life; given the crowds, so did a private lavatory. Compared to these chambers, the hall, which was the central focus of public life, was marked out by its size, its large fireplace and the quality of details like doors and windows; these last in particular were large and often had seats built into their sides for people to talk in more comfort and privacy. Rooms used by the servants or for storage will have none of these features; a chapel will be recognisable by having the same fittings as a church, and often by facing east.

The changing standards of living in the century after the 1180s are well illustrated in the Earl of Ulster's castles. The first castle at Carrickfergus had its hall, still marked by its fine windows, on the east side of the courtyard. John de Courcy's chamber where he slept and led his private life was on the third floor, a splendid room with fine windows; his household

256

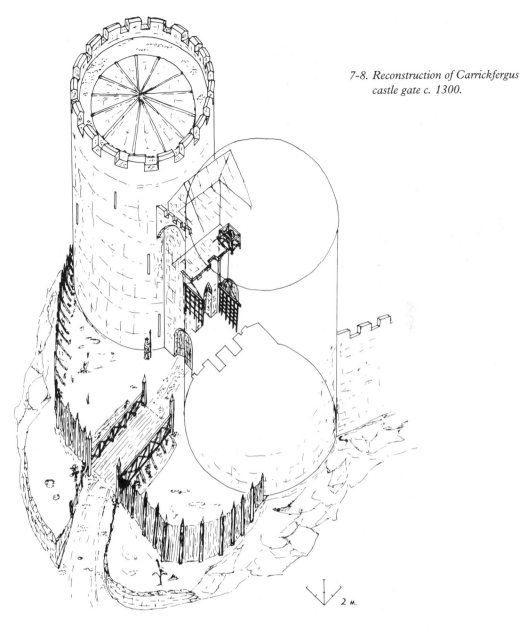

7-8. Reconstruction of Carrickfergus castle gate c. 1300.

2 M.

probably lived in the less well-appointed room below, protecting his privacy from the general castle servants and garrison going to and from the well in the entry floor. Hugh de Lacy, the next Earl, built Greencastle, Co. Down in the 1230s. It has no keep, but the whole castle is built around the great hall, raised to the first floor over storehouses, now somewhat rebuilt in the 15th and 16th centuries. It is still possible to make out its arrangements, however (Ill. 7-9): a big rectangular room lit by high windows on its two long sides and perhaps at one end. It was entered at one end while at the other was a raised platform on which the Earl's table stood across the hall: the fireplace was set nearer that end, too. From the cross-

257

7-9. *Greencastle, Co. Down: interior of hall in the late 13th century.*

table would have stretched two long tables at which the lesser people sat during feasts, on benches; up above the room was open to the roof. While the Earl was in his hall for his public life, he probably spent most of his time in the rooms built against the castle curtain wall to the east. Here instead of John de Courcy's single chamber, we find that Hugh de Lacy had two, for men's desire for privacy was increasing. There is a larger chamber where Hugh would have had his private meals and dealt with private business, and a smaller one, his bedroom. When Richard de Burgh built Greencastle, Co. Donegal in 1305 he made even more elaborate provision for his private accommodation, taking over the whole gatehouse. On each of two floors the same layout of rooms is repeated, an entrance lobby, a large chamber and two bedrooms. One floor was probably for the Earl, his wife (in the second bedroom) and his private business, while the other was probably for an important guest, for a lord would travel with quite a household too. The tower at the other end of the castle from the gatehouse was set aside for a suite of rooms for the Earl's main officer, his steward, with private rooms for other officials in the lesser towers. The hall was

7-10. *Arms of De Lacy.*

258

against one of the inner courtyard walls, still important as the setting for public affairs, but now functioning as the centre piece of a whole series of other rooms and suites of rooms.

In all this, the changes we can see in the Earl's castles, their defences and the increasingly complex and hierarchical pattern of his daily life and that of his household, is precisely like those of a great lord in contemporary England or Europe. When an Earl married his daughter off to an English or Scottish baron (and out of two of Richard de Burgh's daughters, one married the Earl of Gloucester and the other Robert Bruce, who later became king of Scots) they need not have felt any sense of inferiority when their sons-in-law came to stay. We cannot say the same about their chief tenants, their "barons". These men held substantial tracts of land in return for acting as officers in the Earl's wars, for administering justice locally and for giving the Earls the benefit of their advice in his court. They were the men who built most of the castles that can now be seen in the Ulster countryside.

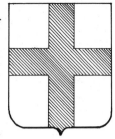

7-11. Arms of De Burgh.

The castles of the Barons

These castles however are quite unlike the great stone castles of the Earl, and must now survive as simple mounds of earth (Ill. 7-12). This is essentially what they were originally, for the mound served to provide a platform usually about 15 metres across raised some 4 metres high all around and approached only up a bridge or by steps up the steep and slippery slope of earth. The platform was protected by a strong wooden palisade around it and often had a wooden tower on it, while the mound was surrounded by a ditch. The result was a fortification easily and quickly erected, for it required only men with spades to build the mound and carpenters for the fence and tower using wood found nearby, with no costly

7-12. Red Hall motte, Co. Antrim.

259

7-13. Reconstruction of Clough motte and bailey.

skilled masons and slow quarrying or hauling of stone required (Ill. 7-13). Fifty men could put up a medium sized motte in under two months, especially if they were being encouraged by other men with swords. These earth castles, known then and now as mottes, were however becoming increasingly rare in the rest of Europe from the later 12th century onwards, for their timber works were easily burned and provided little serious threat to the more professional armies of the time. Only in troubled areas, like Ireland and the English border with Wales, were they still popular; for as well as being cheap and quick they provided a real defence for a few men (a family and their servants) against the kind of small raiding party of Irish or Welsh men that was the main threat in those parts.

The first point to be made in understanding these castles is the very fact of their existence; the Earl may have lived in stone castles, but even his principal barons apparently did not. Whether this was because the Earl stopped them building such things which might have been a threat to his power, or whether they simply were beyond what a baron of Ulster, with much smaller resources than the Earl, could afford, we do not know; the first seems more likely. This would tell of a very real power over his men which was distinctly unusual elsewhere. The second point is that of their distribution. Any list made of field monuments is inaccurate, most obviously because there has always been some which have been destroyed, and mottes are no exception to this rule. The rate of destruction is probably less than that of other sites, because until recently when earth-moving machinery has become common, removing a motte was no easy task: the amount of land gained was not large either, compared to the area gained by removing a rath, for example.

There is a further problem here, however, that of identification. A motte is a round flat-topped mound of earth; all the rest of its features were of timber and have gone. As we saw in the last chapter, raths could develop into mounds looking just like mottes to the archaeologist before excavation. It was quite possible for the crucial 8th century site of Deer Park Farms to appear among a published list of probable mottes, because this list was (as it stated) simply a list of round, flat-topped mounds of earth. This said, the overall pattern of distribution is likely to be correct (Ill. 7-14). Ulster has a dense distribution of mottes by the standards of the British Isles. It is not uniform, however; the mottes are densest on the ground towards the boundaries of the Earldom, especially at the north-east corner of Lough Neagh. This is similar to the other areas of dense distributions of mottes in Ireland and Britain; they typically proliferated in areas of tension and borders. The lesson from this is that they were built most commonly not because the Earl of Ulster's men were so much afraid of internal risings by the peasants of their lands, whether English or Irish, but of raids from outside, from the neighbouring Irish lordships.

There is little precise evidence as to their date. Some, probably the majority, were erected very soon after the English lords first seized land in Ulster, i.e. the later 12th century; they continued to be built, to judge from their distribution in north Antrim, after they seized land there in the 1230s, but perhaps not later. They continued in use in some cases until the early 14th century. Only Clough in Co. Down shows signs of being made the base for later fortifications in stone, evidence that their lords were either prevented from so building, or that there continued to be little resistance from the peasantry to the English seizure of land from their former lords.

7-14. Distribution of mottes.

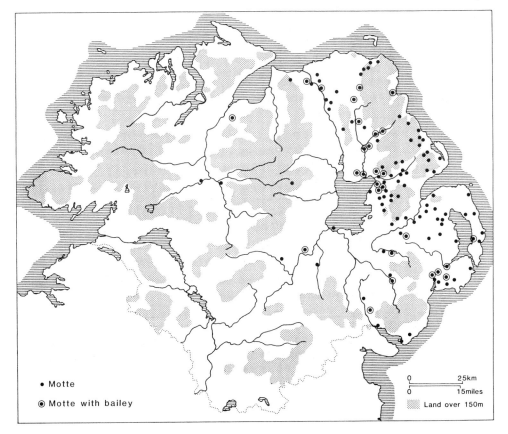

Motte

Motte with bailey

Land over 150m

0   25km
0   15miles

Elsewhere, in England or in Europe, mottes are usually found attached to baileys, the name given to courtyards surrounded and defended by a bank and ditch. The motte served as a refuge strong-point (like the keep in a 12th century stone castle) but the bailey was where most daily life went on. The hall and chamber of the lord was found there, as were the barns and sheds of the yard from which he ran the farming of his estates. In common with the rest of Ireland, relatively few of the mottes of Ulster now have baileys attached. Some 20 or 25% of mottes are found with baileys, as opposed to over 80% in Britain. The baileys in Ulster are also much smaller than those of Britain, (in England an average area might be 2000 square metres: the largest in Ulster is 750 square metres). As such they appear very small to contain the lord's living accommodation and the farmyard of a centralised estate. The baileys of Ulster, like those of Meath, are found, not evenly distributed within the Earldom but concentrated on its borders. This suggests that baileys in Ireland frequently had a military role rather than being the living enclosure attached to a strong point, as in the English model. They may have been for the quartering of small numbers of soldiers stationed there when a raid from the neighbouring lordship might be expected. As such, they could have been succeeded in this role during the later 13th century by a number of small enclosures, built of mortared stone along the borders, such as Seafin in Co. Down or Doonbought in Co. Antrim (Ill. 7-19). The Ulster barons were living in halls like their counterparts elsewhere: two have been excavated from the mottes of Clough and Lismahon in Co. Down. These were, however, on top of the mottes, and only Clough had a bailey.

The English won their battles in Ulster because they had better weapons than the Irish. The English had archers (the Irish threw stones) and their knights were mounted on strong horses (the Irish fought on foot). The knights carried swords and were protected by chain armour; the Irish fought with axes without armour. Of this equipment, arrow heads are common on excavations and so are the horse trappings, especially horseshoes. We have no armour from Ulster nor portrayals of a knight of the 12th or 13th century: our knowledge is derived from literary accounts or else from remains found in other countries.

Farming and settlement in the Earldom

If we suggest a picture which has the mottes of Ulster being used either as the bases on which lords lived perched up on their halls, or as strong points for border forts, it is clear that we are a long way from the standard English model of the motte. There it was the base for a defensive tower, attached to the hall and farming centre of the lord's estate contained in the bailey below. This bring us to the nub of the next question: while we can see from his castles that the Earl's life was that of an English magnate of the period, can we say the same for the rest of his men? Did the occupation of the Earldom of Ulster by English lords, whose motive for seizing land was to profit from producing grain for the rest of Europe, succeed in introducing an English pattern of centralised farms and estates into Ulster, to replace the relatively dispersed pattern of Irish settlement? Did the presence of a motte in the Ulster countryside mean the same type of lord's estate as it did in England?

In the south and east of Ireland, there are found two types of sites, which have yet to be convincingly identified in Ulster. One of these is the "moated site", a rectangular enclosure defined by a bank and ditch, which is, as the name implies, often wet. The second type is the deserted village. The moated sites, in particular, are common, numbered in their hundreds in counties such as Tipperary or Wexford. A few rectangular sites have been noted in the Ulster countryside, but none is in the sort of situation (topographical or political) that we would expect if they were 13th century moated sites; the only one to be excavated, Carnaghliss in Co. Antrim, is high in the Belfast hills and failed to produce evidence of date. Remains of abandoned houses are also found, sometimes not far from a motte as at Killyglen in Co. Antrim, but they are not at all like the organised settlements that we find in the south of Ireland, or would expect from England. There, the moated sites are usually found away from the main estate centres; they represent the farms of men pushing agriculture to the margins of contemporary fields. They are clear evidence of the success of the settlement, in English terms, of the south-east of Ireland. Their absence from Ulster carries with it the conclusion that the settlement and agriculture here was not so successful.

We cannot give unequivocal answers to the nature of settlement and agriculture in the Earldom. Clearly the mottes represent the existence of numerous small lordships and tenancies in the countryside. The coincidence of mottes with churches and mills named in surveys in such an area as east Antrim, and their siting in places which are still recognisable as centres of a sort, such as Carncastle, Kilwaughter or Raloo, shows that there were centres of estates which meant enough perhaps for them to survive down to modern times. This would argue that the system of land holding established at this time had a real impact on later patterns, and, perhaps that there was a definite shift to the centralising of the agriculture. The key to that question lies with the siting of the mills mentioned in the documents. They were, to judge from the written records, the source of a large amount of the income that the lords drew from their lands. This may have come simply from the fees charged to their tenants for grinding their corn, but it is more likely that this represents the way that the clerks recorded the levying of rents in kind from the tenants; that they paid by giving up a proportion of their corn crop at the mill each year.

This would allow us to have a centralised administration of an estate, with a physical centre, the lord's hall, without having to assume that the settlement pattern and agriculture was also centralised. Certainly, there is documentary evidence of lands which form part of an estate being physically detached, by up to several miles, from the estate centre. If we were to visit a knight living in Ulster in 1300, we should perhaps have found him living, not like an English knight in a hall with a large farmyard beside it, and set within, or at the edge of, a village of the peasants who worked the land around. Instead in Ulster he might well be living in a more or less isolated hall, perhaps set on a motte, or else beside one (by 1300 the motte would probably be no longer maintained) near to a mill, but with his peasants scattered over the countryside in no such close relationship as a village. It is in fact quite likely that many of these would be the descendants of the families who had worked the land before the English came, simply carrying on under a system not greatly changed. There were new aristocrats in the countryside but not a new population.

Towns

Monasteries in Ulster had been the focus of populations of craftsmen larger than that of their own monks, and, as we have seen, they have been called towns, dating to before the time of the English Earldom. Whether this is reasonable or not, there can be very little doubt that the Earldom was responsible for the introduction of what was at the least a new type of town into Ulster. The only one which has been examined through archaeology is Carrickfergus, although the documentation makes it clear that Coleraine, Downpatrick, Newtownards and Antrim were also towns in the same sense. This sense is that they were built for a community of people whose principal source of income was commerce, rather than crafts servicing a monastery or the aristocrats of the area. Above all these communities were self-governing and to some extent self-contained, not appendages to a monastery. Carrickfergus may appear to be in such a relationship to the Earl's castle (I11. 7-3). If we look at the plan of the town, it shows that this is not so. It is centred along a spine made up of the wide High Street and Market Place. The latter leads up to the church of St. Nicholas, which seems to have been started under John de Courcy as a pro-cathedral for the bishopric of Connor. The castle was a crucial element in the town, just as the existence of a harbour and a routeway from it through the Carnmoney gap to the hinterland of Antrim was crucial to the siting of both castle and town. The presence of the castle was only one element, however, in the foundation and continued prosperity of the town. Its existence depended on the trade of its market place; the Earl and his household when he was in residence must have been massive spenders, but they were not there all the time, and they were not the only customers.

Excavation during the 1970s by Tom Delaney of a number of sites within Carrickfergus clarified the history of the town considerably. They were almost entirely situated along the spine we have noted, with two particular results. They demonstrated that the plan of these streets went back to the origin of the town; there was no time when people lived on streets laid out in a different alignment. On at least two sites the boundaries of the properties, and probably the street frontages, had remained in exactly the same place since the 13th century. This shows the power of a continuous community, organised by a town council, which upheld the boundaries between the properties and each other and the street. There are still considerable areas to be explored: we do not know how far housing spread east or west along the line of High Street/Market Place, nor how far to the north it extended back from this line. The actual houses have yet to be uncovered, of any class let alone to investigate the mixture of upper, bourgeois, houses and those of the lower classes. These present targets for future work in the town, similar to the expansion of these results by the excavation of other Ulster towns of the Middle Ages, notably Downpatrick, Coleraine or Newtownards. No excavation on their urban settlement has yet taken place, and indeed recent development may mean that the chance has now been lost in crucial sites. None of these places was large; Carrickfergus may have had a maximum population (derived from a guess based on the valuation of the rental in 1333, the available evidence of the area and intensity of the occupation) of something over one thousand, and it was the largest place in the Earldom. At the other end of the scale are such places as Carnmoney, Belfast or Portrush, which were constituted formally, according to the surviving documents, as boroughs, but which were probably towns only in name, being in fact entirely agricultural in their economy and with the population simply of a small village in Europe.

The communities of the towns in a real sense led lives based on trade, either internal or with the world outside Ulster. That extensive trade took place we know from documents; but the archaeological evidence for trade in general is more restricted. The main exports were perishable and they have perished; even if they had not, something like a piece of Ulster leather found in an excavation in England, could never be traced back to its country of origin. The sale of these exports provided the money to bring either goods that could not be made or found in Ulster, or the men who could make them. Trade and the establishment of industries are closely linked economically. Archaeologically there are considerable problems in discussing these imports. We have the same defect in the evidence of perishables as we do with exports; neither wine nor the barrels it travelled in from France, as we know from documents it did, are likely to survive. There is the question of the individual object such as the altar vessel made at Limoges in western France and found at Bright in Co. Down (Ill. 7-15). That an individual might have brought such an object from France to Ireland is unremarkable in the 13th century but if many churches had imported altar vessels it would tell us much of the extent and value of trading links. In these ways the individual object is much less informative than the common one. The commonest of all archaeological objects are sherds of pottery. The most distinctive imports are the pots from France, mostly tall jugs of white clay with a bright green glaze. To judge by what we find on excavations, about one in ten jugs on Ulster tables in the 13th century came from France. This is a much smaller proportion than is found in Dublin or Cork, and rather less than from a seaport on the south coast of England like Southampton. The pots came in the ships whose main business was to bring wine from the lands near Bordeaux; had the ships not

7-15. Altar vessel from Bright (ht. 13 cms.).

been coming anyway the pots would not have justified the expense of the journey. Archaeologists excavating in inland English towns however find few French pots, for the processes of trans-shipment and land transport would have made their price prohibitive and any superiority in quality which they had over local products would have been wiped out. Ulster lies between the two situations. The lesser proportions of imports as compared to Dublin probably means that the wine (and so the pottery) was carried up not directly from France but in coastal shipping after trans-shipment in southern Irish ports. A further factor involved was how successful the local industry was in satisfying the needs of the home market and so inhibiting the French imports. Trade cannot be separated from the home industry, and it was, as noted above often based on the importing of craftsmen.

Mediaeval industry

Archaeology does not inform us about the majority of industries; again the raw materials were frequently perishable, and we lack the excavations of the sites which would have told us of them. Pottery looms large, as do the industries using stone, with some information about iron-working. When the English came to Ulster the native Irish potters were producing only the crude cooking pottery, souterrain ware. If a man wanted to drink wine, he needed glazed jugs on his table and would have had to get them from outside Ulster at first. At some time after the establishment of the Earldom, potters come over to supply the Ulster market, faced of course with the problem that by then people had acquired a taste for imports. Nor can it be said that the potters who set up the new industry in Ulster were the foremost practitioners of the art. Two kilns, the principal remains of their production centres have so far been found in Ulster, one at Carrickfergus and one at Downpatrick. Both sets of potters, to judge by the broken pieces of failed pots ('wasters') found in great numbers by the excavators, produced a mixture of simple cooking pots and glazed jugs (Ill. 7-16).

7-16. Pots from Downpatrick and Carrickfergus kilns.

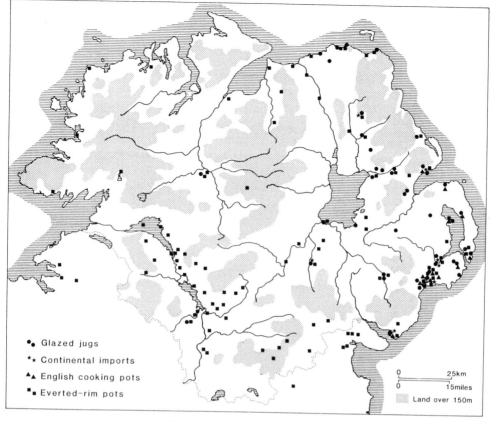

7-17. Distribution of mediaeval pottery.

The shape of an object and the technical tricks used in its manufacture should betray the tradition in which its maker was trained. Both Carrickfergus and Downpatrick potters produced jugs whose simple barrel shape, mostly undecorated, and whose details of finishing the neck, rim and handle are the same as those made in the Chester area, and so we can say that that is where they came from. It cannot yet, however, be said when they came and set up the industry; how long after the political conquest that this part of the economy followed.

The distribution of the pots they produced sheds light on communications (Ill. 7-17). Jugs travelled further from the kilns than the cooking pots. The native tradition continued to be unable to produce jugs (which required kilns and a knowlege of glazing) and so provided no competition; distance may have increased the price of jugs, and so restricted the number of people able to buy them, but there was no competition to replace them. Cooking pots on the other hand could suffer from Irish competition, if men tried to market them too far from their production point. A second, rather depressing, point should be made. The numbers of shapes of cooking pot produced at Downpatrick and Carrickfergus are fewer than those of a kiln in England, and some shapes have not been found on other excavated sites. It would seem probable that cooking in Ulster was more boring than in other parts of the mediaeval world, dominated by stews.

267

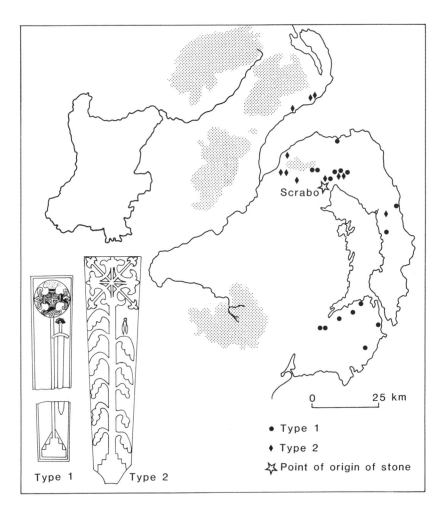

7-18. Grave slabs.

Type 1   Type 2

0   25 km

● Type 1
♦ Type 2
☆ Point of origin of stone

Scrabo

The branch of stone masonry which produced ornamental slabs to mark graves was another case of a craft introduced into the Earldom (Ill. 7-17). It was based on the quarries of sandstone at Scrabo, Co. Down, which provided some of the best stone for carving in Ulster. Again the designs used at Scrabo are those that were found in the north of England, particularly the north-west, including Chester. The carvers presumably came, like the potters, from there. The slabs themselves are found only in eastern Co. Down and at Carrickfergus and Kilroot. They must have depended largely on boats sailing on Belfast and Strangford Loughs for their distribution, which centred on the town of Newtownards. They were transported by land for short distances from there, but apparently not, for example, into the English areas of south Antrim, nor did they reach Coleraine and north Antrim. Clearly communications by land, perhaps dependant on pack-horses as much as on carts, which call for better road surfaces and gentler gradients, were not such as to encourage widespread economic movement of goods. It is not that personal travel was difficult, for the documents are full of travellers, but that the goods traffic was expensive.

268

English and Irish

The largest gap in the archaeology of this period is the absence of any secular site which straddled the incursion of the English. We may speculate as to what, if one were to be found within the area of the Earldom, and excavated, results it might show. If it were an aristocratic site, we would expect it to be displaced by an estate centre, perhaps marked by a motte, of the incoming English lord. On the other hand, if it were a peasant site (house or hamlet), we might, as we have seen above, find very little effect at first, until some of the goods imported through the new commercial networks filtered through into the people's lives. Outside the area of the Earldom the Irish lordships were by no means uniformly hostile to the English and vice versa. There are as many records of alliances as there are of wars between them, although the documents are often written dividing the two groups up and look as though they are set on hostility. This is particularly true of the Irish of those parts of Counties Antrim and Down who shared a boundary with the Earldom, and who were normally allied to the English against their main enemies, the O'Neills from west of the Bann.

Archaeologists in the past have made a fundamental assumption, a mixture of archaeological dogma and English and Irish nationalistic prejudices, that the Irish did not build castles in the 200 years after the English introduced them to Ulster. The distribution of mottes (or what look like them) in the modern Ulster countryside extends far beyond the known borders of the Earldom. This has been explained as the result of English armies building mottes while conducting a campaign or raid. This is most unlikely: the point of a motte is to provide a very strong defensive site for a few people. The area of the top is too small for anything other than a very small raiding party, which would be too few to build it or to stay for long, while it is very difficult to protect your horses on a motte. These mottes outside the Earldom must be the work of the local, Irish lords. Some are most impressive: Harryville in Ballymena and Managh Beg near Derry, respectively the work of O'Flynns and O'Cahans, are as big as any motte of the Earldom (Ill. 7-19).

Excavation has identified two sites as being occupied by Irish lords in the 13th century. Doonbought in mid Antrim is a fort set on a spur of the Antrim hills, looking out over the strategic junction of the valleys of the river Main and the Clough Water which seems to have marked the border between the Earldom's lands in north Antrim and the satellite Irish kingdom of the O'Flynn's, to the south (Ill. 7-20). The area excavated was quite limited, but it showed that there were two periods of occupation: an inner enclosure surrounded by a dry-stone wall at the crest of the spur, with an outer enclosure defined by a mortared wall and a ditch cutting off the lines of approach along the spur; the inner enclosure was succeeded by one enclosed by a polygonal, mortared stone wall. The second period was probably one of a number of such sites erected by the English along the Earldom's borders in the middle and late 13th century (the best known is

7-19. Harryville motte.

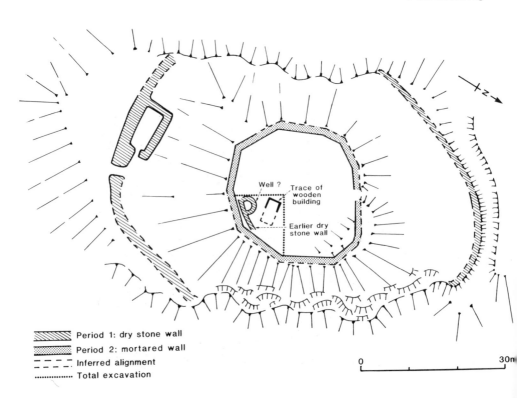

Well ?　Trace of
　　　　wooden
　　　　building

Earlier dry
stone wall

▨ Period 1: dry stone wall
▨ Period 2: mortared wall
- - - - Inferred alignment
.... Total excavation

0　　　　　　　　　30m

Seafin castle, Co. Down), but the earlier phase would seem, with its reliance on dry-stone walling and anomalous design, Irish. Unfortunately, not enough of the interior was excavated to say more than that there were timber framed structures in the inner enclosure.

Coney Island, in the south-west angle of Lough Neagh, is clearly in an area away from the Earldom. There, the excavations by Peter Addyman uncovered a lengthy sequence of occupation, from the early prehistoric period to the later 16th century. In the 13th century a small motte-like mound was erected, which had no trace of occupation left on the top, while elswhere on the island there were several furnaces for iron smelting. Exactly what the nature of the settlement was, whether it was primarily established to work bog iron ore, or whether it was principally a lordly residence, somewhat in the nature of a crannog, where iron smelting was also carried on, was left unclear because of the limited nature of the excavations. In neither case, at Doonbought or at Coney Island, do we have the evidence of whether there was a lordly residence on the site. This gap prevents us from seeing whether a Gaelic lord lived in a house like a lord's hall in the Earldom or in one of an Irish tradition.

Three stone buildings survive above ground which may be dated rather later, to the 13th or 14th centuries, and which may be attributed to the Irish, again to lords. Castle Carra, in Cushendun, Co. Antrim, is probably an isolated first floor hall building, a very small example a type known from England but commoner in Scotland and in the west of Ireland, where they were built by the lesser lords (Il1. 7-21). It lies in a part of the country, the north Antrim coast, which may have been held either by the Anglo-Scottish family of the Bysets, tenants of the Earl, or by the O'Flynns, or indeed, as it certainly was later, by Highland Scots. Who built Castle

7-21. Castle Carra.

7-22. *Harry Avery's castle.*

Carra, or when (the answer to the one question would give the answer to the other), is unknown. It is significant that this is so, because it shows how we cannot identify a "typical" Irish site of the period. All that is visible now of Elagh castle, west of the city of Derry on the Donegal border, is a semi-circular tower at the end of a steep-sided rock outcrop, probably part of a gate house. It is traditionally associated with the O'Doherty's.

Outside Newtonstewart in Co. Tyrone, is Harry Avery's castle, taking its name from an O'Neill lord of the late 14th century. It is the best preserved of these three sites, a polygonal mortared wall enclosing a glacial hill or mound (Ill. 7-22). At one end of the enclosure is a double-towered building with the entrance between; behind the towers is a single hall at the first floor, while there were chambers at first and second floors in the two towers. It is not quite a gate-house, however, for the only communication with the courtyard of the enclosure, at the first floor level of the tower, was reached only by a stair from the ground floor room behind the towers. The lay-out is a simplified version of the English castle gate-houses of the time, notably of Greencastle, Donegal, which also had a gate which was on a level below that of the main courtyard. It is however very much a simplified version. Not only is the "gate-house" itself much simpler, but there are no signs of the great hall and lodgings within the courtyard, which a castle of the Earl might have.

These sites all have one thing in common; they show that the Irish lords who had them constructed were well aware of the innovations of the English lords of the Earldom and were prepared to imitate them, apparently from an early period. Here we see the absurdity of those who like to

272

argue that the Irish would ignore the English developments. This was not just a matter of the form and building of the new sites, the presence of a motte, or the stone construction of a gate-house, but the idea of a permanent stronghold. The survival of the lordship of the O'Flynns in mid Antrim, surrounded to the north, east and south by the Earldom during the later 13th century when the English were expanding into the similar lands of north Londonderry, may have been in part because they were prepared to build mottes, strong points which made the seizure of their lands a more daunting prospect. Harry Avery's castle is set in an area which was in constant dispute between O'Neills and O'Donnells during the 13th and 14th century. Henry Aimredh O'Neill, after whom the castle is named, was a son of the ruling O'Neill, who founded a dynasty in the area; he may have been deliberately given land by his brother, both to satisfy his aspirations and to secure it from the O'Donnells (Ill. 7-2).

This idea of lordship, where there is a firm association between a strong castle, a tract of land and a lordship, was not traditional to Irish society, but comes from the English and European developments of the 10th and 11th centuries, which we call feudalism. The early castles of Irish Ulster come from a period of considerable change there. Not only is the late 12th to 13th century the time when the major families emerged who were to dominate Ulster politics until the early 17th century - O'Neills, O'Donnells, O'Cahans or Maguires - but they took other steps to reinforce their power. The later 13th century sees the beginning of the recruiting of Highland mercenaries by the Ulster lords, the galloglass (Ill. 7-23); they also abandoned their

7-23. Two galloglass from the Dungiven tomb.

273

pretensions in the 13th century to kingship as opposed to a stronger grip over their lands. Castles had a clear role to play in this increasing military power and control over land as opposed to the traditional ties of lordship based on relationships with the people alone.

The artifacts of the period show that it was not only the Irish lords who were prepared to adopt new ways of life from the English. English coins of the 13th and 14th centuries have been found right across Ulster, although some at least could be there because of modern coin collectors. Similarly, it is difficult to interpret the significance of such finds as that of a 13th or 14th century sword blade from the river Blackwater, which had been made in Germany or Poland (Ill. 7-24). It travelled there in antiquity, but was it lost by an Englishman on a raid, was it a gift to an Irish lord, acquired by an Irish mercenary abroad, and was it new or even hundreds of years old when it was lost? Sherds of jugs of English or European manufacture or tradition have also been found at sites such as Armagh or Coney Island, showing that some Irish at least were prepared to import them, presumably along with wine. These might be evidence purely of some of the upper classes making occasional contact with the English, the archaeological expression of the political alliances and inter-marriages which we know from the documentary sources were a regular feature of Ulster, and Irish, life. At Doonbought in particular, but also at Coney Island, as well as at the church site of Killyliss in the extreme north-west of Co. Down, three styles of pottery were found together.

There were the glazed jugs, but no cooking pots, of English style. The cooking (or boiling water at least) was apparently done in pots made by Irish potters. Some were the souterrain wares of the tradition going back to the 8th century in the east of the province, but there was also a second group, the so-called everted rim pots. These were made without using a wheel, of similar clays and firing to the souterrain wares but their different shapes were different, the result of the makers of the earlier ware imitating the imported English cooking pots. The quality was markedly inferior to the English cooking pots, like those of Downpatrick and Carrickfergus, but this does not seem to have prevented them competing successfully with them in the remoter parts of the Earldom. Not only was there this minor change of shapes by the potters but their area of activity expanded rapidly. Everted rim pottery, unlike souterrain ware, is found over the whole of Ulster. The pottery craft probably involved only a few people but it does show the local Irish coming to terms with, and indeed profiting from, the incomers and their economy. Admittedly it would help to understand the significance of the people of central and western Ulster beginning to use pottery after centuries of not doing so, if we knew what souterrain ware had been used for in the past and what the purpose of everted rim ware was.

The remains of the Church

Nowadays we tend to isolate the role of religion in life; in the Middle Ages it was all-pervasive. The individual clerics were much more closely associated with lay people: ties of class and kinship were as important to them as their clerical status. An aristocratic bishop or abbot had more in common with a lay lord (likely to be his relative) than he did with a parish priest from a peasant background. The relationship of the church to the establishment of the English Earldom is an interesting illustration of the complexity of the lay relationships with the Church. We have seen that the great movement for the reform of the Irish church got under way early in the 12th century. Its aim of bringing Ireland into line with the contemporary European church made the reformers naturally sympathetic, in some sense at least, to the idea of the English lordships. Nor could the Church admit to the division of the country into two blocks, the Irish and the English, for they both belonged to it. On the other hand it was obviously easier to work with the lay powers than to oppose them, especially as some were bound to be helpful, and so there was a tendency to organise the Church in line with the divisions of lordships. Bishoprics had been modelled on Irish kingdoms before the English arrived, and they could be remodelled to take account of the Earldom. We see this in the establishment of the bishopric of Dromore for those parts of the bishopric of Down which lay outside the Earldom; the Irish of Connor bishopric were accommodated in a separate deanery (Ill. 7-25). This said, the Church was a powerful medium of communication between the Earldom and the Irish lordships outside it. Churches cost money, and the Church was always a wealthy element in society. Constructing the buildings commissioned by the houses of monks

7-25. Ecclesiastical map of Ulster.

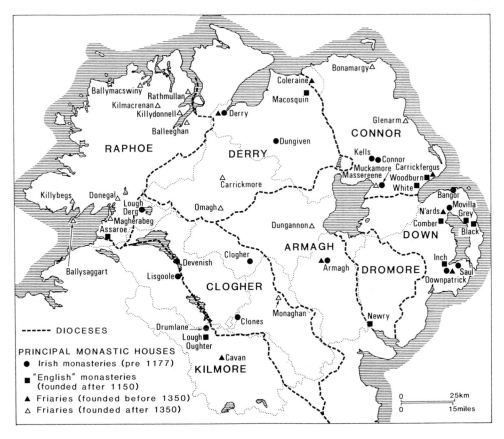

7-26. Air photograph of Inch with Downpatrick in the background.

and friars, and by the parish clergy and cathedrals, was a major industry, similar to the erection of castles, requiring the assembly of workmen from different areas, while the remains of the buildings can show, by their remains, the purposes and aspirations of the churchmen involved.

Abbeys and Friaries

John de Courcy was a strong supporter of the Church and founder of abbeys; to him we owe the remains of the two Cistercian abbeys of Inch and Grey in Co. Down from the end of the 12th century (Ill. 7-26). Inch he founded in the early 1180s, after he had burned its predecessor in 1177; Grey Abbey was founded by his wife some ten years later. Their buildings illustrate well the interlocking of the monastic regime and ideals, and the influence of the lord who paid for it. Both churches and cloisters conform to the European standards of the Cistercian monks, well proportioned and orderly in their planning, in sharp contrast to the traditional Irish monastery. The church lies to the north of the complex, originally divided into two; the choir, transepts and crossing for the literate, superior choir monks, and the nave for the lay brothers, who were illiterate and did much of the hard physical labour of the community. The building along the east of the cloister was the chapter house, where the community met each day for business, with the choir monks' dormitory running over it, linked by a stair into the south transept so that monks could go direct into the choir for night offices. The south side of the cloister was occupied by the monks' refectory,

276

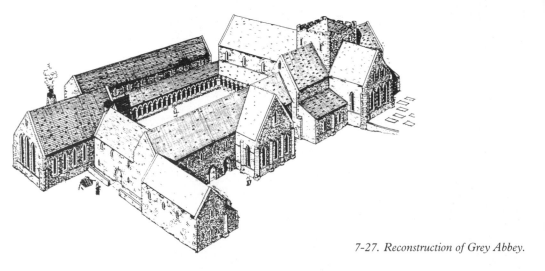

7-27. Reconstruction of Grey Abbey.

while the lay brothers' dormitory and refectory was set along the west side (Ill. 7-27). Right across Europe the houses of the Cistercian order were arranged in the same way, in total contrast to the individual, not to say muddled arrangements of the Irish tradition.

At Inch Abbey, the east and south sides of the cloister have their buildings (now reduced to foundations) but the west range may have been built only in wood; the choir monks' needs took precedence. The east end of the church is well preserved. Grey Abbey is less elaborate, however, than Inch and seems to have taken much longer to build, even to have had its plans changed during its building to make the whole church and cloister smaller (Ill. 7-28). The reason may well lie in the fact that Inch had a ready organised estate, taken over from the earlier monastery, when it was founded, and it also was in existence for nearly twenty years of John de Courcy's patronage as Earl; Grey Abbey had only been founded for ten years when Hugh de Lacy replaced him. The scale of both, especially the

7-28. West door of
Grey Abbey.

7-29. Inch Abbey.   large church that seems to have been intended at Grey Abbey, are eloquent evidence of the confidence of the new English regime in the economic future of the Earldom.

It must have been De Courcy's political aims which made him link the two monasteries to houses in northern England, rejecting equally the traditional, but Irish supremacy of Mellifont over other Cistercian houses in Ireland, and links with southern English houses too open to royal influence. These northern links show in the architectural style of Inch (I11. 7-29). The pointed (not round headed) windows, the carving of the stones of the arches and the form of the vaulting over its chapels all belong to the Gothic style of northern England. The pointed heads of the windows and arches were visual effects which made the visitor's eye follow the lines of the building upwards not so much along its length. This visual effect was combined with the structural demands of a new method of vaulting in France in the middle of the 12th century to give us the Gothic style which gradually replaced Romanesque over Europe in the succeeding decades. Inch marks the arrival of the new style in Ulster, and maybe Ireland, presumably because monks from the north of England came in to man John de Courcy's new monastery. Direct evidence of other new men and their skills can be seen in the individual marks that the masons left on the stones they carved, signing them as their work, for inspection or payment; these abbeys were built by professional masons.

278

Monasteries tended to lose the interest and support of society during the 13th century, to be overtaken by friaries. Friars, unlike monks, went out into the world to preach and look after the poor; they were rather like the Salvation Army transported to the mediaeval world. At first they concentrated on the towns in Europe where poverty was most obvious and where the parish system worked least well among the men flocking in from the over-populated land. The first orders of Friars were founded in the 1210s; within two decades they had started houses in Ireland. Because they worked in towns, their houses have been particularly prone to destruction, sometimes by reformers but usually by men looking for readily available building material. The churches remain of two of the six friaries founded in Ulster in the 13th century, at Newtownards and Armagh (I11. 7-30). Both were originally simply rectangular buildings, with an aisle added later. The churches were simple structures, with only a little elaboration of the arches built to open into the aisles. The site of Newtownards Friary is very restricted, but it has been possible to explore that of Armagh. The contrast between its small cloister and restricted buildings, and the more elaborate cloister at Inch with ancillary buildings outside it is the contrast between a community with no land and one which was running a large agricultural estate.

The secular church

The 12th century reform had established the secular, non-monastic side of the church firmly all over Ireland, and (which was more of a break with tradition) located its churchmen in a particular tracts of land, the priest in his parish and the bishop in his diocese. The parish was the clearest innovation of the period and with it the parish church. This latter, however, could be the church of an earlier small monastic foundation, with slim

7-30. Reconstruction of Armagh Friary.

endowments perhaps now eroded, taken over to serve the new parish possibly in a way that it had informally done before. Certainly the churches that were built as parish churches provide little contrast with the traditional small rectangular buildings with narrow windows and simple doors. As a result unless a particular church happens to preserve some individual feature which reflects a dateable fashion or technological innovation it may be difficult to say when it was built. Some do have such features; for example, Ballywillin church outside Portrush (as large as any at 25 by 6.75 metres) has narrow pointed windows of the 13th century, while the church at Maghera, Co. Down, had timbers set within its walls to stabilise them while the mortar was setting, a technique occasionally found in the same century: without these features the churches could be anything from 10th to 16th century.

There is one notable exception to this, the large parish church of St. Nicholas, Carrickfergus which has transepts and had aisles divided from the nave by arcades and is the only one in Ulster to approach in scale or elaboration a normal parish church of feudal Europe (Ill. 7-31). The

7-31. Reconstruction of St. Nicholas' church, Carrickfergus in the 14th century.

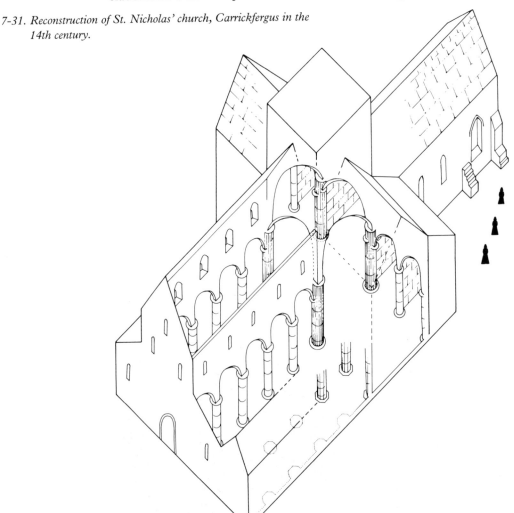

reason for this may lie in the wealth of Carrickfergus town but is more likely to come from its position in the political geography of the 13th century church. It lay within the diocese of Connor but Connor itself lay outside the Earldom. St. Nicholas' church certainly acted at times as the cathedral for the diocese and probably normally did so, keeping the bishop in close contact with the Earl. Both the plan and the details, where they survive, recall contemporary Cistercian work.

Time has been hard on the mediaeval cathedrals of the seven dioceses of Ulster (I11. 7-32). This is a result mainly of Ulster's turbulent history, for cathedrals were frequent targets in war, but it is also partly a result of the number itself. Because of the political pressures to provide bishops for many lordships, and because of a typically 12th century mood of optimism about the possibilities of economic growth in Ireland, the Irish church of the 12th century saddled itself with more cathedrals than it could afford. The English were capable of the same fragmentation; Dromore was a diocese detached from the area of Down, to cater for those parts of Down not occupied by John de Courcy; it was always very small and poor as a result. There were to be none of the splendid buildings of the rest of northern Europe in Ireland. In Ulster we have some remains of two cathedrals, at Armagh and Downpatrick. Of Armagh, the plan is really all that is mediaeval, the present building being almost entirely the result of an early 19th century restoration.

Downpatrick, too, was drastically rebuilt around 1800, after being roofless since the later 16th century. It appears to have started as a simple, aisleless building with transepts, built probably in the later 12th century, with affinities to the new cathedral at Iona. During the 13th century it was replaced by a building which has formed the core of the structure since, an aisled choir without either transepts, or a formally divided nave. This was

7-32. Eighteenth century view of Downpatrick cathedral.

put up by the English Benedictine monks brought in under the Earldom, to staff the cathedral as monks often did in England, but their building was not English in style. It had thick piers between the aisles and the main body of the church, decorated with shafts and capitals only on the north and south sides; the windows of the story above were sited over the piers not over the arches between them. Both of these are features associated with Irish Cistercian practice, rather than English style, although the details themselves are those of contemporary English work. Excavations on the rest of the hilltop have shown that at least two other large stone buildings existed near the cathedral itself. Much of the present appearance of a circular enclosure (identified in the past as a prehistoric hill fort) may date from the pattern of terracing the hillside for the buildings of the cathedral community; curiously there is no evidence yet for the square cloister that we would expect from English Benedictines.

In general one may draw several conclusions about the nature of mediaeval Ulster society from its churches. The first and most powerful impression is that of the poverty of that society. The churches are elaborate and large when compared with the buildings of the Irish church before the reform movement, and they do thus represent a considerably greater commitment of resources than before. To compare them, however, with the parish churches, abbeys or cathedrals of the rest of Europe shows them up cruelly. It is not that Ulster, or Irish, men in general, devoted less effort to their churches in proportion to their resources, but that the money and the skilled craftsmen just were not there. Not only were the buildings modest but, again in contrast to the rest of Europe, they were not often rebuilt in later centuries, although they might be destroyed. It is this that makes Ireland fertile ground for those who want to study, for example, 12th century Cistercian monasteries. Secondly, there is no sign of difference in the kind of church archaeology between Ulster and western Europe; the church was no different as an institution. In this respect the 12th century reform was a complete success. Thirdly, the church straddled the division between Irish and English; although there were some cases of nationalistic antagonism, they were largely confined to the closed world of the monks and friars. Archaeologically we can see no change across the line. In the 13th century, the house of Augustinian canons at Dungiven decided to add a chancel to their church. The new chancel deployed the moulded stone shafts, lancet windows and rib vaulting of the contemporary English Gothic style, just as the nave had been open to English Romanesque style in the 12th century. As far as we can see, the political divide did not affect the cultural contacts of Irish or English craftsmen in the building industry.

The fourteenth century divide

This has long been recognised as a disastrous century in the history of Ireland. The reasons have usually been linked to political events, and to the drastic decline in the power of the royal government in Dublin. In Ulster, 1315 saw the Scots under Edward Bruce, flushed with their success at

Bannockburn, invade Ireland via Larne and stay, pillaging and burning, until Edward's death in 1318. William de Burgh, the last resident and effective Earl of Ulster, was killed near Belfast in 1333, which is often said to have ended the English settlement, already weakened by the Bruce invasion. This is not so; although it left the Earldom without an Earl, royal officials continued to administer it in his daughter's name. It is not until the 1370s that we find the settlement under real pressure, and then from a combination of problems. The main one was not political, but social and economic; the consequences of the Black Death of 1348-9. This and later plagues over all Europe killed about one third of the population, a loss which was not replaced for 150 years at least. Europe's population in 1400 was probably about one half of its size in 1300. Land was no longer scarce in England or in Ireland and men drifted away from marginal areas like Ulster to richer and more peaceful lands: once started, the movement would gain momentum as neighbours left and there was even less chance of making up the gaps by fresh immigration.

Historians have also linked the evidence of political turbulance to the signs of the decline of English royal power in Ireland, in some cases assuming that a decline in royal power was the same as a decline in English settlement. Out of this has arisen the idea of a "Gaelic Resurgence", a re-assertion of Irish culture, rejecting the innovations of the English lordships. Ulster is often given as a key instance of this process. The Earl is killed, and then a faction of the O'Neill royal family was driven out of Tyrone and took land to found the dynasty of the O'Neills of Clandeboy. In point of fact, this was initially at the expense of the Irish O'Flynns of mid Antrim, and only later at the expense of English lords, principally the Savages, driven from south Antrim to the Ards of Down. This took place thirty or forty years after the death of the last Earl, while the same replacement of English lords by Gaelic ones could happen peacefully, as when John MacDonnell married the heiress of the Byset family and inherited the Glens of Antrim. We must not exaggerate this process, which was essentially a matter of changing landlords not the people as a whole, while some areas of the Earldom, Carrickfergus and south east Co. Down always remained at least nominally English.

More to the point, we must not assume that the political changes of lordship affected the whole of life in Ulster. The idea of a Gaelic Revival rests in part on the premise that the 13th century Irish were opposed to the culture of the English. As we have seen, archaeology can point to evidence of their imitation of, and economic co-operation with, the English. Worse still, some archaeologists have picked up the historical picture of the 14th century as a century of collapse, and applied it to archaeology, denying the possibility, for example, of any serious building during the period. On an all-Ireland scale this can be shown to be patently untrue; only the two decades after the Black Death itself show a gap in the founding of new friaries, let alone a stop in reconstruction work on existing sites. In Ulster, we have seen Harry Avery's castle as a probable 14th century building.

7-33.
*Cumaighe na Gall
O'Cahan's tomb,
Dungiven.*

The controversy is summed up in the ascribed date of the tomb of an
O'Cahan in Dungiven Priory (Ill. 7-33). Traditionally, the tomb is of
Cumaighe (Cooey) na Gall O'Cahan, who died in 1385. It consists of a
stone effigy of the man, laid on a tomb chest which is decorated with the
figures of standing warriors, the whole being set below a traceried canopy.
The effigy is of a type which is found from the mid 14th century to the 16th
in the West Highlands. The smaller figures of the tomb chest are set in a
similar way to the knights on a late 13th or early 14th century tomb at
Athassel in Tipperary, while the tracery is of a style first used in early 14th
century England, but which lasted a long time in Ireland. The detailed

mouldings are of 13th or 14th century type rather than later. Modern opinion has agreed that it is a 15th century tomb, rejecting the traditional date, mainly because of the idea that the 14th century produced little, yet it could easily be late 14th century. The problem arises from exaggerating the role of political history. Other countries saw both the Black Death and serious wars in the century: in Britain the Anglo-Scottish wars and the Hundred Years War did not stop it being a period of major cultural achievement. Historians and archaeologists have tended to confuse three separate things in the century: the English royal government's loss of power to the great lords (Anglo-Irish and Gaelic), the individual disasters such as the Black Death, and the long-term demographic decline with the re-organisation of society after it.

The Late Middle Ages

This period, from the late 14th to the mid 16th centuries, is again one which presents the archaeologist with problems and challenges, mainly connected with the assessment of the 14th century. The rest of Europe saw large-scale economic and social changes in response to the decline in the population. Instead of each country and region attempting to produce a full range of the goods needed by the large numbers of people, and with a cheap labour force, they moved much more to specialization, producing those things best suited to the resources of the region. Much land which had been maintained as arable, when it was perhaps not well suited to it, went over to pasture; only the good land stayed with large-scale corn growing. In much of the drier land of the south of Britain, which was taken out of arable farming moved to sheep, while the wetter lands were given over to cattle rearing. These changes stood to benefit Ireland. Here there was natural cattle country, particularly with the mild winters, and an obvious role as a major supplier of hides (leather was a vital commodity in the middle ages) to Europe, rather than attempting to produce corn for the market as well. More land could be deemed as first rate in the new agricultural conditions, while fewer people are required for cattle than corn. In the rest of Ireland we can see in part the consequences: a new pattern of dispersed land-owning by lesser lords, who advanced from being tenants into being effectively freeholders, and a modest but genuine level of prosperity for them. The areas where we can observe this happening are in the south and west, where there had been a strong English settlement in the 13th century, succeeded by a re-organisation of land holding. It does not seem to have happened in Meath, where the continuity of the lesser lordships from the 13th century is in contrast to the creation of the major lordships of Ormonde, Desmond (both Anglo-Irish) or the Burkes who were more Gaelic.

We have not yet found the evidence from Ulster to test whether the same happened here. In part this is because it is not clear whether the English settlement was as nucleated and innovative as it was in Kilkenny, for example. In part it is because we have only a restricted range of the sites of the period. We have towns, Carrickfergus and Ardglass in particular, which clearly continued to provide the communications for the province which had been opened up at the end of the 12th century. In the south-east of Co. Down there are a number of the towers of the lesser lords, who still considered themselves in some sense the heirs of the Earldom. Over the rest of the province we have a number of the towers and castles of the Irish lords, and a smaller number of church sites. However, there are many fewer of both than we would expect in a similar-sized area of the rest of Ireland. More serious is the lack of connections between them; we do not have even a reasonable proportion of the secular sites in a single lordship, let alone both them and the church sites. Above all, we are confronted with the old problem that we have only the sites of the lords, with no evidence about the rest of the people, and, with virtually no excavation of them, no information on the artifacts or the natural environment. We have sites which are sitting alone without their context.

The towns of the 15th and 16th centuries

The main power in Ulster was now in Irish not in English hands, but as we have already seen, the Irish had been in social and economic contact with the Earldom for at least two hundred years by 1400. The result can be seen in the archaeology of towns. Here the position badly needs clarification in some of the 13th century towns, such as Antrim, Newtownards and particularly Coleraine, to know how far they continued. Carrickfergus and Downpatrick certainly did, while Ardglass grew from a place of little note in the 13th century to a modestly prosperous port of the 15th century. Downpatrick had been primarily a religious centre, a group of monasteries and they clearly survived the political changes of the later 14th century. Carrickfergus remained English although isolated (Ill. 7-34). Its urban nature is demonstrated by the continuing existence of the 13th century streets and properties through the period. The prosperity of some at least

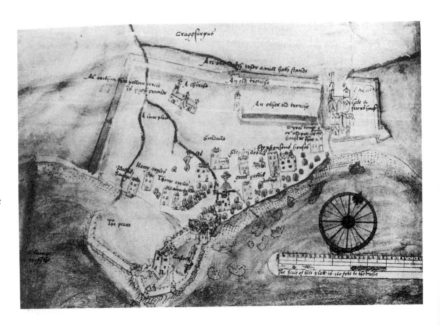

7-34. Map of
Carrickfergus
in 1567.

7-35. Ardglass warehouses.

of the town's families is witnessed by the ten or a dozen tower houses in the town shown on views of it drawn in the 1560s and 1570s. These have now all been removed but some survive at Ardglass, where Jordan's castle is a fine tower-house comparable in its size and detail with the Bishop of Down's tower nearby at Kilclief. Considerably rarer, and so perhaps more interesting is the block of warehouses at Ardglass, known now as Ardglass Castle, and incorporated in the golf club (Ill. 7-35). This was built to provide thirteen spaces behind the quay, guarded by towers at each end, and which could presumably be let out to visiting or resident merchants. This is the standard European pattern, that we find in stories like those of Boccaccio: a merchant sets out with a ship-load of goods and leases a building to store them at his destination, while he gradually sells or exchanges them with local traders.

Maps and documents of the 16th century make references to several towns in the purely Irish areas of Ulster. Armagh and Derry were ecclesiastical and traditional centres of a kind known since at least the 11th or 12th centuries. Cavan under the O'Reilly's was different, a more secular site, built around the castle of the lord. A map of the end of the 16th century shows it as a symmetrically planned small town, of four streets meeting at a square with a market cross in the centre. One street led to the castle in one direction, and to the river crossing, with a suburb beyond, in the other. As with the other sites, we can only regret that there has been no effort as yet to excavate Cavan and exploit the possibilities for exploring the houses, life-style and trade of a Gaelic Irish community.

Trade in the fifteenth century

As with the earlier period there is no direct archaeological evidence of the principal trading goods and so no evidence of the patterns of the trade, for the main exports were perishable hides, wool and fish; again pottery looms very large in the archaeological record. The crannogs investigated in south-western Ulster a hundred years ago apparently produced few imported objects, such as pottery, but the records made were far from good. Not many mottes have been excavated but at least some have: no rural tower houses or their sites have been. Because we have few systematically examined sites of the 15th century we have few ideas of the pottery prevalent then and how to recognise it from the earlier glazed wares, for example. As a result we cannot use stray finds of sherds as we can for the 13th century, until the 16th century when distinctive German jugs and mugs in brown stone ware appear. Like the glazed jugs of the 13th century, these seem to have been readily traded throughout Ulster. Within Ulster the production of pottery has no sites of kilns associated for the period. One thing is clear, that every part of Ulster used the Irish-manufactured everted rim pottery for cooking with (Ill. 7-36, 7-17). It was not produced at one centre for the pottery of Fermanagh and the south-west is quite distinct from that of the east. It is not clear how far the English style of cooking pottery continued to be made and used outside Carrickfergus.

7-36. Everted rim pot (ht. 22 cm).

The lords' sites in the countryside

Life in the towns is relatively easy to define, either in terms of what we know or what we do not. The countryside presents us with a much less clearly focussed picture. The role of a town is clear, but we are not sure of the roles of some of the rural sites, even when we identify them. To a lesser extent this applies to the best known of them, the great castles of the Earl, Carrickfergus, Dundrum and Greencastle, Co. Down. All remained in the hands of English officials. Their role, however, was purely a garrison one, or the centre of an official, and the great state functions were not held, so while the main buildings were kept in some sort of repair there was no new building at all. The case of Dunluce is more complex. Although its origin is often attributed to around 1300, it seems clear from surveys of the 1350s that it was not in existence then. It may well owe its first buildings, the corner towers and curtain wall of the inner enclosure, to the MacQuillans when they took over the area in the late 14th or earlier 15th century. Like Elagh or Harry Avery's castle, Dunluce shows that there were Gaelic lords willing to put up castles considerably more elaborate than the simple towers of many of their contemporaries (Ill. 7-37). We do not know whether Dunluce in its early phases provided its lord with accommodation for more than himself and a small household, but the area enclosed alone argues that there were a number of separate buildings within it. We know that there was a major centre of the O'Neills at Dungannon, and the O'Reilly town and castle at Cavan was the centre of an important Irish lordship. If we could only know what they consisted of we would be a real

7-37. Reconstruction of Dunluce castle.

step forward in understanding late mediaeval Gaelic lordship. As it is, the majority of the sites of the period are tower houses.

The effigy at Dungiven shows us a late mediaeval Gaelic lord in full battle array (Ill. 7-34). He is dressed in a padded mail tunic with a reinforced shoulder protection and carries a long sword slung from a belt. Below him stand his Scots mercenaries, the galloglas, shown as similarly equipped although their traditional weapon was an axe. They and their lords fought on foot, their horses were not for cavalry like 12th century knights. Apart from this, a helmet survives from Lough Henney crannog, apparently a 14th or 15th century piece, and probably imported.

Tower houses

The prevalent monument from the secular life of 15th century Ireland is the tower-house, a simple, isolated square block of three or four storeys, usually 5-8 metres square and about twice as high (Ill. 7-39). They were built to resist some attacks for their windows are small, they have stone boxes projecting from their battlements over the doors so that men inside can drop rocks on unwelcome callers, and their ground floors are normally vaulted in stone so that any firebrands thrown in would not set fire to the floors above. They were built in the 15th century when European armies had cannon, however, and a whole range of siege techniques: tower houses were not built to resist them. Like the mottes of the earlier Earldom they aimed to provide a building where a family and its servants could hold out against a raid from their local enemies. They are commonest in south-east

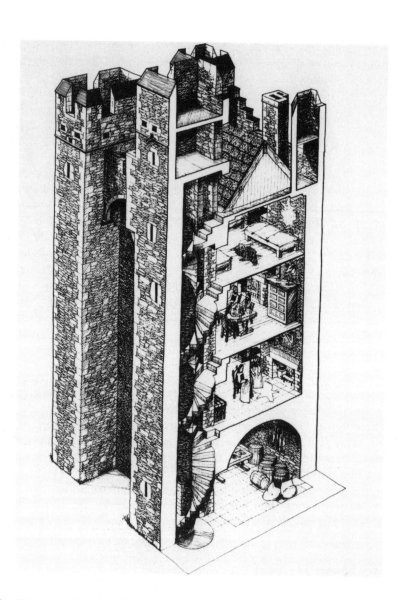

7-38. *Cutaway view of a tower house.*

Co. Down, rather than in the west of Ulster, a common feature of life in the lands which remained English or which had been taken from them; this is the pattern in the rest of Ireland also. Like the mottes they were (as can be seen in their numbers) built not by the few great lords but by the lesser ones. Also like mottes, tower-houses make little or no provision for a complex administrative lordship; the courtyards attached to them, known as bawns, are small and do not look like extensive farmyards with barns etc.

Tower houses are not a type of building confined to Ireland, but are found in other parts of Europe where central administration was weak in the 15th century: the Scottish border country of England and those parts of France fought over by French and English. They combine the move being made by lords from the later 12th century onwards towards living in chamber towers isolated within the castle complex, and the universal resort of men in troubled times to living in a small, strong tower for safety. The actual buildings however vary from region to region so it can only have been the idea of towers that was copied, not a direct imitation nor is there evidence of men being brought in to build them. They are part of a society adapting to a certain common way of life in these places, which had been more or less traditional in Ulster under the Earldom, the way of the frontier, shared by English and Irish alike. The towers of Co. Down have been compared with those of Tipperary and the comparison is illuminating. The Ulster examples share the basic form with those of Munster, a vaulted ground floor, a large room on each upper floor with few lesser chambers, etc., or with none. The Tipperary towers have a fine array of battlements and turrets at roof level, while the Down ones are plainer. On the other hand, the elaborate defensive display of the Tipperary towers is largely for show; frequently access from the battlements on one side of the tower is partially blocked by the roof and gable. In Co. Down the gable is kept within the line of the battlements, so that there is clear all round circulation, at the cost of a more cramped and poorly lit upper floor. In Ulster defensive realities take precedence over the show (and expense) of military strength and some domestic provision.

Our knowlege of Ulster tower houses is heavily weighted towards the Anglo-Irish examples of Co. Down, simply because they are closer to Belfast, and also because they are densely distributed there; counties Antrim and Donegal also have a number of towers dating to before 1600 (Ill. 7-39). The relative absence of towers from central Ulster is interesting. In part this is due to later destruction but it also reflects the situation

7-39. Burt castle.

that the Gaelic lordships, where they were long established did not tend to produce many towers. The O'Cahans, for example, seem only to have had three centres, at Lough Enagh, Limavady and on the west bank of the Bann at Coleraine; likewise the O'Neills of Clandeboy only had two (Shane's Castle and Belfast) before the construction of Castle Reagh early in the 16th century. The Gaelic lords seem to have been successful in preventing the fragmentation of their power, perhaps more so than the Anglo-Irish lords with their tradition of a hierarchy of tenants. The proliferation of towers in Antrim and Donegal reflects the smallness of the areas of the lordships, but mainly the intrusion of Scots into the region, respectively MacDonalds and MacSweeneys.

An impression of prevailing insecurity is reinforced by the fact that a number of crannogs were refurbished in the 15th and early 16th centuries. Several have dates from tree-rings to show building activity in the last quarter of the 15th century or the earlier 16th. Many have produced everted rim pottery, while a number of others, like Loughislandreavy, Co. Down have produced 16th century German pottery. Crannogs have a clear military role; it is, after all, only their usefulness in wartime that would persuade anyone to live on a crannog at all, while they certainly did prove effective in the Tudor wars of the later 16th century. Our problem is that all we know is that the crannogs were refurbished or occupied; we have no idea how, why or by whom. It could easily be that, as there is evidence from annals and the story of the Tudor wars, that they were simply used in an emergency, rather as bolt holes when the fighting was going against a lord. Against this, apparently a number of crannogs are sited close to places which were used as estate centres later; the implication may be that crannogs of the late Middle Ages were aristocratic residences, as they had been in the 7th century. At the centre of this debate would be the questions of how far the society was dominated by the need for refuge from frequent raids (the implication of the lists of such things which dominate the annals) or whether the sort of estate structure which might feed through products for trade was present. Again, as with the towers, and with the position earlier, there is the question of the relationship between Gaelic Irish lords and their lands or power.

The archaeology of the late mediaeval church

Ireland as a whole is remarkable for the number of friaries founded during this period, many of them Franciscan, often of the so-called Third Order, which started as a supporting fraternity for laymen but then developed into full friaries. Not only were there many foundations, but also unlike the rest of Europe, in Ireland the later friaries occupy rural situations, rather than sites in the towns as they had in the 13th century. In Ulster the pride of place among these friaries must be taken by Donegal which not only has the best preserved remains, but also was the home of the friars who assembled the Annals of the Four Masters (I11. 7-40). The individual details are not well preserved, and most of the walls are partially ruined, but

7-40. Donegal Friary.

they do give an idea of the scale and layout of the friary. The church had a nave with an aisle and transept, cut off from the choir by a tower. The cloister was small (about 20 metres square) with a dormitory, refectory and kitchen in the east and north ranges; the west range is now ruined, but may have contained the prior's lodging. The hallmarks of a friary are there: the large nave and associated areas in the church, to accommodate the lay people who came to the services (the clear barrier between this and the choir is another result of the presence of laymen in the church), and the simplicity of the buildings attached to it. Many of the lesser friaries were even simpler: the relatively well-preserved friary at Bonamargy, outside Ballycastle in Co. Antrim, apparently only ever had stone buildings along two sides of the cloister (Ill. 7-43).

7-41. Bonamargy Friary.

It has sometimes been suggested that one reason for the number of foundations of friaries was that they were needed to compensate for a collapse in the parish system in the Irish countryside, caused by the Gaelic resurgence, and that the Irish pattern of dispersed settlement re-asserted itself, so that fixed parishes became difficult to maintain. Ulster provides little evidence of this. Documentary evidence shows that parishes continued to exist, while archaeology shows that some at least were vigorous enough to renew the parish church. We have already seen that the simplicity and lack of fashionable details in the buildings makes Ulster parish churches difficult to date, but still fragments exist to show the activity (Ill. 7-44). Banagher church, in Co. Londonderry, had its east end remodelled; there are windows of 15th century style at Kinawley in Fermanagh, Drumlane in Cavan or Culfeightrin in Antrim (Ill. 7-42, 7-43); Aghalurcher in Fermanagh was rebuilt, partly because it was the burial place of the Maguire lords . The little church of Layde, in an idyllic situation on the Antrim coast, is often described as being a Franciscan church, but there is no documentary evidence of this. There is a tower at the end of the church, which was clearly a residence; the church is probably both an example of a parish church, and a case of a priest building what was in effect a small tower house for himself (Ill. 7-44). If so, here we have evidence of a priest living in a house similar to a merchant or the lord of a small estate, a position like that of some priest on the Anglo-Scottish border of the period, who also put up tower houses. None of these were large undertakings, but their existence disproves the theory of the decline of the parish system.

As for the other institutions, while we cannot date work detected at Down cathedral closely, it is clear that it, too, was reconditioned in the later middle ages. The houses of the older monastic orders, as opposed to those of the friars were not neglected either. In Fermanagh, the Augustinians of Devenish rebuilt their church, aisleless but with a low tower at the junction

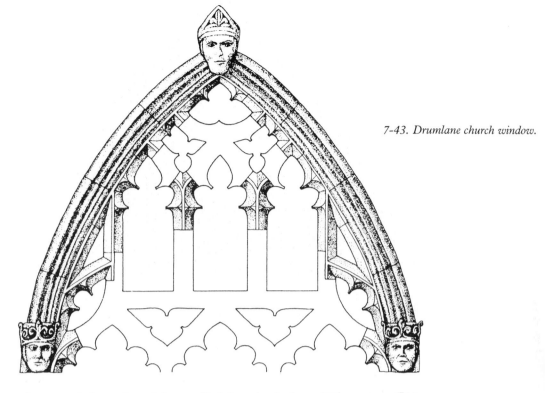

7-43. Drumlane church window.

of nave and chancel, and the small cloister in the later 15th century (Ill. 7-45). The canons of the same order at Dungiven gave the nave of their church a new traceried window. The Cistercians at Inch cut the size of their church in half, demolishing the aisles and cutting off most of the nave, those parts used by the lay brothers: the population decline of the 14th century meant that few peasants felt impelled to seek the harsh life of Cistercian lay brother in return for security.

7-44. Layde church.

There are two lessons from the study of the church remains. The first concerns the style of the work, and the tradition of the craftsmen. The windows, when they have tracery, are typical of those of the rest of Ireland in the period. They have tracery designed with a series of individual sections, culminating in flowing tracery of stone. These designs may sometimes be very close, as with the two windows of Bonamargy (Antrim) and Balleeghan (Donegal), both friaries of the Franciscan Third Order (Ill. 7-46). The designs derive from the work of the English masons of the earlier 14th century, just as the late Gothic designs of the rest of Europe do. Like the rest of Europe, they do not show much signs that the Irish masons were interested in the English developments of the later 14th century, the so-called Perpendicular style. The debate over the date of the Dungiven tomb and of the question of amount of building of the 14th century in general also revolve around this. If building was continuous throughout the period from the early 14th to early 15th centuries, then we can understand how the style could be continuous too. If the masons had had to start again in the early 15th century, their use of 14th century designs seems very odd. In this context the east window of the church of Culfeightrin is interesting. It has horizontal bars across the vertical lines of stone in the tracery, emphasised by two arches below; the upper parts have fairly simple tracery. This design, in particular the emphasised horizontal bar cutting across the vertical lines is reminiscent of the ideas of the English Perpendicular style, one of the few examples in Ireland.

The other point is more general. In the rest of Ireland, the Friars could point to finer buildings than those of Ulster; the Cistercians of Munster saw major rebuildings of at least two of their monasteries, Holy Cross and Kilcooly. The work on Ulster churches was modest in scale, both in terms

7-46. Windows at Balleeghan (left) and Bonamargy.

of the size of the works undertaken and in terms of the elaboration of their detail. This links to the relatively poor remains of the secular buildings of the period. Ulster was the least developed of the four provinces of Ireland. The 15th century may have seen a new economic regime rise from the disasters of the 14th century, and one which may have offered some prosperity, but it was a very modest advance, even in Irish terms, let alone those of Europe.

All through this period, from the 12th to the 16th centuries, we are hampered by the nature of our evidence from having a balanced view of the society and economy. We have sites of every date, it is true, and they are reasonably distributed geographically but they are not evenly distributed as to class. We lack any houses, let alone settlements of the peasantry, whether Irish or English. There are no remains of fields, datable to the period. We lack large deposits of animal bones from any site, let alone from a variety of environments; either from town houses as opposed to rural ones, or a series from the same place over a lengthy period. There have been virtually no pollen studies from deposits, such as wet ditches, of the period. We remain as a result quite ignorant of the details of the organisation of the basic economic activity of the period, the livelihood of almost all the people, agriculture. As with trade, we have to infer the patterns of the economy from the buildings of those who profited from it, the castles and towns, rather than studying it directly.

297

In one sense, this may be seen as reflecting the conditions of the times. The lords and the few merchants did indeed dominate the lives of the rest of the peasants. The poverty of Ulster was probably mainly a reflection of the poverty of resources here, above all the relatively low population, especially in the later Middle Ages. The instability of the political system, the way of life of the dominant lords, had also a part to play in the impression of diminished resources. The increasing militarisation of the political world, and its connection with the insecurity created by having no system of succession to the lordships were both factors. The situation was unstable, rather than truly chaotic; life in early 16th century Ulster was not in a state of anarchy. As the 16th century continued, however, it was this political instability which came to dominate life more and more, so much that it ushered in a new period altogether.

8 *Planters and Capitalists 1550 - 1800 AD*

The legacy of the Middle Ages in Ulster politically was a situation, not of chaos as is sometimes stated, but of instability. We have seen the archaeological evidence that there was not a wholesale sweeping away of the commercial contacts of the 13th and 14th century, represented by the new towns, such as Carrickfergus. The reinforcement of the powers of individual lordships were strengthened by the construction of small castles; their unity expressed in the lack of proliferation of these castles in the Gaelic areas. The instability of the political structures was caused by the competing of several powers, each too weak to assert a single control over Ulster, but strong enough to prevent anyone else from doing so (Ill. 8-1). The O'Neills were by far the strongest Irish power, but with rivals in the O'Donnells, and difficulty in enforcing their will over lesser lords such as the Maguires, O'Cahans or the O'Neills of Clandeboy. The MacDonnells of Antrim controlled a relatively small area of Ulster; before 1550 only the Glens of Antrim, but they had wide lands and resources in the Highlands and Islands of Scotland which they could call on if they needed to. The

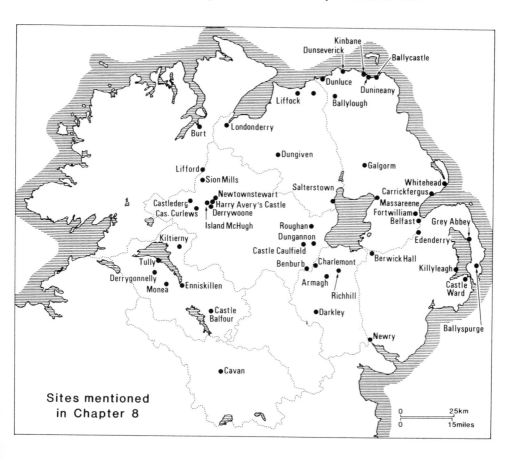

Sites mentioned
in Chapter 8

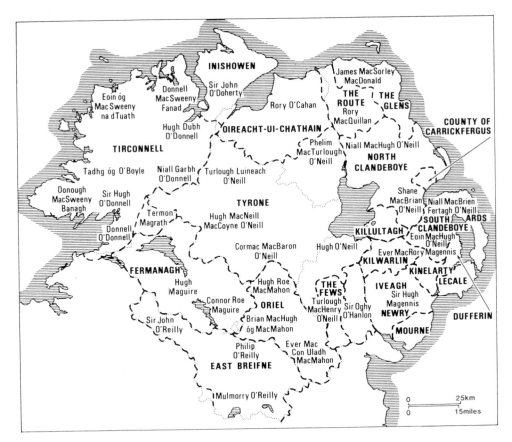

INISHOWEN

James MacSorley
MacDonald

Sir John
O'Doherty

THE
ROUTE
Rory
MacQuillan

THE
GLENS

Donnell
MacSweeny
Fanad

Rory O'Cahan

COUNTY OF
CARRICKFERGUS

Eoin óg
Mac Sweeny
na dTuath

Hugh Dubh
O'Donnell

OIREACHT-UI-CHATHAIN

Phelim
MacTurlough
O'Neill

Niall MacHugh O'Neill

NORTH
CLANDEBOYE

TIRCONNELL

Tadhg óg O'Boyle

Niall Garbh
O'Donnell

Turlough Luineach
O'Neill

Shane
MacBrian
O'Neill

Niall MacBrien
Fertagh O'Neill

Donough
MacSweeny
Banagh

Sir Hugh
O'Donnell

TYRONE

SOUTH
CLANDEBOYE

ARDS

Termon
Magrath

Hugh MacNeill
MacCoyne O'Neill

KILLULTAGH

Eoin MacHugh
O'Neill

Donnell
O'Donnell

Cormac MacBaron
O'Neill

Hugh O'Neill

Ever MacRory Magennis

KILWARLIN

KINELARTY

LECALE

FERMANAGH

Hugh
Maguire

Hugh Roe
MacMahon

THE
FEWS

IVEAGH
Sir Hugh
Magennis

Connor Roe
Maguire

ORIEL

Turlough
MacHenry
O'Neill

Sir Oghy
O'Hanlon

NEWRY

DUFFERIN

Sir John
O'Reilly

Brian MacHugh
óg MacMahon

MOURNE

Philip
O'Reilly

Ever Mac
Con Uladh
MacMahon

EAST BREIFNE

Mulmorry O'Reilly

0   25km

0   15miles

8-1. Lordships in 16th
century Ulster.

English King (or Queen) was by hereditary right Earl of Ulster and acknowleged King of all Ireland by all parties, on their understanding that he did not use it. He had by far the greatest power of all, if he was prepared to spend it on Ulster, where Carrickfergus provided him with an enclave which could be a base to transform vague claims into actual power. Into this unstable mix of political rivalry was added the threat to England of Continental attack through Ireland, and the heady motivation of religious strife of the 16th century Reformation.

The result was a great build up of military forces by all sides, culminating in the Nine Years War between the English Crown and the combined Gaelic lordships, led by Hugh O'Neill of Tyrone, from 1594 to 1603. War did not break out at once; it was preceded by forty years of manoeuvre and escalation with each side attempting to reinforce their position. This was bound to lead to fortification, for what was at stake ultimately was military power over the land, the ultimate reason for building forts or castles. It was not total war at first, as can be seen in the fortifications of the 1560s to 1580s. In the Gaelic world men had refurbished crannogs since the 15th century partly for use as permanent residences but mainly, perhaps, as refuges and strong points in time of war.

At Coney Island, in the south-western part of Lough Neagh, closest to the heart of the O'Neill lordship at Dungannon, Shane O'Neill built a fortified enclosure with a strong stone tower. The O'Neill power rested on

300

his control, through the extensive use of paid soldiers and mercenaries, of his own lands, and the overawing of the lesser lordships of Ulster: his aims were to intensify his power rather than extend it, for his was the most powerful force actually in Ulster, as opposed to others whose power had to be brought into the country. This meant conquest, which we can see in north Antrim. Here the MacDonnells gradually forced out the MacQuillan lords, not in a single conquest but through a steady expansion of power. To consolidate their expansion, they built a number of small castles along the north Antrim coast, such as Dunineaney and Kinbane (Ill. 8-2). These are cliff-top enclosures with a small tower in the case of Kinbane and Dunseverick, not easy to reach but above all offering very limited space inside. This is in marked contrast to the MacDonnell work at Dunluce. When they gained control of this castle, it marked the final success of their attempts to gain control of the valuable north Antrim Route. They celebrated by putting up a magnificent manor house within the fortress, with a fine great hall on the English model, to provide a fit setting for their household and ceremony (Ill. 7-37). If they needed it then, after 1586, why did they not need it before? Like Shane O'Neill at Coney Island, Gaelic lords, who commanded wide areas and power, and could put an army of thousands in to the field, put very little stress on their houses. Their permanent households must have been small, and their tradition did not require permanent structures for their housing; it is from this period that we hear of halls of wattle being erected for specific occasions alone, like the occasion of the marriage of Turlough Luineach O'Neill, Shane's successor.

The English royal government was interested in Ulster, but only in an indirect way at first, hoping to manage and control the local lords from a distance. To do this they needed bases and local agents: there were two,

8-2. Kinbane castle.

the Bagnalls at Newry and the governors of Carrickfergus, principally Captain Pers, or Piers. Our knowlege of Newry derives entirely from descriptions and maps; it was based on the Cistercian abbey and its lands which were given to the Bagnalls after they were seized by Henry VIII; from these developed a small town strung out along the line of Castle street, Upper North street to Trevor Hill. The castle was the base of royal power at Carrickfergus. Piers refurbished it, and his work gives a fair idea of his, and the government's, priorities. He started by repairing the keep, presumably so that he could have a decent house to live in, re-flooring it and replacing the timber divisions at each level with a stone wall, or arch on the third floor. He then turned his attention to the outer walls. He wanted to install artillery, as the obvious modern means of defence, but he then hit the problem of money; Queen Elizabeth was notoriously hostile to anyone other than herself spending it. Piers wrote asking for £4,000 for the works: the Queen's reply was typical both of her own style and more recent ones: "you make mention of a very great sum to be expended in this year, if there be not in the writing some mistaking...". He patched up the gate house with new walls at the back of the towers: the guns he had to mount as far as possible in ports made by adapting earlier arrow slits; they were not well sited but they were cheap (I11. 8-3).

The period of uneasy, limited war and peace gave way at the end of the 16th century to full-scale war between the English and the Irish lords. This culminated in ruthless campaigns by Lord Mountjoy, the English commander, who mobilised the full English strength by combining attacks from Derry, Carrickfergus and Louth devastate the heartland of Tyrone from Dungannon northwards (Ill. 8-4). In 1603, he achieved the total surrender of the Irish, led by Hugh O'Neill, but any permanent settlement between the Irish and the Crown proved impossible. O'Neill and others fled to Spain in 1608, and King James seized six of the nine counties of Ulster. His government decided to divide these lands up and grant them in blocks of 1000, 1500 or 2000 acres each to a mixture of lesser Irish lords,

8-3. Gunloops at Carrickfergus castle.

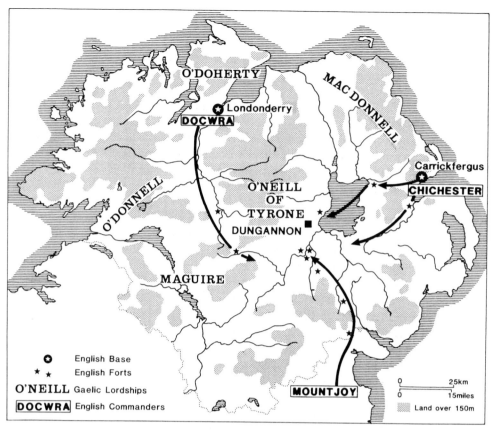

8-4. The campaign strategy of Mountjoy against Tyrone.

English soldiers and governors who knew Ireland, but principally to a whole new group of Scottish and English land owners. These men were to build strong houses and enclosures (bawns) for themselves and to bring over British tenants to settle the land from new: the Plantation of Ulster. The scheme was always too ambitious. The new lords found it difficult to attract British settlers in sufficient numbers to satisfy the requirements of their grants; building up the infrastructure of the local economy so that the lords could get a return on their investment was even harder. Simultaneously, in counties Antrim and Down, which were not part of the formal Plantation scheme, there was a major influx of British settlers, mainly Scots. In Co. Down and in south Antrim, this was led by English and Lowland Presbyterian lords, such as the Hamiltons: in north Antrim, it was under the control of the MacDonnells, Earls of Antrim, who, although both Gaelic and Roman Catholic, did well out of the 1603 peace.

In 1641 came a rebellion led by the Irish lords who had been accommodated into the new regime; it rapidly got out of hand and became a series of massacres and attacks on the new settlers. After the English Civil War was ended with the restoration of the Stuart kings in the person of Charles II, the British settlements were re-established and a new wave of settlers, mostly Scots, came into Ulster. This was based again mainly in the east of the country, where the settlers had never lost control in 1641. These arrangements were again challenged, at the end of the century, as part of the renewed English civil war between the two kings, James II and William III. The protestant, in Ireland British as well, cause prevailed and the power of England was reinforced over Ulster. This was linked to continuing efforts to develop the economy along the lines which the settlers saw as bringing them profit, either through producing goods for British and European consumers, and marketing them, or through producing things which the settlers themselves wanted.

Sites of the Plantation

These are all events of political history; how far are they relevant to archaeology? The Plantation of Ulster was a major political and administrative effort for the period. It generated a series of surveys of conditions, both before the actual settlement itself, but more importantly after it as the government tried to find out what was actually happening in Ulster, and whether the lords were carrying out the terms of their grants. We have a real knowlege of conditions from written sources that we have not from earlier periods; does this mean that archaeology is redundant from the early 17th century on for our knowlege of Ulster? For example, is it justifiable to spend money and effort on the excavation of a site which is represented on a contemporary detailed map or picture? If the object of the exercise is simply to check whether the map is "accurate", then the answer must surely be no. Even if the physical remains are well enough preserved to be able to be sure that the representation does not correspond to what it purported to show, this is hardly very serious. It would be very rash for anyone to argue that the details of a 16th or 17th century map or drawing were so accurate as to be more than a statement to the effect that "there is a fort (town or whatever) in this place of this sort of order of size and (maybe) containing these features, or that I am told that they will soon be built". Testing such a source on the ground is of little value. Again demonstrating that there was a 17th century house in a field in Ulster is of little value in itself, for we know that there were houses then; only its precise form, or its position in the overall pattern of settlement and if it changed our view of it, would be of much point. Only a standing building, as opposed to foundations and a ground plan, will give us the detail we need. This means craftmanship of roofs, windows or doors etc., or the specific arrangement of space in rooms. Only this level of information is useful as a basis of comparison with the other, standing 17th century buildings elsewhere.

The most basic contribution of the archaeology of this post-mediaeval period is that of explaining features present in the modern world. The campaigns of Mountjoy, especially his main force advancing from the Newry pass through Armagh to the crossing of the Blackwater between Benburb and Charlemont and so to Dungannon, caused many more or less permanent fortifications to be built in the country (Ill. 8-4). The later

wars had the same effect. An archaeologist who ventures into the field unaware of the possibilities of small forts or gun emplacements set up during one of these campaigns being the explanation of what he sees before him, is taking a serious risk of making a fool of himself. While the classic form of these should have one or more rectangular or spear-shaped bastions projecting from the angles, as at Fortwilliam in north Belfast, Charlemont or Enniskillen, they are not always present (Ill. 8-5). The best indications are probably the siting, which should be overtly military and strategic, rectangular plan even if without bastions, and the comparative freshness of the earthworks. Almost all the towns of Ulster have their origin, in the sense of a continuous history as towns, in the period, and in it are to be found the period's archaeology. There are places where the pattern of rural settlement also was created at this period: the strip fields in the countryside north of Carrickfergus were laid out shortly after 1600. High up in the hills are the remains of temporary houses, built for occupation during the summer, when whole communities moved their herds to exploit the upland grazing. Excavation has shown, along with the evidence of documents, that these sites, known as boolies (the practice of moving the herds into the uplands in the summer being called booleying) are often to be dated to the late mediaeval period, continuing down into the 18th century (Ill. 8-6). Field boundaries of this antiquity are almost certainly rare in Ulster, but the possibility of estate boundaries from the 17th century still surviving is high: the deer parks of Massareene near Antrim or Kiltierney in Fermanagh, date from Plantation estates (Ill. 8-7).

8-6. Plan of booley house from north Antrim.

305

8-7. Air photograph of Massareene deer park, distinctive because of its large modern fields.

We have already seen how the castles of the later 16th century can show the way that the lords of Gaelic society seem to have set less store by large permanent castles for display and accommodating their households, than did the lords in other mediaeval European societies. So, too, we can use the sites of the end of the 16th and early 17th centuries for the light they shed on other aspects of life before then. The excavation of sites known to have been used, or better constructed in this period gives us a view of the material culture prevailing then; a base line for comparison with secure dating. In pottery, for example, the end of the local hand-made ware, everted rim pottery in the face of the English wares brought in by the Plantation could tell us of the state of the craft in the earlier 16th century. Invasions, when they are well documented, always are able to provide a set of dated horizons for reference in other, less well-dated periods or sites. The plantation of Ulster was only one of the 17th century English colonies; another was in north America. The results and methods used in one place are of interest to the archaeologists in the other: it is no coincidence that teams from the United States have excavated in Ulster; at the Londonderry Plantation sites of Dungiven and Salterstown.

Fortifications

Actions speak louder than words. The policy of individuals and groups, even in political affairs is reflected in the physical remains. The reluctance of Queen Elizabeth to commit resources to Ulster in the 1560s is clearly shown by the parsimony of the fortification of Carrickfergus. Under James I the London companies charged with the defence of the city of Derry did build walls around it. They were weak by contemporary standards, however. Such artillery as was mounted was put along the battlements and not in ground level cannon ports; there was no outer line of defence beyond the wall, and only the bastions were backed with earth to mount the guns. The fortifications at Coleraine, excavated by Nick Brannon, were never more than a bank faced with sods. There were no major royal forts, such as Charles Fort at Kinsale to defend the Ulster coasts from foreign armies landing with a proper siege train. Clearly to the men who took the decisions about the threats to the political settlement of Ulster after 1603 saw internal, disorganised rebellion as the chief problem, not major warfare.

The same confidence can be seen in the individual houses and castles built by the incoming lords, which display a range of emphasis on military defence, or its lack. Sir Arthur Chichester (later Earl of Donegall) at Belfast and Carrickfergus built very grand Jacobean houses with splendid bay windows and quite indefensible; Sir Toby Caulfield at Charlemont and Castle Caulfield built similarly (Il1. 8-8). On the other hand, others put up tower houses which were equally clearly designed with defence in mind: tall buildings with few openings, especially at ground level, and those few loops for hand-guns, and with the doorway particularly defended. The Hamilton castle at Monea is well provided with loops at ground floor level, and the entrance is protected by a high machicolation arch between two towers, after the manner of a mediaeval castle gate. It could be that the men who were experienced in Irish campaigns and administration were less

8-8. Castle Caulfield.

nervous than the new arrivals, and so put up less defensive works. One of Chichester's major tenants and former army officer, Sir Moses Hill, however, erected a strong tower at Castle Chichester (Whitehead, Co. Antrim). The same man could display confidence in one building but not in another. Sir John Davies, writer, politician and lawyer, put up a defensive house at Castlederg, with loops and defended bawn, but at nearby Castle Curlews allowed himself the luxury of one bay window at least, negating its defence (Ill. 8-9, 8-10). General rules are clearly inapplicable, but the study of the individual designs both tells of the hopes and fears of the man concerned, and shows up the range of responses from those responsible for the Plantation; clearly not all saw it as a conquest to be maintained against a permanently hostile population.

8-9. Castle Derg.

8-10. Castle Curlews.

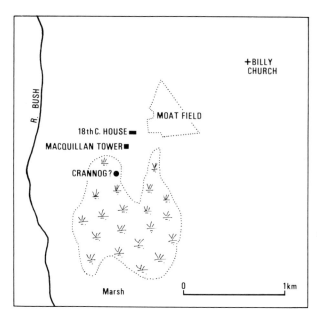

+BILLY
CHURCH

R. BUSH

MOAT FIELD

18th C. HOUSE ▬

MACQUILLAN TOWER ■

CRANNOG? ●

Marsh

0   1km

8-11. Ballylough
estate.

Settlement and houses

The archaeology of settlement from the 17th century onwards again hinges
on the role played by the new lords, and how far the Plantation represented
a total break with the preceding period. In the east of Ulster the fact that
a number of the places noted as the centres of manors or estates in the 13th
century are still found as significant centres implies that the settlement,
could well be built on an existing structure. Ballylough in Co. Antrim has
a crannog, a possible motte site, a MacQuillan tower house of the 15th

*8-12. Monea: crannog
and Plantation
castle.*

century, and the estate house of a lowland Scottish tenant of the MacDonnells established in the early 17th century, all close to each other. The parish church (Billy) is nearby, lending force to the indications that what we have here is an estate which has changed hands numbers of times, but which has remained as a unit notwithstanding (Ill. 8-11). If the estate could survive, might not the tenants too, with only the lords being affected by the changes? A number of Plantation castles are set near to crannogs, such as Monea or Roughan in Tyrone, which might argue for the same idea of continuity, as well as giving an indication that the crannog concerned was a place of importance when the new lord arrived (Ill. 8-12). By its nature this is a hard thing to demonstrate: how near must two sites be for us to accept a relationship? How many such associations are simply the result of the fact that many sites are bound to be near another, given the size of Ulster? How much are we seeing the fact of geographical factors asserting themselves in successive periods, that a good area for agriculture will always be so? The collection of sites in and around Newtownstewart may be such: the mediaeval stone castle at Harry Avery's, the crannog of island MacHugh, the Plantation castles of Derrywoone and Newtownstewart, all near each other in an area of obvious attraction to any settler. A curious case of adaption and continuity occurred at Dungiven. Here excavation and documentary research by Nick Brannon has revealed the house that Sir Edward Doddington built in 1611, attached to the end of the former Augustinian priory church (Ill. 8-13, 8-14).

8-13. *Dungiven: early 17th century view.*

8-14. *Dungiven: excavated plan.*

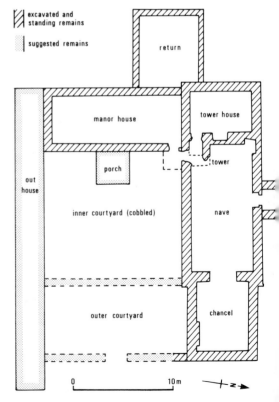

Archaeology can serve to emphasise the elements of survival through the political upheavals. The study of vernacular buildings surviving to the present day shows patterns both of construction and internal organisation of the houses and also of differing geographical patterns of some of the features. This is not the venue to discuss these features, but their existence and study is clearly a part of one form of archaeology. The traditions and patterns noted do not seem to be explained by patterns within the plantation scheme itself, such as areas of mainly Scottish or English settlement, or techniques of the incoming settlers, but either relate to adaptations made independently in different localities or else to pre-existing patterns of material culture. It reminds us again that the Plantation did not take place in a vacuum, nor was it responsible for a wholesale new settlement of people over much of Ulster. The new features are most prominent in the culture of the lords and the upper classes, irrespective of their background: the MacDonnells of Antrim with their English manor house and estate centred at Dunluce stand constantly to remind us that the cultural boundaries were not impermeable, and that class boundaries existed as strong as them. A timber-framed house in Coleraine was investigated by Philip Robinson, Nick Brannon and Mike Baillie. It was built of timbers felled in 1673 or 1674, replacing an earlier one of 1611 whose foundations survived to be excavated. The carpenter who built it adapted a basically English tradition of construction to Ulster conditions. Some fifty years after it was built much of the rubbish of the house, pottery, food bones or shells, etc. were swept into a single pit, a classic sealed deposit. A house nearby, at Liffock, again dated by dendrochronology, to 1691 or a few years later, was built in a different, northern English, style, with stone walls and a timber roof (Ill. 8-15). Houses of the Plantation

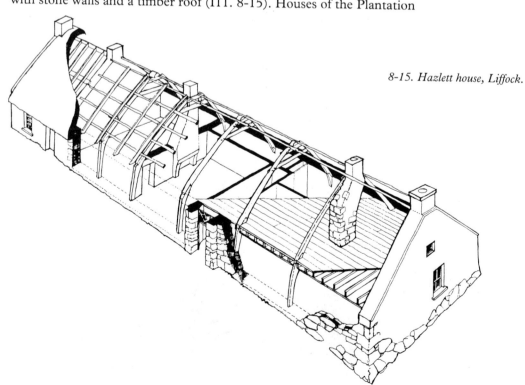

8-15. Hazlett house, Liffock.

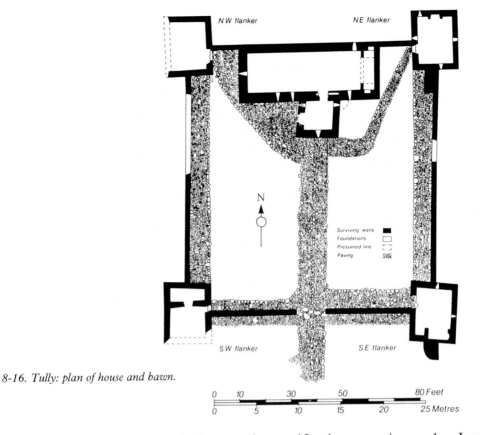

8-16. Tully: plan of house and bawn.

lords mostly lay between the grand Jacobean mansions such as Joymount or Dunluce and the emphasis on fortification given by the tower houses. Tully castle in Fermanagh, built between 1610 and 1618 and ruined in 1641 has a common arrangement: a defensible house set across one side of a bawn (Ill. 8-16, 8-17). The house had two main floors and an attic storey; defence was provided by loops for hand guns in the house - which also had corbelled rounds projecting over the bawn wall - and in the towers at the angles of the bawn. The house had a simple plan, a rectangle with a projecting block for the entrance and staircase. The vaulted ground floor has a large fireplace for the kitchen: the rest of the space was lit only by narrow loops, and was probably for storage. The first floor has two rooms:

8-17. Tully: house.

312

a major one - the descendant of the mediaeval hall - and a lesser one, a parlour or chamber. The attics have windows but no fireplaces; their use must have been purely as bedrooms. Excavations in the bawn has revealed the pattern of its pavements, paths running around all four walls and down the middle to link the bawn entrance to the house door. The corner towers of the bawn have fireplaces and were clearly meant to act as lesser houses or rooms. The paving along the walls shows that there were no lean-to buildings as you might expect: the central space divided by the path from the entrance, could have had buildings on either side, but it is very tempting to see it as a garden. The house and bawn were built for a Scot, Sir John Hume, but the house shows a mixture of English and Scottish design: its rubble walls and ground floor vault show that Irish masons built it.

The houses of the Plantation gentry during the first half of the 17th century tended to be informally designed in a mixed tradition, reflecting a life style that looked back to the middle ages. After the settlement of the late 1650's and 60's their heirs adopted more formal designs. Alexander Colville built a double pile house of later 17th century style - essentially two gabled houses built side by side with the thick central wall carrying the chimney stacks - at Galgorm near Ballymena. At Richhill in Co. Armagh Edward Richardson built a house whose plan, of a central rectangular block with side wings projecting forwards and a stair tower projecting behind, went back a long way. It was, however, planned and decorated with rigid symmetry, while the door was given classical features and the gables shaped in line with Dutch taste. At Killyleagh castle in Co. Down, the Hamiltons' Scottish tower house of the 1620's was converted into a symmetrical composition by adding a matching tower and shifting the door to the centre in the 1660's. The path lay on to the adoption of English of Continental fashions with the classical "Georgian" country houses of the 18th century.

Further down the social scale, evidence is less available, as the buildings merged with an insubstantial vernacular tradition. The house built by a member of the Savage family at Ballyspurge in Co. Down is not much smaller in area than Tully. It has no vault, and only one main floor with an attic, however, and while it has hand gun loops in the house, the bawn lacks flanking towers and is more like a simple walled farmyard. The ground floor had two rooms - hall and kitchen, perhaps - with large fireplaces; leaving the attic floor, which also had fireplaces, to provide the bedrooms. The informality in design of Berwick Hall, near Moira, Co. Down, and its thatched roof distance it from the self-conscious contemporary architecture of the larger late 17th century houses. The Hazlett house, at Liffock in Co. Londonderry, was built for the rector of the parish.

The 17th century church buildings follow a similar pattern. The new cathedral of Londonderry was a grand design of the 1620's interestingly in a purely Gothic style, comparable to a contemporary Oxford college like Wadham. The parish churches were much plainer, simple rectangular

8-18. Galgorm
church.

gabled structures such as Jeremy Taylor's church at Ballinderry, or St John's, Island Magee, both in Co. Antrim. They could show elements of formal design. The Colvilles at Galgorm built a fine west door to the church beside their house (Ill. 8-18); Doddington rebuilt the chancel arch at Dungiven when he converted the priory to a parish church; Sir John Dunbar gave his church at Derrygonnelly in Fermanagh in 1623 a doorway decorated with facetted blocks in a high Renaissance style. Tombs gave the lords fine opportunities to display their wealth and knowledge of fashion: from the finest imported English shop work for Chichester at Carrickfergus, through local work to a pattern book design for Montgomery at Grey Abbey, Co. Down, or a more homely affair for Sir Richard Hansard at Lifford, Co. Donegal.

Many of these buildings show the use of a new building material, which still dominates Ulster visually; brick. Its earliest use appears to be at Carrickfergus castle in the 1560's. The Plantation saw a great expansion in its use; it was well suited for the needs of the time, more permanent (and inflammable) than timber but yet easier and cheaper to build with than stone. Local brick works were set up in many parts of the Province but particularly in the east along the wooded valleys of the Bann and Lagan rivers. As such they helped in the cutting of these woods. One item links the exploitation of clay, social changes of peoples' lives and the colonisation of Ulster and America. This is the clay tobacco pipe, common on sites from the later 17th century onwards; their small size in the 17th century a reminder of the price of tobacco (Ill. 8-19).

From the early 17th century comes our earliest preserved examples of clothing which we can think of as typical. In the 1960's a farmer near Dungiven recognised the bits of cloth he found while digging out a bank as being both old and of clothing (Ill. 8-20). They proved to be a pair of trews, a jacket and a cloak. It cannot be proved that they belonged together

8-19. Tobacco pipe from Belfast, c. 1700.

314

8-20. Dungiven costume.

in the past but they may well have. All had been patched and repaired and they represented a mixture of traditions. The trews may have been from the Scottish Highlands, the jacket an Irish version of an essentially European (or English) garment, but the cloak undoubtedly Irish. Taken together they explained contemporary descriptions (the trews in particular would have hung low just as observers say they did) and give a good idea of the sort of clothes, partly cast-offs perhaps, that a follower of the O'Cahans in the early 17th century might have worn.

Behind the estates and the people working them lay the economic system within which the agriculture operated. Direct study of the intensity or the regional variations of agriculture are difficult. It would be most informative if we could estimate from the evidence of pollen analysis either the extent of the forest cover at the start of the 17th century or when it was cut down, whether to feed tanneries with oak bark and iron works with charcoal, leaving a cut-over scrub land, or whether the land was opened up quickly for agriculture. The problems are those inherent in the method of pollen analysis, imprecision of dating and uncertainty as to the geographical source of the pollen and so the size of the region to which the results apply, with an added one for this period in particular. If we seek our evidence from peat bogs, the normal source for preserved pollen, we must face the fact that most of the top layers of the bogs (which contain the pollen of this period) have been cut away for fuel, especially in the bogs close to the lowland areas good for agriculture, which would be those we would want to examine.

Towns

Contemporaries and modern scholars have seen the Plantation as crucially connected to the position of towns in Ulster. One of the aims of the settlement was to introduce a market society into Ulster in a way which was different from the Gaelic economy, and also a class of people rare in the Gaelic world, a bourgeoisie. We have seen that the Gaelic hostility to towns has been exaggerated; Carrickfergus survived the 15th century because of its usefulness to the O'Neills of Clandeboye. Likewise maps and descriptions both show that the O'Reilly's had a town at Cavan before the Plantation. Nor does the designation of a place by the Planters as a town necessarily mean that it was an instant economic success, and developed away from an essentially agricultural economy, or that it grew beyond the size of a village. Here excavation has a clear role; to define the limits of the settlement over time, before the onset of a steady set of maps in the 19th century, and to examine the density and stability of the urban plots and their boundaries. Just as with an earlier period, we need to see the permanence of plots as evidence of the maintenance of a steady property control, while their subdivision is clear evidence of a growing population demanding more houses or shops. As well as these aims, evidence of garden cultivation in the rear of the plots, or of industrial activity have a clear bearing on how we judge the economy of the towns. The Archbishops of Armagh have preserved a series of leases in parts of Armagh city which seem to show both that the core of the modern city, around Market Place, was both a deliberate piece of planned development of the 1620s and that there was a more substantial population west of the Cathedral before the Plantation than the accounts of the devastation of the wars would indicate. Excavation in Armagh by Chris Lynn, near the Market Place and down Scotch Street, which is one of the principal streets off it, would seem both to confirm the evidence of the new development. However, by providing evidence of a shallow pond at the top of the street, where the leases seem to show a house from the mid 17th century on, there seems to be a conflict between the documents and the results of excavation. If the evidence of detailed leases is not conclusive about the state of urban life, clearly the rest of the towns of Ulster, which do not have that, but only more general descriptions by visitors, have a need for additional sources of information.

Two sites in Belfast show the possibilities of excavation. Behind the street frontage of High Street, the gardens of the 17th century houses, themselves the most substantial in the town, were found, with the rubbish pits dug for the domestic refuse. In Waring Street itself laid out later in the 17th century than High Street, excavation behind the frontages showed a different pattern. Instead of the gardens of specific houses, there was an area of waste ground until the middle of the 18th century, on which accumulated the rubbish of the surrounding industries. The evidence of the difference of the two sites was seen in both the animal bones and in the pottery, those two classics of excavational evidence. The animal bones at High Street were mainly those of food animals, and the bones relating to food joints in particular; as well there were the bones of a dog, probably a domestic animal. At Waring Street the bones were mainly those of cattle, not the bones of food joints, but predominantly skulls, the by-product of the local tanneries, which were also responsible for the cattle hair found scattered over the site. As well as the evidence of the tanning there were also wasters and other pieces of pottery derived from the pottery kiln established in the area just before 1700 (Ill. 8-21). No products of the kiln were known, but it can now be seen that it was producing blue and white tin-glazed plates and other shapes, in imitation of the London and Dutch delftware factories of the 17th century. In fact the Belfast pottery was, after Bristol, the first such pottery to be established outside London in the British Isles.

Seventeenth and eighteenth century industry

Those who play tennis at Ballycastle rarely know the reason why the courts they play on dry so quickly after rain. The answer lies in a remarkable case of an early industrial venture, when the landlord of Ballycastle in the early and mid 18th century, Hugh Boyd, tried to set up a whole industrial complex. He mined the coal deposits of Fair Head as the basis for both fuel and as a product for export in its own right. He set up a brewery, tannery and soap works, but most notably a glass works (using local lime, clay and sand), beside a new harbour which he opened at the mouth of the Margy river, which he diverted for the purpose. The harbour is now occupied by

8-21. Early 18th century pottery made in Belfast.

8-22. *Drumbridge lock,*
Lagan Navigation canal.

the tennis courts, which drain so well because of the sand which has silted it up; the dunes behind cover his glass works. Neither the Belfast pottery nor the Ballycastle industrial complex succeeded, but both were part of the attempts of the 18th century to establish manufacturing industry in Ulster. The entrepreneurs concerned were trying to get the economy away from a reliance purely on agricultural produce and on importing the manufactures from Britain, just as the rise of the tanning and salt beef trades were attempts to respond to the English farmers' success in banning the trade in live cattle from Ireland to England. The new enterprises, above all the linen industry, needed good internal communications. In 1742 the Newry canal, still visible through most of its length from Newry to Lough Neagh, was opened to bring Tyrone coal to Dublin: the Lagan Navigation followed in stages during the latter half of the century (Ill. 8-22). It was during the later 18th century that the basic road network of Ulster was laid out.

8-23. *Edenderry village,*
Co. Down.

In the next century, the spread of the factories, above all of the textile industries is well documented. The actual construction of the factories and the machinery within them is less well so and requires the physical evidence for its elucidation. More obvious are the houses which grew up around the factories, some of them in the towns, but better preserved in the purpose built villages, such as Edenderry, Darkley or Sion Mills (I11. 8-23). These must constitute one of the primary pieces of evidence, not of the growth of the factories, but of the social consequences for the people who moved into the new settlements in search of work. They provide an interesting example of the contact of industrialisation (the actual construction of the houses was based on bricks and timber, no longer the products of the immediate locality), with the social patterns of the countryside, expressed in the actual arrangements and size of the houses themselves. The new factories made money, for their owners and for the middle classes in general. The result was the expansion of the suburbs with their substantial villas, exemplified by those of south Belfast (I11. 8-24). In the countryside the numerous 19th century farmhouses stand witness to the rising prosperity of the farmers of the period, just as the replacement of their farm buildings by modern pre-fabricated sheds symbolises the rise of industrial farming.

Detecting immigration

Communications in the sense of the means by which ideas were spread around within society has always been a key concern of archaeologists. The English conquest and Plantation saw a massive influx of people into Ulster, perhaps equal to a third or more of the Irish population: can we see in their archaeology, the way that ideas also travelled? Some, their nervousness in the face of possible attack, the extent and means by which they transformed the economy, we have already looked at. There remain the evidence of the sources of ideas linked to crafts, either the influence of the Plantation on traditional ones or the start of new ones. The buildings of the period are

8-24. Late 19th century villas, south Belfast.

319

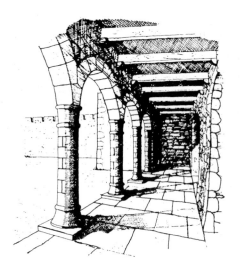

8-25. Dunluce: Italianate loggia.

the best starting point. The Plantation was not the only means of the spread of ideas and styles from outside into Ulster. The O'Docherty castle of Burt in Donegal is shown on a drawing of 1601; in plan it is a square tower with round turrets at two diagonally opposed corners (Ill. 7-39). This is a design aimed at giving flanking fire down all four walls without the expense of building four corner turrets. It is a Scottish plan, the so-called Z plan, but here used by an Irish lord before the Plantation. The MacDonnelll castle of Dunluce is a much more spectacular example of the influx of designs in the late 16th century (Ill. 7-37). The main block is a manor house of fine late 16th century English type, marked by its splendid bay windows and the internal arrangement of hall, great upper chamber and the rooms servicing the hall. The manor house cut across an earlier and more exotic structure, however. This was a line of classical columns, part of an Italianate *loggia*, facing north in the proper fashion, to protect the MacDonnells from the heat of the north Antrim sun (Ill. 8-25). Its design was a reflection of Scottish fashion again, the result of the close links between early 16th century Scotland and Renaissance France.

The incoming lords of the Plantation came from both England and Scotland. The combination of their own cultural background and that of the workmen whom they employed, gave a complex mixture of design. The English tradition resulted in manor houses, more or less undefended, and built to provide a fine hall and chambers, such as a great chamber or a large parlour, even perhaps a long gallery, all well lit by large windows and with large fireplaces. The Scots brought with them a tradition based on their tower houses, marked often by ultimately French motifs such as a fondness for small turrets corbelled out at roof level, or rather heavy roll mouldings around doors. As a rule, the Planters of the two nationalities built in their own styles, just as their tenants tended also to be of their nationality, which also confirmed the stylistic division, for the tenants often included the actual craftsmen.

320

8-26. Turrets at Monea (left) and Claypotts.

The top storeys, square turrets oversailing the round entrance towers below, of Monea castle in Fermanagh, built by the Scot, Malcolm Hamilton, are clearly derived from the castle of Claypotts in Fife, although the rest of the castle is quite different (Ill. 8-26). Castle Caulfield is equally English in its style, the work of Sir Toby Caulfield. The complete picture is not quite as simple as that, however. There are castles, such as Castle Balfour in Fermanagh, built between 1618 and 1625, which combines an English bay window with Scottish details. Other sites combine Irish details of construction, notably the practice of constructing vaults on a bed of mortar supported by wicker mats, which leave their imprint on the underside of the vault. Significantly, the signs of Irish workmanship seem to occur most frequently on the earliest monuments, a result both of the fact that the early Planters brought no workmen with them and of the spread of English or Scottish techniques through the craft as the numbers of incoming masons built up. The idea of the bawn is similar to the Scottish barmkin, also a courtyard attached to tower houses, but the decision of the Government to require the Planters to build one as well as a strong house or castle on their estates is derived from Irish, not Scottish, experience. It is actually quite difficult to point to a building of the Plantation or its period in Ulster which is very similar to one built for a man of the same class in Britain; all show some admixture of styles and adaptation to the local conditions. The same is true of the churches that they erected. There are some very splendid individual items of imported style, most notably the magnificent Chichester tomb in St. Nicholas' church in Carrickfergus (Ill. 8-27). There is only the one church which, as a whole, belongs to Britain in its style; the cathedral at Derry, which is a very successful essay in the latest Gothic manner, even if its scale is that of an English parish church rather than a cathedral (Ill. 8-28).

8-27. Chichester tomb,
Carrickfergus.

The way that building styles reflected both what those who paid for them knew of fashions outside, and the associations of those fashions, continues down through time as much as other aspects. Fashion dictated the layout of the gardens and parks attached to the great houses of the 18th century aristocracy. The change and importance of style is nowhere better exemplified than at Castle Ward, where the new house replaces a tower house as

322

8-28. Londonderry walls and the Church of Ireland Cathedral.

the centre of the estate. The house remarkably "combines" classical and 'Gothick' fashions, the first the choice of Lord Bangor, the latter the choice of his wife; the old taste and the new romanticism. At the same time the park was re-planned with formal planting of trees and the creation of a lake in the latest English style; none of the elements of the house or gardens have their origin in Ireland (Ill. 8-29). In the 19th century, the Gothic style had clear High Church, Anglican or Catholic associations, and the Presbyterians and other Non Conformists were consequently reluctant and slow to build in it. The style in both cases reflects the cultural identity of the people involved, as it still does, whether in a new church or even in a new housing estate where each house is equipped with a "Georgian" porch.

We have strayed far from what many people see as the correct objectives of archaeological study, into the remits of social and economic historians, historical geographers, the students of the history of vernacular building, architecture, industrial archaeology or of folk life. This is true, but it is impossible to draw chronological lines across the subject. Archaeology studies the human past through the material remains of that past and so in a sense it continues down to the present. This is only partly the case, however, for there is clearly a difference between those periods when archaeology is the only source of evidence, and the more recent times when our knowlege of the past is overwhelmingly derived from contemporary accounts of events. This leaves out one further role for the study of the material remains, well exemplified in the popularity of the Ulster Folk Museum. The rebuilt houses and exhibits here evoke a rural world which has now all but disappeared in a way that a book cannot. Direct experience of the objects and sites from the past can stimulate interest in that past much more keenly for some people than can a written account. In this way, the study of archaeology goes beyond simply illustrating the past into encouraging a direct contact with it and interest in it. In the study of recent fashions, also, we can see the way society is always subject to change, and that past times were not all the same, a sort of uniform, perennial and featureless existence into which we may project our ideas taken from a variety of different periods all mixed together and either romanticised or treated with contempt. As individuals, our past clearly goes into making us what we are today; so it is with societies, and so we need to know what happened in the past if we are to understand the present, let alone cope with the future.

8-29. Castle Ward.

9 Retrospect and Prospect

Although any attempt to draw lessons from archaeology places us in a virtual minefield, we cannot avoid some form of summing up. After all, there is no other discipline that provides such a long look at the evolution of human society and such a work as this would hardly be complete without a few comments about the development of both Ulster society and the discipline of archaeology within Ulster.

The Identity of Ulster

Throughout this book we have taken the present geographical borders of Ulster as our guide and among the questions we have asked is to what extent the archaeological record supports the notion that a distinct cultural province evolved here. In general, our conclusions have been less than clear and archaeological remains have often emphasized either regionalism within Ulster itself or the fact that Ulster participated in the same type of cultural behaviour that we often find outside its borders. The lessons of archaeology are comparable to those of history: Ulster has always been very much a movable feast. If we search for it in the distribution of megalithic tombs, Neolithic and Bronze Age ceramics, Early Bronze Age burials, or Early Christian raths and souterrains, it is virtually invisible unless we invoke territorial claims over land that has never been regarded as Ulster. To be sure, there have been artifacts whose distribution seems to be distinctly confined to Ulster - Neolithic Goodland bowls or Early Christian souterrain ware - but these are not found over all of Ulster but are confined to certain territories within the province. In the Iron Age we have seen traces of some form of early political boundary if that is indeed how we may best interpret our linear earthworks but even then Ptolemy reminds us that those who gave us the name of Ulster itself, the Uluti of Armagh, south Down and Louth, were only one of the tribes who lived north of the Black Pig's Dyke, albeit they may have been the most powerful. Moreover, in the Iron Age when our evidence for some form of 'Ulster' is strongest, it is still exceedingly difficult to argue that it was 'culturally' distinct from its immediate neighbours of north Connacht and Leinster. If cultural divisions must be made for prehistory, they are far easier seen between Munster and all that lies north rather than between Ulster and its immediate neighbours to the south.

The historical circumscription of Ulster continued with the Early Christian Ulaid, the dynasty that pseudo-historical tradition once credited as rulers of Emain Macha, who were confined to Antrim and Down. The Ulaid in turn gave way to the English Earldom of "Ulster", which covered the coastal regions of Down, Antrim and north Londonderry. At the end of the Middle Ages came the claims (and pretensions) of the O'Neills. The current geographical boundaries of Ulster are nothing more than the legacy of Queen Elizabeth's map-makers. Whatever ethnic or cultural identity lurks behind the name of Ulster today is more a subject for study by political scientists or social-psychologists than the archaeologist who can readily see that the term Ulster means very different things to different people both within and outside the present borders of the province.

What is our legacy from the past? This is an even harder question than the first although here we can make some concrete statements. We hope that this book has shown to what extent the very landscape of today's Ulster is essentially the result of thousands of years of settlement. Man's impact on the Ulster landscape since the Neolithic has been severe enough to render this land one of the most treeless in Europe and although the denudation of our forests received a final blow in the 17th century, much of it had long since disappeared under the hand of Neolithic and Bronze Age farmers. It was also the activities of man, coupled with climate, that is responsible for much of the extensive boglands that cover the province.

Another obvious legacy of the past is the identity of the modern population of Ulster. How far the roots of this identity stretch back in time is debateable but the Neolithic makes a convincing starting point. Prior to the arrival of the first farmers, the population of Ireland is unlikely to have ever been very large. As we have already seen, Mesolithic communities had to live a mobile way of life and depend on natural resources for their subsistence. This would have tended to keep population levels quite low. However, with the arrival of the first farmers in Ireland we would expect that the population would have begun to climb quite rapidly. By the end of the Neolithic most of Ireland would have been well settled with different farming communities. Whether they all spoke the same language or different languages we can have no idea. What is important is that they established the major population basis of this island. By this we mean that no subsequent immigration to Ireland is ever likely to have contained anywhere near the number of people as were already settled in Ireland before they arrived. Whether we accept the putative movement of Bronze Age peoples or a variety of Iron Age Celtic populations, subsequent Vikings, Scots, Huguenots, or English, each was invariably only an intrusive minority to the already existing population of Ulster. Neither this island nor this province has ever been ethnically 'pure' - be it Gaelic, Cruthin, or whatever the modern political propagandist might hope to summon up - but rather it is a compilation of preceding identities coupled with however its contemporary population chooses to see itself.

Retrospect

The first extensive recording of antiquities in Ulster as with most other areas of Ireland is probably to be associated with the work of the Ordnance Survey of the 1830s. Depending on county or parish, the members of the Ordnance Survey collected an unparalleled record of 'Druidical Altars'

9-1. 'Druidical altar' (court tomb) on Browndod Hill by James Boyle in the
    Ordnance Survey Memoir for the parish of Donegore, 1838.

(Ill. 9-1), 'Druidical Circles', 'Dane's Forts', and other monuments, many
of which have since been destroyed. The visit to Ulster by the British
Association for the Advancement of Science in 1852 prompted both a
major display of antiquities that had been assembled by various collectors,
including a catalogue, and stimulated certain gentlemen to found the *Ulster
Journal of Archaeology* whose first series ran from 1853 to 1862. The scope
of the journal then reflected the greater range of antiquarian interest and
included not only archaeological monuments but historical, literary and
folkloric material that have since found homes in their own more specialised
journals. Similarly, the second series of the *Ulster Journal of Archaeology*
(1894-1911) showed a comparable diversity in scope. Much of the
directed research was in the hands of members of the Belfast Natural
History and Philosophical Society and the local field clubs, especially the
Belfast Naturalists' Field Club. From the 1870s into the early 20th
century, these organizations spearheaded the investigations into the raised
beaches at Larne and determined at least during which geological time
man first established himself in Ulster.

In 1874 the Belfast Naturalists' Field Club also began publishing
summaries of the antiquities of Ulster for both the visit of the British
Association for the Advancement of Science and their own guide to Belfast
and adjacent counties. These accounts along with an updated version from
1902 are similar in their contents, and indeed in their arrangement. They
are primarily concerned to list examples of the various types of monuments
and artifacts found in the province. The individual types, particularly of
the monuments, include sites which we would now distinguish: for
example, the category of forts includes anything with a bank or ditch, such

as the Giant's Ring or Navan, along with sites identified from mentions in the historical annals, such as Dunluce or Dunseverick. The section on castles includes, without discrimination, the early ones such as Carrickfergus or the later tower houses. Dates are very rare, and derived from documentary references. This is particularly surprising for the church sites, where the sequence of the development of architectural styles in Europe had been well studied, certainly by the end of the 19th century. Although the authors recognized that what often passed in common speech as forts built by the Danes were actually earlier, they still lacked a firm chronology for many of their monuments. One of the more fascinating errors was the assumption that souterrains were constructed by prehistoric Ulstermen who had become too populous for life in natural caves which, on analogy with southern Britain, were presumed to be the earliest habitations of the people of this island.

As for artifacts, the adoption of the Danish Three-Age system provided some order for prehistoric antiquities which could at least be arranged into Stone, Bronze and Iron ages but the association between historical sites and objects was still hopelessly unclear; each was isolated as though in its separate collection cabinet and its value was normally reckoned in 'its interest to antiquarians'. Ulster archaeology was reminiscent of a stroll through a museum gallery rather than an account of how society had developed through time.

During the interwar years archaeologists in Ulster began addressing the problems of relating objects to sites. They undertook excavations, such as those at Nendrum monastery by Henry Lawlor, which were aimed, however unsuccessfully in practice, at establishing dates and linking artifacts with settlements. Lawlor was able to follow Goddard Orpen's work over the rest of Ireland and identify mottes as English castle mounds, separate from earlier forts. It was also Lawlor who wrote the first independent account of Ulster's archaeology. His *Ulster: Its archaeology and antiquities*, the published account of a series of lectures broadcast by the BBC, appeared in 1928. Although very much out of date, Lawlor's account is an attempt to narrate the development of Ulster from what today we would term the Mesolithic through at least the 16th century.

The first colonists, according to Lawlor, came essentially in search of the Antrim flint and then only later began penetrating the interior of the province, sailing up the Bann and Lagan in their coracles. Lawlor pondered whether the earliest Ulstermen knew fire and whether they cooked their meals in ceramic vessels, since the concept of a period that was subsequent to the Palaeolithic but prior to the Neolithic was not yet commonly known or accepted in Ireland. Lawlor began man's colonization about 10,000 years ago which was not far off the mark. His Bronze Age, which he began rightly about 2500 BC, was marked by distant contacts between metal-using communities of Ireland and the Near East and the erection of the megalithic tombs which we know today to belong essentially to the Neolithic. In this way Ulster archaeology could in some way be 'explained' by its distant Asian contacts, so much so that Lawlor could propose that one of the marks on the Knockmany tomb could be read as 'waves, the sea' in Egyptian hieroglyphics and that one could trace the spread of Akhnaton's sun-cult westwards to Ireland. The megalithic monuments were interpreted as 'funereal memorials over graves of persons of great importance'. It is also in the Bronze Age that Lawlor would see the introduction of what we now term a Neolithic economy based on stockbreeding and agriculture. Today an understanding of the origins and structure of the subsistence economy of a people is of the highest importance; in Lawlor, he could dismiss the evidence for coastal sites as 'resorts' and liken them to summer holidays by the sea. In general, Lawlor accounts for Ulster's prehistoric development as a distant outpost of Near Eastern civilization, continuously brought into contact with more highly developed peoples through trade and immigration which culminated in the arrival of the Celts about 400 BC and whose culture, he imagined, developed 'fairly free from foreign influence' up to 800 AD. His account of the historical period relies very heavily on the documentary sources, so much so that the evidence of archaeology seems more for illustrative purposes rather than his primary source of evidence.

The major figures of Ulster archaeology of the 1930s and 40s were Oliver Davies (Ill. 9-2) and Estyn Evans (Ill. 9-3) who pioneered a more scientific approach to archaeology and re-established the *Ulster Journal of Archaeology* in 1938 which has since become the longest continually published local journal in Ulster. Both Davies and Evans identified areas requiring

9-2. Oliver Davies on Browndodd Hill, Co. Antrim.

9-3. Estyn and Gwyneth Evans surveying Goward court tomb, Co. Down, in 1932.

further research and undertook an ambitious course of excavation of megalithic monuments, especially court tombs, as well as encouraging the work of others. While Evans also made major contributions to the study of Ulster folklife, Davies who was trained originally as a classical archaeologist, undertook an indefatigable programme of study of all periods of Ulster's archaeology. In his concern to continue the study of archaeology down into the 17th century, Davies refused to follow the normal practice of English archaeologists of the time, who stopped either at the end of the Roman Empire, or with the Vikings. This is evident from his numerous site reports but also for his valedictory summary of the archaeology of Ulster based on a course given to the Workers' Educational Association in Armagh in 1946-47 and published in the *Ulster Journal of Archaeology* for 1948 and 1949. Davies account provides a useful benchmark in the history of Ulster archaeology.

Davies emphasizes the importance of Ulster's environment on the development of its society although he sometimes takes it a peculiar distance, for example, when he notes how 'the warm moist climate which prevails today ... has created a heavy atmosphere which produces mental stagnation and laziness, which form a drag on the natural capabilities of the people'.

In Davies' account, the Mesolithic was a well-known concept and he began the settlement of Ulster with the 'Larnian' about 5500 BC and, interestingly, reversed the technological evolution of the Mesolithic by having microliths introduced into Ireland towards the end of the Mesolithic. It was also at this time that he believed pottery to have been adopted by hunter-gatherers in Ulster from their neighbours in Scotland. An actual immigration of farmers was not held to have occurred until after 1500 BC. They were primarily associated with the various types of megalithic tombs, all of which Davies derived from the Mediterranean. Indeed, Davies envisaged a series of migrations emanating from Sardinia or France that eventually made their way to Ulster. The economic basis of society was viewed as primarily pastoral, even semi-nomadic, and socially Ulster was divided into tribes, ruled by priest-chiefs, for whom the megalithc tombs were presumably erected. Davies believed that the 'megalithic folk were obsessed with the cult of the dead'; it might be fairer to say that it is archaeologists who have been so obsessed, at least with respect to mega-lithic tombs.

Because of the discovery of Bronze Age objects in megalithic tombs, Davies believed that the society that built them persisted through the Bronze Age, the larger megalithic tombs ultimately 'degenerating' into portal tombs, which we now know date to the Neolithic, and the more typical Early Bronze Age cists. Without absolute techniques for dating, the chronology of the Bronze Age was unclear, especially because of the re-use of earlier megalithic tombs. Hence Davies envisaged Beaker intruders entering Ulster from 1500 to 800 BC and dated the stone circles to approximately this same period.

Davies saw 900 BC as a watershed in Ulster's prehistory. This was not only the date which he assigned the beginning of the Late Bronze Age but also the Celtic invasions (Davies suspected that these were the Cruthin of early Ulster history) midst a 'catastrophic deterioration of the climate'. Davies' Celts seemed to have been primarily the result of Late Bronze Age population movements with some subsequent Iron Age tribal incursions and the introduction of the La Tène art style after 500 BC. The frontiers of the 'state of Ulster' could be seen in the erection of linear earthworks such as the Black Pig's Dyke, which Davies assumed had been erected in imitation of Roman frontier-works.

Because of his own extensive fieldwork, especially in the south of the province, Davies was able to distinguish between various types of raths, either by their form or by their siting. Again his excavations, uncovering either souterrain ware or everted rim ("crannog ware") pottery, linked the raths to the first millennium A.D., along with the introduction of the Christian church. The distribution of raths, in the lower lands of Ulster, showed to Davies that settlement had moved down from the uplands of prehistoric farming. Crannogs he linked to the same period, again as the result of excavation, but he saw their origins as earlier, and recognised, too that they remained in use until the 16th century, the epitome of the Gaelic Irish world. Davies, too, was concerned to place the archaeology of Ulster into the context of a general picture of the historical archaeology of Europe, in terms of craftsmen and the builders or inhabitants of the sites. Castles were an indication of the immigration not only of their lords but of tenants, brought over in the 13th century to establish a fully English manorial settlement system. Following Leask, he interpreted the late church remains and the tower houses very much in terms of a Gaelic revival of the 15th century: archaeology reflected documented political events of history, such as invasions.

The period between 1930 and 1948 was very much a pioneering effort which saw the successful co-operation between professionals such as

Evans and Davies and numerous amateurs who assisted them, published excavations and helped produce the *Preliminary Survey of the Ancient Monuments of Northern Ireland* in 1940. In the years following the departure of Oliver Davies, a more formal role for archaeology within Northern Ireland was seen in the establishment of a Department of Archaeology at Queen's University in 1949 with the appointment of Martyn Jope and, in the next year, the founding of the Archaeological Survey which set in motion the invaluable contributions of Dudley Waterman (Ill. 9-4) and Pat Collins (Ill. 9-5). The collaboration between these three resulted in the monumental *Archaeological Survey of Co. Down*. Published in 1966, this produced a complete inventory of all sites in the county, except for raths, and a broad summary of the archaeology of Ulster which clearly indicates how far Ulster archaeology had come since even Davies' time.

The current generation of archaeologists has enjoyed great advances in the recovery of information and the dating of archaeological sites but it is not clear that this great increase in the quality and quantity of information has led to a great change in the interpretations offered. This is something that we have become painfully aware of in writing this book; Irish archaeology offers sites and objects galore but few original ideas and interpretations. If Lawlor and Davies tracked down the ultimate origins of Ulster's societies to the Near East and Mediterranean, interpretations of

9-4. Dudley Waterman (left) with T. G. F. Paterson of the Armagh Museum.

332

9-5. Pat Collins.

Irish archaeology, when attempted at all, have largely looked to theories and methods employed in Britain rather than been generated at home.

The search for explanations, which has characterised this century, has shown one thing. The original aim of some that the study of the material remains of the past would act to fill in the gaps when documentary history failed, has proved illusory. Archaeology tells us about long-term social and economic trends, not about the political events which dominate much of our historical record, and so we cannot write the same sort of historical story from the physical evidence. On the other hand, the material remains of the past are just as dominated by the leaders of society as the documents; archaeology, like history, informs us little about the poor and the losers of society.

The one clear lesson from this brief survey of the development of archaeology in Ulster is that whatever follows it in another twenty years will obviously be very different from what we have produced. Archaeologists should never be so obsessed with the past that they neglect the future and in concluding this volume, we ask ourselves where archaeology in Ulster should be going.

Prospect

At the turn of this century those interested in archaeology seemed content to merely tick off the types of sites and objects that we possessed, often applying them to a check-list of British sites. We have seen that among the major contributions of this century are the establishment of what types of objects associated with what types of sites, the development of better chronologies, and the extensive planning of the distribution of sites. We should now be more concerned with establishing contexts for our sites and artifacts. This means moving away from seeing sites as individual entities on their own, and working towards a view of the nature of the connections between them, whether the physical landscape in which they were built or the social position which their builders held in society. To establish the physical environment, we should be looking at the varying site types for this. Some are in certain specialised environmental locations: uplands or coastal sandhills, for example. These are economic niches within, or alongside, the general system of exploitation of the country's resources and we are still very uncertain how they inter-relate within either the pattern of seasonal hunter-gatherer movements or lowland agriculture. The arsenal of palaeoenvironmental techniques is already being employed to resolve some of these problems and it is a safe prediction that any future archaeology of Ulster will be both more concerned and better able to discuss the patterns of settlement within Ulster with respect to soils, environments, climate, and patterns of subsistence economy.

The questions of the links between sites through the physical environment must be augmented by referring to their links within society. We have become aware of the emergence of increasingly hierarchical societies from the Neolithic onwards, and by the time of the historic period, we are conscious of an outright class structure, often described in documentary sources. The people whose sites and artifacts we study lived within these structures and we must expect the archaeology to be related to them. This means exploring the ways in which we might be able to assign certain sites to certain classes; to understand the system of patronage and status that might lie behind the production of individual artifacts. If we can begin to see such distinctions, then it becomes possible that we might be able to see the hierarchy of society functioning at a certain period in a particular area, either an estate or a group of them. To do this, of course, will require us to be clear about chronology, of whatever period. We have seen the problems that trying to work in such a direction from maps alone in the Early Christian period leads to; without being reasonably sure that sites were occupied at the same time we cannot evaluate their occupants' social relationships. Dendrochronology offers us such a tool, which makes it possible in certain circumstances, to say the year in which a house or other wooden structure was erected.

But it is unlikely that for the more distant past that we will be able to date sites more precisely and we may have to be content with more general associations between, for example, megalithic tombs and the settlements of their builders. In the later periods, also, we cannot be too hopeful of a complete picture. One of the stubbornest problems remains the invisibility in archaeology of the lower classes of society. In the absence of enclosed or nucleated settlements which we can identify from remains above the surface, we are always groping for the houses of the bulk of the population.

These aims of exploring environmental and social links lead towards the intensive study of a particular area. This could be studied either at a certain chosen period, where sites can be identified, such as megaliths, raths or mottes, or else through time. The more we think of such questions, the more we are led to demand that we study sites where organic remains might be preserved in wet conditions. In either case the study would require two things. One is a long-term commitment to it by a team of people with expertise, not just in the field of the archaeology of the period, but also of environmental study and documentary evidence. The second commitment would be that this would be done as a matter of research, as opposed to a response to a threat of destruction. It is possible that such a threat to a whole district might emerge, as with the proposals for open-cast mining of lignite or the like, but it is unlikely. Rather, we would wish to see archaeologists teamed with other disciplines identifying and studying specific local areas through time. To some extent this has already begun with the work of the Navan Research Group which has been making an intensive study of the archaeology and environment of the Navan complex coupled with the available historical and literary sources. But Navan is a unique monument and perhaps a better parallel might be drawn with the Carnlough project which investigated patterns of both lowland and upland settlement around the Glencloy river from the Mesolithic up into the historical period. A future *Archaeology of Ulster* should be able to present detailed case studies of the various different environments of Ulster through time such as coastal occupation along Donegal, lakeland settlement in the Erne basin, or upland settlement in Antrim and Tyrone, where areas would take precedence over the pigeon-holing of sites by chronology.

One obvious goal of any local approach is to investigate how the various sub-regions within Ulster developed and what prompted their existence. We have seen over time the establishment of particular cultural areas, at least they would appear so if our distribution maps of artifacts and site types are anything to go by, within the province itself. County Antrim, for example, often exhibits particular artifact types - Beaker wrist bracers, Collared Urns, etc. - that suggest the presence of some form of cultural border along the lower Bann. Similarly, central Ulster marks itself during the Late Neolithic or Early Bronze Age with its major concentration of stone circles but, during the Early Christian period, is almost entirely devoid of souterrains which are densely concentrated in Antrim, north Londonderry and south Down-Armagh-Louth and more sporadically in the west in Donegal. The mechanisms responsible for such distributions may be in part the product of geographical barriers promoting particular cultural regions, in part social and reflective of particular tribal territories, and part economic indicating where certain schools of craft specialists operated.

From a theoretical point of view, tackling all these issues should promote more thought about Ulster archaeology and help stimulate archaeologists to think more about what their sites and artifacts actually mean within their own region. This means not only more and better data but also more thought. How is this to be accomplished?

The future of archaeology in Ulster is very much a question of resources, not so much financial as human. Archaeology has now become too much the preserve of a small group of professionals who are responsible for the vast bulk of the research being carried out. This is something which we must hope will change, and work towards this end. As we have already seen, it was not always so: the first of the accounts of Ulster archaeology, that of 1874, was written by members of the Belfast Naturalists' Field Club, and much of the work between the wars, culminating in the *Preliminary Survey of Ancient Monuments*, was done by unpaid, amateur (in the best sense of the word) workers. With the emphasis on excavation and high standards of recording has come an impression that archaeology is no longer the sort of study where amateurs may join in and publish research alongside professionals. This emphasis on pure professionalism is not only unwarranted but very much out of step with other countries who invest far more in archaeology. In both America and Britain, for example, amateur associations and volunteer assistance often provides both the backbone and stimulus for much of archaeological research. This is a position that professionals in Ulster should seek to emulate.

There are two fundamental reasons why we need greater amateur involvement. The first is a practical one. The period when archaeology has been dominated by professionals, since around 1950, has not been particularly successful in one of its most basic tasks: the preservation of the monuments of our past. During this time, there has been a steady attrition of sites, by farmers, developers and others, which has seemed beyond the power of the legal protection of Historic Monuments Acts or the activities of the few archaeologists to prevent. There are many reasons for the pressure on the physical remains of our past, from the social upheavals of the steady desertion of the countryside by people moving to the town, to the availability of earth-moving equipment or the application of the economies of scale to farming. It is one of the ironies of life that the increase in education has led to a decline in superstition, which served well to protect our monuments. Archaeology has failed, in Europe as a whole, not just in Ulster, to take its place in the general pressure for the conservation of the environment, along with the other groups. By becoming concerned with professional standards, archaeology has risked losing touch with the support of people, who will ultimately ensure, much better than the actions of professionals, that there is archaeology left for future generations to study.

The second reason for the need to revitalise the amateur involvement in the subject is academic. Professionals will always be few and stretched with other demands on their time, administration, teaching or whatever. They are never going to be able to know a region or locality as well as those who live in it and spend their days moving about it. These are the people who have in the past been on hand to walk the fields after they have been ploughed, or look down new drainage cuts, or the foundations for buildings. In this way many of the major discoveries have been made, such as the Ballynagilly prehistoric site or the Downpatrick pottery kiln of the historic period, and the way we will make the key ones in the future. We identified two areas of likely advances in knowlege in historic archaeology: the intensive study of the sites of a single area and their inter-relationship with the environment, and the finding of lower-class settlement. These are both likely to happen as the result, not of a full-scale professional research project, at least at first, but as the result of an interested amateur. He, or she will find the site or identify a promising area for study, and be able to relate sites to environment through their daily practical knowlege and experience better than a theoretical, professional approach. The two will have to work together, but at present a subject relying on a few professionals alone for its research is condemning itself to a limited and ineffective future; the future lies with amateurs.

Guide to further reading

Abbreviations

Anglo-Norman Ulster = Anglo-Norman Ulster, T. E. McNeill, 1980, Edinburgh.
Barry = The Archaeology of Medieval Ireland, T. B. Barry, 1987, London.
Catalogue = A Catalogue of Irish Iron Age Antiquities, B. Raftery, 1983, Marburg.
Dixon = Ulster Architecture, H. Dixon, 1975, Belfast.
Donegal = An Archaeological Survey of County Donegal, B. Lacey et al., 1983, Lifford.
Down = An Archaeological Survey of County Down, E. M. Jope et al., 1966, Belfast, HMSO.
Green = The Industrial Archaeology of County Down, E. R. R. Green, 1963, Belfast.
Hickey = Images of Stone, H. Hickey, 1976, Belfast.
H.M.N.I. = Historic Monuments of Northern Ireland, HMSO, 1983, Belfast.
Hoards = Hoards of the Irish Later Bronze Age, G. Eogan, 1983, Dublin.
IARF = Irish Archaeological Research Forum.
INJ = Irish Naturalists Journal.
Irish Antiquity = Irish Antiquity, Essays and Studies presented to M. J. O'Kelly, Ed. D. Ó. Corráin, 1981, Cork.
JIA = Journal of Irish Archaeology.
JRSAI = Journal of the Royal Society of Antiquaries of Ireland.
Landscape = Landscape Archaeology in Ireland, Ed. T. Reeves Smyth and F. Hamond, BAR British Series 116, 1983, Oxford.
Monaghan = Archaeological Inventory of Co. Monaghan, A. Brindley, 1986, Dublin.
PBNHPS = Proceedings of the Belfast Natural History and Philosophical Society.
Pieces = Pieces of the Past, Ed. A. Hamlin and C. Lynn, 1988, Belfast.
PPS = Proceedings of the Prehistoric Society.
PRIA = Proceedings of the Royal Irish Academy.
Studies = Studies on Early Ireland: Essays in Honour of Michael V. Duignan, Ed. B. G. Scott, 1982, Belfast.
UJA = Ulster Journal of Archaeology.

General Reading:

There are three general prehistories of Ireland available: M. J. O'Kelly's *Early Ireland*, Cambridge Univ. Press (1989), Peter Harbison's *Prehistoric Ireland*, Thames and Hudson (1988) and the recently reprinted but somewhat dated *Ireland in Prehistory* by Michael Herity and George Eogan, Routledge and Kegan Paul (1977). To these should be added Frank Mitchell's excellent *The Shell Guide to Reading the Irish Landscape*, Country House (1986). The most recent prehistory of Ulster is Laurence Flanagan's *Ulster* (1970) in the Regional Archaeologies series. For the Early Christian period see Maire and Liam de Paor's *Early Christian Ireland*, Thames and Hudson (1958) which will appear soon in revised form: N Edwards' *The archaeology of Early Christian Ireland*, Batsford (1990) gives a detailed view based on excavation. The mediaeval period is surveyed in T. E. McNeill's *Anglo-Norman Ulster*, John Donald, 1980, and T. B. Barry's *The Archaeology of Medieval Ireland*, Methuen (1987).

Ulster Archaeology:

Many of the most important monuments of Northern Ireland are to be found in *Historic Monuments of Northern Ireland*, 1983, HMSO, Belfast, and monuments in the Republic are treated in general in Peter Harbison's *Guide to the National Monuments of Ireland*, 1970, Dublin. Three Ulster counties have published surveys beginning with the monumental *Archaeological Survey of County Down*, 1966, HMSO and two recently published Site Inventories: *An Archaeological Survey of County Donegal* (1983) by B. Lacey et al and the *Archaeological Inventory of Co. Monaghan* (1986) by A. Brindley.

Chapter 1: The Colonization of Ulster

The basic survey is to be found in Peter Woodman's *The Mesolithic in Ireland*, British Archaeological Reports British Series 58 (1978) which supplanted Hallam Movius' *The Irish Stone Age*, Cambridge Univ Press (1942). Woodman also discusses the initial colonization of Ireland in *Irish Antiquity*, 93-110 and more recently *UJA* 49 (1986), 7-17 where he also discusses changes in economy and settlement patterns through the Mesolithic. Mesolithic faunal remains are reviewed by L. van Wijngaarden-Bakker in 'Faunal remains and the Irish Mesolithic' *The Mesolithic in Europe* (Ed. Clive Bonsall), John Donald, Edinburgh, 1989, 125-133. The somewhat 'notorious' Riverford Culture is treated by A. Mahr in *PPS* 11 (1937), 283-331.

Sites:

Bay Farm I, Co. Antrim; P. C. Woodman, *Landscape*, 30.

Castleroe, Co. Londonderry; P. C. Woodman, *Excavations at Mount Sandel 1973-77*, HMSO, 1987, 199-200.

Culbane, Co. Londonderry; A. Mahr, *PPS* 11 (1937), 292-293.

Curran Point, Larne, Co. Antrim; H. Movius, *The Irish Stone Age*, Cambridge Univ Press., 1942, 132-136; H. Movius, *UJA* 16 (1953) 7-23.

Dalkey Island, Co. Dublin; G. D. Liversage, *PRIA* 66C (1968), 53-233.

Dunaff Bay, Co. Donegal; P. Addyman and P. Vernon, *UJA* 29 (1966), 6-15.

Dundonald, Co. Down; P. Carr, *UJA* 48 (1985), 122-123; *UJA* 50 (1987), 157-158, 160-161.

Lough Boora, Co. Offaly; M. Ryan, *Antiquity* 54 (1980), 46-47.

Mount Sandel, Co. Londonderry; P. C. Woodman, *Excavations at Mount Sandel 1973-77*, HMSO, 1987.

Newferry, Co. Antrim; P. C. Woodman, *PPS* 43 (1977), 155-199.

Portglenone, Co. Antrim; A. Mahr, *PPS* 11 (1937), 293-295.

St. John's Point, Co. Down; Dep. of Archaeology Teaching Collection.

Toome Bay, Co. Londonderry; G. F. Mitchell, *UJA* 18 (1955), 1-16.

Windy Ridge, Co. Antrim; P. C. Woodman, per. comm.

Chapter 2: Early Farmers in Ulster

No general survey of Neolithic settlement specifically within Ulster has appeared since H. Case in *UJA* 32 (1969), 3-27. The palynological background is surveyed by Mitchell in *The Shell Guide to Reading the Irish Landscape* (1986) while J. Pilcher's patterns of agricultural use are presented in *Science* 172 (1971), 560-562. G.

Cooney's Leitrim field survey can be found in *Landscape*, 179-194 while an earlier account of the north Mayo field systems by S. Caulfield can be found in the same place, pp. 195-216. Porcellanite axes are surveyed by E.M. Jope in *UJA* 15 (1952), 31-60 and A. Sheridan in *UJA* 49 (1986), 19-32; maceheads have recently been surveyed by D. Simpson in *JRSAI* 118 (1988), 27-52; javelin heads by A. E. P. Collins in *Irish Antiquity*, 111-133; and L. Flanagan's analysis of hollow scrapers is in *UJA* 29 (1966), 82-90; Neolithic pottery: undecorated wares are surveyed by H. Case in *PPS* 27 (1961), 174-233 and updated for Ulster in *UJA* 32 (1969), 3-27; decorated wares are covered by M. Herity in *PRIA* 82 (1982), C. No. 10, 247-404.

The general chronology of Irish megalithic tombs is discussed by A. Ap Simon in *JIA* 3 (1985/86), 5-15. Court tombs are surveyed by R. De Valera in *PRIA* 60 (1960), C, No. 2 and finds from the tombs by M. Herity in *PRIA* 88 (1987), C, No. 5, 103-281, while A. E. P. Collins discusses their 'eastern' origin in *Megalithic Graves and Ritual* (1973, Ed. G. Daniel and P. Kjaerum), 93-103. A general discussion of portal tombs is to be found in ´O Nualláin *JRSAI* 113 (1983), 75-105 while M. Herity in *JRSAI* 94 (1964), 123-144 covers the finds. Passage tombs are surveyed in M. Herity's *Irish Passage Graves*, Dublin 1974 and A. Sheridan in *JIA* 3 (1985/86), 17-30 while the standard work on megalithic art is E. Shee Twohig's *The Megalithic Art of Western Europe* (1981), Oxford. A. Burl's *The Stone Circles of the British Isles* (1976), London, presents a general survey while R. McConkey's 'Stone Circles of Ulster' (MA Dissertation, 1987, Queen's University, Belfast) provides the most recent survey of the Ulster evidence. D. Startin's work on labour estimates for monument building occurs in *Settlement Patterns in the Oxford Region* (1982, CBA Research Report 44; Ed. H. J. Case and A. W. R. Whittle), 153-156, while T. Darvill's study of court and passage tomb distribution is published in *Man* 14 (1979), 311-327.

Sites:

Aghalane, Co. Tyrone; A. Burl, *The Stone Circles of the British Isles* (1976), London, 243, 367.

Aghanaglack, Co. Fermanagh; O. Davies, *JRSAI* 69 (1939), 21-38.

Altanagh, Co. Tyrone; B. B. Williams, *UJA* 49 (1986), 33-88.

Annaghmare, Co. Armagh; D. Waterman, *UJA* 28 (1965), 3-46.

Audleystown, Co. Down; A. E. P. Collins, *UJA* 17 (1954), 7-56; *UJA* 22 (1959), 21-27.

Ballyannan, Co. Donegal; *Donegal*, 29.

Ballyalton, Co. Down; E. E. Evans and O. Davies, *PBNHPS* 1933-34, 79-104.

Ballybriest, Co. Londonderry; A. Burl, *The Stone Circles of the British Isles* (1976), London, 366.

Ballygalley, Co. Antrim; D. Simpson, pers. comm.

Ballygalley Hill, Co. Antrim; A. E. P. Collins, *UJA* 41 (1978), 15-32.

Ballyglass, Co. Mayo; S. ´O Nualláin, *JRSAI* 102, 49-57.

Ballykeel, Co. Armagh; A. E. P. Collins, *UJA* 28 (1965), 47-70.

Ballymacaldrack (Dooey's Cairn), Co. Antrim. Evans, *UJA* 1 (1938), 59-78; Collins, *UJA* 39 (1976), 1-7.

Ballynagilly, Co. Tyrone; A. ApSimon, *JRSAI* 99 (1969), 165-168; *Dissertationes Archaeologicae Gandenses* 16 (1976), 15-30; J. Pilcher and A. G. Smith, *Phil. Trans. Royal Society* 1979, 286 (1979), 345-369.

Ballynoe, Co. Down; W. Groenman-van Waateringe and J. J. Butler, *Palaeohistoria* 18 (1976), 73-110.

Ballyreagh, Co. Fermanagh; O. Davies and E. E. Evans, *UJA* 5 (1942), 78-89.

Ballyrenan, Co. Tyrone; O. Davies, *JRSAI* 67 (1937), 89-100.

Ballyscullion, Co. Antrim; J. R. Pilcher, *Science* 172 (1971), 560-562.

Bavan, Co. Donegal; L. N. W. and D. E. Flanagan, *UJA* 29 (1966), 16-38.

Bay Farm II, Co. Antrim; J. P. Mallory, unpublished.

Beaghmore, Co. Tyrone; A. McL. May, *JRSAI* 83 (1953), 174-197; J. Pilcher, *UJA* 32 (1969), 73-91, *UJA* 38 (1975), 83-84; A. S. Thom, *UJA* 43 (1980), 15-19.

Behy/Glenulra, Co. Mayo; S. Caulfield, *Landscape* 195-215.

Boviel (Cloghnagalla), Co. Londonderry; I. J. Herring and A. McL. May, *UJA* 3 (1940), 41-55.

Brockley, Co. Antrim; J. Dawson, *INJ* 10 (1951), 156-161.

Carrowkeel, Co. Sligo; R. A. S. Macalister et al., *PRIA* 29C (1912), 311-347.

Carrowmore, Co. Sligo; G. Burenhult, *The Archaeology of Carrowmore, Co. Sligo*. Stockholm.

Céide Fields, Co. Mayo; S. Caulfield, *Landscape*, 195-216.

Clady Halliday, Co. Tyrone; O. Davies and C. A. R. Radford, *PBNHPS* 1935-36, 76-85.

Clones, Co. Monaghan; G. Coffey, *JRSAI* 34 (1904), 271-273.

Clontygora Small Cairn, Co. Armagh; T. G. F. Paterson and O. Davies, *UJA* 2 (1939), 55-60.

Cohaw, Co. Cavan; H. E. Kilbride-Jones, *PRIA* 54C (1952), 75-88.

Creggandevesky, Co. Tyrone; C. Foley, *Pieces*, 3-5.

Croghan/Kilmonaster, Co. Donegal; S. 'O Nualláin, *JRSAI* 98 (1968), 1-29.

Cuilbane, Co. Londonderry; M. Yates, *UJA* 48 (1985), 41-50.

Culbane, Co. Londonderry (axes); W. Knowles, *PRIA* 30C (1912), 219.

Donegore Hill, Co. Antrim; J. P. Mallory and B. N. Hartwell, *Current Archaeology* 92 (1984), 271-275.

Dunaff Bay, Co. Donegal; see Chap. 1.

Dundrum Sandhills, Co. Down; A. E. P. Collins, *UJA* 15 (1952), 2-26; *UJA* 22 (1959), 5-20

Druid's Stone, Ballintoy, J. M. Mogey, *UJA* 4 (1941), 49-56.

Dun Ruadh, Co. Tyrone; O. Davies, *PBNHPS* 1 (1936), 50-75.

Fallyhogy, Co. Londonderry; A. G. Smith and E. H. Willis, *UJA* 24-25 (1961-62), 16-24.

Farranmacbride, Co. Donegal; S. 'O Nualláin, *JRSAI* 106 (1976), 93-95.

Giant's Ring, Co. Down; A. E. P. Collins, *UJA* 20 (1957), 44-50.

Goodland, Co, Antrim; H. Case, 'A ritual site in north-east Ireland' in *Megalithic Graves and Ritual* (Ed. G. Daniel and P. Kjaerum), 1973, 173-196.

Gortcorbies, Co. Londonderry. A. McL. May, *UJA* 13 (1950), 28-39.

Island MacHugh, Co. Tyrone; O. Davies, *Excavations at Island MacHugh* (Belfast, 1950); R. J. Ivens et al., *UJA* 49 (1986), 99-103.

Killaghy, Co. Armagh; E. E. Evans; *UJA* 3 (1940), 139-141.

Killybeg, Co. Antrim; P. C. Woodman, *UJA* 30 (1967), 8-14.

Knockmany, Co. Tyrone; A. E. P. Collins and D. M. Waterman, *UJA* 15 (1952), 26-30.

Knowth, Co. Meath; G. Eogan, *Knowth and the Passage-tombs of Ireland*, Thames and Hudson, 1986.

Langford Lodge, Co. Antrim; D. M. Waterman, *UJA* 26 (1963), 43-54.

Largantea, Co. Londonderry; I. Herring, *UJA* 1 (1938), 164-188.

Loughash, Co. Tyrone; O. Davies, *UJA* 2 (1939), 254-268.

Loughaveema, Co. Antrim; E. M. Jope, *UJA* 15 (1952), 39.

Lough Enagh, Co. Londonderry, O. Davies, *UJA* 4 (1941), 88-101.

Lough Gur, Co. Limerick; S. P. ´O Riordáin, *PRIA* 56C (1954), 297-459.

Maguire's Bridge, Co. Fermanagh; J. Raftery, *JRSAI* 97 (1967), 1-28.

Malin More, Co. Donegal; R. de Valera, *PRIA* 60C (1960), 108.

Malone Hoard, Belfast; *PRIA* 34C (1917-19), 84.

Millin Bay, Co. Down; A. E. P. Collins and D. M. Waterman, Millin Bay: *A Late Neolithic Site in Co. Down*, H.M.S.O., 1955.

Navan, Co. Armagh; C. J. Lynn, *Emania* 1 (1986), 11-19.

New Grange, Co. Meath; M. J. O'Kelly, *Newgrange*, Thames and Hudson, 1982.

Lyles Hill, Co. Antrim; E. E. Evans, *Lyles Hill, a late neolithic site in Co. Antrim*, HMSO (Belfast); D. Simpson and A. Gibson, *Current Archaeology* 114 (1989), 214-215.

Mad Man's Window, Co. Antrim; P. C. Woodman, pers. comm.

Raphoe, Co. Donegal; L. N. W. Flanagan, *UJA* 31 (1968), 9-15.

Scotch Street, Co. Armagh; C. Lynn, *Pieces*, 8-10.

Sess Kilgreen, Co. Tyrone; E. Shee Twohig, *The Megalithic Art of Western Europe*, 202-203.

Slidderyford (Wateresk), Co. Down; *Down*, 82.

Slieve Croob, Co. Down (pollen); S. M. Kirk, *UJA* 36-37 (1973-74), 99-100.

Slieve Croob, Co. Down (tomb); M. Herity, *Irish Passage Graves* (1974, Dublin), 229.

Slieve Donard, Co. Down; M. Herity, *Irish Passage Graves* (1974, Dublin), 229-230.

Slieve Gullion, Co. Armagh; A. E. P. Collins and B. C. S. Wilson, *UJA* 26 (1963), 19-40.

Slieve Gullion (pollen), Co. Armagh; A. G. Smith and J. R. Pilcher, *UJA* 35 (1972), 17-21.

Sluggan, Co. Antrim; I. Goddard, The Palaeoecology of Some Sites in the North Of Ireland (MSc dissertation, 1971, QUB).

Tankardstown, Co. Limerick; M. Gowen, *Archaeology Ireland* 1 (1987), 6-10; M. Gowen and C. Tarbett, *Archaeology Ireland* 2 (1988), 156.

Ticloy, Co. Antrim; E. E. Evans and E. Watson, *UJA* 5 (1942), 62-65.

Tievebulliagh, Co. Antrim. E. M. Jope, *UJA* 15 (1952), 31-55; A. Sheridan, *UJA* 49 (1986), 19-32; J. P. Mallory, *UJA* 52 (forthcoming).

Well Glass Spring (see Largantea)

White Park Bay, Co. Antrim; W. J. Knowles, *JRSAI* 17 (1885-86), 104-125.

Windy Ridge, Co. Antrim; P. C. Woodman, pers. comm.

Chapter 3

A general survey of the Early Bronze Age in the British Isles is to be found in Colin Burgess' *The Age of Stonehenge* (1980), London. For a survey of the Early Bronze Age in Ulster see A. ApSimon, *UJA* 32 (1969), 28-72. Most of the funerary ware has received catalogue treatment by R. Kavanagh, i.e. encrusted urns in *PRIA* 73C (1973), 507-617, collared and cordoned urns in *PRIA* 76C (1976), 293-403, and pygmy cups in *JRSAI* 107 (1977), 61-95, while J. Waddell's survey of food vessels in now in press. Edward Watson's study of settlement patterns in Antrim is to be found in UJA 8 (1945), 80-118. For a general survey of metalwork in the British Isles see R. Tylcote *The Prehistory of Metallurgy in the British Isles* (1986), London and J. J. Taylor's *Bronze Age Goldwork of the British Isles* (1980), Cambridge, while the various theories concerning the origins of Irish metalworking are discussed by A. Sheridan in *JIA* 1 (1983), 11-19. For moulds, see A. E. P. Collins in *UJA* 33 (1970), 23-36. Catalogue treatment of Early Bronze Age metalwork can be found in P. Harbison *PRIA* 67C (1968), 35-91, and his *The Daggers and Halberds of the Early Bronze Age in Ireland* (1969), Munich, and *The Axes of the Early Bronze Age in Ireland* (1969), Munich. General discussions of cemeteries are to be found in L. Flanagan *IARF* 3, 2 (1976), 7-20 and J. Waddell *JRSAI* 100 (1970), 91-139, and in *Irish Antiquity* 163-172. For Middle Bronze Age metallurgy see Greer Ramsey's 'Middle Bronze Age Weapons' (Ph. D. thesis, Queen's University, Belfast, 1989). The identification of the Topped Mountain gold work is to be found in J. Taylor in *From the Stone Age to the 'Forty-Five'* (1983; Ed. A. O'Connor and D. V. Clarke), 57-64.

Sites:

Altanagh, Co. Tyrone; B. B. Williams, *UJA* 49 (1986), 33-88.

Ballyclare, Co. Antrim; L. N. W. Flanagan, *UJA* 33 (1970), 15-22

Ballycroghan, Co. Down. H. W. M. Hodges, *UJA* 18 (1955), 17-28.

Ballynagilly, Co. Tyrone; A. ApSimon, *JRSAI* 99 (1969), 165-168; Dissertationes Archaeologicae Gandenses 16 (1976), 15-30; J. Pilcher and A. G. Smith, *Phil. Trans. Royal Society* 1979, 286 (1979), 345-369.

Ballynahinch moulds, Co. Down; A. E. P. Collins, *UJA* 33 (1970), 24-25.

Ballymacaldrack, Co. Antrim; O. Davies and J. J. Tomb, *UJA* 1 (1938), 219-221; O. Davies, *UJA* 4 (1941), 63-66.

Bay Farm III; J. P. Mallory, unpublished.

Beaghmore, Co. Tyrone; A. McL. May, *JRSAI* 83 (1953), 174-197; J. Pilcher, *UJA* 32 (1969), 73-91, *UJA* 38 (1975), 83-84; A. S. Thom, *UJA* 43 (1980), 15-19.

Beltany, Co. Donegal; *Donegal*, 72-73.

Carrickanab, Co. Down; A. E. P. Collins and E. E. Evans, *UJA* 31 (1968), 16-24.

Carrownacaw, Co. Down; A. E. P. Collins, *UJA* 20 (1957), 37-42.

Carryglass, Co. Tyrone; *Preliminary*, 250-251.

Church Bay, Rathlin, Co. Antrim; *Pieces*, 14-15.

Cloughskelt, Co. Down; L. W. Flanagan, *IARF* 3,2 (1976), 7-20.

Coney Island, Lough Neagh; P. V. Addyman, *UJA* 28 (1965), 78-101.

Corkey, Co. Antrim; W. J. Knowles, *JRSAI* 19 (1889), 109-110.

Cullyhanna, Co. Armagh; H. W. M. Hodges, *UJA* 21 (1958), 7-13.

Dalkey Island, Co. Dublin; G. D. Liversage, *PRIA* 66C (1968), 52-233.

Drumnahare, Co. Down; A. E. P. Collins, *UJA* 20 (1957), 37-42.

Drumnakilly, Co. Tyrone; W. F. Wakeman, *JRSAI* 12 (1872-73), 499-512.

Dun Ruadh, Co. Tyrone; O. Davies, *PBNHPS* 1 (1935-36), 50-75.

Gortcorbies, Co. Derry; A McL. May, *UJA* 13 (1950), 28-39.

Killymeddy, Co. Antrim, H. W. M. Hodges, *UJA* 19 (1956), 29-56.

Kilskeery, Co. Tyrone, E. E. Evans and T. G. F. Patterson, *UJA* 2 (1939), 65-71.

Knowth, Co. Meath; G. Eogan, *Excavations at Knowth*, Dublin, 1984.

Largantea, Co. Derry; I. J. Herring, *UJA* 1 (1938), 164-188.

Loughash, Co. Tyrone; O. Davies, *UJA* 2 (1939), 254-268.

Lissane, Co. Londonderry; C. Burgess and S. Gerloff, *The Dirks and Rapiers of Great Britain and Ireland*, Munich, 1981, 54.

Longstone, Ballybeen, Co. Down; J. P. Mallory, *UJA* 47 (1984), 1-4.

Lough Gur, Co. Limerick; S. P. 'O Riordáin, *PRIA* 56C (1954), 297-459.

Mad Man's Window, Co. Antrim; P. C. Woodman, pers. comm.

Magheragallan, Co. Donegal; E. E. Evans, *UJA* 4 (1941), 71-75.

Meadowlands, Downpatrick, Co. Down; A. J. Pollock and D. M. Waterman, *UJA* 27 (1964), 31-58.

Mount Gabriel, Co. Cork; W. F. O'Brien, *Journal Cork Historical and Archaeological Society* 92 (1987), 50-70, 94 (1989), 1-18.

Murlough sandhills, Co. Down; A. E. P. Collins, *UJA* 15 (1952), 2-26; *UJA* 22 (1959), 5-20.

New Grange, Co. Meath; M. J. O'Kelly, R. M. Cleary and D. Lehane, *New Grange, Co. Meath* (BAR 190), Oxford, 1983.

Straid, Co. Londonderry; N. Brannon, *Pieces*, 12-13.

Topped Mountain, Co. Fermanagh; G. Coffey and T. Plunket, *PRIA* 20 (1896-98), 651-658.

Urbalreagh, Co. Antrim; D. Waterman, *UJA* 31 (1968), 25-32.

White Park Bay, Co. Antrim; W. J. Knowles, JRSAI 17 (1885-86), 104-125.

Chapter 4

For the Navan complex see the interim publications that regularly appear in *Emania*; for the ramifications of Hekla 3 see M. G. L. Baillie and M. Munro in *Nature* 332 (1988), 344-346, M. G. L. Baillie in *Archaeology Ireland 2* (1988), 154-155, and J. P. Mallory and R. B. Warner in *Emania* 5 (1988), 36-40. For Late Bronze Age metallurgy in Ulster see H. Hodges in *UJA* 17 (1954), 62-80, *UJA* 19 (1956), 29-56 and *UJA* 20 (1957), 51-63. The hoards are catalogued by G. Eogan in his *Hoards of the Irish Later Bronze Age* (1983), Dublin, who also provides us with a *Catalogue of Irish Bronze Swords* (1965), Dublin, and special treatment of lock-rings in PRIA 67C (1969), 93-148, sleeve-fasteners in *Prehistoric Man in Wales and the West* (1972, Ed. F. Lynch and C. Burgess), 189-209, pins in *JRSAI* 104 (1974), 74-119, and gold discs in *Irish Antiquity*, 147-162. The shields are treated by J. Coles in *PPS* 28 (1962), 159-190 and their effective use is also discussed in his illuminating *Archaeology by Experiment* (1973), London; Coles also discusses bronze horns both in *PPS* 29 (1963), 326-356 and *JRSAI* 97 (1967), 113-117, while Simon 'O Duibhir's experiments are recorded in *Archaeology Ireland 2* (1988), 135-136. R. Bradley's interpretations of hoards/votives can be found in *Man* 17 (1982), 108-122 while Late Bronze Age regional groupings are discussed by G. Eogan in *Archäologisches Korrespondenzblatt* 4 (1974), 319-328.

Sites:

Arboe, Co. Tyrone; *Hoards*, 158-159.

Armoy, Co. Antrim; M. Dunlevy, *Dress in Ireland* (1989, London), 15-16.

Altnahinch, Co. Armagh (pollen); A. Goddard, 'Studies of the Vegetational Changes Associated with Initiation of Blanket Peat Accumulation in North-East Ireland' (PhD. thesis, 1971, QUB).

Ballybeen, Co. Down; J. P. Mallory, *UJA* 47 (1984), 1-4.

Ballyutoag, Co. Antrim; O. Davies, *UJA* 3 (1940), 8 and B. B. Williams, pers. comm.

Bay Farm III, Co. Antrim; J. P. Mallory, unpublished.

Bishopsland, Co. Kildare; *Hoards*, 36-38.

Ballycroghan, Co. Down; H. Hodges, *UJA* 18 (1955), 17-28.

Cathedral Hill, Downpatrick, Co. Down; V. B. Proudfoot, *UJA* 17 (1954), 97-102; *UJA* 19 (1956), 57-72; *UJA* 20 (1957), 70-72.

Clogher, Co. Tyrone; R. B. Warner, pers. comm.

Crevilly-Valley, Co. Antrim; *Hoards*, 52-54

Deer Park Farms, Co. Antrim; *Pieces*, 44-47.

Derryhale, Co. Armagh; *Hoards*, 57-60.

Dowris, Co. Offaly; *Hoards*, 117-142.

Drumbest Bog, Co. Antrim; *Hoards*, 54-55

Glastry, Co. Down; *Hoards*, 82.

Gortcorbies, Co. Derry (pollen); I. Goddard, 'The Palaeoecology of Some Sites in the North Of Ireland' (MSc dissertation, 1971, QUB).

Haughey's Fort, Co. Armagh; J. P. Mallory, *Emania* 4 (1988), 5-20.

Inishowen hoard, Co. Donegal; *Hoards*, 31-33.

Island MacHugh, Co. Tyrone; O. Davies, *Excavations at Island MacHugh* (Belfast, 1950); R. J. Ivens et al., *UJA* 49 (1986), 99-103.

Killymoon, Co. Tyrone; J. Raftery, *JRSAI* 100 (1970), 169-174.

Kilmahamogue, Co. Antrim; E. M. Jope, *UJA* 14 (1951), 62-65.

King's Stables, Co. Armagh; C. J. Lynn, *UJA* 40 (1977), 42-62.

Knockaulin, Co. Kildare; B. Wailes, *Emania* 7 (1990), 10-21.

Kurin, Co. Londonderry; *Hoards*, L. N. W. Flanagan, *UJA* 27 (1964), 92-93.

Lacken Bog, Co. Down; S. Holland, 'Pollen Analytical Studies concerning Settlements and Early Ecology in Co. Down, N. Ireland' (Ph.D. thesis, 1975, QUB).

Largatreany, Co. Donegal; *Hoards*, 33-34.

Lattoon, Co. Cavan; *Hoards*, 64-65.

Lisdromturk, Co. Monaghan; unpublished, in Monaghan County Museum.

Long Lough, Co. Down (pollen); V. Hall, *New Phytologist*, 115 (1990), 377-383.

Lough Eskragh, Co. Tyrone; A. E. P. Collins and W. A. Seaby, *UJA* 23 (1960), 25-37; B. Wiiliams, *UJA*. 41 (1978), 37-48.

Lough MacNean, Co. Fermanagh; B. Williams, per. comm.

Lyles Hill, Co. Antrim; D. Simpson and A. Gibson, *Current Archaeology* 114 (1989), 214-215.

Mullaghmore, Co. Down; J. M. Mogey, *UJA* 12 (1949), 82-88; J. M. Mogey et al., *UJA* 19 (1956), 11-28; *Irish Antiquity*, 175-177.

Navan, Co. Armagh; C. J. Lynn, *Emania* 1 (1986), 11-19.

Rallagh, Co. Londonderry; R. B. Warner, per. comm.

Seacon More, Co. Antrim; *Hoards*, 55-56.

Slieve Gallion, Co. Tyrone (pollen); J. R. Pilcher, *New Phytologist* 72 (1973), 681-689.

Sluggan, Co. Antrim (pollen); I. Goddard, 'The Palaeoecology of Some Sites in the North Of Ireland '(MSc dissertation, 1971, QUB).

Tobermore, Co. Londonderry; H. Hodges, *UJA* 17 (1954), 64.

White Park Bay, Co. Antrim; W. J. Knowles, *JRSAI* 17 (1885-86), 104-125.

Chapter 5

For various interpretations of Ptolemy's map see T. O'Rahilly's *Early Irish History and Mythology* (1946), Dublin, J. Pokorny in *Zeitschrift für celtische Philologie* 24 (1954), 94-120 and L. Gogan in the *Capuchin Annual* 1974, 128-142. Iron Age Navan is covered extensively in the reports of *Emania*. For a listing of other Iron Age sites see R. Warner, J. P. Mallory and M. G. L. Baillie in *Emania* 7 (1990), 46-50. For an annotated bibliography on Ulster linear earthworks see C. J. Lynn in *Emania* 6 (1989), 18-21. Bee-hive querns are discussed by S. Caulfield in *JRSAI* 107 (1977), 104-138. On the origins of iron metallurgy in Ireland see both B. Scott in *IARF* 1, 1 (1974), 9-24 and 1, 2 (1974), 48-50 and R. Warner in *IARF* 1, 2 (1974), 45-47. Full catalogue treatment and discussion of La Tène metalwork in Ireland can be found in B. Raftery's *A Catalogue of Irish Iron Age Antiquities* (1983), Marburg, and his *La Tène in Ireland* (1984), Marburg. For other discussions of La Tène metal work see E. M. Jope in *UJA* 17 (1954), 81-91, on the Toome scabbard and idea of warrior-adventurers, and *UJA* 18 (1955), 37-44, on horse-bits and paired draft. R. Warner's interpretation of the Broighter hoard is to be found in *Studies*, 29-38, and his discussion of art is to be found in *From the Stone Age to the 'Forty-Five* (1983; Ed. A. O'Connor and D. V. Clarke), 160-187. Iron Age burials are surveyed by B. Raftery in *Irish Antiquity*, 171-204 and stone heads are discussed by E. Rynne in *The Iron Age in the Irish Sea Province* (1972, Ed. by C. Thomas), 79-98. For discussions of archaeology and the Ulster Cycle see K. Jackson's *The Oldest Irish Tradition* (1964), Cambridge, and J. P. Mallory in both *Studies*, 99-114 and *Proceedings of the Seventh International Congress of Celtic Studies* (1986, Ed. D. Ellis Evans et al.), 31-78, and N. B. Aitchison in *Journal of Medieval History* 13 (1987), 87-116. For a recent discussion of the literary sources on early Ireland see K. McCone's *Pagan Past and Christian Present* (1990), Maynooth. The whole problem of Irish origins is surveyed by J. P. Mallory in *JIA* 2 (1984), 65-69; see also C. Renfrew's *Archaeology and Language* (1987), London. For the Cruthin see I. Adamson's *The Cruthin* (1974), Belfast. Roman material in Ireland is surveyed by D. Bateson in *PRIA* 73C (1973), 21-97, and discussed by R. Warner in *PRIA* 76C (1976), 267-292.

Sites:

Altartate Glebe, Co. Monaghan; *Catalogue*, 209.

Ardbrin, Co. Down; *Catalogue*, 241.

Ballinrees, Co. Londonderry; D. Bateson, *PRIA* 73C (1973), 21-97.

Ballybogey Bog, Co. Antrim; see Ballymoney.

Ballymoney, Co. Antrim; *Catalogue*, 198.

Ballymulholland I, Co. Londonderry; J. P. Mallory and F. McCormick, *UJA* 51 (1988).

Ballyness, Co. Donegal; D. Bateson, *PRIA* 73C (1973), 21-97.

Ballyshannon, Co. Donegal; *Catalogue*, 89.

Bann disc; E. M. Jope and B. C. S. Wilson, *UJA* 20 (1957), 95-102.

Bay Farm II, Co. Antrim; J. P. Mallory, unpublished.

Beltany, Co. Donegal; E. Rynne, *Irish Sea Province*, 79-93.

Black Pigs Dyke, Co. Monaghan; A. Walsh, *Emania* 3 (1987), 5-11; F. Williams, *Emania* 3 (1987), 12-19.

Boho, Co. Fermanagh; *Catalogue*, 110.

Broighter hoard, Co. Londonderry; R. B. Warner, *Studies*, 29-38.

Carrickfergus, Co. Antrim; *Catalogue*, 216.

Clogher, Co. Tyrone; R. B. Warner, pers. comm.

near Clogher (Killyfaddy), Co. Tyrone; *Catalogue*, 243.

Corlea, Co. Longford; B. Raftery, *Trackways through Time*, Dublin, 1990.

Corleck, Co. Cavan; E. Rynne, *Irish Sea Province*, 79-93.

Derrykeighan, Co. Antrim; *Catalogue*, 271.

Diamond Hill, Killeshandra, Co. Cavan; B. Raftery, *The La Tène in Ireland* (1984), Marburg, 136.

Dorsey, Co. Armagh; C. J. Lynn, *Emania* 6 (1989), 5-10; M. G. L. Baillie and D. M. Brown, *Emania* 6 (1989), 11.

Drumlane, Co. Cavan; *Catalogue*, 207-208.

Dunadry, Co. Antrim; B. Raftery, *Irish Antiquity*, 181-183.

Dunfanaghy, Co. Donegal; T. B. Graham and E. M. Jope, *UJA* 13 (1950), 54-56; D. Bateson, *PRIA* 73C (1973), 21-97.

Feigh Mountain, Co. Antrim; D. Bateson, *PRIA* 73C (1973), 21-97.

Killycluggin, Co. Cavan; B. Raftery, *UJA* 41 (1978), 49-54.

Kiltierney, Co. Fermanagh; *Pieces*, 24-26.

Knockaulin, Co. Kildare; B. Wailes, *Emania* 7 (1990), 10-21.

Lisnacrogher, Co. Antrim; *Catalogue*, 287-288

Lough Mourne, Co. Antrim; *Catalogue*, 218.

'Loughey', Co. Down; E. M. Jope and B. C. S. Wilson, *UJA* 20 (1957), 73-95.

Loughnashade, Co. Armagh; B. Raftery, *Emania* 2 (1987), 21-24.

Mount Sandel, Co. Londonderry; R. Warner and N. F. Brannon, in *Excavations at Mount Sandel 1973-77*, P. C. Woodman (1985, Belfast), 193-195.

Mullaboy, Co. Londonderry; B. B. Williams, *UJA* 44-45 (1981-82), 29-46.

Navan, Co. Armagh; C. J. Lynn, *Emania* 1 (1986), 11-19; J. P. Mallory, *Navan Fort*, Belfast.

Newry, Co. Down; *Catalogue*, 177.

Ralaghan, Co. Cavan; *Catalogue*, 265-266.

Rath Croghan, Co. Roscommon; J. Waddell, *Emania* 5 (1988), 5-18.

Scrabo hill, Co. Down; *Down*, 147, 178-180.

Tandragee, Co. Armagh; in St. Patrick's (Church of Ireland) Cathedral, Armagh.

Toome Bar, Co. Antrim; *Catalogue*, 218.

Turoe stone, Co. Galway; J. Raftery, *JRSAI* 74 (1944), 23-52; M. V. Duignan in *Celtic Art in Ancient Europe* (1976, Ed. P-M. Duval and C. F. C. Hawkes), 201-217.

Whiterocks, Co. Antrim; *Catalogue*, 137-138.

Chapter 6

This period has generated a lot of writing, although very few overall surveys, rather than studies of individual aspects. The archaeology of royal sites is surveyed by R. B. Warner in 'The archaeology of early historic Irish kingship', in S. T. Driscoll & M. R. Nieke (eds.), *Early Medieval Britain*, Edinburgh, 1988. A. E. P. Collins' article 'Settlement in Ulster, 0-1100', in *UJA* 31 (1967), 53-58 gives an introduction to the site types. Raths in particular are the subject of two articles by V. B. Proudfoot, 'The economy of the Irish rath' in *Medieval Archaeology*, 5 (1961) 94-122, and 'Irish raths and cashels; some notes on chronology, origins and survivals', in *UJA* 33 (1970), 37-48. Houses are discussed in C. J. Lynn, 'Early Christian period domestic structures: a change from round to rectangular plans?' in *I.A.R.F.*, 5, (1978), 29-45. Several of the essays in Hamond & Reeves-Smith: *Landscape*, concern this period: B. B. Williams, 'Early Christian landscapes in Co. Antrim', pp 233-46; D. 'O Corráin: 'Some legal references to fences and fencing in early historic Ireland', pp. 247-52: F. McCormick, 'Dairying and beef production in Early Christian Ireland: the faunal evidence', pp. 253-68; T. McErlean, 'The Irish townland system of landscape organisation', pp. 315-40. K. Hughes & A. E. Hamlin: *The Modern Traveller to the Early Irish Church*, S.P.C.K., 1977 introduces the church sites; H. G. Leask, *Irish Churches and Monastic Buildings*, vols I and II, (Dundealgan, 1955 and 1960), cover the period; A. Gwynn and R.N. Hadcock, *Medieval Religious Houses; Ireland*, Longman, 1970, summarises the documentary evidence about each monastery. The art history of the objects from the period are the subject of a three volume study by F. Henry, published by Methuen: *Irish Art, I, in the Early Christian Period, to A.D.800* (1965); II, *During the Viking Invasions* (1960); III, *In the Romanesque period*, 1020-1170 (1960). The stone carving around Lough Erne are the subject of H. Hickey: *Images of Stone*, Blackstaff, 1976. The documentary history of Ulster is the subject of C. Brady, M. O'Dowd and B. Walker (eds.), *Ulster, An Illustrated History*, Batsford, 1989. General historical works which are relevant include D. 'O Corráin, *Ireland before the Normans*, Gill and MacMillan, 1972, and F. Kelly, *A Guide to Early Irish Law*, Dublin Institute of Advanced Studies, 1988.

Sites:

Antiville, near Larne, Co. Antrim; D. M. Waterman, *UJA*, 34 (1971) 65-76.

Antrim, Co. Antrim; *H.M.N.I.*, 71.

Arboe, Co. Tyrone; *H.M.N.I.*, 140.

Armagh; C. Gaskell Brown and A. E. T. Harper, *UJA* 47 (1984) 109-61; *Pieces*, 57-61.

Ballylough, Co. Antrim; T. E. McNeill, *UJA* 49 (1983), 101-128.

Ballynarry, Co. Down; B. K. Davison, *UJA* 24-25 (1961-62), 39-87.

Ballyutoag, Co. Antrim; B. B. Williams, *UJA* 47 (1984), 37-49; *Pieces*, 36-38.

Ballywee, Co. Antrim; *Pieces*, 32-35.

Banagher, Co. Londonderry; D. M. Waterman and A. E. Hamlin, *UJA* 39 (1976) 25-39.

Bangor, Co. Down; O. Davies, *UJA* 9 (1946), 101-104.

Big Glebe, Co. Londonderry; *Pieces*, 41-44.

Boa Island, Co. Fermanagh; Hickey, 24.

Budore, Co. Antrim; E. E. Evans: *Prehistoric and Early Christian Ireland*, Batsford, 1966, 45-46.

Carndonagh, Co. Donegal; *Donegal*, 249-251.

Clogher, Co. Tyrone; R. B. Warner in: 'The archaeology of early historic Irish kingship', in S. T. Driscoll & M. R. Nieke (eds.), *Early Medieval Britain*, Edinburgh, 1988.

Craig Hill, Co. Antrim; D. M. Waterman, *UJA*, 19 (1956), 87-92.

Deer Park Farm's, Co. Antrim; *Pieces*, 44-47.

Derry Church, Co. Down; D. M. Waterman, *UJA* 30 (1967), 53-75.

Derry, Co. Londonderry; B. Lacy, in G. MacNiochaill and P. Wallace (eds.), *Keimelia*, Galway 1988, 378-396.

Devenish, Co. Fermanagh; C. A. R. Radford, *UJA*, 33 (1970) 55-62; Hickey, 59-60.

Donaghmore, Co. Tyrone; *H.M.N.I.*,140; E. Brennan, *Impressions of a Cross*, Irish World, Monaghan, 1988.

Donaghrisk, Co. Tyrone; *H.M.N.I.*, 143.

Downpatrick, Co. Down; *Pieces*, 61-64.

Drumaqueran, Co. Antrim; A. E. Hamlin, *UJA* 35 (1972), 22-7.

Drumard, Co. Londonderry; M. G. L. Baillie, *UJA* 38 (1975), 25-32.

Drumaroad (White Fort), Co. Down; D. M. Waterman, *UJA* 19 (1956), 73-86.

Drumena, Co. Down; *H.M.N.I.*, 93.

Dundrum, Co. Down; D. M. Waterman, *UJA* 14 (1951) 15-29.

Duneight, Co. Down; D. M. Waterman, *UJA* 26 (1963) 55-78.

Dungiven, Co. Londonderry; O. Davies *UJA* 2 (1939) 271-87; *H.M.N.I.*, 127-8.

Dunmisk. Co. Tyrone; *Pieces*, 27-29.

Dunseverick, Co. Antrim; T. E. McNeill, *UJA* 49 (1983) 101-128.

Dunsilly, Co. Antrim; *Excavations Bulletin* 1974, 8-9; 1975-6, 6-7.

Fahan, Co. Donegal; *Donegal*, 268-269.

Finner, Co. Donegal; *Donegal*, 173-176.

Gransha, Co. Down; C. J. Lynn, *UJA* 48 (1985), 81-90.

Grianan of Ailech, Co. Donegal; *Donegal*, 111-2.

Inishmacsaint, Co. Fermanagh; *H.M.N.I.*, 118-119.

Island MacHugh, Co. Tyrone; R. J. Ivens, D. D. A. Simpson and D. Brown, *UJA* 49 (1986), 99-102.

Kilbroney, Co. Down; *Down*, 303.

Killadeas, Co. Fermanagh; Hickey, 50-51.

Killealy, Co. Antrim; *Excavations Bulletin*, 1970, 2-3.

Kilmore, Co. Cavan; Hickey, 54, 60.

Kilnasaggart, Co. Armagh; *H.M.N.I.*, 82-83.

Larne Viking grave; T. Fanning, *J.R.S.A.I.*, 100 (1970) 71-78.

Lisnagade, Co. Down; *Down*, 116.

Lissue, Co. Antrim; G. Bersu, *UJA* 10 (1947), 30-58; *UJA* 11 (1948), 131-133.

Maghera, Co. Londonderry, *H.M.N.I.*, 128-129.

Movilla, Co. Down; O. Davies, *UJA* 8 (1945), 33-38; M. Yates, *UJA* 46 (1983), 53-66; R. Ivens, *UJA* 47 (1984), 71-108; *Pieces*, 50-51.

Nendrum, Co. Down; *Down*, 292-5.

Port Bradden, Co. Antrim; E. E. Evans, *Prehistoric and Early Christian Ireland*, Batsford, 52.

Rathmullan, Co. Down; C. J. Lynn, *UJA* 44/45 (1981-2), 65-171.

Saint John's Point, Co. Down; N. F. Brannon, *UJA* 43 (1980), 59-64.

Sallagh Fort, Co. Antrim; *P.B.N.H.P.S.*, (1937-38), 27-33.

Scotch Street, Armagh; *Pieces*, 57-61.

Scrabo, Co. Down; *Down*, 147, 178-180.

Tullyhogue, Co. Tyrone; G. A. Hayes-McCoy, *UJA* 33 (1970), 89-94; *H.M.N.I.*, 142-143.

Tullylish, Co. Down; *Pieces*, 55-56.

White Island, Co. Fermanagh; D. Lowry-Corry, *UJA* 22 (1959) 59-67; Hickey, 34-39, 43-49.

Chapter 7

Much of the evidence for the first part of the period is summarised in T. E. McNeill, *Anglo-Norman Ulster*, John Donald, 1980; many of the sites not listed below are dealt within it. Some of the works cited for the last chapter are relevant for this one as well: Brady et al. for the history, Gwynn and Hadcock for church sites and

Hickey for Lough Erne stone carvings. H. G. Leask, *Irish Churches and Monastic Buildings*, vols II and III (Dundealgan) cover the period; the Cistercian abbeys are the subject of R. A. Stalley, *The Cistercian Monasteries of Ireland*, Yale, 1987. H. G. Leask, *Irish Castles*, provides a sketchy introduction to the subject. Books on the documentary history include the two relevant volumes of the Helicon series, published in 1981: R. Frame, *Colonial Ireland, 1169-1369*, and A. Cosgrove, *Late Medieval Ireland, 1369-1541*. Two specific aspects of history are covered in the Gill history series, published in 1972: J. Watt, *The Church in Medieval Ireland*, and K. Nicholls, *Gaelic and Gaelicised Ireland in the Later Middle Ages*. K. Simms, *From Kings to Warlords*, Boydell, 1987, is a more detailed account of Gaelic lordship.

Sites:

Aghalurcher, Co. Fermanagh; *H.M.N.I.*, 116.

Ardglass, Co. Down; *Down*, 220-225.

Armagh; C.J.Lynn, *UJA* 38 (1975), 61-80; *Pieces*, 57-61.

Balleeghan, Co. Donegal; *Donegal*, 328.

Banagher, Co. Londonderry; D. M. Waterman and A. Hamlin, *UJA* 39 (1976), 25-41.

Blackwater sword; B. G. Scott: 'A decorated sword blade from the river Blackwater, between the townlands of Copney, Co. Armagh and Derrygalley, Co. Tyrone', in G. MacNiochaill & P. Wallace (eds.), *Keimelia*, Galway, 1988, 193-217.

Bonamargy, Co. Antrim; *H.M.N.I.*, 72-3.

Bright, Co. Down; *Down*, 141.

Carnaghliss, Co. Antrim; Barry, 85-86.

Carrickfergus, Co. Antrim; T. E. McNeill, *Carrickfergus Castle*, H.M.S.O., 1981; M. Simpson and A. Dickson, *Medieval Archaeology*, 25 (1981), 78-89; *Anglo-Norman Ulster*, 47-50.

Castle Carra, Co. Antrim; T. E. McNeill, *UJA* 49 (1983), 101-128.

Castle Reagh, Co. Down; T. E. McNeill, *UJA* 50 (1987) 123-128.

Clough, Co. Down; D. M. Waterman, *UJA* 17 (1954), 103-163.

Coney Island, Lough Neagh; P. V. Addyman, *UJA* 28 (1965) 78-101.

Culfeightrin, Co. Antrim; E. M. Jope, *Ancient Monuments in Northern Ireland not in state charge*, H.M.S.O., 1952, 25.

Derry, Co. Londonderry; B. Lacy and G. MacNiochaill and P. Wallace, *Keimelia*, Galway, 1988, 378-96.

Devenish, Co. Fermanagh; C. A. R. Radford, *UJA* 33 (1970), 55-62; D. M. Waterman, *UJA* 36-37 (1973-74), 100-102; *UJA* 42 (1979), 34-50.

Donegal Friary, Co. Donegal; *Donegal*, 330-32.

Doonbought, Co. Antrim; T. E. McNeill, *UJA* 40 (1977), 63-84.

Downpatrick, Co. Down; A. J. Pollock and D. M. Waterman, *UJA* 26 (1963), 79-104; *Pieces*, 61-64.

Dundrum, Co. Down; *Down*, 207-11; D. M. Waterman, *UJA* 27 (1964), 136-139.

Dungiven, Co. Londonderry; O. Davies, *UJA*, 2 (1939), 271-87; *H.M.N.I.*, 127-128.

Dunluce, Co. Antrim; A. McL. May, *Dunluce Castle*, H.M.S.O., 1966; *H.M.N.I.*, 74.

Elagh Castle, Co. Londonderry; *Anglo-Norman Ulster*, 75, 114.

Greencastle, Co. Donegal; D. M. Waterman, *UJA* 21 (1958),74-88; *Donegal*, 365-367.

Greencastle, Co. Down; *Down*, 211-9; *Anglo-Norman Ulster*, 24-7; C. Gaskell-Brown, *UJA* 42 (1979), 51-65; *Pieces*, 66-69.

Harry Avery's castle, Co. Tyrone; E. M. Jope, H. M. Jope and E. A. Johnson, *UJA* 13 (1950), 81-92; S. G. Rees-Jones and D. M. Waterman, *UJA* 30 (1967), 76-82.

Inch Abbey, Co. Down; *Down*, 279-81; A. E. Hamlin, *UJA* 40 (1977) 85-88.

Kilclief, Co. Down; *Down*, 233-5.

Kinawley, Co. Fermanagh; *H.M.N.I.*, 56.

Layde, Co. Antrim; *H.M.N.I.*, 75-76.

Lismahon, Co. Down; D. M. Waterman: *Medieval Archaeology*, 3 (1959) 139-176.

Newtownards, Co. Down; *Down*, 284-287.

Rathmullan, Co. Down; C. J. Lynn, *UJA* 44/45 (1981-2) 65-171.

Seafin, Co. Down; D. M. Waterman, *UJA* 18 (1955), 83-104; *Down*, 219-20.

Tullylish, Co.Down; *Pieces*, 55-56.

Chapter 8

The buildings of the late 16th and 17th centuries are discussed by E. M. Jope in two general articles: 'Scottish influence in the north of Ireland: castles with Scottish features, 1580-1640', *UJA* 14 (1951) 31-47, and 'Moyry, Charlemont, Castleraw and Richhill: fortification to architecture in the north of Ireland', *UJA*, 23 (1960) 97-123. The Plantation castles of Fermanagh are considered by J. J. Johnstone in *UJA* 43 (1980) 79-89. The building history of Ulster as a whole is covered by H. Dixon, *Ulster Architecture*, U.A.H.S., 1975; in the north-west by A. Rowan, *The Buildings of Ireland; north-west Ulster*, Penguin, 1979. Towns are discussed in G. Camblin, *The Town in Ulster*, Mullan, 1951. The industrial archaeology is covered by E. R. R. Green, *The Industrial Archaeology of Co. Down*, H.M.S.O., 1963, and by W. A. McCutcheon, *The Industrial Archaeology of Northern Ireland*, H.M.S.O., 1980. The historical background is given in C. Brady et al.; P. Robinson, *The Plantation of Ulster*, Gill and MacMillan, 1984; R. Gillespie, *Colonial Ulster*, Cork University Press, 1985, and in C. Brady and R. Gillespie (eds.), *Natives and Newcomers*, Irish Academic Press, 1986.

Sites:

Armagh; Camblin, 1951; *Pieces*, 57-61.

Ballycastle, Co. Antrim; C. Dallat: *The Glynns* 2 (1974) 28-32; 3 (1975) 7-13.

Ballylough, Co. Antrim; T. E. McNeill, *UJA* 49 (1983), 101-128.

Belfast; *Pieces*, 79-81.

Benburb, Co. Tyrone; *H.M.N.I.*, 144-5.

Burt, Co. Donegal; O. Davies and H. P. Swan, *UJA* 2 (1939) 188-93; *Donegal*, 370-371.

Carrickfergus, Co. Antrim; Camblin, 1951; *Dixon*, 1975, 16; T. E. McNeill, *Carrickfergus Castle*, H.M.S.O., 1981.

Castle Balfour, Co. Fermanagh; D. M. Waterman, *UJA* 31 (1968), 71-76.

Castle Caulfield, Co. Tyrone; E. M. Jope, *UJA* 21 (1958), 101-107.

Castle Curlews, Co. Tyrone; D. M. Waterman, *UJA* 23 (1960) 89-96.

Castlederg, Co. Tyrone; D. M. Waterman, *UJA* 23 (1960) 89-96.

Castleward, Co. Down; *Down,* 356-61; *Dixon,* 1975, 40.

Charlemont, Co. Antrim; E. M. Jope, *UJA* 23 (1960), 97-123.

Coleraine, Co. Londonderry; P. Robinson and N. Brannon, *UJA* 44/45 (1981-82), 173-178; *Pieces,* 78-79.

Coney Island, Lough Neagh; P. V. Addyman, *UJA* 28 (1965), 78-101.

Derrywoon, Co. Tyrone; E. M. Jope, *UJA* 14 (1951), 44.

Dungiven castle, Co. Londonderry; N. Brannon and B. S. Blades, *UJA,* 43 (1980), 91-96; *Pieces,* 81-84.

Dungiven costume, Co. Londonderry; A. S. Henshall and W. A. Seaby, *UJA* 24/25 (1961-62), 119-142.

Dunineaney, Co. Antrim; T. E. McNeill, *UJA* 49 (1983), 101-128.

Dunluce, Co. Antrim; A. McL. May, *Dunluce castle,* H.M.S.O., 1966; *H.M.N.I.,* 74.

Dunseverick, Co. Antrim; T. E. McNeill, *UJA* 49 (1983), 101-128.

Enniskillen, Co. Fermanagh; *H.M.N.I.,* 120.

Fortwilliam, Belfast; E. M. Jope, *UJA* 23 (1960), 116.

Harry Avery's Castle, Co. Tyrone; E. M. Jope, H. M. Jope and E. A. Johnson, *UJA* 13 (1950), 81-92; S. G. Rees-Jones and D. M. Waterman, *UJA* 30 (1967), 76-82.

Kiltierney, Co. Fermanagh; M. J. Daniels and B. B. Williams, *UJA* 40 (1977), 32-41.

Kinbane, Co. Antrim; T. E. McNeill, *UJA* 49 (1983), 101-128.

Lagan Navigation; *Green.*

Liffock, Co. Londonderry; D. McCourt and D. Evans, *UJA* 35 (1972) 48-56.

Londonderry; H.M.N.I., 131.

Monea, Co. Fermanagh; E. M. Jope, *UJA* 14 (1951) 42-3; *H.M.N.I.,* 121.

Newry, Co. Down; *Down,* 419-420.

Newry Canal; *Green.*

Newtownstewart, Co. Tyrone; H. A. Meek and E. M. Jope, *UJA* 21 (1958), 109-114.

Roughan, Co. Tyrone; E. M. Jope, *UJA* 14 (1951) 43.

Salterstown, Co. Londonderry; E. M. Jope, *UJA* 23 (1960) 97-123.

Tully castle, Co. Fermanagh; D. M. Waterman, *UJA* 22 (1959) 123-126; *H.M.N.I.,* 121-122.

White House, Ballyspurge, Co. Down; *Down,* 256-257; *H.M.N.I.,* 114-115.

Illustration Credits

Unless otherwise credited, illustrations are courtesy of the authors or the illustrator. Special thanks to: Barry Raftery for permission to reproduce directly illustrations from his *Catalogue of Irish Iron Age Antiquities* (=Cat.); George Eogan for permission to reproduce from his *Hoards of the Irish Later Bronze Age*; and the editor of the *Ulster Journal of Archaeology* for permission to reproduce many illustrations; the Historic Monuments and Buildings Branch of the D.O.E. (N. I.) and the Ulster Museum for supplying many of the photographs reproduced in this volume.

Chapter 1

3. After F. Mitchell, *Shell Guide to Reading the Irish Landscape*, 1986, 50; **4.** List after R. Savage, *Irish Naturalist Journal* 15 (1966), 117-130; **5.** After Woodman, *UJA* 49 (1986), 9 with additions; **6.** Photo, J. P. Mallory; **7.** Photo, B. N. Hartwell; **9.** From *The Belfast Natural History and Philosophical Society, Centenary Volume*, 1924, 78; **10.** From *The Belfast Natural History and Philosophical Society, Centenary Volume*, 1924, 79; **11.** After Woodman 1987, 15; **12.** Reconstruction by S. Conlin; **13.** After L. van Wijngaarden-Bakker, 1989, 127; **14.** After Woodman, *Mount Sandel*, 1987, 168; **15.** After Woodman, *Mount Sandel*, 1987, 37; **16.** After Woodman, *Mount Sandel*, 1987, 39; **18.** After Woodman, *Mount Sandel*, 1987, 49; **19.** After Woodman, *Mount Sandel*, 1987, 44; **20.** After Woodman, *Mount Sandel*, 1987, 44; **21.** After Woodman, *Mount Sandel*, 1987, 42; **22.** After Woodman, *Mount Sandel*, 1987, 42; **23.** Drawings by S. Conlin; **24.** After Woodman in *Irish Antiquity*, 97; **26.** After Woodman, *UJA* 49 (1986), 14; **27.** Drawing by B. N. Hartwell; **28.** After H. Movius, *The Irish Stone Age*, 160; **29-30.** Drawn by S. Conlin; **31-32.** Dep. of Archaeology Teaching Collection; **33.** After Mitchell, *UJA* 18 (1955), 15.

Chapter 2

2. After Ap Simon, *Dissert. Archaeol. Gandenses* 16 (1976), 15-30; **3.** Reconstruction by S. Conlin; **6.** Photo. D. D. A. Simpson; **9.** Reconstruction by B. N. Hartwell; **10.** After H. Case in *Megalithic Graves and Ritual*, 1973, 174; **11.** After *Pieces*, 9; **15.** After Mitchell, 1986, 100.; **16.** After *Landscape*, 187; **17.** After *Landscape*, 199; **23.** After Herity and Eogan, 41; **24.** After Sheridan, *UJA* 49 (1986), 20; **25.** Photo courtesy of the Ulster Museum; **27.** After Evans, *Lyles Hill*, 52; **28.** After Collins, *Irish Antiquity*, 118; **29.** After Herity, *PRIA* 87 (1987), 250; **30.** After Evans, *Lyles Hill*, 53; **32.** Drawn by B. N. Hartwell; **33.** Drawn by E. Brennan; **34.** After Collins, *UJA* 28 (1965), 58; **35.** After Case, *PPS.* 27 (1961), 190; **36.** After Herity, *PRIA* 82 (1982), 379; **37.** After Herity, *Irish Passage Graves*, 1974, 288; **38.** After O'Kelly, *Early Ireland*, 86; **39.** After de Valera, *PRIA* 59, pl. xix; **40.** After de Valera, *PRIA* 59, pl. xxiv; **41.** After de Valera, *PRIA* 59, pl. xvii; **42.** After de Valera, *PRIA* 59, pl. xvii; **43.** After Collins, *UJA* 39 (1976), 2; **46.** After O'Kelly, *Early Ireland*, 93; **47.** After *Donegal*, 34; **49.** After Evans and Watson, *UJA* 5 (1942), 62; **50.** After O'Kelly, *Early Ireland*, 98; **51.** After Sheridan, *JIA* 3 (1985-86), 22; **52.** After Sheridan, *JIA* 3 (1985-86), 18; **53.** Photo by J. Pilcher; **54.** Photo by B. C. S. Wilson; **55.** After *Ancient Monuments of Northern Ireland*, vol. II, 1963, 11; **56.** After van Hoek, *UJA* 50 (1987), 32; **58.** After O'Kelly, *Early Ireland*, 116; **59.** After Herring and May, *UJA* 3 (1940), 43; **60.** After McConkey, 'Stone Circles of Ulster', fig. 1;

62. After Groenman-van Waateringe and Butler, *Palaeohistoria* 18 (1976), 78 and 82; **63-64.** Courtesy Historic Monuments and Buildings Branch; **67.** After Darvill, *Man* 14 (1979), 317.

Chapter 3

1. After R. Harrison, *The Beaker Folk*, 1980, 12; **2.** After P. Harbison, in *The Origins of Metallurgy in Atlantic Europe* (Ed. M. Ryan), 1978, 100, with additions; **3.** After Herring, *UJA* 1 (1938), pl. xx.; **5.** QUB Archaeology Teaching Collection; **6.** After P. Harbison, in *The Origins of Metallurgy in Atlantic Europe* (Ed. M. Ryan), 1978, 100; **7.** After *Down*, 35 and Kavanagh 1973, 579; **8.** After Ap Simon, *UJA* 32 (1969), 45; **9.** After *Down*, 41; **10.** After *Down*, 37; **11.** After Ap Simon, *UJA* 32 (1969), 36 and 38 with additions; **12.** After Ap Simon, *UJA* 32 (1969), 41 and 44 with additions; **13.** After Pollock and Waterman, *UJA* 27 (1964), 36; **14.** After Waterman, *UJA* 31 (1968), 27; **17.** Courtesy D. D. A. Simpson; **19-20.** After Harbison, *The Axes of the Early Bronze Age in Ireland*, 1969, nos. 7, 884 and 1864; **21.** After Harbison, *The Daggers and the Halberds of the Early Bronze Age in Ireland*, 1969, no. 1; **22.** Drawn by E. Brennan; **23.** After Collins and Seaby, *UJA* 23 (1960), 34; **25.** Courtesy of Ulster Museum; **28.** Photo by J. Pilcher; **29.** After Hodges, *UJA* 21 (1958), 8; **30.** After Hodges, *UJA* 21 (1958), 12; **31.** Photo by M. G. L. Baillie; **32.** Courtesy of the Ulster Museum; **33.** After Hodges, *UJA* 18 (1955), 18; **34-35, 37.** QUB Archaeology Teaching Collection; **38-39.** After Ramsey, 1989, no 48 and no 748. **41.** After Herity and Eogan, 1977, 160-161.

Chapter 4

2. After Lynn, *Emania* 1 (1986), 15; **3.** Reconstruction by S. Conlin; **4.** Courtesy Historic Monuments and Buildings Branch; **9-10.** Drawn by D. Warner; **14.** From *Pieces*, 20; **15.** Courtesy R. B. Warner; **17-18.** After Williams, *UJA* 41 (1978), 37, 42; **19.** Courtesy Historic Monuments and Buildings Branch, D.O.E.N.I.; **20.** After Williams, *UJA* 41 (1978), 42; **21.** After Herity and Eogan, 1978, 102; **22.** Courtesy M. G. L. Baillie; **23.** After Hodges, *UJA* 17 (1954), 67; **24.** After *Hoards*, 234; **25-26.** After Eogan, *Catalogue of Irish Bronze Swords* (1965), figs. 21 and 91; **27** QUB Archaeology Teaching Collection; **28.** After Jope, *UJA* 14 (1951), pl. 8; **29.** After *Hoards*, 237; **30.** Drawn by E. Brennan, after P. V. Glob, *The Mound People*, 86; **31-34.** After *Hoards*, 225, 224, 241, and 304; **35.** From *Hoards*, 25, with kind permission of the author; **36-37.** After *Hoards*, 239 and 236; **39.** After *Hoards*, 226; **40.** After Herity and Eogan, 206; **41.** After *Hoards*, 314; **42.** After Mallory, *UJA* 47 (1984), 3; **43.** After Eogan, *Swords*, 67; **44.** After Eogan, *Archäologisches Korrespondenzblatt* 4 (1974), taf. 80.

Chapter 5

2. After Lynn, *Emania* 1 (1986), 17; **3.** Reconstruction by S. Conlin; **4.** Wailes, *Emania* 7 (1990), 14; **5.** From *La Tène*, 137; **6.** Reconstruction by S. Conlin; **8.** After Walsh, *Emania* 3 (1987), 5; **9.** After Lynn, *Emania* 6 (1989), 6; **11.** After Walsh, *Emania* 3 (1987), 7; **12.** *Cat(alogue)*, 184; **13.** *Cat.*, 166; **14.** *Cat.*, 101; **15.** *Cat.*, 105; **16.** *Cat.*, 244; **17.** *Cat.*, 111; **18.** *La Tène*, 109; **19.** *Cat.*, 125; **20.** *Cat.*, 120; **21.** *La Tène*, 20, fig. 10; **22.** *Cat.*, 89; **23.** *Cat.*, 99; **24.** *Cat.*, 99; **25.** From Raftery *Trackways through Time*, 1990, pl. vii; **26.** *Cat.*, 209; **27.** *Cat.*, 129; **28.** *Cat.*, 130; **29.** *Cat.*, 131; **30.** *Cat.*, 134; **31.** *Cat.*, 141 and 231; **32.** *Cat.*, 148; **33.** *Cat.*, 203; **34.** *Cat.*, 213;

35. *Cat.*, 232; **36.** *Cat.*, 233; **37.** From *PPS* 1937, pl. xxvi; **38.** *Cat.*, 228; **39.** St. Patrick's Cathedral (C. of I), Armagh; **40.** After *Pieces*, 25; **42.** *Cat.*, 119; **44.** Reconstructions by B. N. Hartwell; **46.** *Cat.*, 152; **47.** After N. Edwards, 1990, 102.

Chapter 6.

1. After Lynn 1985, 86; **2.** Photo courtesy of Ulster Museum; **3.** Photo, B. N. Hartwell; **4.** Photo, B. N. Hartwell; **5.** Drawn by B. N. Hartwell; **6.** Photo, B. N. Hartwell; **7.** Photo, B. N. Hartwell; **8.** B. Clayton in *UJA*, 36-7 (1973- 4), 43. **9.** Drawn by B. N. Hartwell; **10.** Drawn by D. Warner; **11.** Photo, B. N. Hartwell, courtesy of Historic Monuments & Buildings Branch, D.O.E.N.I.; **12.** After Jope, unpublished; **13.** From *Pieces*, 33; **14.** After V.Buckley, *UJA*, 49 (1986), 109; **15.** Courtesy of Ulster Museum; **16.** Photo, B. N. Hartwell; **17.** Photo, B. N. Hartwell; **18.** *Pieces*, 36; **19.** After C. Gaskell-Brown & N. Brannon, *UJA*, 41 (1978), 82 ; **20.** E. Watson in *Belfast in its Regional Setting* (British Association), 1952, 94; **21.** Photo, B. N. Hartwell; **22.** Courtesy of A. E. Hamlin; **23.** *Pieces*, 53; **24.** Courtesy of Historic Monuments & Buildings Branch, D.O.E.N.I.; **25.** Drawn by B. N. Hartwell; **26.** Photo courtesy of the National Museum of Ireland; **27.** Photo courtesy of Ulster Museum; **29.** Photo, B. N. Hartwell, courtesy of the Ulster Museum; **30.** Photo, B. N. Hartwell; **31.** After Hamlin, 1972, 23; **32, 33.** Photo, B. N. Hartwell; **34.** Drawn by E. Brennan; **35.** After *Donegal*, 269; **36.** After *Down*, pl.73; **37, 38.** After Lowry-Corry, 1959, plates 6 & 7; **39.** After Edwards, 1990, 74; **40.** After T. McErlean, unpublished; **41.** After Fanning, 1970; **42.** Photo courtesy of Ulster Museum; **43.** After Raftery, *JRSAI,*, 99 (1969), 134; **44.** After Kenny, *PRIA*, 87C (1987), 524; **45.** Photo, B. N. Hartwell; **46.** Drawn by B. N. Hartwell, after Henry, II, pl. 58. **47.** Drawn by B. N. Hartwell, after Henry, III, pl. 22, 24; **48.** Drawn by B. N. Hartwell, after Henry, III, pl.36; **50-52.** Photo, B. N. Hartwell; **53.** Photo courtesy of Historic Monuments and Buildings Branch, D.O.E.N.I.; **54.** After Hamlin, *UJA*,1977, pl.8; **55.** After Waterman and Hamlin, *UJA*, 1977, 30, & photo, T. E. McNeill; **56.** Photo courtesy Historic Monuments & Buildings Branch, D.O.E.N.I.

Chapter 7.

3. Drawn by T. E. McNeill; **4.** After *Anglo-Norman Ulster*, 10; **5.** Drawn by T. E. McNeill; **6-7.** Photo, B. N. Hartwell; **8.** Drawn by T. E. McNeill; **9-10.** Photo B. N. Hartwell; **13.** Drawn by D. Warner; **14.** After *Anglo-Norman Ulster*, 66 (with changes); **15, 16.** Photo courtesy of Ulster Museum; **17-18** After *Anglo-Norman Ulster* 112, 44; **19.** Photo, B. N. Hartwell; **20.** After McNeill, *UJA*, 1977, 65; **21.** Photo, B. N. Hartwell; **22.** Photo, T. E. McNeill; **23.** Photo courtesy of Historic Monuments and Buildings Branch, D.O.E.N.I.; **24.** Drawn by T. E. McNeill, after Scott, 1988, 195, 201; **26.** Photo B. N. Hartwell; **27.** Drawing courtesy of Historic Monuments and Buildings Branch, D.O.E.N.I.; **28, 29.** Photo, B. N. Hartwell; **30.** Drawing courtesy of Historic Monuments and Buildings Branch, D.O.E.N.I.; **31.** Drawn by M. Pringle; **32.** After *Down*, pl. 88; **33.** Photo courtesy of Historic Monuments & Buildings Branch, D.O.E.N.I.; **34.** Trinity College, Dublin, ms 1209 (26); **35.** After *Down*, pl. 49; **36.** After Waterman (Devenish), 1979, 42; **37-38.** Drawings courtesy of Historic Monuments and Buildings Branch, D.O.E.N.I.; **39-42.** Photo, B. N. Hartwell; **43.** After Hickey, 82; **44-5.** Photo, B. N. Hartwell; **46.** After *Donegal*, 328 and Historic Monuments & Buildings Branch, D.O.E.N.I.

Chapter 8.

1. After Hiram Morgan; **2-3.** Photo, B. N. Hartwell; **5.** Photo B. N. Hartwell; **6.** After Williams, *UJA*, 46 (1983), 31; **7-10.** Photo, B. N. Hartwell; **11.** After McNeill, 1983, 116; **12.** Courtesy of Historic Monuments & Buildings Branch, D.O.E.N.I.; **13-14.** *Pieces*, 82, 83; **15.** Evans and McCourt, 1972, 49; **16-17.** Courtesy of Historic Monuments and Buildings Branch, D.O.E.N.I.; **18.** Photo, B. N. Hartwell; **19.** Drawn by T. E. McNeill; **20.** Courtesy of the Ulster Museum; **21-24.** Photo B. N. Hartwell; **25.** Courtesy of Historic Monuments and Buildings Branch, D.O.E.N.I.; **26.** After Historic Monuments and Building Branch, D.O.E.N.I., *Guide Card*; **27-9.** Photo B. N. Hartwell.

Chapter 9.

1. After O.S.Memoir, *Parish of Donegore*; **2-3.** Courtesy of Mrs. G. Evans; **4.** Photo by A.E.P.Collins; **5.** Courtesy of Mrs. F. Collins.

Index

Adamson, I. 177
Addyman, P. 95, 271
adzes (flint): 15
aerial photography 35
Aghalane, Co. Tyrone 71
Aghalurcher, Co. Fermanagh 294
Aghanaglack, Co. Fermanagh 81
Agricola 178
Ailech 239
Airgialla 124
alder 126, 132
Altagore, Co. Antrim 187
Altanagh, Co. Tyrone 81, 98–99
Altartate Glebe, Co. Monaghan 155
Altnahinch, Co. Armagh 127
amber 135, 208
Annaghmare, Co. Armagh 60
annals 1, 86, 167, 227, 230–32
Annals of Ulster 213
Antiville, Co. Antrim 231
antler 15, 36, 54, 66, 82
Antrim 232, 264, 286, 305
ape 119, 146
apples 12
ApSimon, A. 31, 71, 92
Arboe, Co. Tyrone 135, 214–15
Ardagh chalice 210
Ardbrin, Co. Down 160
Ardglass, Co. Down 286–87
Ardstraw, Co. Tyrone 246
Armagh 37, 204–06, 213, 219, 231,
    234–37, 241–46, 274, 279, 281,
    287, 304, 316
armour 228, 262
Armoy, Co. Antrim 133
Arran, Scotland 49
arrows (flint): 15, 24, 28, 30, 36, 49–
    50, 57, 59, 90, 102, 132; (metal):
    262
Arthurs, W. 100
ash 126, 189
Athassel, Co. Tipperary 284
Audleystown, Co. Down 57, 59, 60–
    61, 81, 96
Augustinians 244–47, 282, 294, 310
awls (bronze): 97, 136
axes (flint): 15; (stone): 22, 24–26,
    30, 44–47, 57, 59, 70, 83;

(copper): 86, 101; (bronze): 89,
    101, 109–110, 126, 130–31, 133,
    135–36; (iron): 155, 227
Bagnalls 302
baileys 262
Baillie, M. G. L. 107, 129, 147, 151,
    311
Ballintoy, Co. Antrim 69
Ballyannan, Co. Donegal 63
Balleeghan, Co. Donegal 296
Ballinderry, Co. Antrim 314
Ballinrees, Co. Londonderry 178
Ballyalton, Co. Down 52–53, 59
Ballyalton bowls 52, 54
Ballybeen, Co. Down 138
ballybetagh 221–23
Ballybogey Bog, Co. Antrim 158
Ballybriest, Co. Londonderry 71
Ballycastle, Co. Antrim 9, 293, 317–
    18
Ballyclare, Co. Antrim 102
Ballycroghan, Co. Down 109
Ballygalley, Co. Antrim 33, 49
Ballyglass, Co. Mayo 32
Ballykeel, Co. Armagh 54, 64
Ballylough, Co. Antrim 231, 309
Ballymacaldrack (Dooey's Cairn),
    Co. Antrim 58–59
Ballymacaldrack, Co. Antrim 112
Ballymena Field Club 10
Ballymena, Co. Antrim 269, 313
Ballymoney, Co. Antrim 155
Ballymulholland I, Co. Londonderry
    150, 153
Ballynagilly, Co. Tyrone 31–32, 40,
    57, 77, 88–89, 96, 337
Ballynahatty, Co. Down 69
Ballynahinch, Co. Down 101
Ballynarry, Co. Down 231
Ballyness, Co. Donegal 179
Ballynoe, Co. Down 71–73
Ballyreagh, Co. Fermanagh 61
Ballyrenan, Co. Tyrone 64
Ballyscullion, Co. Antrim 40
Ballyshannon, Co. Donegal 156, 168
Ballyspurge, Co. Down 313
Ballyutoag, Co. Antrim 127, 200
Ballywee, Co. Antrim 194, 231
Ballywillin, Co. Antrim 280
Banagher, Co. Londonderry 227,
    246, 294

Bangor, Co. Down 205, 222, 237, 242, 245–46
Bann flake 24, 27
Bann river 14, 16, 24–27, 85, 93, 111, 130–31, 139, 141, 145, 156, 161, 167, 210, 269, 292, 314, 328, 335
Barber, J. 128
barley 35, 38, 89, 122, 190
basin stones 68, 82
battle–axes 227–28, 262, 289
Bavan, Co. Donegal 49
bawns 290, 303, 308, 312–13, 321
Bay Farm I, Co. Antrim 24
Bay Farm II, Co. Antrim 33, 150
Bay Farm III, Co. Antrim 89, 97, 127
beads 54, 57, 59, 99, 135, 160, 164, 173
Beaghmore, Co. Tyrone 40, 105
Beaker culture 70, 87–91, 102, 141, 174, 331
beakers 87
beetles 122
Behy/Glenulra, Co. Mayo 42
Belfast 27, 49, 69, 75, 202, 265, 268, 283, 291–92, 305, 307, 316–19, 327
Belfast Naturalists' Field Club 23, 327, 336
Belfast Natural History and Philosophical Society 10, 327
bell 217, 232, 235
Beltany, Co. Donegal 104, 163
Benburb, Co. Tyrone 304
Benedictines 244, 282
Bersu, G. 195
Berwick Hall, Co. Down 313
Big Glebe, Co. Londonderry 187
birch 5, 46, 125, 126
birds 16–17, 27, 200
Bishopsland, Co. Kildare 131
Black Death 281–83, 285
Black Mountain, Belfast 49
Black Pigs Dyke, Co. Monaghan 150–52, 165–66, 325, 331
Blackwater river, Munster 5, 21
Blackwater river, Ulster, 274, 304
Boa Island, Co. Fermanagh 163, 213
boats 20–21, 31, 159, 178, 226
Boho, Co. Fermanagh 157
Bonamargy, Co. Antrim 293, 296

Book of Armagh 213
Book of Kells 212
Book of Lindisfarne 212
Book of Mac Durnan 213
Boviel (Cloghnagalla), Co. Londonderry 70
Boyd, H. 317–18
Boyne river 65–66, 68–69, 78–79, 82, 142, 144, 171
bracelets (jet): 126, 164; (gold): 131, 134, 159; (bronze) 160; (glass): 164, 173
Bradley, R. 140
Brannon, N. F. 98, 307, 310, 311
Breac Maodhog 237
Brian Boru 234
brick 314
Bright, Co. Down 265
Britain 20, 21, 26, 28–29, 31, 36, 46, 48, 50, 52, 54, 60, 62, 75, 87, 91, 93, 101–02, 138, 141, 143, 156–57, 168, 173, 177, 183
British Association for the Advancement of Science 327
Brittany 62, 65, 68, 90
Brockley, Co. Antrim 44
Broighter hoard, Co. Londonderry 159–161
bronze 86–87, 115
brooches 164, 179, 183, 209–10, 217, 225, 229, 230
Bruce, Edward 256, 282–83
Bruce, Robert 259
buckets 130–31, 136, 142
Budore, Co. Antrim 186
bung 121
Burgess, C. 139
burins 16
Burt, Co. Donegal 320
Bush river 145
Burenhult, G. 69
Bysets 271, 283
Campbeltown, Scotland 49
canoes 21, 126, 136
Carndonagh, Co. Donegal 214, 217
Carlingford, Co. Louth 56, 77
Carnaghliss, Co. Antrim 263
Carncastle, Co. Antrim 263
Carnlough, Co. Antrim 24, 33, 43, 97, 127, 225

Carnmoney, Co. Antrim 265
Carrickanab, Co. Down 97
Carrickfergus, Co. Antrim 155, 253–
    56, 264–68, 280–81, 283, 286,
    288, 299–300, 302, 305, 307, 314,
    316, 321, 328
Carromore, Co. Sligo 65, 69, 82
Carrowkeel, Co. Sligo 53
Carrowkeel ware 38, 53, 54, 66, 74
Carrownacaw, Co. Down 103
Carryglass, Co. Tyrone 98
Case, H. J. 37, 60
Cashel, Co. Tipperary 243–44
cashels 187, 225
Castle Balfour, Co. Fermanagh 321
Castle Carra, Co. Antrim 271–72
Castle Caulfield, Co. Tyrone 307,
    321
Castle Chichester, Co. Antrim 308
Castle Curlews, Co. Tyrone 308
Castle Reagh, Co. Down 292
Castlederg, Co. Tyrone 308
Castleroe, Co. Londonderry 14
Castleward, Co. Down 322–23
Cathach 235–36
Cathbar O'Donnell 235
cattle (wild): 4, 6, 25; (domestic)
    30–31, 38, 50, 89, 95, 98, 121,
    123, 153, 157, 189–91, 194,
    196–97, 220, 222, 285, 317
cauldrons 130–31, 136–37, 141, 155
Caulfield, S. 41, 42, 78, 154
Caulfield, Sir Toby 307, 321
causewayed camps 36, 78
Cavan 162, 287–88, 316
Céide Fields, Co. Mayo 42
Cellach 245
Celts 87, 139, 141, 148–49, 155, 160,
    162, 168, 170–78, 225, 331
Cenel Connaill 170, 235
Cenel Eoghain 235, 238–40, 246–47
Cenfaelad 235
cereals 41, 141, 154, 219, 249–51,
    262–64, 285
chape 118, 131, 156
chariots 157–58
Charlemont, Co. Antrim 304–05, 307
chert 9, 68
Chichester, Sir Arthur 307–08, 314
chisel (flint): 15; (bronze): 130–31,
    136; 219

Church Bay, Rathlin, Co. Antrim 96
Ciannachta 246
Cistercians 244–47, 276–78, 281–82,
    295–96
Clady Halliday, Co. Tyrone 57
Claudy, Co. Londonderry 98
Clogher, Co. Tyrone 124, 146, 150,
    160, 165, 167, 179, 183, 211
Cloghnagalla, Co. Londonderry 70
Clones, Co. Monaghan 52
Clontygora Small Cairn, Co. Armagh
    65
Clough, Co. Down 261–62
Cloughskelt, Co. Down 98
Clough Water 269
clubs (stone): 26
Clyde–Carlingford culture 57
coarse ware 107, 116, 118, 124–27
Cohaw, Co. Cavan 57
coins 178–79, 210, 229, 274
Coleraine, Co. Londonderry 11, 210,
    26–65, 268, 286, 292, 307, 311
Coles, J. 132
Collared Urns 32, 92–93, 97, 141,
    335
Collins, A. E. P. 50, 59–60, 67–68,
    73, 76, 103, 125, 332
Columba 235
Colville, A. 313–14
comb 154
Comber, Co. Down 202
Coney Island, Lough Neagh 95, 271,
    274, 300–01
Connacht 225, 229
Cooney, G. 41
copper 86–87, 99–100, 154–55
Cordoned Urns 89, 91, 95–96, 98–
    99, 112
Corkey, Co. Antrim 97
Corlea, Co. Longford 158
Corleck, Co. Cavan 162
Cormac Mac Carthy 244
Cormac's chapel 244–47
Cornwall 99
court tombs 50, 56–65, 79–83, 96,
    330
Craig Hill, Co. Antrim 231
crannogs 124–25, 185, 192–93, 199–
    202, 220–22, 224–25, 231, 288,
    292, 309–10, 331
Creggandevesky, Co. Tyrone 61, 81

Crevilly–Valley, Co. Antrim 130
Crickley Hill, England 36
Croghan/Kilmonaster, Co. Donegal 65
Cross of Cong 237
croziers 210, 217, 229–30
Crumlin, Co. Antrim 3
Cruthin 176–78, 331
Cú Chulainn 139, 146, 167–68
Cuduilg 235–37
Cuilbane, Co. Londonderry 72
Culbane, Co. Londonderry 26, 27, 45
Culfeightrin, Co. Antrim 294, 296
Cullyhanna, Co. Armagh 107–08
Cumaighe na Gall O' Cahan 284
Cumbria 20
Curran Point, Larne, Co. Antrim 24
Cushendall, 44, 46
Cushendun, Co. Antrim 271
daggers (bronze): 97, 102, 111
Dál nAraidhe 222, 242
Dál Fiatach 177, 222, 240–42
Dál Riada 175
Dalkey Island, Co. Dublin 88
Dane's Cast 150–51
Darini 145
Darkley, Co. Armagh 319
Darvill, T. 79–82
Davies, Sir John 308
Davies, Oliver 33, 57, 61–62, 70, 89, 126–27, 153, 231, 329–33
Davison, B. 231
de Burgh, Richard 258–59
de Courcy, John 249, 252, 256, 258, 264, 276–78, 281
de Lacy, Hugh 255, 257–58
de Valera, R. 62
Deer Park Farms, Co. Antrim 118, 193, 219–20, 261
Delaney, T. 264
dendrochronology 107–09, 128–29, 152, 199–202, 220, 224, 230, 292, 311, 334
Denmark 134
Dermot Mac Murrough 248–49
Derry Church, Co. Down 207–08
Derry, Co. Londonderry 205, 239, 241, 269, 272, 287, 302, 307, 321
Derrygonnelly, Co. Fermanagh 314
Derryhale, Co. Armagh 135

Derrykeighan, Co. Antrim 161–62
Derrynaflan chalice 210
Derrywoone, Co. Tyrone 310
Devenish, Co. Fermanagh 232, 235, 237, 243, 294
Diamond Hill, Killeshandra, Co. Cavan 160
discs 134–35
Doddington, Sir Edward 310
dog 38, 95, 103, 121, 123, 317
Domnaill Mac Amhalgadha 235
Domnaill Mac Lochlainn 235
Donaghadee, Co. Down 158, 179
Donaghmore, Co. Tyrone 214
Donaghrisk, Co. Tyrone 240
Donegal Friary, Co. Donegal 292–93
Donegore Hill, Co. Antrim 35–36, 50, 52, 54, 57, 78, 95, 124
Dooey's Cairn, Co. Antrim 38, 58 (see Ballymacaldrack)
Doonbought, Co. Antrim 262, 269, 271, 274
Dorsey, Co. Armagh 150–51, 166
Downpatrick, Co. Down 95, 134, 165, 206, 240–43, 245, 264–67, 281, 286, 294, 337
Dowris, Co. Offaly 131
dress–fasteners 130, 134
Drogheda, Co. Louth 5
Dromore 202, 275, 281
Drowse river 142
Druid's Stone, Ballintoy, Co. Antrim 69
Drumaqueran, Co. Antrim 214
Drumard, Co. Londonderry 201
Drumaroad (White Fort), Co. Down 193
Drumbest Bog, Co. Antrim 137
Drumena, Co. Down 187
Drumlane, Co. Cavan 155, 294
Drumnahare, Co. Down 103
Drumnakilly, Co. Tyrone 92
Dublin 230
Dubtach 213
Dún Ailinne (see Knockaulin) 119, 166
Dun Ruadh, Co. Tyrone 75, 98
Dunadry, Co. Antrim 164
Dunaff Bay, Co. Donegal 49
Dunbar, Sir John 314

Dundonald, Co. Down 11, 103, 138
Dundrum Sandhills, Co. Down 32, 200
Dundrum, Co. Down 130, 288
Duneight, Co. Down 241
Dunfanaghy, Co. Donegal 179
Dungannon, Co. Tyrone 157, 288, 300, 302, 304
Dungiven costume, Co. Londonderry 314–15
Dungiven, Co. Londonderry 246–47, 273, 282, 284–85, 295–96, 306, 310, 314
Dunineaney, Co. Antrim 301
Dunluce, Co. Antrim 288, 301, 311–12, 320, 328
Dunmisk. Co. Tyrone 184, 208
Dunseverick, Co. Antrim 165, 185, 198, 231, 301, 328
Dunsilly, Co. Antrim 193
earrings 131
Edenderry, Co. Down 319
eels 12, 14, 17
Elagh, Co. Londonderry 239, 272, 288
elm 189
elm decline 40
Emain Macha (see Navan) 38, 118, 146, 152, 165, 167–69, 325
Encrusted Urns 89, 93, 98
England 7, 46, 52, 59, 79, 154, 157, 174, 201, 209–10, 224–27, 229, 243, 248, 262–63, 282, 296, 311, 313
Enniskillen, Co. Fermanagh 305
Eoghan, G. 141
Erdini 145
Erenagh, Co. Down 245–46
Evans, Estyn 33–34, 57–59, 80, 329–330, 332
everted rim ware 274, 288, 331
E–ware 183, 200, 201
exchange and trade 25, 46–51, 93, 102, 112–13, 178–79, 183, 229, 250–51, 265–68, 286–88, 316–17
Fahan, Co. Donegal 214, 216
Fallyhogy, Co. Londonderry 40
Farranmacbride, Co. Donegal 57
Feigh Mountain, Co. Antrim 179
Ferdomnach 213

fibula 159, 167, 173
field systems 41–43, 77–78, 154, 191, 200, 305
Finn McCool 47, 107–08
Finner, Co. Donegal 186
Fir Bolg 141, 176–77
fish 15, 17, 27, 288
fishing 6, 16, 24, 26–27, 200
Flanagan, L. 50, 98, 164
flax 55, 190
flint 5, 7–10, 15, 17, 22–25, 27, 30, 32, 36–38, 43, 48–51, 68
Foley, C. 164
Food Vessels 91–98, 102, 112
Fortwilliam, Belfast 305
Foyle river 90, 93, 145, 254
France 20, 70, 156, 174, 200, 226, 237, 278, 290
Franciscans 292–94
friaries 279
fulachta fian 109
Gaelic revival 283–85
Galboly, Co. Antrim 43
Galgorm, Co. Antrim 313
galloglass 273, 289
Giant's Ring, Co. Down 69, 75–77, 83, 328
Giraldus Cambrensis 170
glass 160, 164, 173, 208, 210
Glastry, Co. Down 130
Glenariff, Co. Antrim 4
Glenarm, Co. Antrim 9, 32
Glencloy river 335
goats 30, 31, 38, 121
Gogan, L. 145
gold 86–87, 99–100, 113, 115, 122, 130, 229, 236
Goodland, Co, Antrim 37, 53, 61
Goodland bowls 53, 77, 325
gorgets 141
Gortcorbies, Co. Londonderry 89, 127
Gothic architecture 278, 282, 296, 321–22
gouge 130, 136
Graig Llwyd, Wales 46
Grainger, J. 10
Gransha, Co. Down 183, 231
grass 35, 40, 128
graver 131

Gray, W. 10–11, 23
Great Langdale, Cumbria 46
Greencastle, Co. Donegal 254–55, 258–59, 272
Greencastle, Co. Down 254–55, 257–58, 288
Greene, D. 174
Grey Abbey, Co. Down 276–78, 314
Grianan of Ailech, Co. Donegal 239
Grimston ware 52
Gweedore, Co. Donegal 95
halberds 102
Hall, V. 140
Hallstatt 141, 174
Hamiltons 303, 307, 321
hammer 131, 136
Hansard, Sir Richard 314
Harbison, P. 55
Harper, Alan 204, 231
harpoon (flint): 15
Harry Avery's Castle, Co. Tyrone 272–73, 283, 288, 310
Harryville, Co. Antrim 269
Hartwell, B. 35, 76, 79
Haughey's Fort, Co. Armagh 120–24, 135, 146
hazel 5, 12, 17, 26, 30, 192
helmets 228, 289
henges 74–77, 79, 98, 118
Henry Aimredh O' Neill 273
Herity, M. 52, 68
Herring, I. 89
Hiberno–Scottish (Drumnakilly) series 92–93
hill–forts 118, 120
Hillam, J. 107
hoards 130–31, 133–35, 229–30
Hodges, H. 107–09
horns 131, 137–38, 141, 160
horse–bits 157
horses (wild): 3–4; (domestic) 89, 95–96, 121, 157, 170, 269, 289
Hume, Sir John 313
Iberia 90
Inch Abbey, Co. Down 276–79, 295
Inishmacsaint, Co. Fermanagh 214
Inishowen, Co. Donegal 134, 234
interlace 210, 229, 235–36
Irish language 171–78
iron 141, 155, 271, 315

Isamnion 145–46
Island MacHugh, Co. Tyrone 33, 50, 125–26, 185, 310
Island Magee, Co. Antrim 314
Islandbridge/Kilmainham, Co. Dublin 227
Isle of Man 20, 22, 160, 179, 227
Ivens, R. 127, 184
Jarrow, Co. Durham 212
javelins (flint): 30, 49–51, 57, 102; (bronze): 132
jet 126
Jope, E. M. 157, 161, 163, 173, 332
Joymount, Carrickfergus, Co. Antrim 307, 312
juniper 5
Kells, Co. Meath 235
Kilbroney, Co. Down 214, 216
Kilclief, Co. Down 287
Killadeas, Co. Fermanagh 217
Killaghy, Co. Armagh 81
Killealy, Co. Antrim 231
Killybeg, Co. Antrim 50
Killycluggin, Co. Cavan 161–63
Killyglen, Co. Antrim 263
Killyleagh, Co. Down 243, 313
Killyliss, Co. Down 274
Killymaddy, Co. Antrim 111
Killymoon, Co. Tyrone 130
Kilmahamogue, Co. Antrim 132, 136
Kilmore, Co. Cavan 243
Kilnasaggart, Co. Armagh 214
Kilroot, Co. Antrim 268
Kilskeery, Co. Tyrone 94
Kiltierney, Co. Fermanagh 159, 164, 305
Kilwaughter, Co. Antrim 263
Kinawley, Co. Fermanagh 294
Kinbane, Co. Antrim 301
King's Stables, Co. Armagh 122–23, 129, 139, 146, 149
Kirk, S. M. 41
knives (flint): 50, 59; (bronze): 97, 136
Knockaulin, Co. Kildare 119, 148, 153, 166
Knockmany, Co. Tyrone 68, 320
Knowles, W. 10, 23, 45, 54, 95
Knowth, Co. Meath 48, 66, 82, 88
Kurin, Co. Londonderry 135

La Tène 155–58, 161, 166–67, 174, 177, 331
Lacken Bog, Co. Down 140
Lagan Navigation 318
Lagan river 77, 79, 144, 171, 314, 328
landnam 40–41
Largantea, Co. Londonderry 89
Largatreany, Co. Donegal 134
Larne, Co. Antrim 4, 23–24, 227, 233, 283, 327
Larnian 24, 330
Lattoon, Co. Cavan 134
Lawlor, H. C. 9, 328–29, 332
Layde, Co. Antrim 294
lead 130
Leask, H. 331
Leinster 166, 225, 229
Liffock, Co. Londonderry 311, 313
Lifford, Co. Donegal 314
Limavady, Co. Londonderry 292
Limerick 88
linear earthworks 150–53, 165, 167, 325, 331
linen 55
Linkardstown cists 54
Lisburn, Co. Antrim 195
Lisdromturk, Co. Monaghan 137
Lismahon, Co. Down 262
Lisnacrogher, Co. Antrim 156–57, 166
Lisnagade, Co. Down 186
Lissane, Co. Londonderry 110
Lissue, Co. Antrim 195
Long Lough, Co. Down 140
Longstone, Ballybeen, Co. Down 103
Lough Beg 24
Lough Boora, Co. Offaly 17, 20
Lough Enagh, Co. Londonderry 33, 125, 292
Lough Erne 25, 131, 139, 145, 165, 217, 235, 243
Lough Eskragh, Co. Tyrone 125–26, 136
Lough Gur, Co. Limerick 88
Lough Henney, Co. Down 289
Lough MacNean, Co. Fermanagh 127
Lough Mourne, Co. Antrim 155
Lough Neagh 20, 37, 95, 189, 261, 271, 300, 318

Loughan, Co. Londonderry 210
Loughash, Co. Tyrone 70, 89
Loughbrickland, Co. Down 103
Loughey, Co. Down 158, 173
Loughislandreavy, Co. Down 292
Loughnashade, Co. Armagh 149, 160
Loughnatrosk, Co. Antrim 33
lunula 102–03, 112
Lyles Hill, Co. Antrim 33–36, 46, 49–50, 52, 54, 57, 59–60, 78, 94, 124, 150
Lyles Hill Ware 52–54
Lynn, C. J. 37, 118, 123, 125, 151–52, 193, 204, 219, 231, 242, 255, 316
Mac Donalds 292
Mac Donnells 299–202, 230–31, 233–34
Mac Lochlainns 238
Mac Quillans 288, 301, 309
Mac Sweeneys 292
Macalister, R. A. S. 52
maceheads (stone): 47–48, 83
Mad Man's Window, Co. Antrim 32, 89
Maelbrigte Mac Tornian (Durnan) 213, 228
Maghera, Co. Down 280
Maghera, Co. Londonderry 246–47, 280
Magheragallan, Co. Donegal 95
Maguire's Bridge, Co. Fermanagh 46
Maguires 273, 294, 299
Main river 269
Malin More, Co. Donegal 57
Malone Hoard, Belfast 47, 83
mammoth 3, 4, 6
Managh Beg, Co. Londonderry 269
Manannan 160
manuscripts 211–13, 228, 233, 237
McLean, A. 236
megalithic yard 105
megaliths 38, 41, 55–74, 79–83
Mellifont, Co. Louth 245, 278
microliths 6, 15–16, 20, 22
Millin Bay, Co. Down 73–74
mills 189, 199–202, 230–31, 233–34, 263–64
mirror 158, 164
Misach 235–36

Mitchell, G. F. 26
Moira, Co. Down 313
Monea, Co. Fermanagh 307, 310, 321
Monkwearmouth, Co. Durham 212
mottes 241, 259–64, 269, 288–89, 309, 328, 335
moulds 70, 89, 100–01, 111, 123, 126, 129–130, 155, 209
Mount Gabriel, Co. Cork 99
Mount Hekla, Iceland 128–29, 139
Mount Sandel, Co. Londonderry 11–17, 20, 27, 31–32, 38, 150
Mountjoy 302, 304
Mournes 100
Movilla, Co. Down 205, 242
Movius, H. 24
Moyola river 100
Muircetach Mac Lochlainn 246
Muirchetach O'Brian 248
Mullaboy, Co. Londonderry 154
Mullaghmore, Co. Down 138
Munster 90–91, 101, 137–38, 141–42, 173, 225, 229, 244–45, 296, 325
Murlough sandhills, Co. Down 89
Navan, Co. Armagh 38, 116–124, 139, 146–150, 153–54, 157, 159–60, 165–67, 176, 328
Navan Research Group 385
necklaces 159
Nendrum, Co. Down 205–07, 233, 242, 328
New Grange, Co. Meath 66–67, 82, 88–89, 105
Newcastle, Co. Down 53
Newferry, Co. Antrim 24–25, 28
Newry, Co. Down 160, 163, 167, 202, 246, 302, 304, 318
Newry Canal 318
Newtownards, Co. Down 264–65, 268, 279, 286
Newtownstewart, Co. Tyrone 272, 310
Northumbria 212
Ó Duibhir, S. 137
O' Cahans 246, 269, 273, 284, 292, 299, 315
O' Dochertys 320
O' Dohertys 272

O' Donnells 238, 273, 299
O' Flynns 239, 269, 271, 273, 283
O' Hagans 240, 246
O' Heaneys 246
O' Laverty, J. 85, 111
O' Neills 238, 269, 272–73, 288, 299, 300–02
O' Neills of Clandeboye 251, 292, 299, 316
O' Rahilly, T. 145, 172–73, 176
O' Reillys 288–89, 316
oak 31, 107–09, 125–26, 129, 146, 200, 219, 315, 326
oats 190
ogham 173–74, 179, 189, 213, 225
Ordnance Survey 67, 326
Orkneys 48, 65
Orpen, G. 328
palstaves 70, 110, 135
palynology 39–40, 55, 88–89, 96, 118, 127–28, 135–36, 140, 188–89, 297, 315–16
Partholon 40, 176
passage tombs 53–54, 65–69, 81–83
Perpendicular style 296
Petrie Crown 161
picks (flint):15; (antler): 36
Piers, W. 302
pigs (wild): 6, 12–17, 27; (domestic) 30, 38, 89, 95, 98, 121, 123, 153, 189–190
Pilcher, J. R. 41, 96, 107
pine 26, 46
pins (antler): 54, 66, 82; (metal) 130, 133, 135, 167, 183, 211, 233
pipes 314
pitchstone 49
Pokorny, J. 145
Pomponius Mela 153
poplar 155, 189
porcellanite 44–47, 57, 83
Port Bradden, Co. Antrim 200
portal tombs 63–65, 331
Portglenone, Co. Antrim 26, 46, 85
Portpatrick, Scotland 49
Portrush, Co. Antrim 265, 280
Posidonius 139
pottery 28, 30, 32, 34, 36–38, 43, 51–54, 183, 200–01, 217–19, 265–67, 274, 288

promontory forts 199

Ptolemy 143–45, 165, 171–72, 177, 325

punch 131

Pygmy Cups 92

Pytheas 172

querns 122, 126, 154, 166–67, 189

Quig, J. 179

Quoile river 240

rabbits 103

radiocarbon 2, 31, 36, 41, 59, 83, 105, 108, 123, 125–26, 139, 150, 200, 220

Raftery, B. 158, 161, 167

raised beach 23

Ralaghan, Co. Cavan 162–63

Rallagh, Co. Londonderry 124

Raloo, Co. Antrim 263

Ramsey, G. 101, 110

Raphoe, Co. Donegal 49

rapiers 110–11, 131

Rath Croghan, Co. Roscommon 153

Rathlin Island 44, 46, 96, 145

Rathmore, Co. Antrim 221, 231

Rathmullan, Co. Down 231

raths 185–86, 191, 197–203, 211, 219–25, 231, 241, 260, 325, 331, 335

Ravarnet river 241

razors 111–12, 133

red deer 6, 16–17, 25, 27, 29, 36, 95

Regia 146

reindeer 3, 4, 6

Renfrew, C. 79, 174

Richhill, Co. Armagh 313

ring–forts (see raths)

Ringerike 235–37

rings 130, 135, 141, 173, 183

Robinson, P. 311

Roe river 145, 159, 163

Romanesque 243–44, 278, 282

Rossory, Co. Fermanagh 230–31

Roughan, Co. Tyrone 310

round towers 206, 232–33

Rudraighe 2, 141

Saint John's Point, Co. Down 26, 207

Saint Malachy 237, 242, 245–46

Saint Manchan's shrine 237

Saint Molaise 235

Saint Patrick 178, 181, 205, 213

Saint Patrick's bell 235–37

Sallagh Fort, Co. Antrim 231

salmon 12, 14, 17

Salterstown, Co. Londonderry 306

Sandhills Ware 53, 70

Savages 283, 313

saw 131, 136

scabbards 131, 156, 161, 167, 174

Scandinavia 135, 138

Scotch Street, Armagh 37, 204, 242

Scotland 4, 7–8, 20, 46, 49, 55, 57, 59, 62, 65, 88–89, 113, 124, 128, 141, 145, 154, 157, 160, 173–75, 179, 185, 212, 224–26, 228–29, 248, 290, 292, 303, 313

Scotshouse, Co. Monaghan 152

Scrabo, Co. Down 150, 185, 268

scrapers 16, 50, 55, 57, 59, 70, 97

sea–level 3, 5, 20, 23

Seaby, W. A. 125

Seacon More, Co. Antrim 135

Seafin, Co. Down 262

Sess Kilgreen, Co. Tyrone 68

Severn–Cotswold tombs 62

Shane's Castle, Co. Antrim 292

sheep 30, 31, 38, 50, 54–55, 89, 95, 121, 123, 153–54, 189–91

shellfish 95, 200

Sheridan, A. 46–47, 69, 82

shields 130–32, 136, 156, 217

sickles 111, 118

silver 168, 178–79, 210, 229–30, 234–35

Simpson, D. D. A. 32–33, 48, 75, 98, 118, 127

Sion Mills, Co. Tyrone 319

Six Mile Water 33, 36, 196

Skellig Michael, Co. Kerry 205

Slaght, Co. Antrim 186

Slane, Co. Meath 232–33

sleeve–fasteners 134–35, 141

Slidderyford (Wateresk), Co. Down 64

Slieve Croob, Co. Down 41, 68

Slieve Donard, Co. Down 68, 205

Slieve Gallion, Co. Tyrone 127

Slieve Gullion, Co. Armagh 67

Slieve–an–orra, Co. Antrim 100

Slieve–na–miskan, Co. Down 100

Sligo 56
Sluggan, Co. Antrim 127
Smith, A. 96
snakes 178
Soiscel Molaise 237
Solinus 155, 178
souterrains 188, 195–96, 231, 325, 328, 335
souterrain ware 201–02, 217–20, 224–25, 231, 233, 240, 266, 274, 325, 331
Spain 177
spear–butts 157, 166, 168
spearheads (flint): 24, 49; (bronze) 101–02, 109–111, 118, 130–32, 135, 156–57, 168
Sperrins 100, 239
standing stones 103–04, 139
Startin, D. W.A. 77
stone circles 71–74, 104–05, 139, 141, 163, 331, 335
Strabo 164, 178
Straid, Co. Londonderry 98
Strongbow 248
sword (bronze): 118, 123, 126–27, 131–32, 135, 139; (iron): 155–56, 167–68, 174, 211, 217, 227, 262, 274, 289
Táin 167
Tandragee, Co. Armagh 163
Tankardstown, Co. Limerick 32
Tara 119
Tara brooch 210, 221
Taylor, Joan 102
Taylor, Jeremy 314
Templepatrick, Co. Antrim 33
terret 157
textiles 54–55, 133, 319
Thom, A. S. 105
Thomsen, C. 85
Three Collas 167
Ticloy, Co. Antrim 64
Tievebulliagh, Co. Antrim 44–46
tin 86, 99, 154–55
Tipperary 291
Tobermore, Co. Londonderry 130
Toome Bar, Co. Antrim 155
Toome Bay, Co. Londonderry 26
Topped Mountain, Co. Fermanagh 102, 113

Torbach 213
torcs 134, 159
tower–houses 287–92, 294, 307, 309, 312–13, 321, 328, 331
trackways 136, 158
Trewhiddle style 210, 229
Trinity Island, Co. Cavan 243
trout 12
túath 170
Tullahogue, Co. Tyrone 239–40, 246
Tully castle, Co. Fermanagh 312–13
Tullylish, Co. Down 207
Turlough Luineach O'Neill 301
Turlough O'Connor 237
Turoe stone, Co. Galway 161
tweezers 158, 173
Uí Néill 167
Uí Tuirtre 238–39, 251; see O'Flynns
Ulaid 145, 167, 222, 238–41, 246, 249, 325
Ulster Journal of Archaelogy 48, 327
Uluti 145–46, 177, 325
Urbalreagh, Co. Antrim 96
Urnes style 236–37, 246
van Giffen, A. E. 72
Vennicnii 145
Voluntii 145
Waddell, J. 112
Wailes, B. 148
Wales 7, 20, 46, 55, 65, 179, 185, 224–25, 260
Walsh, A. 152
Warhurst, C. 204, 255
Warner, R. B. 109, 121, 124, 160–61, 174, 177, 179
water lily 12, 30
Waterman, D. 37–38, 60, 73, 96, 116, 149, 169, 193, 231, 332
Watson, E. 96
wedge tombs 69–71, 89, 141
Weir, D. 118
Wessex 113
whales 27, 153
wheat 30, 38, 89, 190
wheeled vehicles 136, 157–58
White House, Ballyspurge, Co. Down 313

White Island, Co. Fermanagh 217, 243
White Park Bay, Co. Antrim 32, 89,
 127
Whitehead, Co. Antrim 308
Whiterocks, Co. Antrim 150
Williams, B. B. 98, 125–27
willow 5
Wilson, B. C. S. 68, 161, 173

Windy Ridge, Co. Antrim 33
wine 183, 265, 274
wolves 171, 197
Woodman, P. C. 11–12, 14, 16, 21,
 24, 27
wrist–bracers 90, 141, 335
yokes 157
Yorkshire 93, 112

200320735